450 Legal Problems Solved

About the author

Keith Richards, a barrister, writer and broadcaster on consumer affairs, worked for many years as a senior lawyer, and legal editor of the journal *Consumer Policy Review*, at Consumers' Association. He is the author of several consumer law books, and for ten years provided regular legal advice on BBC Radio 2's *Jimmy Young Show*, as well as being the GMTV consumer lawyer. Currently Head of Consumer Affairs at ABTA, the travel industry regulator, he has served on a number of statutory bodies including the Architects Registration Board, the statutory body for that profession. He sits on DPTAC, the government's advisory body on access to travel and the built environment for disabled people, and is a member of the Department of Trade and Industry sustainability pioneers group developing sustainable development strategies across various industries.

450 Legal Problems Solved

Keith Richards

which

Which? Books are commissioned by
Consumers' Association and published by
Which? Ltd, 2 Marylebone Road, London NW1 4DF
Email: books@which.co.uk

First edition of *350 Legal Problems Solved* October 1993, revised 1995
First edition of *401 Legal Problems Solved* March 1998, reprinted April 1999 with some
updating
First edition of *420 Legal Problems Solved* May 2000
Bound in new cover 2003
First edition of *450 Legal Problems Solved* May 2004
Reprinted June 2005

British Library Cataloguing in Publication Data
A catalogue record for *450 Legal Problems Solved* is available from the British Library

ISBN 0 85202 974 8

This book provides general guidance only. Before taking action it is advisable to seek financial
and/or legal assistance by contacting one of the organisations listed on pages 23–24.

Help at hand
If you have ever been faced with the sorts of problem described in this book, you'll be glad
to know that *Which?* has a service, open to all, whereby you can consult a qualified lawyer
by telephone Monday–Friday (9 a.m.–5 p.m.). For details of how to subscribe to Which?
Legal Service, either write to Consumers' Association, Gascoyne Way, Hertford X, SG14
1LH or telephone (01992) 822828. Information about *Which?* and its sister magazines can
be obtained from the same address.

Editorial and production: Robert Gray, Ian Robinson, Mary Sunderland
Index: Marie Lorimer
Original cover concept by Sarah Harmer
Cover illustration by Corbis, adapted by Jason Harris

Typeset by Saxon Graphics Ltd, Derby
Printed and bound by Creative Print and Design, Wales

Contents

How to use this book

If you already have a consumer problem to which you want to know the answer, check the **contents** listing first to find out which chapter would cover it. Or, if you want to check a point of law, use the **index**. The questions and answers throughout the book explain how the various laws apply in practice.

For an overview of how consumer legislation works, read the **introduction**, which also includes a *Which?* Guide to Complaining: this takes you through the practical process of making a complaint, whatever the problem, and explains how to deal with the most common excuses made by shops and traders to fob off customers.

For matters which cannot be simply resolved, you should read **Chapter 13**, on taking a case to court and alternative ways of settling disputes. The meaning of various terms used in the book, or in legal documents you may come across, is clearly explained throughout.

The names, **addresses,** telephone numbers and websites of the most important contact organisations are listed at the end of the book, and where these appear in the text they are marked with an asterisk(★).

Introduction

This book is your source of consumer legal wisdom. What does 'without prejudice' mean? Can you get out of a contract once you have signed it? What information do companies hold about you and what rights do you have to know? Here you will find the questions most frequently asked, with concise, easy-to-understand answers that show you, first, exactly what your legal position is, and, if it looks like you have a case, how to proceed. Each chapter deals with the sorts of problems you may encounter in situations ranging from buying everyday items, through tackling holiday problems, to dealing with a rejected insurance claim. Mobile phone contracts, the Internet, train delays, hospital treatment, disability discrimination, timeshare and wheel-clamping all present particular problems and these issues, plus many more, are covered in this book.

In our complex, busy world few of us have time to gain expertise in areas outside our chosen interests or careers. We may think we know our rights, but things are changing rapidly. The high street shops and mail-order companies are being challenged by Internet shopping and for consumers this can throw up new risks. The latest statistics for 2003 (Office for National Statistics) show that just about half of the 24 million households in the UK had access to the Internet and over 91 per cent had access at work, with over half of UK consumers having shopped online. The most popular purchases were travel, books, tickets for shows and events, music and e-learning materials.

In a country where you can buy your gas from an electricity company, your electricity from a gas supplier, and get a loan from the supermarket, consumer confusion over which companies provide what services these days is understandable. Yet today's consumers are increasingly willing to question standards and to complain when things go wrong. But who do you complain to?

There is a plethora of organisations, schemes and associations to which the wronged consumer can turn for help – codes of practice, charters, mediation, arbitration schemes, and ombudsmen. *450 Legal Problems Solved* explains about those that can help you and what they can do for you. The objective is to provide the ammunition for you to fight your own consumer battles, thus saving sizeable lawyers' fees. For most disputes there simply is no need to pay lawyers for advice, particularly as research for *Which?* magazine has repeatedly shown that many solicitors know little about consumer law. And if you need to go to court, the book explains how to do it yourself.

If you do need a lawyer there are ways of keeping the costs down. Since Legal Aid was all but abolished in 2000 the number of companies helping people claim compensation on a 'no win, no fee' basis has increased enormously. No problem there – these deals are worth having in some cases. The idea is simple. You arrange with your lawyer that he'll take on your case on the basis that, if you lose, he will not get any fee, although you will still have to pay your opponent's costs. Insurance cover is available to pay for these. If you win the lawyer gets his 'normal' fee plus an additional 'success' fee based on a percentage of his 'normal' bill – this is agreed in advance and could be up to another 100 per cent. The insurance premium and the success fee can be recovered from the losing party (pp. 112–3).

General figures from the Office of Fair Trading (OFT)* show that in 2002 alone we made over 830,000 official complaints about goods and services to Trading Standards and Environmental Health Departments. In the context of all complaints about unsatisfactory transactions these are just the tip of a very large iceberg. The biggest area of complaint is home maintenance and improvements with second-hand cars and electrical goods close behind. No surprises there. And these are areas that the government has specifically targeted to improve consumer protection and redress. Even so, the chances are that most transactions will not cause us any problems. But when things do go wrong we need to know our rights and be able to act quickly. And if we are making a big purchase – buying a house or having building work done, say – we need to think about protecting ourselves in advance. For both future protection and sorting out problems, *450 Legal Problems Solved* is the answer.

There is nothing magical about the law. It is largely based on common sense. *450 Legal Problems Solved* explains the law as it applies in everyday consumer situations, dispels the myth and mystique and shows you how to use the law to your advantage.

Knowledge is a shield to protect us from being ripped off and a sword to help us pursue our rights. *450 Legal Problems Solved* continues the long *Which?* tradition of fighting for a better deal for consumers. It works on one simple assumption: that consumer law exists for the benefit of consumers, not lawyers. The book enhances your bargaining power when dealing with shops, businesses, professionals – and even your neighbours. Regular research carried out by *Which?* magazine shows that people with a legal problem who make the legal system work for them by getting good advice from the right source at an early stage have an excellent chance of getting redress, and may not need to take any significant financial risks.

Like a Highway Code for consumer disputes, this book is a guide to avoiding getting into difficulty and to making confident use of the law when any disputes arise, so that they can be successfully resolved. Stick to the golden rules – be persistent, be reasonable and be clued-up.

The Which? Guide to Complaining

The following action points should help you to make an effective complaint in most circumstances. We also list the most common excuses you may come up against when you do complain, and advise you how to deal with them.

- **Act quickly** Don't let your complaint go stale as this can affect your rights (pp. 11, 22 and 32–3). If you discover a defect in goods, say, go straight back to the shop or, if that is inconvenient, write.
- **Know your rights** Check in this book what you are entitled to so you can let the person to whom you are complaining know the legal basis of your claim.
- **Target your complaint** Write or insist on speaking to someone in authority – the manager of a local branch, for example, or the managing director of a company. Don't vent your anger on the telephonist or the cashier: he or she may not have the authority to make a decision about the problem.
- **Keep a record of your action** Even if you complain in person, or by phone, make sure you keep a record of what was said and when, together with a note of the name and position of the person you dealt with.
- **Follow up in writing** Unless your problem is resolved immediately, follow up your complaint by letter, and keep a copy. By sending your letter to a named individual you reduce the risk of it being passed around the organisation and perhaps being ignored or lost. Type (or write as neatly as possible), date it, and, if appropriate, give the letter a heading (if it is an insurance or holiday dispute, say, state the name and number of your insurance policy, or your holiday booking reference and so on). Use this heading, and any reference given by the organisation, every time you write.

  To avoid committing yourself by mistake when negotiating settlement terms, write '**without prejudice**' at the top of that part of your letter, but don't use it on all your letters as this may cause problems (p. 21).

  You may be sent a cheque in '**full and final settlement**' of your claim. If this happens, be very careful: even if you do not consider the amount to be enough, by cashing the cheque you will have accepted it, in settlement of your claim, so you will be unable to claim any more (p. 161). If the amount proffered is not sufficient, it is best to send it back.
- **Keep to the point**
  - A brief letter setting out the facts in short paragraphs, rather than an angry or emotional letter making personal remarks, will help your claim. But be firm.
  - Quoting the relevant law, such as the Sale of Goods Act 1979 if you are complaining about faulty goods or the Supply of Goods and Services Act

1982 in respect of inadequate services, shows you are aware of your rights and mean business.

- State what redress you want: if you want your money back, a repair or a replacement, or if you want financial compensation, spell it out.
- Give a reasonable deadline for a response: 14 days for a simple matter, but longer if it's a more substantial problem such as building work.
- Use recorded delivery and keep copies of all documentation.

- **Get evidence** Get and keep any evidence you can to support your claim: receipts, invoices, brochures, contract terms and conditions, advertisements, estimates, bills, statements from witnesses, photographs of damage, etc., and technical expert evidence if appropriate.

- **Be persistent and don't be fobbed off** If you are not happy with the response to your complaint, or you've had no response at all, write another letter. Don't fall prey to attempts to fob you off with less than you're entitled to. Here are some of the most common excuses:

  - **'You're too late. You should have complained within 30 days'** Don't accept time limits of this sort. Whether it is goods or services, or a bad holiday you are complaining about, your rights to claim compensation for breach of contract or negligence last for six years (five years in Scotland), and three years in personal injury claims (p. 22). So, even if you have lost the right to reject faulty goods, say, because the 'reasonable' period of time has elapsed (pp. 32–3), you can still claim compensation or opt for a replacement or repair (p. 33). Even if there's a term in a contract (for example, a holiday brochure) and you don't complain within the set time limit, you may be able to challenge this under the Unfair Contract Terms Act 1977 (p. 81) or refer such terms to one of the 'qualifying bodies' with the power to challenge them under the Unfair Terms in Consumer Contracts Regulations 1999 (p. 88).

  - **'We don't give refunds'** If you have bought goods that are faulty, unfit for their purpose, or not as described, you are entitled to a refund if you act quickly enough (pp. 32–3). Notices saying 'No refunds' or anything else which implies that you can't get your money back under any circumstances, are against the law. If you have the right to reject defective goods and demand a refund, that right can never be taken away (pp. 32-3). So don't be put off by such notices and report any you see to your local Trading Standards Department.

  - **'We don't guarantee our products'** Ignore this. Your rights as a consumer in all circumstances apply whether you have a written guarantee or not (pp. 32–3).

  - **'You caused the problem, not us'** Don't be deterred by this. For example, a pair of children's shoes should be designed to withstand the rough and tumble of the playground, so if they fall apart soon after purchase the trader cannot blame the way your child used them. But if it's not as clear-cut as this you may need an independent test on the product or service.

- **'It's not our problem. Try the manufacturer'** If you have bought something faulty, it is up to the retailer to deal with it, not the manufacturer. But all too often the retailer will try to pass you on to the manufacturer or force you to claim on the manufacturer's guarantee on the grounds that 'we only sell them'. While manufacturer's guarantees are now legally enforceable (p. 38), they often give you far more limited rights than you have against the retailer anyway. So you're usually better off telling the retailer that it is his or her legal responsibility to address the problem (pp. 32–3). This also applies to complaints about goods supplied via services – for example, materials used in work done for you by a builder or plumber.
- **'We can't do anything without a receipt'** There is no legal requirement to have a receipt, but you may have to prove when and where you paid for the goods or service. So if the trader asks for proof of payment, a receipt is useful. But a credit-card voucher, say, would be legally acceptable.
- **'No refunds on sale items'** If you buy goods in a sale you still have your normal rights. If you buy goods that are seconds you cannot expect them to be perfect, but they must still be of satisfactory quality (i.e. free from hidden defects, pp. 32–3) and as described. But you cannot complain about any defects which were pointed out to you or which you could have spotted before buying (p. 36).

• **Be reasonable** Be prepared to come to a compromise if you receive a fair offer, even if it is not exactly what you wanted. But be warned that once you have accepted an offer of compensation you cannot ask for more later (p. 161).

• **Follow the right complaints procedure** If you cannot come to an agreement it is time to let somebody else decide on the rights and wrongs of your complaint, such an ombudsman. Or, if the trader is a member of a **trade association** which operates a **code of practice**, you may be able to get help there (pp. 272–4). Most have a free conciliation service to help settle disputes.

Many industries and professions now have their own formal mechanisms for dealing with complaints. You'll find detailed explanations in the relevant chapters of this book. Broadly, the following courses of action may be open to you (see Chapter 13):

Ombudsmen In many professions and industries there are ombudsmen (sometimes called commissioners) available to handle complaints (pp. 276–7). Some are voluntary, so the trader or company you are complaining about must be a member of the particular ombudsman scheme, and some are compulsory, so check first. The service is free, and you may still be able to pursue your claim in the courts if you are not happy with the final decision (p. 277).

Mediation Disputes can be mediated by an independent mediator. There are some ready-made schemes around or you and the other side can always agree to go to a mediator. The outcome is only binding if both sides are able to reach an agreement which they're happy to sign up to. If not then you're free to go to court.

Arbitration If you have a dispute and both you and the other party agree, you can ask for the dispute to be referred to arbitration, which is generally operated by the Chartered Institute of Arbitrators★ (Arbiters in Scotland), so that an independent decision on your dispute can be made. This will be binding, so that you cannot subsequently go to court if you are not satisfied with the outcome. And it can also be expensive. But many trade and professional bodies offer their own low-cost schemes, so check first (pp. 271–4).

Court In almost all cases you'll have the option of going to court. The small claims track (part of the county court) offers a cheap and relatively informal way of dealing with fairly straightforward cases (p. 276). If you have reached the end of your negotiations, the final stage before starting court action is to send a 'letter before action' or 'letter of claim', telling the other party that unless you receive redress within a specified period (usually seven days) you will take the matter to court. But before doing so most claims will be subject to what is called a 'pre-action protocol'. This may delay the beginning of your legal action but the aim is to make sure that you and the other side have explored all the alternatives to court first. For example, you are expected to disclose as much information about your claim to the other party as you can as early as possible, including details of how you have calculated the amount of compensation you're asking for, and the facts to prove it. If you don't comply with these protocols you could be penalised over your costs and expenses, even if you subsequently win your case.

Q *Where does consumer law come from?*

A There is a huge body of law specifically designed to help the individual consumer, some made by Parliament in the form of **statutes**, some by judges in the form of cases argued out by lawyers in the court room (known as **common law**), and some direct from European Union Directives which are brought into force in the UK in the form of **regulations**.

- **Statute law**, set down in Acts of Parliament (such as the Sale of Goods Act 1979) and in Regulations and Orders under the general authority of Acts of Parliament, sets out the rights and duties of specified people in specified circumstances.
- **Common law** is based on the decisions of the courts in actual cases which also set out the rights and duties of people in different circumstances. These are recorded in law reports and form 'precedents' for the future. In this way the courts can adapt the law to new situations without having to wait for Parliament to introduce legislation. And many cases that come before the courts are interpreting and defining the words in various Acts of Parliament.

Q *Which **statutes** and **regulations** give protection to consumers?*

A The following statutes form the main body of legislation aimed at consumer protection:

- **The Enterprise Act 2002** is one of the most wide-ranging pieces of new law. It gives the Office of Fair Trading (OFT) substantial powers to act against unfair business practices (pp. 87–8), take rogue traders out of action, and to support good industry Codes of Conduct (pp. 16–17, 40, 87). It also gives other designated bodies such as Trading Standards and Consumers' Association the legal right to get court orders to stop traders conducting their businesses in breach of consumer legislation (p. 88). It also introduces the new concept of 'super-complaints'. The Act gives 'designated bodies' the power to submit a complaint that 'any feature, or combination of features, of a market in the UK for goods and services is or appears to be significantly harming the interests of consumers'
- **Sale and Supply of Goods to Consumer Regulations 2002** This law updates the Sale of Goods Act 1979 and the Supply of Goods and Services Act 1982 (see below), improving consumers' rights. It brings in new rights in respect of 'free' manufacturers' guarantees, and widens the choice of remedies consumers have when things go wrong (pp. 33–4)
- **Sale of Goods Act 1979** (as amended) Perhaps the most important single piece of consumer legislation, this sets out the obligations on businesses that sell goods to consumers (pp. 32–6). Goods supplied by a trader must be of 'satisfactory quality', and 'fit for their purpose'. In brief, the goods must be durable, safe and free from major and minor defects
- **Supply of Goods and Services Act 1982** This Act defines the standard of the service consumers can legally expect when engaging a trader to provide a service; it also covers the quality of the materials used and other criteria such as price and timescale (pp. 67–9)

- **Privacy and Electronic Communications (EC Directive) Regulations 2003** These provide important consumer protection from unsolicited advertising or marketing faxes, phone calls, text messages and 'spam' emails (p. 259). They are enforced by the Information Commissioner★

- **Arbitration Act 1996** If a disputed sum of money is for £5,000 or less consumers are not legally bound by clauses in contracts which state that any dispute must be referred to arbitration; they have the choice of court or arbitration (pp. 273–4)

- **Consumer Credit Act 1974** This regulates credit agreements and stipulates that advertisements for credit schemes must show true rates of interest without hidden extras; it also confers upon purchasers the right to pay off the debt earlier than the time for payment laid down in the agreement; and it gives purchasers who sign a credit agreement at home a 'cooling-off' period during which they are allowed to change their minds and cancel the agreement (pp. 142–3). The Act is in the process of a review by the UK government

- **Consumer Protection Act 1987** and, in Northern Ireland, the **(N.I.) Order 1987** This states that (1) manufacturers are strictly liable if the products they make are defective and cause personal injury, or damage to property over £275, and (2) all goods must comply with a general safety requirement (pp. 48–51); it also (3) provides guidance to prevent traders quoting misleading prices for goods and services (pp. 29, 62)

- **Consumer Protection (Cancellation of Contracts Concluded Away from Business Premises) Regulations 1987** This gives purchasers a seven-day cooling-off period during which they have the right to cancel certain contracts made during an unrequested visit by a salesperson to their home even when they are not buying on credit (pp. 20 & 43)

- **Occupiers' Liability Act 1957** This gives individuals the right to claim compensation if they are injured due to negligence while visiting someone's premises (p. 255)

- **Misrepresentation Act 1967** and, in Northern Ireland, the **Misrepresentation Act (N.I.) 1967** If purchasers enter into an agreement on the basis of a statement purporting to be a fact but which turns out to be untrue, they have the right to cancel the deal and get their money back if they act quickly, or to claim compensation. The Act does not apply to Scotland. However, Scottish law is broadly similar (pp. 52, 268–9)

- **Unfair Contract Terms Act 1977** The small print in contracts for the sale of goods cannot take away purchasers' rights under the Sale of Goods Act. These and other notices or conditions in contracts which exclude or restrict liability for financial loss or damage to property have to be fair and reasonable. If they are not, they will be invalid under the Act and will not affect a claim

- **Unfair Terms in Consumer Contracts Regulations 1999** These add to the rights consumers have under existing laws, in particular the Unfair Contract Terms Act 1977. The regulations make it clear that terms in standard consumer contracts can be relied on by businesses only if they are 'fair'. They give qualifying bodies such as the Office of Fair Trading (OFT)★, Consumers' Association★, Trading Standards departments, and those regulating specific industries such as OFGEM★ (formerly OFGAS and OFFER), OFCOM★ and OFWAT★, the power to have standard contract terms declared 'unfair' by the courts, which means they must be removed from a company's contracts or altered (pp. 58 & 88–9).
- **Unsolicited Goods and Services Act 1971** This gives recipients of unrequested and unwanted goods the right to get rid of them without paying for them
- **Consumer Protection (Distance Selling) Regulations 2002** These are designed to give basic legal protection to consumers who buy goods and services via the Internet, mail order, telephone, or any other distance contract. Consumers have the right to basic pre-contract information about the name and address of the supplier, the characteristics of the goods or services, the price, etc., as well as having a seven-day cooling-off period in which to withdraw from the contract (pp. 59–60).

Certain **criminal laws** also affect consumers.

The most relevant laws are:

- **Consumer Protection Act 1987** This stipulates that only safe goods should be put on sale and prohibits misleading price indications
- **Food Safety Act 1990** This covers food standards and hygiene wherever food is manufactured, prepared or sold, as well as other aspects of food and drink
- **Trade Descriptions Act 1968** This makes it a criminal offence for traders to make false statements about the goods they sell
- **Weights and Measures Act 1985** and, in Northern Ireland, the **(N.I.) Order 1988** This stipulates that (1) all weighing and measuring equipment should be accurate; (2) many commodities (especially foods) should be marked with the quantity supplied, and that certain commodities should be sold only in certain specified quantities; and (3) all aspects of quantity control in trade should be open to official inspection.

Q *Surely the law changes all the time. How do I know that the contents of this book are still up-to-date?*

A The list of statutes and regulations (see above) shows that most of these laws have been with us for some time, many for more than ten years, some longer. But of course the law is not static and some important proposals are currently under consultation, aimed at plugging some of the loopholes in the law – for example, those that allow unscrupulous traders to prey on consumers, or simply aimed at updating the law to keep it in line with developments such as new selling techniques or the rise in the Internet and electronic commerce (pp. 59–63).

There is no one single consumer Act of Parliament. This means that there are many different sources of consumer rights with loose ends that need tying up. The last few years have brought some significant changes. And some of your rights described in this book will develop over the next few years, hopefully for the better. You can keep up to date on most issues, particularly those listed below, by contacting any of the main government bodies responsible for the changes, or by asking at your local advice centre, Citizens Advice Bureau or Trading Standards department, or Consumers' Association★. The government currently has its own 'Consumer Gateway' Internet site where you can get easy access to key consumer sites and information at *www.consumer.gov.uk*. This will soon be replaced with a new initiative called 'Consumer Direct'. If you don't already have access to the Internet at home or work, you may be able to access it via a computer in your local library, or there are an increasing number of touch-screen kiosks in supermarkets, railway stations and shopping centres, as well as Internet cafés and other outlets around the country.

Q *What are the areas where I should look out for changes in consumer protection?*

A There is likely to be an increase in consumer education and better informa-tion for consumers about their rights, backed by government initiatives, which should also improve the services provided by the local authority Trading Standards Officers (TSOs). TSOs have the job of policing a lot of the laws covered in this book, as well as providing consumer advice.

The Enterprise Act 2002, which came into force in April 2003, is a wide-ranging piece of law which gives the Office of Fair Trading (OFT)★ the power to act against businesses which act unfairly towards consumers and to take swift action against the rogues who simply rip consumers off. Other bodies, such as Consumers' Association, can also get court orders to stop traders conducting their businesses in breach of a whole range of consumer laws. You can get full details from the OFT.

Below is a list of the main areas about to change or where change is in the pipeline:

- throughout 2004 and 2005 the Office of Fair Trading will be launching and expanding its OFT Codes Accreditation regime. This will provide an 'at-a-glance' hallmark to identify businesses and trade associations that guarantee good service through codes of conduct. It includes the requirement that there is an Alternative Dispute Resolution (ADR) mechanism to help consumers put things right if they go wrong. The OFT will police the codes hallmarking and will help publicise those traders who qualify, to help consumers make informed decisions about which trader to deal with
- the Consumer Credit Act 1974 is under review and new proposals coming from the European Commission are set to harmonise consumer credit laws across Europe. This could mean the end of that important protection provided by section 75 (p. 152).

Q *What is the difference between* **civil law** *and* **criminal law***?*

A **Civil law** This is the branch of the legal system which is of most use to the individual seeking compensation and redress. The civil law is concerned with rights and duties that relate to individuals in their dealings with other individuals (including companies and other groups of people). If you suffer loss because someone else breaches these laws then you have a right to redress and are entitled to take that person to court. The main areas of civil law are **tort** (which includes negligence) and **contract**. The courts which deal with civil claims are the **county court** (in which the **small claims track** may be used for general claims of £5,000 or less, and £1,000 or less for personal injury) and the **High Court** for general claims over £15,000 and personal injury claims over £50,000 (pp. 279–80).

Criminal law This is the branch of law which is concerned with offences against the public, such as the Trade Descriptions Act 1968. Criminal law is generally enforced by the police, but the specific criminal law affecting consumers is enforced by public authorities like Trading Standards Departments and Environmental Health Officers (both based at your local council offices). You cannot get compensation directly by reporting a criminal offence such as a false trade description, but evidence of such wrongdoing will lend added weight to your complaint. The courts which deal with criminal matters are the magistrates' courts and the crown courts.

Q *What is a* **tort***, and how does it affect me as a consumer?*

A A tort (in Scotland a 'delict') is a wrongdoing in civil law, entirely distinct from breach of contract. If you suffer a wrong you may be able to claim in tort against the wrongdoer. There does not need to be a contract nor does a criminal offence need to have been committed. The commonest 'consumer' tort is lack of duty of care or negligence – for example, you could tear your clothes or injure yourself in a shop by slipping on a wet floor (p. 256). What is important is the relationship between the wrongdoer and the person who suffered the damage. For example, all road-users owe a legal duty to other road-users and, of course, pedestrians. If they break that duty by being careless, they will be responsible for the consequences.

Q *What does **caveat emptor** ('let the buyer beware') mean in legal terms?*

A This legal principle means that the risk of buying something that is faulty in any way rests with the buyer, so it would be up to the buyer to check the quality of the item before purchase. Any defect that the inspection failed to identify would be the buyer's responsibility. Fortunately, when a consumer buys 'goods' (p. 26) this principle does not apply. The Sale of Goods Act 1979 makes the trader who sells the goods 'strictly liable' for the quality of those goods (pp. 31–34). So there is no legal requirement to inspect goods thoroughly before buying: if you buy goods from a trader and they turn out to be defective, the seller is responsible.

But 'buyer beware' still applies to the sale of property, so the burden is on the buyer of property to check the quality before going ahead with the purchase. If no checks are made by the buyer and the property turns out to be defective, the seller is not generally responsible (p. 125).

Q *Am I better off dealing only with shops and traders who are members of trade associations?*

A Don't assume that you'll be better protected just because a trader belongs to a trade association. Contact the relevant trade association to check that the company is a member and to see what protection is offered. Some will offer you the choice of paying an additional premium which protects your money in the event of insolvency, and occasionally in the event of bad workmanship even if your trader is still in business (pp. 73–4). Some require member traders to follow codes of conduct and offer conciliation or binding arbitration if you have a dispute (p. 272).

Q *How can I find out whether a trader is financially sound?*

A There is no sure way of knowing, and well-known names are no guarantee. Strong signs of trouble are dead phones, being constantly fobbed off with lame excuses, near-empty shelves, endless sales, or hefty deposit demands before the trader will deal with you. If any of these criteria apply to a firm you are thinking of dealing with, it may be best to avoid it, or to take extra precautions, such as paying for goods or services by credit card (p. 152), taking out an insurance-backed guarantee for work (pp. 73–4) or using traders who are bonded as part of their membership of a trade association. Also, contact the Trading Standards Department local to the trader, to see whether it has any further information to help you decide, or if it's a limited company you could carry out a company search with Companies House★.

Q *Does a contract have to be in writing?*

A No. This is probably the greatest misunderstanding of the law of contract. Every day we make contracts without putting them in writing, or even speaking a single word: we buy food in shops, pay taxi or bus fares, etc. All these have the same standing as written contracts and are governed by the same laws as other contracts. Whether written or verbal, a contract is an agreement that can be enforced by the law and gives rise to rights and responsibilities for those involved.

Some rights are always implied into certain transactions: for example, when you buy goods, or when you employ a trader to do work for you, the rights embodied in the relevant legislation automatically come into play and can never be taken away (see below) whether or not you have anything in writing.

Spoken agreements can cause problems if it later becomes necessary to prove the precise terms agreed, such as the price or a delivery date. It is always worth keeping receipts for goods in case you need to prove later where they were bought and how much you paid. If you do not have a proper written contract, keep any evidence you do have. The only contracts which must be in writing are:

- contracts for the sale or leasing of land
- hire-purchase agreements and similar credit and hire transactions (see pp. 141–2).

Q *I've just signed a contract which had lots of terms and conditions on the back. I didn't have time to read everything before signing it and I'm now worried that my rights may be restricted by the **small print**. Am I bound by these terms, whatever they say?*

A If you sign a document you will normally be bound by it whether you have read it or not, and the terms of a written agreement will almost always override anything that you have agreed orally. Even if the terms are contained in a separate document, if you are referred to that document (for example, by the words 'full terms and conditions available on request') you will probably be bound by them, even if you didn't see them and didn't ask to see a copy. You can challenge some of the small print (pp. 80–81), but to avoid such situations:

- *always* ask for a copy of the final agreement bearing both your signature and that of the other person

- *never* sign a document until you have read it. *If in doubt, don't sign.* Ask to take the document away to think about it
- if you are not happy with some of the terms in an agreement cross them out and ask for it to be re-typed, or make sure your amendments are signed by the company representative
- if the small print in contracts for goods or services attempts to take away or limit your rights to claim under the Sale of Goods Act 1979 (pp. 31–32), it is illegal: your statutory rights cannot be taken away
- other notices or conditions in contracts have to be fair and reasonable. If they are not, they could be declared invalid under the Unfair Contract Terms Act 1977 and can be ignored, but do refer them to the Office of Fair Trading (OFT)★, Consumers' Association★, or any other 'qualifying body' under the Unfair Terms in Consumer Contracts Regulations (pp. 80–81)
- if defective goods or workmanship cause death or personal injury, your right to claim compensation can *never* be taken away by a notice or contract term.

Q *Can I cancel the contract I've just signed?*

A Most contracts become legally binding as soon as they are made, and you cannot get out of them simply because you have **changed your mind**. Moreover, most contracts do not have to be in writing and signed, but it prevents disputes about the precise terms agreed if they are written down. Only specific types of contract can be cancelled after signature. They are:

- **credit agreements** The Consumer Credit Act 1974 provides for a five-day cancellation period for credit contracts that are signed anywhere other than at the creditor's or trader's business premises. So if you have just signed a credit contract at your or a friend's home, say, you have five days to cancel if you change your mind (pp. 142–3)
- **timeshare contracts** The Timeshare Act 1992 provides for a 14-day cooling-off period in timeshare contracts signed in the UK and the Timeshare Regulations 1997 allow cancellation within a minimum of ten days elsewhere within the European Union. When you sign you should be given a notice of your cancellation rights and a blank form for you to complete and return. If you cancel during the cooling-off period, you are entitled to recover any money you have paid in connection with the contract (pp. 207–8)
- **contracts made at home** The Consumer Protection (Cancellation of Contracts Concluded Away from Business Premises) Regulations 1987 give you a seven-day cooling-off period during which you have the right to cancel a contract which is made during an 'unsolicited visit' by a salesperson

to your home. An 'unsolicited visit' is one in which you did not make the first contract with the salesperson to request the visit. You have the right to cancel if the appointment was made as a result of unrequested telephone calls or after delivery of a card proposing a visit. And since recent amendments to the Regulations you are protected even if you receive an unannounced visit and agree to the trader coming back – the subsequent visit is also 'unsolicited' under the Regulations. However, if you initiated the visit, you are not protected by the Regulations and can't cancel (pp. 43–4)

- **contracts made at a distance** The Consumer Protection (Distance Selling) Regulations 2000 give consumers who buy goods and services over the phone, Internet, by mail order, or any other contract which is concluded without you and the supplier coming face to face, the right to cancel within seven working days of making the contract without giving a reason. Not all contracts are covered, so you don't have the automatic right to cancel holidays and travel arrangements, or delivery contracts for daily consumption, such as milk (pp. 59–60).

Q *What does 'without prejudice' on a letter mean?*

A Either you or the other party in a dispute may make a 'without prejudice' offer in an effort to reach a settlement. This is useful to avoid making a commitment by mistake when negotiating figures. Any offer in a letter which is 'without prejudice' may not be used against you and may not be revealed if you finally have to go to court to fight the claim. For example, a trader may be asking for £2,000 from you, but you may feel you owe only £750 at the most. If you make an offer of £750 'without prejudice' and this is not accepted by the trader, in the event of the dispute going to court you can still refuse to pay and the judge will never learn that you were prepared to pay anything at all.

It can therefore be useful to put the words 'without prejudice' at the top of a letter in which you're making an offer, since that letter cannot be used against you. But do not use the words on any letter you might later need to prove your case. If you want to make an offer, or if you are responding to an offer from the trader, you could send two letters, one 'without prejudice' which mentions the offer, the other without 'without prejudice' written on it, ignoring the offer completely and pursuing the main basis of your claim.

Q *Have I the right to have my complaint decided in a courtroom, even if the other side doesn't want to, or wants to go to arbitration?*

A Yes. If you have a valid case, it is your choice whether to go to court or choose any alternative means of sorting it out (Chapter 13). If the amount in dispute is £5,000 or less, a company cannot take away your right to go to court.

The Arbitration Act 1996 prevents this. Court action is your right, which would be forfeited only if both sides were to agree to arbitration.

However, if you do want to go to court, the courts are now required to encourage both sides to consider using **Alternative Dispute Resolution** (ADR) (pp. 277–8). When you have issued your claim and the other side has put in its defence, you will have to fill in an **'allocation questionnaire'**. This will ask if the parties want a one-month stay in the claim (that is, to put it on hold) while you attempt to settle it through some form of ADR. A judge can force you to do this and when it comes to the court awarding costs and expenses once the court case is finished, the court must take account not only of the eventual result but also of the conduct of the parties throughout. So, if you don't seriously attempt some form of ADR you might not recover your fees etc. even if you win the case.

Q *How long do I have to start a claim in the courts?*

A This depends on the type of claim, but the Limitation Act does put a time limit on starting a formal claim. Once a claim falls foul of the time limit it is said to become **statute barred**. If you do not issue a court summons against a trader within a certain time, you lose your right to do so. The most common periods are:

- six years for claims for **breach of contract** from the date of the breach (five years in Scotland): this covers any dispute arising from a claim under a contract (for example, those arising under the Sale of Goods Act 1979 or the Supply of Goods and Services Act 1982)
- six years for claims of **negligence** from the date of the negligent act (five in Scotland): this covers any claim for damage, say, to your property where there is no contract between you and the person who caused the damage. Such claims would include, for example, damage caused to your car by another driver
- three years in the event of **personal injury**, whether the claim is for breach of contract or negligence. This would include claims for personal injury under the Consumer Protection Act 1987
- defective design or building work may not become apparent until long after the design or work was done. In some cases the Latent Damage Act 1986 can extend the time period for a claim up to a maximum of 15 years from the date of the work. If your claim is complex, a solicitor may be the best source of advice on this point
- six months for claims of disability discrimination with the possibility of a further two-month extension if, for example, you've been seeking conciliation with the help of the Disability Rights Commission★.

Q *Is the law the same in Scotland, Northern Ireland, England and Wales?*

A No, although most of the rules which apply to the purchase of goods and services are broadly the same throughout the UK. For example, the Sale of Goods Act 1979 applies to the UK as a whole, whereas only part of the Supply of Goods and Services Act 1982 applies in Scotland. Where there are specific differences these are referred to in the relevant question and answer in the book. These are some of the main differences:

- the system of property purchase operates on a model of sealed bids in Scotland. Once a buyer makes an offer and this is accepted by the seller, the contract is binding and this prevents either party pulling out after this stage.
- in Scotland the equivalent of the **county court** is the **sheriff court**
- the **small claims track** in the county court in England and Wales will deal with almost all consumer cases up to a value of £5,000. In Scotland the small claims process is called **'summary cause' procedure** and the limit is £1,500. In Northern Ireland the limit is £2,000
- free booklets are available from all county and sheriff courts which will tell you how to begin your action, and how much it will cost.

Q *Where can I get help with a consumer dispute?*

A Wherever possible you should get clued-up about your rights without having to resort to the expense of using lawyers. This includes knowledge of the alternative ways to solve disputes, such as watchdog and trade association schemes, and ombudsmen (pp. 272–3). Check in this book under the section that relates to your particular dispute. For more personal advice the secret is to go to the right people for help without incurring unnecessary expense. And there are a variety of ways to fund legal action without taking too many financial risks – such as Legal Expenses Insurance (LEI) and 'no win, no fee' arrangements (pp. 110–114). The possibilities for free or cheap initial help include:

- **Citizens Advice★** This is the largest and best-known national network of centres providing free and independent information and advice to people on any legal issue. There are about 1,000 Citizens Advice offices all over Britain, for which addresses and telephone numbers are listed in the local phone directory or on the website. They will refer individuals to solicitors who take part in a fixed-fee interview scheme, or who give initial advice free of charge; or to a Law Centre if the individuals need representation, or where Legal Aid is not available and they cannot afford to pay a solicitor
- **Community Legal Service** This is a government initiative which aims to make it easier to get access to good-quality legal advice (*www.justask.org.uk*)

- **Trading Standards Departments** Part of the local authority services, these are provided by county councils, metropolitan districts and London boroughs, by regional or islands councils in Scotland, and by area Trading Standards Offices of the Department of Commerce in Northern Ireland. Their work can be divided into two categories: helping consumers and enforcing the criminal law. The extent to which they can offer help to consumers varies from area to area, and they may not be as accessible to the public as local advice centres. However, the main job of the departments is enforcing the criminal law as it applies to consumer matters. These include the law on trade descriptions, misleading prices, weights and measures, unsafe or dangerous goods and so on

- **Environmental Health Departments** Another part of the local authority, these enforce the criminal laws on health-related issues including environmental protection, unfit food, and lack of hygiene in restaurants, hotels and other eating places

- **Legal Advice Centres** These informal, non-profit-making legal offices, set up by Citizens Advice, local authorities and various charitable organisations, are staffed by volunteer lawyers who give their services free on a part-time or rota basis. They offer free legal advice but do not generally handle any casework or act for clients in court

- **Law Centres** These are rather like Legal Advice Centres but can take on whole cases and often represent individuals in legal proceedings

- **Which? Legal Service** This is a legal advice line operated by Consumers' Association★. There is a membership fee, and subscribing gives you access to impartial legal advice from a team of highly qualified consumer lawyers. Most issues are dealt with through the telephone advice lines, however, for more complicated cases members receive greatly reduced charges for written legal help. Advice is available on most of the subjects dealt with in this book. See opposite Contents page for further details.

This book's sister publication *160 Letters that Get Results,* also from Which? Books★ could also be very helpful to you.

Q *What rights do I have to get information about others – surely if the local Trading Standards have received lots of complaints about a local trader, for example, I'm entitled to know?*

A There may be a conflict here between the Data Protection Act (which gives individuals, including sole traders, the right not to have personal data passed on to other people), and the Freedom of Information Act 2000 (FoIA), which gives individuals the right to get information from 'public authorities'. These include a wide range of authorities, such as central and local government (including

Trading Standards), police and health authorities, publicly owned companies, the BBC, Bank of England and NHS.

The FoIA was passed in November 2000 but won't be fully implemented until at least January 2005, by which time a general right of access to information held by all public authorities should come into force. Generally you have the right to know if a public authority holds the information you are seeking and, if it's not 'exempt information' then you're entitled to receive it. Even information that's exempted may be disclosed, if it's in the public interest. You may have to pay a fee to cover some of the organisation's costs in collating the information you want or for a copy of a published report.

The FoIA will only apply to those bodies listed in the legislation – there's no general assumption that any body responsible for public services must be open. The Information Commissioner★ oversees the working of the Act.

Follow these guidelines:

- if there is a nominated person or office to deal with an information request write directly to them
- check that the information you're seeking is not already available, on the body's website, or even the National Statistics site (*www.statistics.gov.uk*)
- make your request in writing and give your name and address
- describe the information you're seeking as clearly and precisely as you can. Vague or general requests are likely to be returned for clarification. You don't have to say why you want the information but, if you're happy to do so, it may make it easier to define what you're seeking
- listed bodies generally have 20 working days to reply to your request from the date it is received.

Chapter 1

Buying goods

Most of us buy goods every day – groceries, newspapers etc. – and often clothes, records and so on. Occasionally we buy more substantial and more expensive items, such as furniture and cars. And the way we make our purchases can vary enormously. We may buy from a shop, order over the phone or from a mail-order catalogue, or from a door-to-door trader, or over the Internet. And we may pay the full price, use cash, a cheque or credit card, haggle for a reduction, rummage in the sales for bargains or look in the small ads for something second-hand.

Traders may go bust before they deliver, or may sell us a defective product which causes injury. Goods may not arrive in time, or at all. Fortunately, whatever we buy, wherever we buy, and whatever we pay, the law provides protection when things go wrong.

Q *What are 'goods'?*

A For the purposes of the law, the term 'goods' applies to all personal possessions that are bought and sold, excluding money and property. The Sale of Goods Act 1979 and the Supply of Goods and Services Act 1982 cover a huge variety of products, from cars, electrical goods, toys, clothes and kitchen and bathroom equipment to food. No matter what type of goods you buy, if they aren't up to scratch, your legal rights as set out in those Acts apply (pp. 31–2 and 67–8). However, the Acts do not cover property, so if you buy a house, for example, your rights are very limited and you will have no legal protection from the law on 'goods' (p. 125–6).

Q *I saw a jumper I wanted in a shop window, but when I went to buy it the assistant told me it was wrongly priced. Could I have insisted on paying the price marked?*

A This is a popular belief, but unfortunately it is wrong. Under the civil law a price displayed on the shelf, on the goods themselves, in an advertisement or on a price list, in the window of a shop or even on a website is called an **invitation**

to treat, i.e. an invitation for the public to go to the till or contact the seller and make an offer to buy the goods at that price. But if the shop realises it has mispriced the goods displayed, you cannot insist on buying them at the price marked. In fact:

- as long as it's not on the grounds of sex, race or a disability, a trader can refuse to sell anything to you without giving any reason
- you can try offering the marked price, and the trader *may* agree to sell the item to you at this price
- you can always bargain by offering any price for goods, and if the shop accepts your offer then a contract is made
- if the shop does sell something at the wrong price by mistake, it can't automatically insist you pay the extra later (p. 31 and pp. 61–2).

Under criminal law the trader offering the goods at the 'wrong' price (if the actual price is higher) could be liable to prosecution. The Trade Descriptions Act 1968 makes it an offence to give an indication that goods exposed for sale are being offered at a lower price than that at which they are in fact being offered. Also, the Consumer Protection Act 1987 makes it an offence to give a 'misleading price indication'. You should report cases such as this to the Trading Standards Department at your local council offices. But if the price displayed was a genuine mistake then the shop would not be prosecuted.

Q *When I ordered a sofa, the store asked me for a £100 deposit, which I paid. I was then made redundant and cancelled the order. The store refuses to return my deposit. Can it do that?*

A By placing the order you have made a legally binding contract to purchase the sofa. By cancelling the order you have broken the contract, because you agreed to take delivery of the goods and to pay the balance of the price. In most cases a deposit is taken as security, to make the buyer think twice before attempting to cancel the contract, so the store may be entitled to keep the deposit – particularly if it can show the deposit was a reasonable pre-estimate of the store's loss on cancellation of the order.

In addition, it may be entitled to claim from you any loss of profit over and above the amount of the deposit: for example, if the sofa had been specially made for you to a precise size and could be difficult to sell to anyone else. Fortunately, if the goods are of a standard design and size stores should not have problems selling them on to recover their loss, so you may lose only the deposit.

In certain circumstances you may have the right to challenge the decision of the shop to keep your deposit. If this is part of the standard terms of business of the shop and you think it is unfair contact the Office of Fair Trading (OFT)★ or Consumers' Association★. The Unfair Terms in Consumer Contracts

Regulations 1999 give bodies such as these the power to challenge 'unfair' contract terms and prevent business relying on them.

Q *I paid a deposit for a new sofa, but I've just heard that the store has gone bust. Can I still get my sofa, or at least get my money back?*

A When a business collapses and cannot pay all its debts, a strict order of priority operates concerning creditors. As an ordinary customer, you are what is known as an 'unsecured creditor', and unfortunately you come last in the queue: other creditors, such as the Inland Revenue and the company's employees, are ahead of you. You may miss any chance of getting your deposit back if you do not act quickly. So make a claim to the liquidator or receiver straight away (pp. 160–161). There may well not be enough money to go around, so you could end up getting back less than you paid, or nothing at all. However, all may not be lost in the following circumstances:

- you can get your money back if you paid the deposit by credit card, provided the goods cost more than £100 (the actual deposit paid can be less than this – it is the cost of the goods that counts)
- if the goods had been clearly labelled as yours and put to one side in the store or warehouse when you paid the deposit, they belong to you, not the trader, so you should try to collect them. If you have problems, get in touch with the liquidator or receiver immediately.

Q *I was told that the goods I bought in a sale had previously been £50 but were now £35. I have discovered that they were on sale at £20 just before the sale began. Can the shop do this?*

A The shop may be committing a criminal offence by misleading customers into thinking that they are getting a better deal than they really are. The Consumer Protection Act 1987 sets out guidelines on misleading prices. If a shop is making a comparison with its previous prices:

- the previous price should be the last price at which the goods were available in the previous six months
- the goods should have been available at the higher price for at least 28 consecutive days during the last six months
- the goods should have been on sale at that previous, higher price for that period at the *same* shop.

The law aims to prevent customers being misled. However, retailers can give notice that these conditions do not apply, as long as they spell it out clearly – for example, that the earlier price was only available for one week previously, or that that price had been available only in selected branches. If they don't give you this information and you suspect that you have been misled, report the matter to the Trading Standards Department for the area where the shop is.

Q *I saw a computer advertised on the Internet for £500. Once I had ordered one a message came back to say that the price did not include VAT or the delivery charge, all of which made it almost £100 more expensive than I could buy it for in the high street. As I had no option but to pay these extras, shouldn't they have been included in the advertised price?*

A The Internet can cause a number of problems with tracing the whereabouts of the seller. This will be crucial to whether anything can be done about the pricing practices of the trader.

If the business is outside the UK the law that applies to the deal is very likely to be the law of the country where the business is based. Look at the terms and conditions on the website. If this is an EU country then the laws of that member state which protect consumers are likely to be the same or very similar to those we have in the UK, as many of our own laws come from EU Directives or Regulations. And when it comes to enforcing your rights you can usually sue a company from another member state in your own local court, or use the EEJ-Net to get access to alternatives to court across Europe (pp. 291–2).

If the business is outside the EU, for example in the USA, then the law governing the contract could be very different, and if things go wrong you would have to take legal action in that country to enforce your rights (assuming you can find out what your rights are) and this could be long-winded and costly.

Assuming the trader who was advertising the computer is based somewhere in the UK, you should report the matter to the Trading Standards Officers (TSOs) at the council offices local to the trader's place of business. Under the Consumer Protection Act 1987 a Code of Practice for Traders on Price Indications gives examples of good practice on how to use price indications and avoid misleading consumers. It states that price indications to consumers, by whatever means, must include VAT, and that consumers are to be made fully aware of any extra amounts they have no option but to pay, such as postage, packing and delivery charges, before making a commitment to buy. The Code is a guide to what may or may not be 'misleading'.

In addition, the Price Marking Order 1999 goes some way towards ensuring price transparency by requiring shops to have easily identifiable prices marked on goods for sale – so there should be no need to ask the price. This order implements a European Union Directive which aims to ensure that all EU member states have the same basic level of protection against misleading pricing of goods (it doesn't apply to services). So, similar rights would apply to traders based in the EU and selling on the Internet, say. The Order states that:

- price indications must be unambiguous, easily identifiable and clearly legible
- the selling price must be the final price and include VAT and all other taxes
- the unit price of goods sold by quantity must be given
- extras like postage, packing and delivery charges can be shown separately as long as it is made clear to a prospective purchaser that they are to be added to the price indicated for the products advertised.

Q *I paid £40 each for some theatre tickets from a ticket agent, but have since discovered that the box-office price for the tickets is £19 each. I wasn't told this by the agent. Can I claim the extra back?*

A No. You should expect to pay more when buying tickets from agents – they will add on their commission and there is no limit on the amount of commission agents can charge. And you agreed to pay the £40 price. But the agent has ignored a government code of practice designed to protect consumers from misleading prices, so could be breaking the law. The code, which comes from the Consumer Protection Act 1987, states that if prices are higher than those charged at the box office, then the **face value** of the ticket should be made clear.

This applies to prices given over the phone as well as those quoted in advertisements and so on. Although the code is not mandatory, failure to comply could go against an agency if it is taken to court on a charge of quoting misleading prices.

If you use a ticket agency:

- check prices with the theatre first
- ask the agency what the face value of the tickets is and where the seats are – if it can't, or won't, say, don't buy
- always ring around a few agencies. Prices vary enormously, depending (especially) on the night you want
- if you think you have been misled over price, contact the Trading Standards Department (at the council offices local to the agency).

Q *Is there a difference between an **estimate** and a **quotation**?*

A The words have no legal definition. Nevertheless, there's an increasing tendency for an **estimate** to be a provisional guide to the price for the completed work and a **quotation** to be a firm price. So, if you find you're in dispute over a bill, the real issue is whether the price given was intended to be a rough guide or a fixed amount.

If a trader gives you a document with precise details of the work required plus detailed costs, you should not be charged more once that work is done. Some industries, like the motor trade, have codes of practice which follow this general tendency. So if a dispute arises over the meaning of the words in an agreement the relevant code of practice will provide a useful guideline.

Before you engage someone to do work for you, be sure to get an **exact and firm quotation** in writing, specifying precisely what is to be done.

Q *I ordered a new car last month and, after some discussion, agreed a price of £14,600. The garage rang to tell me the car is ready for collection but say I must pay an extra £900 as they made a* **mistake** *in their original calculations. Should I pay this?*

A No. Because you agreed a fixed price with the garage and knew nothing of its mistake, a contract was made and you can insist on buying the car for that sum. For a trader successfully to argue that its mistake allows it to cancel the contract it must prove that the price mistake was obvious and you could not have really believed the offer was genuine.

If the garage refuses to let you have the car at the agreed price, you should write giving it a time limit of seven days, say, in which to deliver the car. If it doesn't you may buy the same model somewhere else as cheaply as possible, and, if the price is higher, claim the additional sum from the garage (see pp. 61–2).

Q *What happens if, when I buy a car, the manufacturer's recommended price rises between the time I place the order and the time I take delivery?*

A It's important to remember that when you sign a contract you will be bound by the terms of that contract. So you must look at your sales agreement. If this doesn't allow the seller to pass on to the buyer any rise in the seller's costs then you can insist on paying only the original contract price. So check any contract before signing. If there is a term which lets the seller increase the price to take into account increases in the manufacturer's prices, strike it out before you sign and ask the seller to agree the amendments you've made.

You should consider referring contract terms such as these to the Office of Fair Trading (OFT)★ or Consumers' Association★ to be considered under the Unfair Terms in Consumer Contracts Regulations 1999 (p. 58, & pp. 88–9). Under these, the trader could be forced to remove this kind of term from its standard consumer contract if it is considered 'unfair'. The Regulations list examples of terms that are likely to be considered unfair, including situations where a contract allows for the price of goods to be determined at the time of delivery, or allows a seller to increase prices but does not give the consumer the right to cancel the contract if the final price is too high.

Q *I bought a coat to take on my holiday, but after I had worn it only twice the colour started to fade and became rather patchy. I did wear it in the rain, but that's why I bought it. Is the shop responsible?*

A Yes. There's clearly something wrong with a coat that fades and becomes patchy so early in its life, so the shop is responsible. **The Sale of Goods Act 1979** (as amended and strengthened by subsequent Acts – p. 33 & p. 38) is perhaps the most important consumer protection legislation ever passed by Parliament. This says that when you buy goods from a trader (whether they're new, second-hand, or in a sale) those goods must:

- belong to the person selling them – if the seller doesn't have **title** to the goods (i.e. own them) then you won't normally become the owner, even after paying your money
- fit any **description** given of them – whether this was on the label, packaging, in an advertisement, or otherwise. So if you were told the coat was suitable for all kinds of weather it must fit that description
- be of **satisfactory quality** – hence, in good condition and free of minor and major faults, safe and able to do the job expected (taking into account the price, age and so on) and must last a reasonable length of time. So your coat should have been able to withstand ordinary wear and tear
- be reasonably **fit for their purpose** – if you told the seller you needed the coat for a specific purpose (for example, to withstand rain/be waterproof), then it should be fit for that purpose as well as general use
- correspond with any **sample** you have been shown. If you ordered, say, a sofa on the basis of a fabric sample, the goods supplied should accord with the sample.

If the goods don't meet any of these requirements it is the retailer (rather than the manufacturer) who is under a legal obligation to sort out your problem.

Q *Eight months ago I bought a new freezer but the temperature control no longer works properly: last week all the food in it went off. The shop refuses to acknowledge that I have a valid complaint. Can I reject the goods and get my money back?*

A Unlikely, after eight months, although some shops will offer a refund or replacement as a matter of goodwill, and you should check in case you are entitled to a refund under the terms of any retailer or manufacturer guarantee. The problem in this case is that the freezer has not proved **durable** enough, so the seller is in breach of the contractual conditions implied by the Sale of Goods Act 1979 (p.00) and is obliged to compensate you. This problem illustrates a particularly difficult area in consumer law, where defects are not discoverable initially but show up only during the life of the goods. If goods are not up to scratch the law allows you either to **reject** them and claim your money back, plus compensation for any extra loss suffered; or to claim **compensation**, usually the cost of repair; or ask for a repair or a replacement item, plus any extra loss suffered. Note that:

- your right to **reject** the goods and get your **money back** can be lost with the passage of time, regardless of whether you could have known about the defect before it came to light. You lose the right to reject faulty goods once you have '**accepted**' them. The Sale of Goods Act says that you have 'accepted' the goods if you keep them for a '**reasonable**' time before rejecting them. There is no precise legal definition of 'reasonable' – it depends on the circumstances of each case and can be as little as a few weeks. This means that you probably lost the right to get your money back on your freezer a week or so after purchase, even though you didn't know of the problem at that time. In one well-known case it was too late to reject a new car after only three weeks and 228 km (142 miles), even though the defect – which caused the engine to seize up – could not have been discovered earlier. However, in that case, the buyer was fully reimbursed for the **cost of repair** and was also paid compensation for the hassle caused on the day the car broke down. That case was governed by the old Sale of Goods Act before a number of amendments gave consumers stronger rights, so a buyer in a similar situation today would probably be treated better and certainly have a wider range of options (see below)
- even though it may be too late for you to reject your freezer, you still have the right to **compensation**, or to insist on a repair or a replacement. So at the very least the shop ought to pay the full cost of repair of the temperature control plus the cost of the wasted food.

Q *I've complained to the shop about my DVD player. It just stopped working and I'd like a replacement, but the shop is only offering to repair it. What is my position?*

A With faulty goods purchased after 31 March 2003 the Sale and Supply of Goods to Consumers Regulations 2002 apply. The regulations changed the Sale of Goods Act to give consumers very specific rights in relation to defective goods. They amend the existing Sale of Goods Act 1979 (pp. 32–3), and give consumers more choices of redress when things go wrong with goods. The changes include the following:

- manufacturers' guarantees are legally enforceable. This clarifies the previously uncertain position outside Scotland (p. 38)
- if a fault appears in goods during the first six months, it is assumed that the fault was there when the consumer bought the product unless the seller can prove it wasn't. This reverses the previous situation where the buyer had to prove that the goods were defective at the time of purchase (see below)
- if the goods were defective when supplied and the defect comes to light fairly early in their life, the buyer can enforce very specific rights against the seller, including the right to demand a repair or replacement of faulty goods

or a price reduction or refund. There is one important rider to this – if the cost to the seller of repairing or replacing the item is disproportionate, or if repairs are impossible, say, the seller can refuse these remedies. This means you would then be entitled to a partial or full refund – the actual amount would depend on the nature of the defect and the amount of use you'd had of the goods.

Q *I took a newly purchased computer back to the shop where I bought it because it didn't work properly. The manager argued that the shop was not to blame as the staff didn't realise it was defective, and it worked when it was sold to me. Surely this argument is irrelevant?*

A Yes, you can ignore the shop's plea of ignorance. The Sale of Goods Act 1979 imposes **strict liability** on retailers. This means that the goods they sell must satisfy each of the various implied terms, including the satisfactory quality condition. If they don't, they will be liable for **breach of contract**. It is no defence for the seller to claim that he or she did not know about, and could not reasonably be expected to have discovered, the fault. So, although the fault may have been caused by the wiring or a defective microchip which the retailer could not possibly have noticed, the seller is still fully responsible because of his or her contract with the customer.

With purchases made before 31 March 2003 the buyer had to prove that the goods were defective. On contracts made since, the situation has changed dramatically. Under the new regime if a defect comes to light within six months the law assumes the seller is at fault – so the shop has to prove that it was perfect at the time of sale. If you don't discover the fault until after six months the burden of proof rests with you.

Q *When my wife bit into a shop-bought apple pie she started choking. She had swallowed a piece of wire which was inside it. The injury was slight, but what are her rights?*

A If you buy food that is contaminated you should take it to your local Environmental Health Officer (EHO) – at your local council, who will investigate the matter and may recommend a prosecution. But whatever the EHO does, you are still entitled to claim compensation for any injury and possibly for the stress caused. You should complain in writing straight away, and make sure you get the necessary evidence to show that the food was contaminated. If you are injured you may need a report from your doctor to back up your claim. This gives rise to two possible claims:

- under the Sale of Goods Act 1979 against the retailer. The pie was obviously not of satisfactory quality and so the retailer was in breach of contract (pp.

31–2). Claims such as this, even if there is no physical injury, can sometimes lead to substantial compensation for the stress or trauma incurred

- under the Consumer Protection Act 1987 against the manufacturer. The pie was clearly not as safe as you are entitled to expect and there is no need to prove that the manufacturer was at fault in any way (p. 49).

Q *I gave a radio as a* **gift** *to my aunt some months ago. It has stopped working and the shop has refused to repair it for her free of charge, as she doesn't have the* **receipt**. *What can she do?*

A The Sale of Goods Act 1979 says that goods bought from a retailer must be of satisfactory quality). But it's the person who buys the item, not the person who receives it, who has the legal rights if something goes wrong. So the law protects only the purchaser, and the right to claim a refund or the cost of the repair rests with you under the contract of sale between you and the retailer. If the matter went to court you would have to pursue the claim on behalf of your aunt. And as long as you can prove that you bought the radio, there is no legal requirement to produce the receipt – a credit-card slip showing that you bought the item from that shop would do just as well (p. 11). Unless special arrangements had been made at the time of purchase your aunt cannot enforce those rights.

The Contracts (Rights of Third Parties) Act 1999 applies to most contracts entered into on or after 11 May 2000. In certain circumstances it grants the person who receives the gift the right to claim under the sale contract – but these rights are hard to get. In practice, there has to be a written agreement between you and the shop at the time of purchase which specifically agrees that your aunt (the third party) will have the benefit of the goods and that the 1999 Act applies to the purchase. This is unlikely to happen in most consumer contracts.

Q *The carpet we bought has become marked with dark patches. I complained to the shop but they say it is* **shading** *and the carpet is not faulty. Is this right?*

A 'Shading' occurs when some of the carpet pile lies in a different direction from the rest, producing light and dark patches which will not go away. Some retailers (supported by carpet manufacturers) refuse to offer compensation for shading, claiming that it is a normal feature of certain types of carpet and has to be accepted. And it often happens that by the time the shading has become apparent, it is too late to reject a carpet and get your money back, because a period longer than a 'reasonable' time has elapsed (p. 32). So your options could be a claim for compensation, a repair (if this is possible) or a replacement carpet. However, if the cost involved in replacing the carpet is 'disproportionate' the retailer doesn't have to agree. Then you're entitled to a full or partial refund. This will depend on how long you've had the goods, the use you've had and the kind of problem you've got – so it's likely to be partial.

Don't be deterred:

- it may be possible to prove that the problem with your carpet *does* mean that it is of unsatisfactory quality and is unfit for its purpose. You may need to get an expert opinion on this point, so contact a local carpet dealer or the British Carpet Technical Centre (BCTC)*. The BCTC also offers an arbitration scheme to handle complaints about appearance, quality or performance, but if you decide to go to arbitration, you cannot later choose to go to court if you disagree with the decision (pp. 272–3)
- if the shop did not warn you about shading before you bought the carpet, you have a claim against the retailer for breach of contract. You will be entitled to claim the difference between the price paid for the carpet and what it is really worth, taking into account the shading characteristics. So, if the carpet is so bad that it is effectively worth very little, compensation may be substantial enough to allow you to buy a replacement.

Q *I often buy goods in **sales** or marked **bargain, shop-soiled** or **seconds**. How does this affect my rights if they are faulty?*

A You have the same rights as you do when buying goods for the full price (pp. 31–2). You are free to shop for bargains, rummage in sales, or even haggle to reduce the price, without fear of reducing those rights. Even if described as 'seconds' or 'imperfect', goods must always be of 'satisfactory quality', so the seller can't fob you off with rubbish (unless of course the goods are actually described as 'rubbish'!).

Signs like 'shop-soiled' or 'imperfect' imply that the standard or quality may be below what you might otherwise reasonably expect. Usually the imperfection or area of soiling will be pointed out to you or will certainly be apparent, so you buy knowing the defect is there. For example, the pattern in the weave of a sweater may be imperfect so you can't complain about that specific problem later. But if the sweater unravels when you wear it, or a sleeve becomes detached when you wash it, you have a valid complaint under the Sale of Goods Act 1979.

Q *I bought a television to get the free flights that were offered with it. It seemed such a good deal, but I've got to buy accommodation from a list provided and it's all very expensive. It's not such a good offer after all. What is the law on **free offers**?*

A If you buy a product with a 'free' offer attached, you are legally entitled to benefit from that offer, but many free offers will have binding terms and conditions. If you comply with all the conditions to the letter but don't get the goods or services offered, you may have a claim for breach of contract against the company running the promotion. So if you apply for an offer, always read these conditions very carefully before you make your purchase – you might have to pay for accommodation at a specified hotel (not likely to be a cheap one), you might have to take all your meals in an expensive restaurant in the same hotel, you may have only a couple of dates to choose from, or your dates of travel or departure airport may be imposed upon you.

With some offers the choice of dates is **subject to availability**, so you may be unable to rely on travelling on the date you want. If you are attracted by an offer attached to a product, only make the purchase if you want the product and after reading the conditions.

The British Code of Advertising, Sales Promotion and Direct Marketing specifies how these offers are promoted and what information the promoter must give you. If you feel the offer is misleading, report the matter to your local Trading Standards Department, or to the Advertising Standards Authority (ASA)* which administers the Code. The main points of the Code are:

- the terms and conditions of a promotion should be clear, complete and easily seen by consumers *before* purchase
- even if an offer is 'subject to availability' the promoter must take all reasonable steps to avoid disappointing the consumer
- the promoter should have adequate resources to administer the promotion to prevent justifiable complaints
- if the promotion provokes an unexpectedly high level of demand and the promoter is subsequently unable to supply the promised goods, then alternatives must be offered of equal or greater value.

Q *The tiles on our kitchen floor are wearing badly after less than two years. We paid a lot, expecting the floor to last for many years. The showroom rejected our claim for compensation on the grounds that the tiles were not faulty when delivered to us and said, 'You can't expect floor tiles to last forever.' Have we any legal rights against the store?*

A Yes. The Sale of Goods Act 1979 specifically refers to **durability** as a component of satisfactory quality and fitness for purpose. This obligation is a continuing warranty:

- it is not enough for the supplier to deliver goods that are OK at the time of purchase – they must continue to be fit for their normal purpose for a reasonable time. No particular time limits are laid down as these will vary from one type of goods to another and will also depend on the price and the related quality of the goods
- although your tiles may have seemed to be of the right quality when they were delivered, the fact that they have worn out so quickly would indicate

that there must have been a defect in them initially, although the problems didn't reveal themselves until later

- the showroom might suggest that you have misused the floor tiles in some way (pp. 10–11), although that is more usually argued in the case of cars and other mechanical goods where careless servicing and maintenance may be to blame. But floor tiles are designed to be walked on and to get wet, etc., so you can pursue your rights with more confidence

- always be careful not to fall foul of the limitation period laid down by law, which prevents claims being made after the lapse of a specified time – in this case, six years (five years in Scotland) (pp. 22–3).

Q *If I buy an electrical product or a car which is covered by a* **manufacturer's guarantee**, *does this mean that I can't complain if the product goes wrong after the guarantee (usually lasting one year) has expired?*

A Many manufacturers promise to resolve problems in their products free of charge. Some offer money back, others offer a free repair or replacement. Always check the wording of a guarantee to see what is included. The important things to remember about free guarantees are as follows:

- rights under the manufacturer's guarantee are **in addition to your rights** against the seller of the goods under the Sale of Goods Act 1979 and are not in any way an alternative to those rights. The manufacturer is legally obliged to explain this, so you will see phrases like 'this does not affect your statutory rights'

- strangely, in England and Wales, until changes to the Sale of Goods Act were introduced for purchases after 31 March 2003, there was some doubt whether such a manufacturer's guarantee was legally enforceable (Scottish law, on the other hand, has long treated such guarantees as contracts between the consumer and the manufacturer, which makes the terms of the guarantee legally binding). Now England and Wales have been brought into line with Scotland, courtesy of the EU Consumer Guarantees Directive, and manufacturers' guarantees are now legally enforceable. But be careful as they may give you limited rights and limited time to enforce them

- manufacturers are under no legal obligation to give a guarantee and if they do it can be as limited in scope as they wish – check carefully

- the fact that the guarantee lasts for only one year (or six months, or whatever) may give the impression that this is the full extent of the durability which you are entitled to expect. In fact, the extent of the cover offered by the manufacturer has no effect on your statutory rights against the seller .

Q *When goods are faulty, can the shop from which they were bought insist that I take* **exchange goods** *or a* **credit note** *when I would prefer my money back?*

A You are entitled to ask for **money compensation** because the seller has broken a condition of the Sale of Goods Act 1979. This compensation should be in the form of either a full refund of the price or the cost of repair, depending on how long you have had the goods. For goods purchased after 31 March 2003 you also have a choice of other options – repair or replacement. If the shop does offer a replacement or credit note you may prefer to accept this, particularly if it's too late to get a full refund – the decision is entirely yours – but it can't force you.

The usual way to **reject** goods is to return them to the shop and demand an immediate refund, but you don't have to take them back – it's up to the seller to collect them, or pay for them to be returned. If the shop refuses or if it's a large product, like a fridge, send a letter making it clear that you are rejecting the goods and seeking all your money back. Keep a copy of the letter. If that has no effect, in the last resort you will have to sue the retailer (pp. 275–6).

Remember, once you reject goods you must stop using them altogether otherwise you may lose the right to reject them.

Q *Recently I bought a blouse. When I got home I tried it on. I found it didn't fit very well and I've* **changed my mind** *about the colour anyway. I took it back but the shop refused to refund my money. They did offer me a* **credit note***. What can I do?*

A Nothing. If the blouse is of the right quality and perfectly wearable, you can't blame the shop because you made a mistake in choosing the wrong size or colour. You should have tried the blouse on first, if possible, and checked it was the colour you wanted. So the offer of a credit note may be more than you're entitled to.

It would be different if the blouse had been wrongly labelled, so that you bought what appeared to be your size and it turned out to be a size smaller – this would be a breach of 'description' under the Sale of Goods Act 1979.

Some shops operate a return and refund policy that applies whatever the reason for the goods being returned. But they do not have to do this. If the shop does not state that this is its policy and you're worried about the colour or the size, get the sales assistant to write on the back of the receipt that you can return the goods and exchange them for something else if they are unsuitable, or be given a credit note, or even get your money back.

Q *I went back to the shop where I bought a handbag to complain that the strap had broken. The shop had closed down, so I went to the nearest branch. I was told that each* *branch was a separate **franchise** and I could only claim against the branch where I bought the goods. Is this true?*

A If it was a franchise the shop would have been legally obliged to display the name and address of the owner (usually by the till, or on its letterhead if it did business by correspondence). Although all the branches may be using the same logo and name, each one could be a different company. Your contract was with the person or company who owned the franchise to that branch. So, if the company that was running that particular branch has ceased trading, even though there are many other shops with the same name still trading, you are unlikely to recover your money. If you paid by credit card and the price was over £100, you may have a claim against the credit-card company (pp. 153–4).

Q *The television I bought from the local branch of a large electrical store came with a 'free' radio-cassette recorder. The television is fine but the radio has stopped working. The shop manager said, 'You get what you pay for. As it was a **free gift** you can hardly complain that it's rubbish!'*

A The retailer is wrong. The shop has supplied the radio as part of the contract of sale and is responsible for the quality of both the television and the radio. They must both be of satisfactory quality and function properly. The retailer will have to pay for the repair: if he or she refuses, you are entitled to get it repaired elsewhere and send the bill to the shop.

Q *Sometimes when I buy things there are signs claiming that the shop is bound by a **code of practice**. Do these mean anything?*

A The Office of Fair Trading (OFT)⋆ has long encouraged trade associations to prepare codes of practice for their members. Such codes now exist for many types of business including double glazing, travel agents and tour operators, laundries and dry cleaning, mail order, and many areas of retail from electrical goods to cars, footwear, and so on.

But it can be difficult for consumers to know what benefits a code has for them. During 2004 the OFT will launch a new scheme to accredit codes which have proved their value to consumers by meeting the OFT's core criteria for accreditation. These criteria include the way the code sponsor (usually a trade association) is organised, the way the code is prepared and the content decided, how complaints are handled and monitored (consumers must, for example, have access to an independent redress mechanism), and how the code is policed and publicised (*www.oft.gov.uk/Consumer/default.htm*).

The aim of the exercise is to raise business standards by recommending standards of practice. The recommendations in the various codes have no legal force, however, and no legal action can be taken in the courts if a member does not adhere to them. Many codes offer free conciliation by the trade association in the event of a dispute between a member and a customer. Some also offer a system of low-cost arbitration through which the dispute can be resolved instead of going to court.

Q *I traded my old fridge in **part exchange** for a new one and paid the difference in cash. What are my rights if there are faults in the new fridge?*

A Your rights are exactly the same as if you had paid in full for the new fridge. Part-exchange deals are common in the case of cars, cookers, washing machines, cameras and an increasing range of other goods. Whatever the goods, you have the full protection of the Sale of Goods Act 1979 (pp. 31–2).

Q *I ordered and paid for a table from a furniture shop, explaining that I needed it in time for a birthday party four weeks away. What can I do if the table does not arrive in time?*

A There is no legal requirement that goods be delivered within a fixed period, so it's up to you to tell the retailer if you have a deadline. The Sale of Goods Act 1979 says that the seller must deliver the goods to you within a 'reasonable' time. There are no hard and fast rules about what is 'reasonable'. It depends on the circumstances – the type of goods, their availability and so on. Note that:

- if the date of delivery is important you should make **time of the essence** in writing when making the contract. Then, if delivery is delayed by even a day, you are entitled to cancel the contract and receive a full refund of the price paid. And if it costs you more than the price you paid originally to get the same goods elsewhere, you can claim the extra cost from the original supplier

- if no specific date was agreed in this way you can give notice in writing to the shop, imposing an ultimate time limit. The period specified in the notice must be reasonable, and if the goods do not arrive by that deadline you may cancel the contract and get your money and any extra costs back. You would then be within your rights to go to another supplier who has the table in stock and get it immediately. If in doing so you have to pay more, the additional cost can be recovered from the first shop

- sometimes it is clear from the nature of the goods (Christmas cards, or items in an Easter catalogue, say) that the goods ordered are required by a particular date. So even if you have not specified a date, if such goods do not arrive in time then you are entitled to cancel the contract and get a refund of your money plus any extra costs.

Q *The furniture I bought was delivered to my home. I was asked to sign a* **delivery note** *which stated: 'I acknowledge that the goods have been delivered in good order.' When I unpacked the furniture I found it badly scratched. Should I have signed the note?*

A If you have no option but to sign the note, and no opportunity to inspect properly, the safer course would be to add 'goods not examined' or a similar note to the effect that you have not had an opportunity to inspect the contents to see if they are perfect. The Sale of Goods Act gives you the right to reject faulty goods such as this, but you will lose that right once you have 'accepted' the goods (pp. 32–3). The trader could argue that by signing the delivery note you cannot complain and get your money back now. Do not worry. An amendment to the Act makes it clear that whatever you sign you must have a proper right to examine goods before you are deemed to have accepted them. This means a right to unpack them, inspect them, and use them for a reasonable period to make sure they are as described, of the right quality, and free of damage and other defects. So you can still complain and, as long as you take immediate action, you can still reject the furniture and insist on a refund, whatever the delivery note said.

Q *The iron I bought was faulty and I was given a replacement. The replacement is no better and stopped working within a week. The shop has refused to exchange it, saying that the second iron was a gift. Is this correct?*

A No. Although you cannot insist on a replacement, if you are offered one it must be of satisfactory quality and fit for its purpose (pp. 31–2). There is some legal dispute over whether the second goods are supplied under a new contract, or whether this transaction is a continuation of the original contract of purchase – this precise legal point has not been tested, but the fact remains that you are legally entitled to goods of satisfactory quality.

If your goods are replaced by the manufacturer this will give rise to a contractual obligation on the manufacturer to ensure that the goods supplied are of the proper quality. Legally this creates a contract of exchange, and your rights would be governed by the Supply of Goods and Services Act 1982 instead of the Sale of Goods Act 1979 (p. 68).

Q *After my new freezer was delivered I noticed a scratch on the side. Can I reject it and get my money back?*

A This will depend on how bad the scratch is. The Sale of Goods Act 1979 says that to be of 'satisfactory quality' (pp. 31–2) goods must be free from major and minor defects. If the scratch is very small it may be that there is no legal claim. The law will not concern itself with trifles.

Q *A salesman turned up at my home unannounced. He was selling burglar alarms. As I was alone I asked him to come back when my partner was there so we agreed that he would return the following day. When he did I was still on my own but I let him in anyway. He left after three hours and only when I'd signed his contract. When my partner and I talked about it we decided it was far too expensive. But when we rang the company to cancel the contract we were told that it was too late. What can I do?*

A The general rule is that once you've signed a contract you can't cancel it. The law does recognise that in some circumstances this rule would be too harsh (pp. 20–21). In this situation the Consumer Protection (Cancellation of Contracts Concluded Away from Business Premises) Regulations 1987 apply. The Regulations give you seven days to change your mind (a seven-day 'cooling-off' period) and were introduced to help the victims of unscrupulous doorstep traders. To qualify for this thinking time the contract must have been signed at your own or another person's home, or even at your place of work, the goods or services you agreed to buy must cost more than £35, and, most importantly, the contract must have been signed following an '**unsolicited**' visit by the salesperson. The crucial part is that the visit must not have been expressly requested by you. Clearly, if you contact the trader or company yourself and invite them to your home you have no legal right to change your mind once you've signed the contract – you initiated the visit so it wasn't 'unsolicited'. In those cases the law assumes you knew what you were doing and that you had shopped around before choosing which seller to contact and invite in.

The 1987 Regulations were strengthened recently – the original version allowed unscrupulous traders to get around the law, for example by calling unannounced and then persuading potential customers to invite them back another time, or suggesting a revisit, thus removing the 'unsolicited' element. The law is now much stricter:

- even though you receive an unsolicited visit and then arrange for the salesperson to come back at another time more convenient for you this still counts as 'unsolicited' and so any contract you sign is cancellable
- the salesperson commits a criminal offence if he or she does not tell you about your right to cancel. You must be given a written notice of your cancellation rights spelling out what you have to do to cancel and whom to notify. Trading Standards Officers police this area of law and a trader can be fined up to £2,500 for failing to comply.

If you're not told in writing of your right to cancel, then the seven days doesn't start to run until you are. So, not only does the salesperson commit an offence, but the law won't allow him or her to enforce the contract against you. In effect, you can ignore it and are entitled to recover any money you may have paid – you'll have to hand back the goods as well.

Unscrupulous doorstep traders have given honest salespeople a bad name. The kinds of goods and services you're most likely to find on offer from doorstep salespeople are tarmacking drives, roof repairs, vacuum cleaners, double glazing and burglar alarms, general building repairs and maintenance work. A few specific services are not included in the Regulations, such as building contracts for the construction or extension of a building, but most things are covered (pp. 263–4).

Q *I've seen some clothes I'd like to buy but they are only available by mail order and I'm worried about ordering goods by post. What laws can I rely on?*

A In fact, you may have extra protection when you buy mail-order goods:

- you are fully covered by the Sale of Goods Act 1979, so the goods must be of satisfactory quality and be reasonably fit for their purpose, and should correspond with their description in advertisements or catalogues (pp. 31–2)
- you are fully covered by the Consumer Protection Act 1987, so if something you have bought turns out to be dangerous and causes damage to you or your property you can claim against the manufacturer (p. 49)
- the Consumer Protection (Distance Selling) Regulations 2000 cover contracts made by telephone, fax or television, over the Internet or by mail order, and give consumers the right to change their mind and withdraw from most of these contracts within the first seven working days, without giving any reason (pp. 59–60).

In addition to the legal protection you have when buying by mail order there are a number of voluntary schemes in place which can offer even greater protection than the law (see below).

Q *In catalogues and mail-order adverts I've seen lots of logos claiming to offer protection. What should I really look out for?*

A It depends where you saw the advert or what kind of publication you are buying the goods from. The law as described above will always give you a basic level of protection. Many mail-order protection schemes take that protection one step further:

- when you buy from a catalogue or respond to an advert in a magazine or newspaper, you are probably covered by one of the mail-order protection schemes. For example, the Mail Order Traders' Association★ code of practice states that customers should be allowed at least 14 days to return unwanted goods. Not all traders are members of particular schemes. The British Code of Advertising, Sales Promotion and Direct Marketing, administered by the Advertising Standards Authority (ASA)★, covers *all* mail-order traders, including companies selling on the Internet, as long as they are based in the UK (p. 52, pp. 59–60). It says that consumers are entitled to return unwanted goods within seven days for any reason. So you have time to change your mind if you don't like the goods, and if you send them back within the stated time you will be entitled to all your money back. You may have to pay the postage for this, depending on the policy of the company, but if you're returning goods because they are defective you should never have to pay to do so. If you run into difficulty, contact the protection scheme or the ASA as appropriate

- the trade association will usually investigate any complaint against a member, and will offer a conciliation service to you and the member free of charge
- if you have a complaint about goods ordered directly in response to an advertisement in a newspaper or journal, write to the advertising manager at the publication in which the advertisement appeared giving details of the date of publication, the name and address of the company, goods ordered, price, amount of money sent, and nature of the complaint
- if you ordered and paid in advance for goods from a company that goes bust you will be protected if the company belongs to the Mail Order Protection Scheme (MOPS)★. The MOPS logo should be displayed on the advert. There are time limits within which you have to claim, so in such cases you should contact the advertising manager for the publication in which the advertisement appeared as soon as possible. MOPS schemes are run by:
  - the Newspaper Publishers' Association Ltd★, for the national dailies and the Sunday papers
  - the Periodical Publishers Association Ltd★, for most magazine and periodical publishers
  - the Newspaper Society★, for most regional and local papers
  - the Scottish Daily Newspaper Society★, for daily papers in Scotland.

Q *The goods I bought from a mail-order company haven't arrived after six weeks. Can I cancel the contract and get my money back?*

A There is no legal requirement that goods arrive within a particular time. The law merely says they must arrive within a 'reasonable' time (p. 41). The British Code of Advertising, Sales Promotion and Direct Marketing states that mail-order goods should arrive within 30 clear days of order, unless the goods are of a type that may require longer, such as plants or made-to-measure clothing. The timescale should be stated on the advertisement or in the catalogue.

- if you need goods by a particular date, make this date 'of the essence' when you place your original order

- keep a note of the date (as well as the company's name and address and goods ordered) when you order goods so you know when the stated date has arrived or the 28 days are up
- if the goods don't arrive by the stated date, or within the 28 days set out in the Code, you can cancel the contract and recover your money
- if the trader is a member of a trade association contact it for help in sorting out your problem. If it is not a member of any particular association, contact the Advertising Standards Authority (ASA)★. The ASA administers the Code, and although this has no legal force, it is a good indicator of what length of time is 'unreasonable'.

Q *I'm fed up with receiving junk mail and offers for things I don't want. How can I prevent this?*

A The law puts responsibilities on businesses which may have your details or pass them on to others, and also on those businesses which may get hold of your details and want to target you for marketing. The main areas are:

- the Data Protection Act 1998 strengthens and extends the data protection regime that has existed in England, Wales and Northern Ireland since 1984. The Act is enforced by the Information Commissioner and anyone falling foul of the Act faces a substantial fine. The relevant part of the Act here is that any individual is entitled to prevent personal data about themself from being used for direct marketing. Under the Act 'direct marketing' covers any kind of communication of any advertising or marketing material which is directed to particular individuals (pp. 258–9, p. 261)
- If you want to reduce the volume of unwanted mail you receive write to the Mailing Preference Service (MPS)★ and ask for your name to be removed from direct mailing lists. It could take up to three months for the mail to stop. Also, the British Code of Advertising Practice (BCAP) says that any company using a mailing list to send out goods must refer to the MPS register and exclude people who appear on it
- the British Code of Advertising, Sales Promotion and Direct Marketing is administered by the Advertising Standards Authority (ASA)★ and, unlike the Data Protection Act, it doesn't have the force of law. It says that traders must tell you if they might pass your name and address on to other companies and must give you a chance to tell them if you don't want your details used in this way for other traders' promotions
- the Telecommunications (Data Protection and Privacy) (Direct Marketing) Regulations 1998 impose a complete ban on unsolicited advertising or marketing faxes to consumers, unless you've given your prior consent. If you

don't want to receive unsolicited direct marketing calls you can opt out by registering with the Telephone Preference Service★

- direct marketing companies must provide an address or a free phone number for contact when requested by consumers so that you can ask to be removed from their own database. The Regulations are enforced by the Information Commissioner★

- the Consumer Protection (Distance Selling) Regulations 2000 require telephone sales and marketing businesses which cold-call consumers at home to give details at the start of the call of who they are and why they're calling.

Q *I ordered a hair-dryer by mail-order. It was delivered in a battered box and when I opened it the plastic casing of the dryer was smashed. Do I still have to pay for it?*

A In practice, mail-order companies which belong to trade associations generally agree to replace damaged goods free of charge. But there may be no protection if the company is not a member of a trade association and therefore does not subscribe to a code of practice. In such circumstances your rights will depend on whether the supplier can prove that the goods left its premises in perfect condition.

If it is clear that the goods were damaged in transit, you have a claim against the carrier. In the case of the Post Office, you should complete form P58 (available at any post office) and send it to the Head Postmaster. Remember to keep a copy of what you write. If you can show that the parcel was damaged in the post, you are entitled to compensation on a sliding scale, but it may not cover the actual cost of the item.

The Sale of Goods Act 1979 says that where goods are bought by a consumer (rather than a business), the risk of accidental loss or damage to the goods stays with the seller until the goods are delivered to the consumer. So if the goods arrive damaged you can reject the goods and demand your money back.

Q *I received in the post a set of kitchen knives which I didn't order. A letter arrived asking for £60, which I ignored. Now I've received a letter threatening to sue me. What should I do?*

A You should certainly not pay any money. The practice of demanding payment for unsolicited goods was made illegal by the Unsolicited Goods and Services Act 1971 (or, in Northern Ireland, the Unsolicited Goods and Services [Northern Ireland] Order 1976). As long as the goods were sent to you in your private capacity (not to your business) and had not been requested or ordered by you and you have not agreed to acquire or return them, the goods become your property and you are free to do whatever you want with them.

The law makes it a criminal offence for a trader to do any of the following to consumers in relation to unsolicited goods or services: demand payment, threaten legal proceedings, place or threaten to place the consumer's name on a list of defaulters, or instigate a debt collection procedure (see also p.266). You are therefore not obliged to meet demands for payment of the goods or services and should report the matter to the Trading Standards Department at your local council (address in phone book).

Q *We collected tokens from cereal packs, sent them off with 50 pence and waited for our 'free' gift to arrive. A letter from the company told us that they were out of stock. It's now been three months and nothing has arrived. Can we insist on being sent the goods offered?*

A Truly 'free' offers are very rare indeed. If you have to do something in return, such as collecting tokens and/or sending money, this creates a contract between you and the company offering the 'gift'. So by collecting and sending off tokens from the packets of cereal, you have entered into a contract and you are entitled to receive your gift. If the company fails to deliver its part of the bargain, the compensation you can expect to receive should put you in the same position as if the contract had been fulfilled, so you can claim the cost of buying the same item or a similar one elsewhere.

Q *What does the term **product liability** mean?*

A It means legal responsibility for the safety of goods and is generally used to describe the legal position between a manufacturer and the ultimate user of the product, the consumer. This is to distinguish it from the legal relationship between the consumer and the person who sells the product. Usually this is a different person or company. Your rights against the seller are governed by contract law (pp. 31–32). Other than under the terms of a manufacturer's warranty you do not have a contract with the manufacturer. So a different set of legal principles applies if you want to hold the manufacturer responsible for losses you suffer owing to a problem with his or her product. Product liability laws are usually cited if the product in question has proved to be unsafe in some way and has caused either physical injury or damage to property.

Q *My parents bought us a washing machine as a wedding present. The machine burst into flames while we were out. Luckily the emergency services put the fire out quickly but the smoke and fire damage is extensive. It will cost us a good deal to replace everything we've lost and to repair the damage. Who is responsible for this?*

A As you did not buy the machine yourself you have no contract with the shop it came from and therefore cannot claim under the Sale of Goods Act 1979 (pp. 31–32). So any claim will be against the manufacturer under the Consumer Protection Act 1987. This allows you to claim for the damage to your house and any injury to you, but not the damage to the machine itself, for which your parents should claim from the retailer. Had you been injured during the fire you would have needed to obtain medical evidence from your GP or a specialist.

You may also be covered for the damage to the building and contents under your household insurance, so check this carefully.

Q *Do I have to prove the manufacturer was at fault to have a viable claim for injury or damage caused by faulty goods?*

A It used to be the case that to establish a claim against the manufacturer you had to prove the manufacturer had been negligent. This was often very difficult without specialised technical evidence and knowledge of the company's manufacturing processes. The Consumer Protection Act 1987 changed all that. Nowadays:

- you have to prove that the product was **defective** and that it **caused** the injury or damage about which you are complaining
- a product is considered **defective** if it is **less safe** than the consumer is reasonably entitled to expect (for a successful claim, therefore, goods must be unsafe, not merely shoddy)
- the terms of the Consumer Protection Act 1987 do not remove the existing liability of retailers under the Sale of Goods Act 1979 (pp. 31–32)
- the Consumer Protection Act applies to products *supplied* after March 1988
- you cannot claim for damage to the product itself. So if, say, your car breaks down completely but does not damage you or anything else this law will not help you, although you may be able to claim against the retailer for this sort of problem under the contract of sale.

Q *I received severe head injuries following a car accident. My head hit the side door in the crash and I have had to give up my job. The consultant told me that if an air bag had* *been fitted to the car, I wouldn't have received any head injuries. Surely it's the manufacturer's responsibility to fit safety features to products?*

A It is, although much will depend on the age of the car. The Consumer Protection Act 1987 makes manufacturers 'strictly liable' for 'defective' products, so you may have a claim against the manufacturer for damages for the injury you suffered as a direct result of the lack of safety features in the car. Damage to property must amount to at least £275 (a purely arbitrary figure designed to discourage lots of minor claims against manufacturers), but even minor personal injury is covered. Given that you have suffered a serious injury and the fact that side air bags have for years been standard on many cars, there is a strong argument that the overall design of the car does not meet current expectations of safety (p. 49). In any claim for serious injury, you should seek the advice of a specialist personal injury solicitor. Contact the Law Society* or the Association of Personal Injury Lawyers (APIL)*.

Q *I've found out too late that the washer dryer that caused a severe fire in my house was the subject of a **product recall**. I never heard about this. Does the fact that there was a recall strengthen my case?*

A The recall makes it much easier to prove that there was a defect as the evidence has been provided by the manufacturer. It will be difficult for the manufacturer to argue that the product was not defective if the fault that caused the fire in your house is the same as the one that prompted the recall. It may be advisable to have the appliance in question examined by an appropriate independent expert to confirm what the nature of the problem was. The manufacturer will probably also be keener to sort out problems if there has already been the bad publicity of a recall.

At present, product recalls are usually advertised in the national press. If you have such a product you should contact the manufacturer immediately. If it's already too late and the damage is done, ask the manufacturer for compensation.

There are few guidelines for domestic product recalls. Withdrawing an unsafe product from sale is the first step, but this doesn't help those who have already bought one of the items and have it in their home. Serious faults need more urgent and widely published recalls, and some products, including medicines and foods, have special rules to ensure that unsafe products are taken off the market as soon as possible. But what is needed are simple procedures that all manufacturers can follow. At the time of writing discussions are taking place in Europe with a view to forcing producers of consumer products to take appropriate action which would include withdrawing a product from the market, and recalling products already sold. Currently, no one can force a manufacturer to initiate a product recall although the government can make a manufacturer issue a notice warning people about an unsafe product. This is usually enough of a threat to make most manufacturers institute a recall. The Department of Trade and Industry (DTI)★ publishes a 'good practice' guide for industry on how to improve the current practice of recalling products to protect consumer safety, and to encourage all producers to plan in advance for such an event. (Readers may find the DTI Consumer Gateway website★ useful.)

Q *My motorbike broke down completely after six months, and the manufacturer is refusing to repair it or replace it. Isn't it the manufacturer's responsibility?*

A No. Product liability does not help you when goods are merely shoddy or break down. You should go back to the shop and exercise your rights as a buyer under the Sale of Goods Act 1979 (pp. 31–2). The manufacturer will only be liable if:

- the fault was such as to make the vehicle **unsafe** and you actually suffered some damage to yourself or your property (other than the bike) as a result of this
- you received a manufacturer's guarantee when you bought the motorbike. If it has not expired, the manufacturer may put things right under the terms of the guarantee.

Q *I bought a **second-hand** car from a garage last week and signed a form which said 'sold as seen'. It was a low-mileage car and was described as in 'very good condition'. The car broke down as I was driving along the motorway and now needs a new engine. The engineer's report says that the garage would have known that the engine was defective when they sold it to me. But they refuse to pay the repair costs. Is this right?*

A No. When you buy **second-hand** goods from a trader, the Sale of Goods Act 1979 applies, so they must fit their **description**, be of **satisfactory quality**, and be **fit for their purpose** (pp. 31–2). Obviously, a second-hand car won't be in such good condition as a new car, but it should be roadworthy, and the quality you can expect will depend on the age, the price and the description given of the car. In this case the engineer's statement shows that the car was defective at the time you purchased it so it didn't fit its description and was not of satisfactory quality. It also seems likely that there was a **misrepresentation** which led you to buy the car.

If you act quickly enough you are entitled to reject the car and get your money back. If you've lost the right to reject, or if you want to keep the car, you are entitled to compensation for the defective engine, or you can claim a repair or a replacement car (although this may be considered 'disproportionate'). Compensation is usually quantified as the cost of repair anyway. In this case the engine has to be replaced, so the garage will be responsible for this, although you may be asked for a contribution if the engine it puts in is a new one, and therefore better than the old one you thought you were getting.

Q *I had a new gearbox put in my recently purchased car before I realised the car had previously been reported as a stolen vehicle. Can I claim that money back from the true owner?*

A Under the Torts (Interference with Goods) Act 1977 you are entitled to receive compensation for the repairs and improvements you make. This Act can be used like a shield, not a sword, so if the true owner of the car takes you to court to get the car back, the court will make an allowance for the increase in value of the car which is attributable to the repairs and improvements you have made. Your position will be much weaker if you let the true owner take the car back without going to court, because then you cannot use this Act to sue the true owner for your financial outlay on repairs. So while there is a dispute, park the car on your property if possible, and don't give anyone permission to take it away. Try to negotiate a reasonable payment and avoid going to court if you can. But if a court does order you to hand it over you should be able to recover the full purchase price from the person who sold the car to you (see p. 54).

Q *We've just bought a car from a **private ad** in the local paper. The ad described it as reliable, and as having been serviced regularly. The lady who was selling the car said that it had been looked after well. On the first long journey the engine seized up and it's now obvious that it hasn't been serviced for a long time. Will the seller have to pay for the repairs?*

A When you buy goods from a **private seller** the principle of **caveat emptor** ('let the buyer beware') applies. There is no legal requirement that the goods are of satisfactory quality or fit for their purpose. With private sales you will have redress only if:

- the goods don't correspond with any **description** you have been given, or
- the seller was guilty of **misrepresentation**, or
- the seller doesn't really own the goods.

In this case the car was described as being reliable, in good condition, and as having been regularly serviced and looked after well. This is clearly not true and so will give rise to two possible claims:

- **breach of description** This entitles you to reject the car and get your money back, or keep it and ask for compensation (usually the cost of repair)
- **misrepresentation** This entitles you to cancel the contract and get your money back, or keep it and ask for compensation. A misrepresentation is a

statement of fact (not opinion) which is made by the seller before the contract is made. If you relied on that statement when deciding whether to buy and it turns out to be wrong, you can claim.

In any dispute where the seller has made a written or verbal statement about the goods, it is probably best to allege both misrepresentation and breach of contract.

Q *What steps should I take to avoid problems when I buy a second-hand car?*

A When buying a second-hand car, your legal rights may be limited (see above). It is almost impossible to protect yourself fully against hidden defects and legal problems. However, here are a few tips which should help:

- employ an engineer to check the car over and report on the car's condition. This is especially important if you are buying from a private seller. If you are a member of a motoring organisation it may provide a vehicle inspection report if requested
- carry out a search with Hire Purchase Information plc (HPI)★. You can apply to HPI direct and will be charged a small fee for each search. An HPI search does not guarantee that the car you buy is OK, but it will tell you whether the car is recorded:

  - to be subject to an outstanding finance agreement
  - to have had a major damage-related insurance claim
  - to be stolen or subject to fraudulent activity (see below)
  - to have been subject to a registration plate change

- try to make a note of everything that the seller says about the car – it is useful to take an independent witness along with you so that you have proof that any claims made were really said. Also, hang on to the advert if it contains a description of the car
- read the latest *Which?* report on buying a second-hand car: following the advice should help you avoid costly mistakes.

Q *Last year I bought a used car privately. I have now received a visit from the police, who inform me that it had been **stolen** the year before I purchased it. The person I bought the car from doesn't know anything about this either. The original owner wants the car back. Do I have to return it?*

A Possibly yes, but it's a very complicated area. Stolen cars now account for most of the problems over title. In the meantime, always investigate the history of the car, for example via the HPI (see above) or the police, before buying.

The Sale of Goods Act 1979 says that a person who sells goods must be the real owner (have **title**), or have the consent of the real owner to sell (pp. 31–2). Your seller had no right to sell the car, as he or she was not the owner and was not in a position to transfer the ownership to you. The original owner from whom the car was stolen remained the real owner throughout. If you refuse to return the car, he or she will be able to bring a civil action in the courts for 'conversion'. The court may order you to pay the original owner the value of the car at the date you bought it, or, more likely, order you to return the car to him or her.

Even if this happens, all is not lost:

- you may recover the full price from your seller, because under the Sale of Goods Act 1979 the requirement that a seller must own the goods he or she sells means that your seller is in breach of the contract with you. You are therefore entitled to a full refund. It is irrelevant that your seller was completely innocent and had no knowledge or suspicion that the car was stolen: like most of the obligations under the Act, it is a 'strict liability' on the seller to ensure that he or she has the rights of ownership, and hence the right to sell on

- it is equally irrelevant that your seller was a private seller, as the provision as to title applies to private and trade sales alike

- some still talk of the 'market overt' rule which used to allow buyers to keep stolen goods purchased between sunrise and sunset at a market or fair established by charter or custom. This very old and quirky bit of law was abolished in January 1995.

Q *I bought a second-hand car but, unknown to me, it was still on* **hire purchase**. *The finance company is now reclaiming the car. Should I let the company take it?*

A No. Under an HP agreement the goods are still owned by the finance company, and the hirer does not become the legal owner until he or she has paid all that was due under the HP agreement (pp. 148–9). Until then, he or she has nothing more than a right to possession of the car and has no right to sell it. The Hire Purchase Act 1964 offers protection specifically where a motor vehicle which is the subject of an outstanding HP agreement is sold to a **private purchaser**. Provided you (the private purchaser) did not know about the existence of the hire-purchase agreement, or were told about it but informed that it had been paid off, you will obtain a good title to the vehicle and be able to resist the finance company's claims. So if you meet these criteria the car is legally yours to keep. The finance company will have to fight it out with the dishonest seller.

Q *What is the position if I buy goods at an* **auction** *and they turn out to be defective?*

A Although the Sale of Goods Act 1979 applies to auction purchases, its main conditions (pp. 31–2) may be excluded by a notice on display or in the catalogue – so beware, and check the auction house conditions before you bid. If you buy goods at an auction, your rights are against the seller, who could prove difficult to trace and, unlike in an ordinary consumer transaction where your statutory rights cannot be excluded (pp. 19–20), your rights at an auction may be limited.

Q *My car has just broken down and the gearbox needs replacing. The car is only four months old but the garage I bought it from has gone out of business. I used credit to pay for the car. What can I do?*

A It is a sad fact that when a company goes out of business the consumer often loses out (pp. 28 and 159–60). But paying for goods and services on credit can offer some protection (p. 152). The answer here depends on what form of credit you used to buy your car:

- if you entered into a credit agreement that was arranged by the garage that sold you the car, then under section 75 of the Consumer Credit Act 1974 the credit company is liable for any breach of contract or misrepresentation for which the garage would be liable. In this case you can claim that the car was unsatisfactory, but it would be difficult to argue that you could reject the car because you could be deemed to have accepted it, and may have lost the right to reject it after four months' use. In such a case you would still be entitled to the cost of fitting a replacement gearbox and consequential losses
- if the finance was in the form of a hire-purchase or conditional sale agreement your contract is with the finance company and not the retailer, and you have the same basic legal rights as if you had paid cash. With HP agreements these rights are laid down by the Supply of Goods (Implied Terms) Act 1973. However, when it comes to rejecting a faulty car, your rights to claim your money back last longer than if you had bought the goods outright. You have the common law right to reject throughout the time period covered by the HP agreement, as long as you act as soon as you discover the problem. In this case you should stop paying the instalments, write to the HP company saying that the car is unsatisfactory, that you're rejecting it, and that the car is available for collection by the lender. The HP company should then arrange for collection of the car and refund any payments you have made, although you may have to pay for the use you have had of the car during the period it was working properly
- if you arranged a general loan through your local bank, and you used that to pay for the car, then you will not be able to pursue the bank under section

75 of the Consumer Credit Act 1974. The bank is an 'unconnected' lender and has effectively nothing to do with the purchase of the car. In this case you have only two hopes: one is that there will be some money over to pay your claim as you are one of the creditors of the garage (this is unlikely); the other is that any manufacturer's guarantee will cover your claim (look at the wording of the guarantee to see whether it is or not).

Q *I ordered a new car a couple of months ago, but it was badly dented and scraped while being transported to the garage prior to delivery to me. I don't like the colour and I'm upset about the damage. Can I reject the car?*

A Under the Sale of Goods Act 1979 a new or second-hand car should fit its description, be of satisfactory quality and be fit for its purpose, although the standard is higher for a new car. If the car does not meet these requirements you have a claim against the dealer. You can ask for the car to be collected and for your money back. However, you must reject the car straight away because you have only a 'reasonable time' from when you get the car to reject it and get your money back. The Act doesn't say what a reasonable time is, but you should assume it is weeks rather than months. The problem with complex goods like cars is that time may have run out before you discover the fault, although since the Act was strengthened it is now clear that you have a reasonable opportunity to 'examine' the goods before you lose your right to reject. This should mean that you have a reasonable opportunity to use the car for at least a couple of weeks to make sure no faults develop. But if the garage disagrees only a court can make the final decision.

If you are too late to reject you will have to pursue the dealer for compensation, repair or replacement. Whichever remedy you choose you are also entitled to claim compensation for any expenses you incur which were reasonably foreseeable by both you and the dealer at the time of purchase, such as the cost of alternative means of transport while your car is off the road.

Q *I purchased my car on **hire purchase** and now I am trying to sell it on. I've been told that I can't do so until I've paid off all the instalments. Is that correct?*

A Yes, that is correct. The car is still owned by the finance company, and you will own it only when you have paid off all the instalments and purchased it. Your agreement is most probably a consumer credit agreement, which means that you are entitled to settle the agreement early and to obtain a rebate on the interest charges to reflect the early repayment. If you want to do this, write to the finance company for the settlement figure, pay that off, and then the car will be yours to sell. If you do not follow this procedure you will have broken the contract with the buyer under the Sale of Goods Act 1979 and you will be liable to the finance company for wrongfully dealing with its property.

Q *A car dealer sold me a car with a recorded mileage of 45,000 miles. After I had driven the car for about five months, my garage said the engine needed a lot of work, and in their opinion it had done more than the 50,000 miles on the clock. I contacted the previous registered keeper, a company, and they told me that when they sold the car it had at least 120,000 miles on the clock. What can I do?*

A When you purchased the car it had a false odometer reading, and if you were given no warning (a sticker, for example) that the odometer was wrong you have two courses of action open to you:

- you may pursue your rights in civil law under the Sale of Goods Act 1979 (misdescription) (pp. 31–2) or under the Misrepresentation Act 1967 (misrepresentation) (pp. 52–3)
- you should report the matter to the Trading Standards Department at the dealer's local council. Simply threatening to do so may lead to a quick settlement of your case. The Trade Descriptions Act 1968 makes it a criminal offence for dealers to make false statements about the cars they sell. The Act, which is criminal, not civil, law, cannot help you directly if you want to make a claim for compensation, but if the Trading Standards Officer does decide to prosecute you may ask the court for compensation.

This practice of dealers selling cars with false mileage readings, known as **clocking**, is fraudulent. The government has announced a package of measures aimed at tackling the problem. Information on the history of a vehicle would help a new purchaser to identify where clocking has taken place. At the time of going to press the Driver and Vehicle Licensing Agency (DVLA)★ was in the process of rolling out reforms in the MOT recording system, including a requirement that mileage be reported on vehicle registration and vehicle licence renewal forms, and computerisation of the MOT testing system would allow mileage to be recorded at every MOT test station. The Office of Fair Trading (OFT)★ has also announced that it would remove, or refuse to grant or renew, credit licences to car dealers that are shown to undertake unfair practices. These would include selling unroadworthy vehicles, discouraging buyers from examining vehicles, dealing in clocked cars, or routinely using disclaimers about the mileage of cars they sell without checking on mileages themselves.

Q *Six weeks ago I bought a laser printer and agreed to buy an extended warranty. The salesman was very persuasive, saying it would give me 'peace of mind'. But it cost over*

£150 and now I doubt whether it was worthwhile. Can I cancel it before the warranty period starts at the end of the first year?

A Electrical retailers often have incentive schemes encouraging staff to sell this kind of 'extended breakdown insurance', which may account for their powers of persuasion. But, in fact, most electrical products are so reliable these days that there is, statistically, little chance of their breaking down within the first five or six years. If they do, the repair costs are likely to be fairly low. So peace of mind in the form of a warranty is likely to prove expensive.

When you bought the warranty you made a separate contract with the shop. Most contracts become legally binding as soon as they are made, therefore you cannot get out of them simply because you have changed your mind. However, the British Retail Consortium (BRC)★ has a code of practice which is designed to allow customers of member shops to cancel these contracts. Check whether the shop from which you bought is a member. If so, you should have been given information on the possibility of cancellation at the time of sale. However, this code is not legally binding, so if the shop is not helpful about letting you cancel, you cannot get your money back.

Q *I want to buy a mobile phone but the contract for the airtime gives the company the right to increase the price without notice, and if I wanted to get out of it I'd have to give three months' notice. Are all these contracts equally punitive?*

A No. Under the Unfair Terms in Consumer Contracts Regulations 1999 the Office of Fair Trading (OFT)★ and other 'qualifying bodies' have the power to challenge contract terms that are biased against the interests of consumers (pp. 88–9). The idea behind the Regulations is that you should not be bound by an unfair standard term in a contract which you enter into as a private individual buying a product or service from a business. OFT has already taken action against many mobile phone airtime suppliers to ensure that consumers are not penalised by the following types of contract term:

- notice periods that prevent the consumer from getting out of the contract without giving three months' notice, or even longer
- price variation clauses allowing the company to increase prices but still tying the consumer to an unfair notice period if he or she is unhappy with the new prices
- excessive disconnection charges
- tying the consumer into the contract for too long, sometimes well in excess of one year
- 'entire agreement' clauses which attempt to disown any responsibility for what is said to the consumer by the company's salesperson or agents

- small print or generally unintelligible contract terms which are not written in plain English.

Many suppliers have reduced their notice periods to one month and now give consumers a chance to change their minds within 14 days of signing. If you feel that you are being presented with an unfair contract, don't sign, shop around for another supplier, and refer the contract to OFT.

Q *The goods I ordered over the Internet have arrived but now I've changed my mind about them. Can I cancel the contract and get my money back?*

A The Consumer Protection (Distance Selling) Regulations 2002 are designed to give basic legal protection to consumers who buy goods and services via the Internet, through mail order, telephone, or any other contract where you and the supplier do not come face to face. It's important to note that the Regulations don't cover contracts where the seller makes the initial contact at a distance, over the phone or Internet, say, but completes the formalities of agreeing the contract face to face. The whole process must be carried out at a distance. Some contracts are not covered by the main parts of the Regulations, such as those for holiday and travel arrangements, and regular deliveries of goods for everyday consumption, for example, milk. The Regulations also don't cover distance selling of financial services, which has its own regulations.

Under the 2002 Regulations consumers have the right to:

- **basic pre-contract information** This means that before the contract is finalised you must be told the name and address of the supplier, the main characteristics of the goods or services, the price, arrangements for payment, details of your right to withdraw from the contract, etc.
- **written or other durable confirmation of an order** This means, for example, that an electronic mail message from the supplier would be acceptable to confirm an order made by email
- a cooling-off period of seven working days in which to withdraw from the contract, starting from when the goods are received or, in the case of services, when the contract was made. There is no right to cancel in some situations, such as orders for perishable goods, items tailor-made to your specifications, and travel and holidays
- the contract being carried out within 30 days unless you and the supplier have agreed otherwise
- a refund of all money taken through fraudulent use of a credit or charge card. You have the right to cancel whatever contract has been made using your card and you're entitled to recover from the supplier any money that

has been wrongly debited from your account. This provides even better protection than the Consumer Credit Act 1974 and the voluntary Banking Code, as it extends full legal protection to all types of cards (including, arguably, debit cards) and doesn't make you liable even for the first £50 loss.

- a complete ban on the supply of unsolicited goods and services where supply involves a demand for payment
- an opt-out from receiving junk mail, 'spam' email, or junk telephone calls (pp. 258–60).

Q *I have recently connected to the Internet and have come across many businesses with their own websites selling products. If I buy something, am I protected in the same way as if I went into a shop on the high street?*

A Currently, there is no simple answer but consumer rights have been clarified and improved, at least within Europe (pp. 59, 258–60). UK law covers the quality of goods and services and other conditions with which traders must comply when doing business within England, Wales, Scotland and Northern Ireland. And much of the law we all rely on for protection is based on the fact that the businesses we deal with are themselves based somewhere in the UK. So buying goods from a high-street shop, or from a UK-based mail-order company, poses few problems if things go wrong and you wish to enforce your rights. Even with a UK-based Internet trader you get all the usual legal rights when buying goods and services, although, as we shall see, you may not know where the trader actually is or how to track down the people running the show to enforce those rights. But you cannot assume that the Sale of Goods Act 1979, or indeed any other consumer legislation, will protect you in respect of every Internet purchase you make.

The very nature of the Internet blows conventional notions of national or European consumer protection into cyberspace. The Internet opens up a world of possibilities for businesses that want to get straight into the homes of potential customers. And for consumers the attraction of cybershopping from the comfort of home by simply pressing a few buttons is clear. It also opens up a number of opportunities for fraud.

The Internet has no national borders and throws up a number of risks where the law may currently offer little or no protection. On the high street you know where the trader is and how to contact him or her, that the contract you make is governed by UK laws, and that you can use the UK courts if need be. Over the Internet none of this is clear. Until effective regulation is brought in to protect all consumers, many will lose out to unscrupulous or fraudulent traders. However, you can take care to protect yourself:

- the location of the trader may be unclear. A business operating on the Internet may set up in a location of convenience to circumvent regulations or simply use a third party based in yet another location to process orders on its behalf. Be wary of traders who do not give full details of their own address, phone numbers, etc. in their website pages. Always do everything you can to verify the details by phoning, checking in Internet directories, or even ringing local enforcement agencies (the equivalent of Trading Standards) if you can get details (some will have their own websites)

- the identity of the trader is a major concern and one which cannot easily be verified. If you have never heard of the trader's name before try to check it out in a directory, for example. The anonymous nature of the Internet allows fraudulent trading to take place. And once you have given your credit-card details – say, to purchase goods over the Internet – the money may be lost

- when things go wrong it could be very difficult to enforce your rights, depending on the trader's location. If both you and the trader are within the UK and you know the trader's name and address, there should be no problem. Contact the local Trading Standards Department for help. Even if the company is not within the UK but is trading from within the European Union there are means of settling inter-jurisdictional disputes, so in theory you will not be in any worse a position than if you had travelled to that country and brought goods back with you. Serious problems can arise where the trader is based in a country where consumer rights are poor, or may not even exist, or if it has used a third party to process business on its behalf.

Q *I bought some downloadable virus protection software over the Internet at the advertised US price. The company then contacted me to say I'd have to pay the higher UK price. Aren't there laws to stop this sort of thing happening?*

A Unfortunately not. Companies have every right to decide on what basis and price they supply a product to you. The exception to this is if a company has a dominant position in the marketplace, when there are laws governing how much it can charge, and the Office of Fair Trading★ has powers to prevent abuse of that dominant position (p. 13 – Enterprise Act).

Sometimes online companies charge customers in different countries more to cover things like import duty or delivery. But clearly this isn't the case for downloadable software so it proves you should always shop around to make sure you're getting the best deal – whatever you're buying and however you're buying it.

Q *I saw what looked like an unbelievable bargain as I was browsing on the Internet – washing machines advertised for £20. I ordered one over the Net. A week later an email arrived from the company apologising for an error in the price on the website, stating that* *the correct price was £200 and offering to deliver the machine a few days later. Can I insist on getting the machine for £20 as I had already placed the order?*

A It would certainly be worth arguing the point, although the law is by no means clear. There may well be a breach of that part of the Consumer Protection Act which is designed to prevent misleading pricing (pp. 27–9).

Trading over the Internet is booming. The laws that govern the more common ways of buying and selling, over the counter, by mail-order, etc., apply equally to Internet transactions with UK-based businesses. For instance, to have a binding contract you must show that an offer has been made and accepted and a contract has been concluded. Conventionally, goods on offer in shops, and possibly goods offered over the Internet too, are simply invitations to treat. It's you who makes the offer to buy, for example by handing over the money, or by filling in the website order form and then clicking 'OK' or 'send'. Only when your offer has been accepted by the company does a contract exist. So, it depends whether your offer to buy the washing machine has already been accepted. Many sites make it clear that no contract exists until you receive an email confirming this – a simple electronic acknowledgment of your order isn't enough. If your order has been accepted there may still be a way for the company to refuse to sell you the machine for £20 – by claiming that a '**mistake**' has been made.

Generally in law a mistake wouldn't stop you from enforcing your contract. But there are some kinds of mistakes which do make the contract 'void'. The seller has to show that there was a mistake of fact. This can take a number of forms but would require the seller to prove that you must have known that the contract wasn't a true reflection of the seller's intentions. This may mean having to prove that no reasonable person could have believed the offer to be genuine. However, in such price-competitive times it may not be so obviously ridiculous to see a washing machine advertised at £20.

So, as long as your offer to buy at the advertised price was accepted by the seller, you may be in a strong position to claim your machine at the agreed price, even if it was incredibly low. And, if the company refuses to honour it you may have to buy the same machine elsewhere and claim the difference between £20 and the price you had to pay.

Q *What protection do I get when buying from Internet sites which aren't based in the UK? Surely there must be some harmonisation of consumer protection for electronic commerce within Europe.*

A At present the European Commission and Parliament are still running to catch up with the explosion in Internet trading. EU Directives on e-commerce are aimed at making consumer protection more secure and to harmonise the laws of EU member states. The main aims of the Commission are:

- to reduce the risks of illegal activities in Europe by ensuring effective action is taken against the trader in its country of origin. The Office of Fair Trading (OFT)★ has been working with other consumer protection agencies around the world to combat this
- to ensure that consumers are able to make well-informed decisions based on clear and transparent information
- to clarify when an electronic contract comes into being, as this varies between EU member countries and may not even yet be entirely clear in the UK
- to provide better redress by promoting e-commerce codes of conduct and out-of-court settlement of disputes such as conciliation and arbitration (pp. 272–5). If it's a business in another European member state and there's a body responsible for handling disputes, such as an ombudsman or arbitration scheme, consumers can get access through the European Extra-Judicial Network (EEJ-Net) (pp. 291–2 – 'taking your claim further').

The Electronic Commerce (EC Directive) Regulations 2002 offer consumer protection when using 'information society services' – that is, 'any service normally provided for remuneration, at a distance, by electronic means and at the individual request of a recipient'. So, it covers straightforward Internet trading, email, interactive tele-shopping, electronic newspapers and a whole host of electronic services. Certain information has to be provided to the consumer as part of the transaction, such as:

- the name of the service provider
- the address where the service provider is based
- the service provider's email address so that contact can be made
- any company or trader registration number and where that register can be searched. This will depend on the company and commercial laws of each member state but, for example, a UK company will have to give its company registration number and details of how to contact Companies House★
- where the trader is subject to an authorisation scheme, the details of that scheme and how to contact the authorising body. The idea here is that details of self-regulatory organisations such as the Association of British Travel Agents (ABTA)★, the Direct Marketing Association UK Ltd★, or the Radio, Electrical and Television Retailers' Association Ltd (RETRA)★ should be given when the trader deals on the Internet to allow customers to contact the relevant body and access any redress mechanism, such as arbitration

- for regulated professions, the details of the professional body, such as the Law Society★ for an English solicitor, the Architects Registration Board (ARB)★ for a UK-based architect, and so on.

TrustUK is a company set up to oversee a system of 'e-hallmarking'. This grants a hallmark to traders who can guarantee a number of measures to ensure that customers are protected. The hallmark has core principles. These include the requirement to give clear, accurate and not misleading information about goods and services, prices, delivery costs, returns policy etc., to ensure security of payments over the Internet, to make arrangements for protecting personal data, and to avoid 'spam email' (that is, unsolicited electronic messages – see p. 260), as well as giving full details of how to contact the trader including a terrestrial address and phone number. Many of these have been or soon will be included in other new EU directives being implemented in the UK.

Q *A stall in my local market sells food that has passed its 'use by' and 'best before' dates. Surely this is not only illegal but also dangerous?*

A The dates marked on food labels are an important indication of whether a food is likely to be unfit or unpleasant to eat. The law requires most food labels to carry a datemark, which can be a 'best before' or a 'use by' date. However, note that a few foods do not have to carry a datemark at all, and that:

- it is not illegal to sell food simply because its 'best before' datemark has expired. The food could still be sound and wholesome, but it may simply be past its best. The mark merely alerts you to this possibility
- food with 'use by' dates must be withdrawn from sale once that date has passed. It is an offence to sell foods bearing an expired 'use by' date and for anyone to change the date
- whether the 'use by' date has expired or not it is an offence under the Food Safety Act 1990 to sell any food that is not fit for human consumption, or not of the nature, substance or quality that a purchaser might expect from the labelling or packaging
- if the food is not in the condition expected, or it has gone off and is not fit to eat, you also have the right to claim under the Sale of Goods Act 1979 (pp. 31–2).

If you are worried about a particular datemark, tell the stallholder, shopkeeper or manager. In England and Wales the Trading Standards Department of the county council enforces food labelling laws. In metropolitan areas it is the district council; in London it is the London boroughs; and in Scotland and Northern Ireland it is the Environmental Health Department of the district council. You will find these listed in the phone book.

Q *Why are some shops allowed to stay open for as long as they like on Sundays while others, such as the supermarket I use, are not?*

A For well over 40 years the law in England and Wales was specifically aimed at preventing most shops from opening on Sundays. Scotland has not had any similar history of restraints on the shopping habits of the population, except for the sale of alcohol and the services of hairdressers! Few real restrictions remain. South of the border the old law was not simple to understand and so was not adequately enforced. As a result, many shops, particularly garden centres and d-i-y stores, simply flouted the law. The Sunday Trading Act 1994 changed everything and all shops are now allowed to open on Sundays, regardless of what they sell, for at least some part of the day. However, there are some restrictions:

- most 'large shops' (over 280 square metres of display and retail space) are restricted to any continuous period of six hours between 10 a.m. and 6 p.m. The shops affected can choose the six-hour period in which to operate according to when there is greatest demand. Hence, a garden centre might choose 10 to 4 while a record or video shop might choose 12 to 6. There must be a notice in an obvious place spelling out which six-hour period the shop has opted for
- the ban on 'large shops' opening for longer periods on Sunday is not total. Some are allowed to open for longer. These include farm shops, motorway service stations, pharmacies, airport, railway and petrol forecourt shops, and those selling motor supplies
- no loading or unloading at stores open on Sundays may take place before 9 a.m. without local authority consent
- no large shop can open on Easter Day or Christmas Day when it falls on a Sunday. At the time of writing the government was considering proposals to ban shops from opening on Christmas Day no matter which day of the week it falls.

Q *While I was passing a shop that I thought had closed down I noticed a one-off 'sale' going. A man was shouting out the offers and drawing a big crowd. It was like an auction and I soon got caught up in the excitement and spent over £200 on a personal stereo, toaster and camera. I could not get near the goods before paying but other people there seemed to get top brands at bargain prices. When I finally managed to check my goods they were mainly discontinued lines and worth very little. I want to complain, but now I cannot trace the organisers.*

A If this was a real auction your rights would be very limited. But goods bought at one-day sales, liquidation or closing-down sales are covered by full shopping rights. Auction selling methods, and the fact that people often pay before they have had a chance to examine the goods properly, mean it is easy to be misled, particularly over the make or quality of the goods you think you are getting. And because such traders move on quickly to different premises for their next sale it can be difficult to track them down to register any complaints.

The Trade Descriptions Act 1968 makes it a criminal offence for traders to give false descriptions of the goods they sell. In the circumstances you describe, the chances are that prices will not be displayed as in a shop, so you will not know what you will have to pay. Usually goods are sold on the basis of those present competing with each other – a kind of bidding where the first person to throw up his or her hands gets the bag of goodies. If this was the set-up, and you had to pay a couple of pounds to take part, or if goods were given away or offered as gifts to keep you bidding, the whole event may have been illegal under the Mock Auctions Act 1961. And it is more than likely that the people at the start who seemed to get the good deals were part of the whole operation.

Trading Standards Officers face many problems in enforcing the law. Getting evidence and tracing the operators are just two. The Enterprise Act 2002 gives the OFT and other bodies substantial powers to deal with rogue traders and unfair sales practices (pp. 87–8).

Before you get involved in these sales, try to find out the name and address of the trader. Assuming you are given a real name and address, at least you know where to direct any claim. Best of all, if you are not prepared to join in the rough-and-tumble and take a great risk, go and shop where you can take your time to inspect the goods and assess the price before you buy.

Chapter 2

Commercial services

Calling in a plumber, having your hair cut, getting your wedding photos developed, having your car serviced, or installing kitchens, bathrooms or double glazing – all are examples of contracts of service. If a dispute arises between you and the person providing the service, it is the contract which dictates the legal rights and obligations you owe each other, and consumers have rights even if the contract is entirely unwritten. And in areas where rip-off merchants can wreak havoc the Enterprise Act 2002 (p. 13) now gives the Office of Fair Trading, Consumers' Association, Trading Standards and other bodies powers to take swift court action to stop the rogues and even ban them from trading.

Q *When I employ a trader to do work for me, what are my rights?*

A Contracts where the trader provides not merely goods such as spare parts, or materials for repairing, building or constructing something, but also the labour element, are classified in law as contracts for **work and materials**. This covers everything from large building works, to double glazing installation, to servicing a washing machine. Contracts of this type are governed by the Supply of Goods and Services Act 1982, which has been amended and strengthened by various subsequent statutes, including the Sale and Supply of Goods to Consumers Regulations 2002 (p. 13). In England, Wales and Northern Ireland it is the amended 1982 Act that governs your right to good-quality work and materials. In Scotland the Act only covers the quality of materials while the services element is dealt with by the common law, although consumers' rights are very similar to the Act. The law imposes the following legal duty on the supplier of the service:

- to carry out the service with reasonable skill and care
- to carry out the service within a 'reasonable time' where no time limit has been fixed
- to make a 'reasonable charge' for the service where no charge has been agreed in advance

- to use materials which are of satisfactory quality and fit for their purpose, as they would need to be under the Sale of Goods Act 1979 (pp. 31–2).

Q *I've just had new leather soles put on my shoes, but the workmanship is so poor that the soles started to come off the first time I wore them. I don't trust the repairer to do the job properly, but can I get them put right free of charge?*

A Yes, you are entitled to get the job done properly. The **Supply of Goods and Services Act 1982** (and in addition the common law in Scotland) gives you rights when you have work done. The person doing the work for you must carry out the job with reasonable skill and care, and use suitable materials of satisfactory quality.

Clearly the shoe repairer has not fulfilled the first requirement, and you are entitled to take the shoes back and ask for them to be put right free of charge. But if you have really lost confidence in the repairer, have them put right by someone else and charge the cost to the original repairer. If the shoes are beyond repair you should be entitled to compensation, which in this case would be the second-hand value of the shoes and a refund of the wasted repair charges.

If your complaint drags on, find out whether the repairer is a member of a trade association, in this case the Society of Master Shoe Repairers, which subscribes to the code of practice for shoe repairs; if he or she is, you may be able to ask for conciliation, and, for a small fee, get an independent test report. You should try to agree in advance with the trader that you will both agree to follow the findings of the expert. This could then quickly resolve the dispute.

Q *My computer broke down when the hard disk drive failed. A local repairer fitted a new drive, but a couple of weeks later that one broke down as well. The manager has just told me that I will have to pay for the new work because his engineer checked the replacement hard disk drive and he had no reason to think it was faulty. He said he couldn't be held responsible for manufacturing defects. Is that right?*

A No. The repairer should have supplied a disk drive that was of satisfactory quality under the Supply of Goods and Services Act 1982 (p. 67). It is no defence for the repairer to say that his staff were careful and had no reason to suspect that the disk drive was defective. And if a defect in a product comes to light within six months of the date that product was supplied – in this case the date the new drive was fitted – the law assumes it was faulty from the start and it's up to the repairer to prove it wasn't. This comes from the Sale and Supply of Goods to Consumers Regulations 2002 and reverses the normal burden consumers face of proving that goods are defective.

The manager shouldn't charge you again for putting the computer right – you can insist on a replacement, and he should provide the next disk drive and labour free of charge. If he refuses, you are entitled to have the work done else-where and ask the original repairer to pay the bill plus any extra expense, such as computer hire while your computer is out of action.

Q *What difference would it have made if the new hard disk drive had turned out not to be faulty but had been fitted incorrectly by an incompetent engineer, which caused the subsequent breakdown?*

A The repairer would still have to put the computer right free of charge. The Supply of Goods and Services Act 1982 (common law in Scotland) states that the work should be done with reasonable care and skill. As the repairer was under a duty to carry out the repair carefully, it is responsible for the incompetent and careless work of the engineer. There is a possibility that you could have signed away your right to compensation if you signed a contract containing a clause that excluded the repairer from liability for negligence. This clause must be reasonable and it's very likely that a court would not allow the company to rely on it; if it is not reasonable it will have no effect on your rights.

Q *I left my car at a garage for repairs. When I collected it, I noticed that the wing had a big dent in it. The garage denies any responsibility. What can I do?*

A When you take your car into a garage for repairs, the garage must take reasonable care of it. If your car is damaged while in the possession of the garage, or on the garage forecourt, for example, the garage is responsible – unless it can prove that the damage was caused through no fault on its part. This principle is enshrined in the law of bailment (p. 82).

The garage may attempt to restrict your legal rights by referring to a sign excluding loss or damage to cars in its possession. Under the Unfair Contract Terms Act 1977, notices or conditions in contracts which exclude or restrict liability for loss or damage to property will be upheld only if the garage can prove that they are fair and reasonable in the circumstances. This protection is supplemented by laws on unfair contract terms, set out in the Unfair Terms in Consumer Contracts Regulations 1999. It is very unlikely that a court would allow a garage to rely on a notice which tried to exempt it from all responsibility for loss and damage, whatever the cause. You should consider referring any unfair contract terms to the Office of Fair Trading (OFT)★.

Q *I discovered a leaking pipe in my loft, so I had to call a plumber in to do some emergency work. On the phone he said it would probably cost 'around £50' depending on the work needed. He was only here for one hour but handed me a bill for £250. Do I have to pay the extra £200? The plumber's argument is that it was an emergency and he stopped considerable damage resulting, so he can charge what he likes. Is this right?*

A If you're only given a rough guide to the cost, or if no price is agreed at all, the trader may charge only a **reasonable price** in accordance with the Supply of Goods and Services Act 1982. What is reasonable depends on how much work has been done, whether that work was done well, and the type of job that was undertaken. So the fact that the work was a matter of urgency and may well have prevented further damage does not automatically justify the trader increasing the charge except to take account of any lost business caused by dropping everything else to help you out.

If you just give blanket instructions to do whatever was necessary to repair, you must expect the final bill to cover the work actually required. But the bill must still be **reasonable**. Follow these guidelines:

- always ask for a written **exact and firm quotation** before agreeing to the work
- ask the relevant trade association (such as the Institute of Plumbing, *www.plumbers.org.uk*) for guidance on charges
- after the event, get quotes from other traders as to what they would charge for the same work in the same conditions
- finally, send the trader a cheque for what you consider to be the fair price.

If there is evidence that a trader consistently quotes very low prices simply to get the job, only to demand a much higher amount when the job is done, the Office of Fair Trading (OFT)★ and local Trading Standards officers may take action under the Enterprise Act 2002 to stop any action that they consider detrimental to consumer interests (pp. 87–8).

Q *I paid to have my washing machine serviced and the trader overhauled my tumble drier at the same time free of charge. The washer works perfectly but now the drier has packed up. Even though I didn't pay for the work to the drier, can I still complain?*

A Yes. The trader agreed to service both machines as part of the contract for the work and is responsible for the standard of work to both. The Supply of Goods and Services Act 1982 (common law in Scotland) sets out the legal requirements of the work (pp. 67–8). It is immaterial that the trader serviced two machines for the price of one – the work to the drier should have been carried out with reasonable skill and care, and if it wasn't, the trader will have to put the matter right: if he refuses, you are entitled to get the work done elsewhere and send the bill to the trader.

Q *I need some work done on my house. What can I do to reduce the chances of getting into a dispute over the work?*

A Follow these steps:

- problems with the price charged for work, the time it takes to do the job and the standard of the work can be reduced by finding a reliable trader: use someone recommended by a friend or relative, and look for membership of a trade association
- be as **precise** as possible about the problem you have and ask for a clear explanation of what the tradesperson proposes to do to solve the problem
- once you have agreed on what needs to be done, insist on a written **exact and firm quotation** for the job rather than an estimate
- get quotes from more than one trader: three should give you a good guide
- have a written **contract**, especially for bigger jobs such as building work (see model on p. 73)
- ideally, pay only when the work is complete and you're happy with it. It certainly shouldn't be necessary to make any payments until work has begun other than for materials bought on your behalf, but for more complicated work, or work of longer duration, you may have to pay in instalments during the job as stages are completed. If you do agree to this, write the stages into the contract as well as the final payment date. If you're not happy with the work done at any particular stage, then you're entitled to withhold payment for that stage until the work is done to your satisfaction
- be wary of traders who demand too much up front. The OFT★ has investigated many kitchen and bathroom companies for this practice, using powers under the Unfair Terms in Consumer Contracts Regulations.

The Quality Mark Scheme, launched by the government a few years ago, provides a register of qualified and trustworthy traders (*www.qualitymark.org.uk*). Businesses on the register are assessed before being allowed on and are reassessed annually. And all work is covered by a six-year Quality Mark warranty.

Q *What should be included in a contract for work to be carried out on property?*

A If possible, draw up your own contract using the example (p. 73) so you and the trader know exactly what's expected of both of you. Ideally this should include:

- your name and the name and address of the contractor
- a reference to the standard of workmanship ('good and workmanlike manner') and materials to be used, including a statement that the work will be in accordance with any plans and specifications. These specifications may refer to appropriate British Standards or codes of practice

- the date on which the work will start, and the date on which it will be finished. You can also agree that the contractor pays you reasonable compensation if the work is late (while allowing give-and-take in the completion date due to delays caused by unusually bad weather or other circumstances beyond the contractor's control)
- a requirement that the trader should leave the site in a tidy state at the end of the work
- clarification of who (you or the trader) is responsible for applying for Building Regulations or planning permission
- agreement that any changes to the specification are to be confirmed in writing
- a requirement that the contractor must be properly insured
- provision for ending the contract, by you or the contractor
- the total cost of the work and how it will be paid – a lump sum at the end or stage payments as the work progresses
- a requirement that the contractor returns to put right any defects in the work, and any damage caused to your property, at the contractor's expense.

Some tradespeople will present their own terms and conditions in the form of a contract. If they do, read the small print very carefully and check it against the list opposite before signing. Make sure the trader agrees to any changes you make before you finally give the go-ahead for the work. If the trader is only happy to work with lots of exclusion clauses in the contract, he or she is not worth hiring.

Q *We had our house rewired recently, and the electrician accidentally knocked a tin of paint over our carpet and up the walls. The trader has agreed to pay for redecoration, but says that as the carpet wasn't new he won't pay the full cost of replacement as this would put us in a **better position**. Is this right?*

A If someone working on your property carelessly causes damage in the process, you are entitled to claim full compensation for any losses you would not otherwise have incurred. Normally, you may not be able to recover the full cost of replacing an old item with a brand new one as this would put you in a better position as a result. If the carpet was perfectly serviceable and, but for the other party's **negligence**, would not have needed replacing for several years, you may be able to claim the full cost of replacement. If a second-hand replacement is readily available, the amount of compensation will be reduced to take account of **betterment**. But if the carpet was fitted it may not be possible to buy a second-hand carpet to fit, so, even if the damaged carpet was not brand-new, you are still entitled to the full cost of a new replacement.

Contract

1 _____ (contractor)
of _____
_____
shall carry out and complete the work outlined in the attached specification and drawings in a good and workmanlike manner in accordance with all relevant British Standards and Codes of Practice, all for the sum of **£___ plus VAT** at the standard rate.

2 The contractor shall provide all the labour, plant, materials and equipment necessary to complete the work.

3 The work shall start on _____(date) The work shall be completed by __(date)

Time is of the essence with regard to this work. All work must be carried out diligently and on a regular basis. The completion date will be extended only if the contractor is prevented from completing the work by factors outside his/her control. Should the contractor, without good reason, fail to finish the work on time he/she agrees to pay the owner damages which represent actual loss to the owner of £_____[*] for every week or part of a week during which the completion is delayed.

4 The contractor shall remove all rubbish as it accumulates and all tools, surplus materials etc. from the site and leave it in a clean and tidy condition within 14 days of completion of the contracted work.

5 The contractor shall comply with all statutory requirements, local and national regulations and by-laws that relate to the work. He/she shall make all notifications, arrange inspections etc. in connection with the work.

6 The value of any variation to the contracted work should be agreed before it is carried out. Only variations authorised in writing by the owner shall be paid for.

7 The contractor shall take out all necessary insurance.

8 If the contractor's work is not of a reasonable standard, or if the contractor leaves the site without reasonable explanation for more than 4 consecutive days, the owner may terminate the contract paying only for the value of the work done, less compensation for inconvenience or additional expense.

9 Once the contract is completed the contractor shall submit a final account to the owner. This shall be paid within 14 days of receipt by the owner.

10 The contractor shall make good at his/her own expense any damage to the owner's premises caused by him/her and/or his/her agents or employees.

11 Any defects that arise due to faulty work or materials shall be put right promptly by the contractor for no further payment.

12 In the event of a dispute over the cause of defects the owner may appoint an expert to report on the faulty work and/or materials and the contractor will agree to accept the findings of that expert. If the report proves the liability of the contractor for the faulty work and/or material the contractor agrees to pay the cost of that report.

[*£50, say, or whatever sum you think is likely to reflect your out-of-pocket expenses arising from the delay]

Q _I'm considering having an extension built. Are there any steps I can take to **protect my money** if the work is unsatisfactory or if the builder goes bust?_

A If you have paid money in advance you risk losing it, so when you get work done on your home it's wise to ensure you have cover – which goes beyond your basic legal rights – not only for poor work and materials but also in case the company goes bust. Here are some ways to protect yourself:

- if you have no option but to pay something in advance, don't pay too much: 10 per cent would be a reasonable maximum. With large jobs like this it's better to pay at certain stages of the work
- pick a builder who offers an **insurance-backed guarantee scheme**. To benefit from such schemes the customer will have to pay a small percentage of the total cost of the work (usually about 1 per cent or a one-off fee of £40–60) as the insurance premium. Get full documentation of the cover before you give the final go-ahead. There are several different schemes around (including some in specialist areas such as damp treatment and wood preservation and they vary in the cover they provide. For example:
  - the Quality Mark Scheme★: this provides a six-year warranty which protects you against poor workmanship, major defects and insolvency
  - the Independent Warranty Association★: this covers the installation of windows, conservatories and doors and will give protection in the event of the trader going out of business. The scheme will ensure that any uncompleted work is finished, and will make sure any remedial work is carried out
  - the Glass and Glazing Federation★: this ensures that deposits paid to members of the Federation are protected by an insurance scheme which indemnifies customers not only for unsatisfactory materials and workmanship, but also if the company goes bust. It covers payments up to £3,000 or 25 per cent of the contract price, whichever is the lower
  - the Building Guarantee Scheme Ltd★: this offers cover for two-and-a-half years after the completion of the job. It is available for any building work costing between £500 and £100,000, and covers disputes over the quality of that work or the insolvency of the trader
  - the Guarantee Protection Insurance Company Ltd★: this covers treatment for woodworm, wet and dry rot, rising damp and replacement wall ties. All traders are members of the British Wood Preserving and Damp-proofing Association (BWPDA)★ (p. 79). If the customer has a complaint over the quality of the work and the trader has ceased trading, the insurance will pay for remedial work
- pay a deposit with your credit card if the company will accept it, or arrange with the builder for finance to pay for all or part of the work.

Under this last option the credit or finance company is 'jointly liable' with the builder. So if the builder goes bust, or is still trading but breaks the contract in any other way, you can also claim against the credit company which financed the deal. This protection is provided by the Consumer Credit Act 1974 for loans to buy specific goods or services where the lender has a contract with the supplier, such as credit-card purchases (a general loan from your bank will not give this protection as the credit deal has to be made specifically to finance the work). It applies if the cash value of the goods or work is between £100 and £30,000 and the loan is for less than £25,000.

Q *When the builder had finished the roofing work he asked me to sign a note to say 'I accept that the work has been inspected by me and completed to my satisfaction'. The roof looked all right so I signed, but now it's leaking. The builder says I signed so I can't complain now. Is this right?*

A It's best not to sign a '**satisfaction note**' of this sort if you can avoid it. It could make it difficult to claim for defects in the workmanship later. By signing you have admitted that you inspected the work and found no problems, even though you had no idea whether the work was good or bad. If you had no option but to sign, and no opportunity to inspect, the safer course would have been to add 'work unexamined' or a similar note to the effect that you could not say whether the work was satisfactory or not. It is still worth pursuing the complaint, especially if the defect was not of the kind that an inspection by you would have discovered.

Q *The joinery of the extension I had built is appalling. The builder says that the woodwork was done by a **subcontractor** and so he is not responsible. What is my legal position?*

A The argument that the builder is not responsible for subcontractors is incorrect. He has agreed to do the work and it is irrelevant whether he does it personally, either by using employees or by subcontracting. If the job is not done properly the main contractor, the builder with whom you made the contract, is responsible for doing the job in accordance with the express and implied terms of the contract.

The work should have been done in accordance with the technical specifications in the contract as well as any stipulations as to time and cost. The Supply of Goods and Services Act 1982 implies a condition that the supplier shall supply goods that correspond with the contractual description. If the timbers are the wrong size and do not meet this description the builder has broken that contractual condition.

Further, the work should have been carried out with reasonable skill and care. If it was not, the builder is in breach of contract on this score as well. If the builder will not put right the defects, you are entitled to call in another builder to finish the job off properly and deduct the cost from the first builder's account.

There are many trade associations for the building industry which can attempt to resolve a dispute with a member company by conciliation or even

independent arbitration if you wish (p. 273). Some builders who subscribe to
the Building Guarantee Scheme Ltd★ can offer an insurance-backed guarantee
to cover the quality of work, and to protect you in the event of their going out
of business (pp. 73–4).

Q *I took a day's holiday for the repairer to come and mend my television. He promised
to call on Friday so I took the day off specially. He didn't come until Saturday. Will he
have to compensate me for my wasted day?*

A There is certainly a breach of your verbal agreement with the trader. But
whether you can recover compensation for the wasted day rests on the repairer's
knowledge that you would have to take a day off work specially. He might have
assumed somebody would be at home anyway. So if you didn't spell this out at
the time you requested the visit, your loss may not have been a foreseeable one.

If you have a complaint about a trader failing to keep to an agreed deadline,
or indeed any other servicing complaint, and the trader is a member of a trade
association, such as the Radio, Electrical and Television Retailers' Association
Ltd (RETRA)★, the Association of Manufacturers of Domestic Electrical
Appliances (AMDEA)★, or the Domestic Appliance Service Association
(DASA)★, the relevant association may be able to intervene in your dispute and
enforce the standards set out in the code of conduct the trader has signed up to.

Q *My car was taken to a garage for major repairs. It took six weeks to do the job.
Meanwhile, I had to hire a car from another garage, which was surprised at the delay and
said the work should only have taken a fortnight. I accept that I should pay for the work,
but can I recover some of the car hire charges?*

A Under the Supply of Goods and Services Act 1982 the garage should have
carried out the work 'within a reasonable time' (the common law says much the
same in Scotland). In your case, two weeks would seem to be that reasonable
time, in the view of the second garage. The extra four weeks' hire charges, therefore, were caused by the garage's delay and should be recoverable as damages for
breach of contract, as long as the garage was aware that you would be hiring a
car while yours was with them. The general rule is that you can recover only
those items of loss which both parties could have contemplated at the time the
contract was made as being likely to result from any breach. Unless you told the
trader that you would need to hire a car, the trader might have assumed you
would use public transport.

Many garages are members of one of the trade associations which adhere to
the motor industry code of practice (for example, the Retail Motor Industry
Federation★ or the Scottish Motor Trade Association★). If the dealer is a

member and you are having difficulty getting a problem sorted out, tell the relevant association about your complaint as soon as possible. It may be able to resolve the problem. If that doesn't work, you have the choice of going to court or taking your claim to arbitration. Some trade associations run their own schemes in conjunction with the Chartered Institute of Arbitrators★. Your case would be heard by an independent arbitrator, who would study your evidence and the evidence of the dealer and make a decision, but you would not be able to go to court if you are unhappy with the result.

Q *I asked my local garage to give my car a 24,000-mile service, according to the manufacturer's guidelines. When I went to pay for the service, the garage told me that they had also replaced the rear tyres because they were worn. This isn't part of a 24,000-mile service, and I could have got the tyres cheaper elsewhere. Is there anything I can do about this?*

A As you had a contract with the garage to service the car according to the manufacturer's guidelines for a 24,000-mile service, and no other work, you are entitled to tell the garage to remove the new tyres, put the old ones back on and reduce the bill accordingly. Practically, it might be easier to try to get the garage to reduce the bill for the tyres in accordance with the price of the cheaper tyres mentioned, and for you to keep the tyres.

Q *I have to have my car repaired soon, and the garage is not quite sure what is wrong with it, so they don't know how much the work is going to cost. I can't afford a really big repair bill at the moment. Is there anything I can do to limit the cost of the repair work?*

A When you ask a garage to do some work on your car, you only have to pay for the work that you've authorised. So, be clear about what you have agreed before allowing the garage to carry out any work, preferably by putting things in writing. If no fixed price is agreed, the law says that you are obliged to pay a 'reasonable price' for the work. This depends on how much work has been done and the type of repair or service undertaken. If you feel that the price you are charged is too high, you will have to show that the price is unreasonable. You can do this by getting evidence from other garages or motoring organisations, if you are a member.

As you have not yet entered into a contract you could ask the garage to give you an estimate once the problem has been diagnosed. Instead of just asking the garage to put your car right, ask whether the work is going to cost, for example, more than £500. If you are forced to pay as a condition of recovering your car, you should make it clear in writing that you are **paying under protest** and **without prejudice** to any legal rights you may have against the garage. This means that you can pursue the matter further when you have your car back.

Q *I ordered double glazing. The order form stated a delivery period of '10–12 weeks' and stated that 'time for delivery is not of the essence of the contract'. After 14 weeks nothing had happened. I rang to cancel the order, but was told that the windows had been made and if I did not take delivery the company would keep the deposit and sue me for the balance of the price. Could they really do that?*

A Probably yes, because time was expressly stated to be 'not of the essence' and there appear to be no special circumstances which made the delivery date vitally important to you. So, although the company did not meet the delivery date, this did not entitle you to cancel the contract:

- if the goods are not delivered and the work is not started within a 'reasonable' time, you should write giving the company reasonable notice of a deadline – if, say, the windows were not supplied and fitted within two weeks at the latest you would regard the contract as terminated
- in the absence of a notice imposing a strict time limit in that way, you were legally obliged to continue with the contract and let the double-glazing company complete the job
- assuming the windows were in fact ready for fitting the following week and you refused to let the work proceed, you would find yourself saddled with considerable expense: as the windows had been specially made for your house, it is unlikely that they could have been sold to another customer and you would have been liable for the total contract price less the small value of the glass and other materials left on the company's hands
- if you wish a trader to do a job on or by a particular date and have the ability to cancel otherwise, you must ensure that the agreed date is seen to be of importance by stressing in the contract that delivery or completion of work take place precisely on time, by, for example, making 'time of the essence'.

If you run into difficulties, contact the Glass and Glazing Federation★ or another relevant trade association.

Q *The kitchen installation company I've been dealing with has proved to be a nightmare from the start with delayed installations, deliveries containing faulty items and poor-quality workmanship. Is there anyone I can turn to without going to court?*

A There are no guarantees that any company you choose will do a good job but membership of some organisations can make it easier for you to get problems sorted out when they arise. If the company isn't a member of anything then court action may be your only option. Organisations to look out for are:

- the Kitchen Bathroom Bedroom Specialists Association (KBSA)★, which requires members to meet minimum service standards. There's also an insurance-backed deposit protection scheme which protects your deposit if the company goes bust or doesn't supply your goods. But there are time limits and terms and conditions you'll have to comply with to qualify

- Qualitas★ – this is an independent standards body for furniture and floor coverings. If you complain to Qualitas about a member company it will hold 20 per cent of any amount you've already paid during the investigation of your complaint. If it's not resolved there's a conciliation service and if that fails, the dispute can be 'adjudicated' on – this means you'll get a decision which is binding on the company but not on you, so you can still go to court if you're unhappy.

Q *My home is affected by damp, but there are so many damp specialists how can I make sure I find a competent one?*

A You'll find plenty of logos for trade bodies and associations in advertisements in phone books and on company letters and brochures. You can't rely on membership of a trade association as a guarantee of quality, or that you'll get help with any future complaint. It all depends on the trade association. At the time of going to press the government was looking at the way trade associations operate their codes of conduct with the aim of ensuring that they mean something for consumers and provide an effective way for complaints to be dealt with.

The main bodies you'll see referred to that represent damp specialists are:

- the British Wood Preserving and Damp-proofing Association (BWPDA)★: a prominent trade body in the damp industry. Using a member of this association will not guarantee you'll get a good job, but it does provide an arbitration scheme should you be unhappy about the quality of the work. The BWPDA also insists that a company employs qualified surveyors before it grants membership, issues technical briefings on industry developments and standards, and checks the quality of its members' work (though not anonymously). The association also has a guarantee insurance scheme which its members can offer through the Guarantee Protection Insurance Company Ltd (GPI)★ (p. 74). The association has also been developing a bonding scheme to cover customer deposits should a company go bust before a job is completed
- the National Register of Property Preservation Specialists (NRPPS)★ monitors the quality of its members' work and has a free phone advisory service. Also, its members can give insurance-backed guarantees.

Many companies issue guarantees, often for 20 years or more, at no additional cost. The benefit of this is that you can usually transfer the benefits of a guarantee to the new owner if you sell your home. Any standard guarantee will cover only the work done by the company, and won't cover further damp caused by disrepair – such as faulty gutters, pipes or pointing, or condensation problems. The danger here is that if the company disappears, so does the guarantee. Before you give the company the go-ahead, ask whether it has any insurance to back the guarantee, should it go bust during the course of the guarantee – if it does, ask for details.

Q *I asked a builder to build an extension to my house, but we did not agree a starting date. Whenever I manage to speak to him he tells me he is very busy and will fit it in when he can. When can I call it a day?*

A Where no date is fixed for work to be done (or goods to be delivered), the contract contains an implied term that it will be done within a **reasonable time**. Contracts for a service are governed by the Supply of Goods and Services Act 1982 (plus common law in Scotland). It is always difficult to determine what a reasonable time actually is in any particular case. But what is clear is that there is no excuse for the supplier to justify his delay on the grounds that he is busy.

It would be reasonable for you to expect work to begin within a few months of making the agreement. Despite the long delay, you should not cancel the contract without first giving notice by setting a deadline, making time of the essence, by which work must commence: a month hence would seem long enough. If nothing happens by this date, you will be released from the contract as a result of the builder's breach. You could then claim from the builder any additional cost of placing the building contract elsewhere.

Q *Last week when I went to collect my trousers from the dry-cleaners, I was told they couldn't find them. The cleaners are now refusing to pay me any compensation. Can they do this?*

A Under the Supply of Goods and Services Act 1982 (and common law in Scotland), dry-cleaners are under a duty to take reasonable care of your possessions. The fact that they have lost your clothes whilst they were in their care and can provide no explanation as to what happened is evidence that they were negligent. In the circumstances you are entitled to compensation. You should start off by claiming the cost of replacing the lost item but you may find that you have to accept less to take account of wear and tear.

Q *I recently took a silk suit to the cleaners, pointing out a particular stain that needed to be removed. When I got the suit home I noticed that the stain had not been removed and the colour of the suit seemed to have faded in certain parts. I complained but they pointed* *to a notice which said, 'We cannot accept responsibility for loss of or damage to goods howsoever caused.' Can they rely on this notice?*

A The Supply of Goods and Services Act 1982 (and common law in Scotland) entitles you to have articles cleaned with reasonable care and skill, and if they are not you are entitled to claim compensation. However, it is very common in business contracts, particularly contracts for services, to find terms which attempt to limit or exclude liability. These are commonly called **exclusion** or **exemption clauses**. The Unfair Contract Terms Act 1977 and the Unfair Terms in Consumer Contracts Regulations 1999 control these and allow suppliers to hide behind them only if the clause is fair and reasonable. What is fair and reasonable depends on the circumstances of each case. Factors that may be taken into account are the bargaining position of both you and the cleaners, whether you could have got the service elsewhere on different terms, and whether you had ever used that cleaners before. So don't be put off pursuing your compensation claim just because of the sign. Each case depends on the individual facts.

To avoid problems with dry-cleaners follow these guidelines:

- if the garment is stained, point out the stain to the cleaner, stating if possible what caused it and how long it has been there, and get it written on the receipt when you hand over the clothes
- take the garment to the cleaners as soon as you can: in some cases the longer you leave a stain the more difficult it is to remove
- examine the item at the cleaners to check that it has been cleaned properly.

If there *is* a problem:

- take the item back as soon as possible and complain
- if you get nowhere put your complaint in writing, explaining the problem and what you want done
- if the dry-cleaner does not respond or you cannot reach a settlement and the cleaner is a member of the Textiles Services Association Ltd (TSA)★, ask the TSA for a list of independent labs which will consider the problem to try to decide who is at fault. You will initially have to pay a fee, but if the TSA finds in your favour the cleaner will be asked to refund you the lab costs as well as paying you fair compensation
- if you don't want to go to arbitration, or if the cleaner is not a member of the TSA, you will have to go to court in order to get compensation. You can make a claim of up to £5,000 in the small claims track of the county court (£1,500 in Scotland, £1,000 in Northern Ireland).

Q *When I arrived at a hotel the attendant parked my car for me in the hotel car park. I didn't use it all weekend but when I went to collect the car on leaving there was a large scratch on one of the doors that certainly hadn't been there before. Can I get the hotel to pay for the repairs?*

A Since the hotel took possession of your car, it was under a duty to take care not to lose or damage it. This is known as the law of **bailment**. Where goods are lost or damaged, the law assumes that the bailee (in this case, the hotel) has not taken care of them, so it is up to the hotel to prove that the damage was caused through no fault on its part.

If the attendant had parked the car sticking out on a dangerous corner, you would be entitled to compensation for the cost of repairing the car. Even if there had been a notice saying 'The hotel accepts no responsibility for loss of or damage to customers' cars', you could challenge this, particularly as the attendant parked your car for you and the notice was not brought to your attention.

Q *I sent off my holiday photos to be developed. Later, the photoprocessing company wrote me a letter saying they had lost the photos; they offered me my money back and a free film. I challenged this but they pointed to a statement on the envelope which said, 'In the event of loss of or damage to films, the company's liability is limited to the cost of processing and a replacement film.' Am I entitled to compensation?*

A Yes. As you have a contract with the photoprocessing company, the Supply of Goods and Services Act 1982 (plus the common law in Scotland) gives you rights in the event of the photoprocessing going wrong. If your photos were of a once-in-a-lifetime holiday, say, or of an unrepeatable event, such as a wedding or other special occasion, you are entitled to compensation for the value of the film and for the upset, disappointment and loss of enjoyment arising from the loss or damage. The amount of compensation depends upon the importance of the photos to you – so, if it was your wedding, you would get more than for those of a distant relative's birthday celebration. The highest awards have been for hundreds of pounds but this is quite rare.

To have any legal effect on your claim, the term in the small print which attempts to take away or limit your rights must be fair and reasonable, as laid down by the laws governing unfair terms in consumer contracts (pp. 58, 81, 88–9). Many photoprocessors now use small print which offers alternative sorts of service, such as insurance, to cover films that are more valuable to you than the average snaps. Whether this makes the term reasonable depends on the size and legibility of the small print, whether every reasonable effort was made to bring it to your attention, and whether the insurance cover, say, is sufficient and easily obtainable.

Q *Last month I went to a new hairdresser for a perm. The salon owner used a perm solution which reacted with my scalp and within a few days I had a bald patch on the top of my head. The owner blamed it on a bad batch of solution. Can I expect any compensation?*

A The hairdresser was providing a service and so should have used reasonable skill and care when perming your hair. When using chemicals a competent hairdresser should carry out a patch test on a small section of the scalp or on some strands of hair to test for any adverse reaction. If the hairdresser fails to do this and you suffer injury as a result, you will have a claim for compensation.

Even if there was something wrong with the batch of perm solution, the Supply of Goods and Services Act 1982 puts the hairdresser under a strict liability to supply materials suitable for your particular hair and scalp. You should complain immediately in writing, bearing in mind that:

- you will need medical evidence concerning your injuries and the cause, so visit your doctor and, if necessary, a member of the Institute of Trichologists★
- if the hairdresser is a member of the Hairdressing Council★, you may be able to take advantage of this trade association's conciliation and arbitration scheme, designed to deal with complaints against members
- if you cannot reach an agreement with the salon, and the hairdresser is not a member of the Council, your only option will be to go to court. As this would be a claim for personal injury you can't claim more than £1,000 in the small claims track of the county court, despite the general limit for claims being £5,000.

Q *I complained to the Hairdressing Council about the hairdresser I used. They say he's not registered with them. Isn't registration compulsory?*

A No. Anybody can set up a salon and cut hair without any training or experience. In fact, this is typical of many services offered to the public. It is wise to choose a trader who can demonstrate the necessary competence to do the job. The Hairdressing Council★ is the trade association which provides state registration of hairdressers. Under this scheme members must have at least two years' training and expertise. Some salons train their staff, but unless a hairdresser is state-registered, you have no easy way of knowing if he or she is competent.

Q *I made an appointment for a haircut at a busy salon. I decided I didn't have time to get there so I didn't bother to turn up. The salon now wants compensation from me. Do I have to pay?*

A Probably. When you make an appointment with a trader, you are making a contract under which you agree to turn up at the appointed time and the trader agrees to provide whatever services he or she offers. If you don't turn up the trader can claim reasonable compensation for loss of business if he or she is unable to fill the appointment. Traders must prove that they made reasonable efforts to get a replacement customer, and if they did manage to fill the gap they will have suffered little or no loss, so they cannot make a charge.

If you have made an appointment but cannot keep it, tell the trader as soon as possible to give him or her the chance to find another customer. If not, you may be legally obliged to pay what you would have spent if you had turned up.

Q *I am in dispute with a garage over charges for repairs. The garage won't let me have my car back until I pay the bill. Can it do this?*

A Yes. If a garage has carried out repairs and improvements to your car, it has what in law is called a **repairer's lien** over the goods. It is legally entitled to hold on to the car until it is paid for the work. This can create problems, particularly as you may need to get another garage to look at the car in order to get evidence to challenge the bill, or the quality of the work. Check whether the trader is a member of a trade association, and try to enlist the association's help in getting your car back. If that fails, you may have no option but to pay the bill **under protest** in order to recover your car – do this in writing, on the back of the cheque, say – and this will leave you free to claim back the disputed amount later. Again, contact the trade association, and consider the options of arbitration or taking the matter to court.

Q *When I picked my dog up from the kennels after my holiday he was ill and dirty. The sleeping pens looked very badly cleaned and I heard other pet owners complaining. What can I do?*

A Under the Animal Boarding Establishments Act 1963, each kennel and cattery has to be inspected by environmental health officers before being granted a licence. There are then annual visits to make sure standards are maintained. In the worst cases the local authority can close down the business.

Each local authority can apply its own standards but most stick to the 'model licence conditions and guidance for dog and cat boarding establishments' produced by the Chartered Institute of Environmental Health★. If you're unhappy with the conditions your dog was kept in, report the kennels to the local Environmental Health Department and the local council. And if your dog is ill and needs treatment you can argue that the service you received was not of satisfactory quality and seek compensation. This could be simply a reduction in the agreed price, or the cost of treatment for your dog – assuming you can prove that the illness was caused by the poor service and standards provided by the kennels.

Q *We moved home recently. When the removal company delivered our belongings to the new house, many items of china were broken and some items just didn't turn up. The removers also damaged the wallpaper when they were bringing in furniture. What rights do we have?*

A Removal companies must carry out their services with reasonable skill and care, as laid down by the Supply of Goods and Services Act 1982 (plus common law in Scotland). It is clear that this company did not carry out the service properly and is in breach of contract (pp. 67–8). Therefore you are legally entitled to claim against the firm for the loss and damage resulting from its lack of care – this will include the cost of repairs to your possessions, if indeed they are repairable, the cost of replacing the missing items, and redecorating the damaged areas of wall. Note that:

- small print attempting to limit or remove your rights is common in removal contracts, so check this very carefully. You will often find a term limiting liability to a small sum, £20 say, but offering additional insurance cover if you want it. If such insurance is offered and is readily available and you fail to take advantage of it, the courts might well consider that a clause limiting a removal company's liability to £20 is reasonable under the laws governing unfair terms in consumer contracts

- always make a full inventory of your possessions before the company packs and transports or stores them, so that you can identify any missing items

- it is better to let the company's staff pack your belongings so there can be no argument that your packing was inadequate

- make sure you have up-to-date valuations on your possessions to help you assess your claim precisely

- the British Association of Removers (BAR)★ is the trade association for removal firms and provides a conciliation service to resolve disputes with its members. If both parties agree, the Association can appoint an independent arbitrator to give a decision which is binding on both of you.

Q *Is it possible to take over woodworm and similar guarantees when work was done for a previous owner of my home?*

A Almost always, guarantees for all types of specialist treatment to property can be taken over by purchasers, but a guarantee issued by a company is worthless if the company goes bust, unless there is some form of insurance backing for the guarantee. Guarantees are issued following timber treatment, damp treatments, roof sealing and so on. Although many of these guarantees are for impressively long periods, some for up to 30 years, experience shows that not every company that offers such a guarantee itself survives that long. In strict legal terms the guarantee forms part of the original contract for the work between the previous owner and the specialist company, so in every case you have to check the guarantee form:

- it may be necessary to inform the company concerned of the change of ownership, and possibly pay a small registration fee
- it may also be necessary to have a formal written 'assignment' of the guarantee at the same time as the purchase of the property, so check with your conveyancer when you buy
- when you are offered a property with the benefit of one of these warranties, check that the company is still in business, as you will have no benefit at all if it has gone out of business unless the guarantee was backed by insurance.

Q *While my car was in the car wash the water stopped, but the brushes continued revolving and badly scratched the paintwork. The garage manager pointed to a sign stating: 'The garage is not responsible for damage to customers' cars, however caused.' Should the garage pay for repairs?*

A You must prove that the garage failed in its duty to act with reasonable care when providing the service, so you will need to discover why the water stopped. If the breakdown occurred because the garage had failed to have the equipment maintained and serviced properly, that would be evidence enough – but the garage would not necessarily be to blame for the failure of the water supply. You may be able to challenge the exclusion clause under the Unfair Contract Terms Act 1977 (pp. 69, 88–9).

Q *If I **hire** goods, am I protected regarding their quality, safety and so on in the same way as if I'd bought them?*

A Yes. The law governing contracts of hire, often called rental or leasing agreements, is clear:

- the Supply of Goods and Services Act 1982 says that a hire company has to supply goods which are of **satisfactory quality, fit for their purpose**, and as **described** – these are comparable with the provisions in the Sale of Goods Act 1979 (pp. 31–2)
- before hiring, you must explain what you intend to do with the goods and listen to the hire company's advice. That way, you'll be in a stronger position if the goods turn out to be not up to the job and will be able to demand a refund of the wasted hire charges and any extra expenses

- it is a criminal offence, under the Consumer Protection Act 1987, for hirers to supply unsafe goods, or goods without appropriate instructions and safety warnings. If you hire goods which you feel are unsafe, contact the Trading Standards Department at your local council offices.

Q *I paid £50 deposit by credit-card to a local trader to rebuild my garden wall. Two weeks later he demanded the balance of £300 in cash, which I paid. He seems to have abandoned work and does not answer the phone or respond to letters. I have contacted the credit-card company but it has offered to refund only the £50. Is this right?*

A If you meet the requirements of section 75 of the Consumer Credit Act 1974 you can claim the full contract amount from your card issuer (p. 152). The important point here is that the price the builder put on the whole job was more than £100. It does not matter whether you paid the full amount by card or only a small initial deposit – the credit-card issuer is still 'jointly liable' for any breach of contract by the builder up to the full amount of your losses.

Before pursuing the card company, send a recorded delivery letter to the builder making 'time of the essence'. Set a final reasonable deadline for the work to be completed and explain that you will employ a second builder to complete the work and will seek to recover from the first any extra expense over and above the price you agreed. If he doesn't respond, or simply refuses to pay up, you should contact the card company and forward copies of the letters you sent to the builder.

Q *My elderly mother has been ripped off by a roofing firm. However, even though she won her court case the firm haven't paid her money back. Several of her friends have recently lost money to this same firm so I know it is still cheating people with the same scams and practices. How can some traders get away with breaking the law and no one can do anything to stop them?*

A If a trader is a rogue, getting money from him or her is going to be difficult. And even if you've been to court and won there's no guarantee that you'll get your money back. But because of recent changes in the law it is now easier for enforcement bodies to take action against persistent offenders. The Enterprise Act 2002 came into force in June 2003 and gives the Office of Fair Trading (OFT)⋆, Trading Standards Departments and other 'designated' enforcers such as Consumers' Association, a range of powers (see also 'introduction' p. 13). In this context it includes the power to take action against 'rogues' who harm, or have the potential to harm, the collective interests of consumers. So the more examples there are against the same trader the more likely it is that action will be taken and will succeed.

If there is evidence of breaches of consumer protection laws then the enforcement body can obtain an 'enforcement order' from the courts to stop the business carrying on with certain practices, or even take the trader out of action completely. These include breaches of the laws governing consumer credit (p. 141–8), estate agents and property descriptions (pp. 127–131), timeshare (pp. 207–10), the Administration of Justice Act section 40 (pp. 266–7), the Trade Descriptions Act (p. 57), mock auctions (pp. 65–6), package travel regulations (pp. 189–90), unfair terms in consumer contracts (pp. 88–9), sale of goods laws (p. 32) and many more.

If the trader refuses to comply with the terms of an enforcement order he or she faces a hefty fine or going to prison for contempt of court. The EU is also considering introducing a new law to spell out what are 'unfair practices'. There is likely to be a list of 'misleading' and 'aggressive' commercial practices, and the law will aim to ensure that traders who use them can be dealt with quickly.

Q *I am in dispute over some work that was carried out badly, almost a year ago. The company just quotes the standard contract I signed, which says it is not responsible for defects reported more than six months after completion of the work. Can it escape its responsibilities in this way?*

A No. The Unfair Terms in Consumer Contracts Regulations 1999 make it clear that terms in standard consumer contracts can be relied on by businesses only if they are 'fair'. A blanket term that attempts to remove your right to complain after six months is clearly not.

The Regulations govern 'unfair' terms contained in 'standard contracts' between consumers and businesses where the consumer is unable to negotiate individual contract terms. They add to but do not replace existing consumer protection provided by the Unfair Contract Terms Act 1977. But there is a major difference between the two bits of law. The 1977 Act allows you to take your own complaint to court and ask the judge to decide whether a term is unfair. If you win your argument you may get compensation but the trader can carry on using the same contract containing the same term with all its other customers.

Under the 1999 Regulations the power to challenge such terms rests with bodies such as the Office of Fair Trading (OFT)★ and Consumers' Association★. If you report a contract term that you consider unfair to the OFT, for example, it may ask the trader to remove the term from its contracts or amend it. If the trader refuses, the OFT can ask the High Court (Court of Session in Scotland) to grant an injunction to prevent continued use of the term. Assuming the court does agree, the term may not be used or relied on by the trader in any of its existing or future contracts with consumers. A term would be judged unfair under the 1999 Regulations if:

- it is not in plain, intelligible language, or
- it causes a 'significant imbalance' in the parties' rights to the consumer's detriment, or
- there is inequality in the bargaining power of the parties.

The Regulations include examples of contract terms that are likely to be judged unfair – for example, one-sided terms that:

- allow a trader to keep a deposit if the consumer decides to pull out of a contract, without providing equal compensation for the consumer if the trader decides to cancel
- prevent the consumer from taking legal action and instead force him or her to claim through an arbitration scheme
- require the consumer who fails to fulfil his or her obligations to pay a disproportionately high sum in compensation.

These terms, if persistently being used against the collective interests of consumers, can also result in enforcement action being taken under the Enterprise Act 2002 (see above). Although neither the 1999 Regulations nor the 2002 Act will get you compensation, the action outlined above may prompt the company to accept liability. If it refuses you can use the fact that the term has been ruled 'unfair' as part of your claim for compensation.

Q *How does the law protect me from discrimination because of my **disability**?*

A The Disability Discrimination Act 1995 makes it unlawful for anyone providing goods, services or facilities direct to the public to discriminate on the grounds of someone's disability. It doesn't matter if these goods or services are charged for or provided free. Supermarkets and shops, travel agents, restaurants, hotels and banks all are covered.

'Disability' is defined as a physical, sensory or mental impairment which has a substantial and long-term adverse effect on a person's ability to carry out normal day-to-day activities. This includes wheelchair users, the blind and visually impaired, deaf people and those with a hearing impairment. It also covers countless people who may not be on any official register of disabled people and encompasses a huge range of impairments including people with impaired mobility, those with diabetes, epilepsy and asthma, people with ME, facial and bodily disfigurements, and learning difficulties.

The Act has been introduced in stages:

- since December 1996, it has been unlawful for service providers to treat disabled people less favourably for a reason related to their disability. It is illegal to refuse to serve someone for a reason related to his or her disability, or to offer services on different terms, or to provide a service of a different standard or manner

- since October 1999, service providers have had to make 'reasonable adjustments' to the way they operate so that disabled people can use their services. This covers the policies, practices and procedure of their service provider for example taking more time to explain things to someone with a learning disability, or fetching things from shelves that are inaccessible. It also means looking at what can be done to provide their services by alternative methods, such as having a temporary ramp available to help wheelchair access to premises, or providing services over the phone or on an accessible website, say
- from October 2004, service providers have to make 'reasonable adjustments' to the physical features of their premises to overcome physical barriers to access.

A code of practice under the Act gives practical guidance on how to prevent discrimination against disabled people in accessing services or premises. It applies to England, Wales and Scotland. Northern Ireland has a separate but similar code. The code doesn't impose legal obligations. Nor does it claim to be an authoritative statement of the law. Only the courts can decide whether a particular activity or treatment is in breach of the Act. But the code can be used in evidence in legal proceedings.

Access to education services is covered but access to most forms of transport vehicles is not. This means that disabled people can currently be excluded from planes (but see p. 206), buses, ships, ferries and taxis without legal comeback. However, transport termini such as bus and rail stations, and airports, are covered and must take reasonable steps to improve services and accessibility. New-build taxis, buses, coaches, trains and trams have to meet minimum standards set by the government even though people can be refused access to them. At the time of writing, the government had published its proposals to bring access to transport within the Act in the future.

You can complain to the Disability Rights Commission*, which has a duty to encourage good practice and advise the government on how the Act is working, as well as to conciliate in disputes and act as a central source of information for disabled people. Ultimately, you can take the service provider to the county court for compensation, but you have to start any legal action within six months.

Chapter 3

Domestic services

Throughout the 1990s the whole structure of the domestic supply industry changed from one of nationalisation to one of private ownership. Changes have continued with the introduction of competition and consumer choice. The imbalance of power between the large supply companies and the consumer has lessened with the introduction of bodies which provide help and advice and publish league tables of complaints, such as Energywatch★. And then there are the regulatory bodies, such as the Office of Water Services (OFWAT)★, the Office of Gas and Electricity Markets (OFGEM)★ and the Office for the Regulation of Electricity and Gas (OFREG)★ in Northern Ireland. Privatisation and competition have brought substantial improvements in the nature of the relationship between the supplier and the consumer, and introduced new legal obligations. The energy, water and telecommunications markets continue to open up. The law provides for standards of performance to be set by companies and establishes procedures for dealing with complaints. The spread of competition in these markets is pushing up standards still further. And under new laws the regulation of these industries is becoming more consumer-focused.

Q *Our boiler broke down, so I made an appointment for the engineer from my gas supply company to call. I waited in but he didn't show up. I made an appointment for two days later and the repairs have now been done. I'm annoyed that I had to wait in all day. I've read about **fixed compensation schemes**. Is my situation covered?*

A Your situation should be covered under your supplier's own customer standards of service. If the company fails to meet its targets you can in many cases get fixed compensation for the inconvenience caused. However, while this scheme provides for guaranteed compensation in certain circumstances, it does not prevent you claiming if you suffer additional financial loss. The guaranteed compensation scheme includes:

- **missed appointments** You receive £11 compensation if your gas supply company fails to turn up for an appointment, unless you were given 24 hours' notice of cancellation

- **interruptions in the gas supply for safety reasons** Most supply companies promise to put the gas back on within one working day. If you are still without gas after a day, compensation of £20 will be paid for every extra day or part of the day you are without gas

- **special treatment for older, disabled or vulnerable customers** £10 compensation is payable if the supply company cuts off the supply to one of these customers and leaves him or her without adequate heating and cooking facilities.

Ask your gas supply company for full details. This compensation should be claimed through your own gas supply company. National Grid Transco★ owns the gas supply pipes and meters.

Q *My gas supplier missed an appointment to read my meter. I made another appointment, but no one turned up for that either. Am I entitled to compensation?*

A Gas and electricity customers are entitled to £20 if a supplier fails to turn up for a pre-arranged meter reading. If it isn't paid within ten days, you're entitled to a further £20.

Make an official complaint to your supplier. If there's no satisfactory response within ten days, you should complain to Energywatch★ about the supplier.

Q *I'm having some problems with the gas company. How can I get help?*

A If you want to complain about a gas bill, initially you should write to your local gas supply company (the address will be on the back of the bill). If you are not happy with the reply, contact the Customer Relations Manager at the head office. If you're not happy with the way the company responds to your complaint, contact Energywatch★, which can not only comment on all aspects of work done by the licensed gas companies but can also persuade them to respond and provide evidence to back up their arguments.

Energywatch represents the interests of all gas and electricity consumers and provides advice and information on complaints against suppliers. However, while the energy company must provide all relevant information to Energywatch, decisions by Energywatch are recommendations and are not legally enforceable. To ensure that the company complies with its statutory obligations, Energywatch refers more serious or recurring cases which need this sanction to the regulator, the Office of Gas and Electricity Markets (OFGEM)★. OFGEM can investigate complaints about the supply of gas (including payment for supply and disconnection) and gas bills, but not those concerning appliances, or appliance servicing.

Q *I'm disputing a gas bill and have sent the details to Energywatch. Can my supplier cut me off if I don't pay the bill?*

A Yes. The gas supply companies are legally entitled to disconnect a supply for non-payment of a gas bill, and this could mean you have to pay the extra cost of disconnection and reconnection fees on top of the bill. When you disagree with a bill, or if you have trouble paying it, contact the company immediately:

- the supplier must allow a specified period of time from the date when the original bill was sent (this will be part of the supply company's own customer standards and is usually around 30 days), and must then give usually another seven days' notice before disconnecting you
- before disconnection the supplier must offer you alternative payment methods – for example, a pre-payment meter – and allow your past debts to be repaid as part of your future bills
- if you have a genuine dispute, contact Energywatch★
- it may be worth paying the proportion of the bill you think is right while your complaint is considered
- cases of hardship should be dealt with by gas supply companies reasonably and sensitively.

One thing at least is clear – customers over 60 cannot have their power cut off for unpaid bills.

While your complaint is subject to investigation by Energywatch you are unlikely to be cut off. But if you have failed to contact your supplier, or Energywatch, or if you cannot reach agreement with the company, you could be disconnected. Disconnection, incidentally, will not enable you to avoid settling the original bill as you will still be liable to pay it and could be taken to the county court if you fail to do so.

Q *My gas bill is far too high. I was on holiday for a month during the period the bill covers so I didn't use much gas. How can I check whether it is right?*

A If you think your bill is wrong you should always contact your gas company first. Make sure you follow these steps:

- check whether the amount was **estimated**. As you were away the estimate may be higher than the actual usage. Take your own reading as soon as possible after receiving the bill and phone or send the reading to the gas company. It will then send an amended bill

- if the bill has been **assessed**, check back over past bills: the previous one may have been underestimated, so you may have been charged for more than one period
- the meter itself may be inaccurate (see below). Turn off all your gas appliances, including pilot lights. Read the meter and wait as long as you can before turning anything back on. If the meter changes during this time, tell your supplier immediately
- contact Energywatch★: it will help you calculate your gas usage and will assist with your complaint to the company.

Q *How can I get my gas meter checked?*

A Every gas company must check its customers' meters once every two years. In addition to reading the meter the company will check the fittings to make sure the meter is correctly positioned and hasn't been tampered with. If you disagree with the supplier about whether your meter is working properly, you can request a meter examination by the Technical Directorate of OFGEM★ to check that it's working correctly. Your meter and the gas supply will be tested and the meter may be removed for further tests. If the meter is found to have been over-reading you won't have to pay for the test and will be compensated for your over-payment, but if the meter is found to be operating correctly you will have to pay a test fee of about £20. The examiner's decision is final. The Gas Act sets out the amount you can claim, or, if you've been under-charged, the amount you'll have to pay. It says that any backdating can go back only to the last-but-one meter reading which was obtained. However, a gas company can backdate a refund (but not a surcharge) to an even earlier date if there's evidence that the fault started before the last-but-one reading.

Q *I had central heating installed by a gas engineer. It doesn't work properly. What can I do?*

A You have the same rights as you would have when employing any other contractor. Under the Supply of Goods and Services Act 1982 (common law in Scotland), you are entitled to expect the work to be carried out with reasonable skill and care, using materials of satisfactory quality. If the work or materials are not up to scratch you should contact the installer and ask him or her to put the work right free of charge. If he or she refuses or fails to do this, or if you have lost all confidence in his or her ability to do the work competently, you can employ another gas installer to do the work and send the bill to the original trader. Make sure you get all the evidence you can to prove that the original work was done badly. Additionally:

- you can refer the dispute, if necessary, to Energywatch★ (OFGEM cannot investigate complaints about an appliance or appliance servicing)

- if the work was done by a fitter who is a member of a trade association, it may be worth complaining to this organisation
- complaints about the safety of appliances or services should be immediately referred to Energywatch, which has access to technical experts and can, if necessary, provide a report. Alternatively, if the trader is registered with the Council for Registered Gas Installers (CORGI)★, you can refer safety issues to them
- if the matter remains unsettled your only option will be to claim through the courts. If the amount claimed is below £5,000 (£1,500 in Scotland, £1,000 in Northern Ireland), you can use the small claims procedure in the county or sheriff court).

Q *The gas cooker I bought last week from a high-street store has broken down. What are my rights?*

A When you buy goods from a trader, your rights are set out in the Sale of Goods Act 1979. You should complain to the shop straight away. If you fail to reach an agreement, contact Energywatch★, which will help with any dispute over gas appliances and services, wherever you bought them. It will put pressure on the trader and can give an opinion on whether the case is worth pursuing (through the small claims court, for example).

Q *I came home to find that National Grid Transco had entered my premises without my permission. They say there was a gas leak and they had to investigate. Are they allowed do this?*

A If there is a gas leak or some other emergency, employees of National Grid Transco★, or one of the other companies which owns the transmission pipes and equipment, can break in at any time – they don't need your permission. But they must leave your property reasonably secure. However, they do need your permission to enter for non-emergencies like reading your meter, inspecting fittings such as the meter, or disconnecting the supply for unpaid bills. If you don't give permission, they can get a warrant to enter your property. The warrant allows them to use reasonable force to get in. They must show that you were given at least 24 hours' notice that they were coming, and that they have been refused entry or your house is unoccupied. Entry must be at a reasonable time. They can also get a warrant if they suspect that you are tampering with the meter.

Q *Under what circumstances may an electricity company **disconnect** a meter?*

A An electricity company may not cut you off without warning. If the problem is an unpaid bill, the company must first try to find out the reason for non-payment and offer you help and advice:

- if the unpaid bill was an estimated reading you may not be disconnected: owing to the fact that the meter has not been read, there is no precise sum 'due'
- you may not be disconnected if the bill was left unpaid by mistake (because, for example, you failed to sign the cheque)
- you may not be disconnected if the unpaid bill is the subject of a genuine dispute and negotiations are in progress
- if you genuinely cannot afford to pay, the electricity company must first offer you a payment plan that is tailored to suit your individual financial circumstances, rather than simply cutting you off, for example, allowing you to clear the debt in instalments of an amount based on your ability to pay
- where it is safe and practical to provide one, you may be offered the option of having a pre-payment meter. Each time you credit your meter some of the credit would be used to pay off your debt
- even if no agreement can be reached, the company should not disconnect you until 20 days after the date of the first bill
- you should always be given at least 48 hours' notice of disconnection
- if the company does not try to make alternative arrangements for payment or does not give you the required notice, you should take up the matter with the Office of Gas and Electricity Markets (OFGEM)★. OFGEM has powers to make an electricity company change its decisions in its dealings with customers
- even if you have been disconnected you remain legally responsible for the unpaid bill, and the company can still take you to court to recover the amount outstanding.

Q *I live on my own and have gas central heating. My latest electricity bill is almost twice the usual amount. How can I challenge this?*

A All meters are checked before installation, and are replaced at regular intervals. The electricity company therefore assumes that the meter is working properly and that the reading, and hence the bill, is correct. The bill will tell you if the electrical usage figure was an **estimated** or an **actual reading**. So, as for any other meter reading, check the bill first. If it is based on an actual reading, check the meter reading against the bill: mistakes and misreadings do happen. Ask the company to come back and take another reading if you spot an error. If the bill and the meter match, there are three ways of challenging the charge:

- you may be able to show that what you regard as an abnormally high reading is caused by a 'leakage to earth': to do this, turn off all appliances which use electricity; if the meter is still recording usage, tell the electricity company immediately

- ask the company to check the accuracy of the meter
- if you are not happy with the outcome of your complaint, refer the matter directly to the industry regulator, the Office of Gas and Electricity Markets (OFGEM)★, via one of its 14 regional offices, and tell the company that you are doing so. OFGEM will nominate an independent meter examiner to test your meter and send his or her conclusion and report to OFGEM. If you are still unhappy with OFGEM's decision, you will have to pursue the matter in court. The small claims track in the county court (pp. 275–6) is a way of doing this, but you will have to prove that the meter examiner's report is incorrect, which will be virtually impossible.

Q *How can I change my supplier of gas and electricity and will I be penalised for doing so?*

A Changing supplier won't cost you anything. Supply pipes, cables and most meters won't have to be changed, as these will still belong to the public electricity or gas transporting company for your home. For example, currently the biggest gas-supply transporting company is National Grid Transco (which used to be part of British Gas). A new supplier will simply supply the gas or electricity – which will be exactly the same gas and electricity you receive now – via the existing pipes and cables.

To change you must sign a contract with the new supplier. Take time to look carefully at all the competing companies. If you do change you'll be asked to read your meter yourself. You will then receive a final bill from your current supplier, British Gas Trading, say. From then on you will receive bills from your new supplier.

If you do want to switch, don't sign a contract with more than one of the new companies. However, you can change supplier as often as you like – all you have to do is give 28 days' notice before switching. A few companies have cancellation fees. And if you've signed a contract as a result of a visit from a door-to-door salesperson or an unsolicited phone call, the law allows you a seven-day cooling-off period during which you can cancel your contract without penalty. The website *www.switchwithwhich.co.uk* gives information on how to change supplier.

Q *A salesperson talked my elderly father into switching energy suppliers when he didn't really want to. Now the company says he can't cancel it. What are his rights?*

A After signing a new energy contract, you have 14 days to cancel it without penalty. If this cooling-off period has passed, you should contact the new supplier to give it a chance to resolve the problem. If you're unhappy with the outcome of the initial complaint, contact Energywatch★. It can take up your father's complaint with the company concerned and give you free, impartial advice on all energy problems.

If you can prove your father was pressured into it, the supplier should return you to your old company straight away. Unscrupulous selling techniques can be investigated by your local Trading Standards office, which may decide to prosecute.

If he was switched by mistake, you can refer to the 'Erroneous Transfer Customer Charter', jointly developed by OFGEM and Energywatch. This sets out the minimum level of service a customer should expect. It ensures that your new and old supply company will talk to each other and that you will be kept fully informed about what is happening to reinstate your original position (*www.energywatch.org.uk*).

Q *I applied to switch electricity supplier four months ago and I'm still waiting. Can my old supplier prevent me from leaving? And am I entitled to compensation?*

A Switching energy supplier normally takes between four and six weeks. Your present supplier can prevent the switch for only two reasons – if you have an outstanding debt or if you fail to give 28 days' notice. You can request compensation for costs and inconvenience incurred, but unfortunately energy suppliers aren't obliged to pay it.

Q *I want to switch suppliers. But how do I know if the savings I've been promised will last for a reasonable time? Are prices guaranteed or regulated?*

A There are no guarantees that prices won't change if you're on a normal contract. With these, prices are fixed for a set period but during that time you can't switch supplier without incurring a penalty. There's no longer any price regulation in the gas and electricity markets. Suppliers can charge what they like but must give you ten days' notice of price rises.

Q *I haven't received a bill from my electricity supply company for over a year. I've reminded them but still no bill. Does the amount I owe get written off after a time?*

A The fact that you have had a supply of electricity, gas or water for a year, or even longer, without receiving a bill does not mean that you will get away scot free. Utilities suppliers, like most other services, deal with customers on standard contracts. These give rights and responsibilities to both you and the supplier. In exchange for the supply of power you have to pay the amount or tariff agreed under the contract for the electricity used.

Most customers are on 'credit meters'. This means they use the electricity first and pay for it afterwards, usually via a quarterly bill. Once they've used any electricity they become a debtor of the supplier. Any outstanding debts can be called in by the company any time up to six years (five in Scotland) after payment becomes due. So, when does payment become due? In fact, late billing may well delay the start of the six-year limitation period. It can be argued that payment doesn't become due, and so the limitation period doesn't start to run, until the bill is sent out. So even if you wait six years it doesn't necessarily mean that you won't have to pay for the electricity you used six years before. You have to look to the contract to find out billing dates and when payment is due.

Most customers are on what are called 'rolling contracts'. This means the supply of gas and electricity carries on until you terminate it, usually by moving or by switching to another supplier. With this sort of supply, billing is on a rolling timescale. Most contracts are unclear on when bills will be sent, although the norm is quarterly. The amounts demanded are usually estimated as there is only a legal obligation to read the meter every two years.

If the company does ask for backdated or forgotten payments it could catch customers off guard who might struggle to pay a large amount of money they hadn't budgeted for. The strict legal position is that as long as you're still liable to pay for the electricity used you'll have to pay for it all – no concessions and no delays. And failure to do so could affect your credit record. But most companies should give customers a sympathetic ear and agree to instalments. Judges tend to look sympathetically on consumers who can't pay and offer this solution. Customers who simply can't pay a large sum should contact Energywatch★ which should be able to persuade the supplier to allow payments by instalments where appropriate.

Q *Energywatch recommended that my electricity supplier should pay me £500 compensation for a problem I've had. However, the company refuses to pay up, and Energywatch says it can't force it. Is this true?*

A Yes. The powers Energywatch★ has are limited. It has a duty to look into consumer complaints, but can't fine companies or enforce action. If it thinks that an energy company has breached its statutory or licence conditions, it can report the matter to OFGEM★. OFGEM does have the power to take action, for instance by imposing restrictions for bad practice or even fining persistent offenders.

Q *What do 'guaranteed standards of performance' mean in the context of electricity services?*

A The Office of Gas and Electricity Markets (OFGEM)★ has instituted performance standards with which the electricity companies must comply. If they do not, fixed amounts must be paid to compensate for the inconvenience, whether you would have a legal claim or not. Specifically:

- electricity company engineers must keep their appointments: if they fail to, you, the customer, will be entitled to £20
- the company must reply to a billing or voltage complaint in ten working days; if it does not, you will be entitled to £20
- the company must give you five working days' notice if it plans to interrupt the electricity supply (for example, to carry out maintenance work); if it does not, you will be entitled to £20
- following an unplanned cut in the supply you should not be left without power for more than 18 hours; if you are, you will be entitled to £50, plus £25 for each additional 12 hours you remain without electricity (see below).

All the companies must send their customers details of their standards at least once a year. Most payments are automatic and are usually made by reducing the next bill. Some electricity companies also offer rebate and voucher schemes, so check by writing to the address on your bill.

For Northern Ireland, contact Northern Ireland Electricity (in the phone book). If you are not satisfied, contact the General Consumer Council for Northern Ireland★.

Q *I keep experiencing* **power cuts**. *I live in a rural area and sometimes have to cope without electricity for long periods. Am I entitled to compensation?*

A If you suffer a power cut for a **continuous period of 18 hours** or more, you are entitled to £50 compensation, plus £25 for every further 12 hours without power, but only if:

- the power cut is the result of a technical breakdown or negligence on the part of the company – not when severe weather is the cause
- the power cut is **continuous**, so even if you are frequently without power for long periods you can claim only if the power goes off for 18 hours or more each time. Frequent shorter power cuts are not eligible for compensation.

If you suffer loss and damage as the result of a power cut due to the negligence of the electricity company, your claim for compensation is not limited to the guaranteed compensation amount. So if the food in your freezer is ruined, say, you can claim from the electricity company.

It's also worth considering whether you qualify for priority if there's a disruption to your fuel supply. Energywatch★ runs the Priority Services Register. You can join this register if you receive a pension, are chronically sick or have a disability. Energy suppliers will then put your needs first and will provide alternative heating arrangements if needed. Under this scheme you can also get free safety checks of installations and equipment.

Q *I bought a washing machine from my local electrical goods shop and had it installed through them. There's something wrong with it but they won't sort it out. Can I complain to OFGEM?*

A No. OFGEM★ cannot consider disputes over faulty products or defective electrical services. It can deal only with disputes over electricity supply and billing. The Sale of Goods Act 1979 sets out the responsibilities of the retailer, who is liable if the goods sold are defective (pp. 31–2).

Consider referring the matter to the relevant trade association. If that fails to resolve the dispute you can consider whether it is worth starting a claim under the small claims procedure .

Q *If I fail to pay my electricity bill, can the electricity company come into my home to disconnect the meter?*

A If you do not pay your bills, the electricity company can take various steps to make you pay up. Disconnection should be its very last resort. However, ultimately the company can get a warrant which allows it to use reasonable force to enter premises and disconnect the meter. The circumstances which would allow electricity company employees access to your home are the same as for gas company employees.

Q *What level of service can I expect from my local water supply company?*

A Each water company in England and Wales must have a **code of practice** setting out the services offered, charges, what customers should do in an emergency, how the complaints procedure works, and what to do in the event of a leakage or a disconnection. Leaflets on the code of practice are available from your local water company. Water companies are also legally obliged to operate a **Guaranteed Standards** scheme and customers are entitled to a fixed amount of compensation (£20) if those standards are not met. Many companies have their own customer charters that go beyond these, so check first. The Guaranteed Standards scheme states that each company must:

- keep appointments made, or give at least 24 hours' notice of cancellation
- respond to your complaint or enquiry within ten working days of receiving your letter
- restore the water supply, in the event of planned interruption, on or before the date specified
- give at least 48 hours' warning of a planned interruption in the water supply lasting more than four hours
- restore the water supply, if the interruption was unplanned, within 24 hours, unless the burst is on a strategic main.

- in addition to the £20 fixed compensation, provide an extra £10 for each
  additional 24 hours without supply.

Q *I was without water for two days, but I'm not happy with the water company's*
response to my complaint. Whom can I contact?

A If you cannot get satisfaction from the water company, write to the regional
committee of Watervoice (look in the phone book). Watervoice was set up by
OFWAT★, and has ten regional committees which are independent of the
water companies and can deal with the water and sewerage companies in their
locality. The committees will liaise between you and the company concerned
and can force the company to provide information. The committees do not
have power to force the water companies to abide by their decision, but, where
the company refuses to accept a decision by Watervoice, they can refer the
complaint to the Director General of OFWAT.

The water supply is provided in Scotland by the regional and islands councils
and in Northern Ireland by the Department of the Environment Water
Service★. Neither is regulated by OFWAT. In Northern Ireland, rights and
complaints procedures are not as strong as those described above. Contact your
local water supplier for details. In Scotland there is a Water Industry
Commissioner★ to promote the interests of consumers, and each water and
sewerage authority has a Water Industry Consultative Committee.

Q *The water from my tap was yellow and smelled fishy. I complained to the water*
company and it was cleared up quite quickly. But I had to buy bottled water for a couple
of days. Can I reclaim the cost of this from the company?

A The Water Act 1989 says that water companies must maintain a supply of
wholesome water. The quality of water for domestic purposes is also
controlled by regulations which reflect the requirements of the European
Community. It is an offence for a water company to supply water that is 'unfit
for human consumption', so any quality problems should be immediately
reported to the water company. If that fails to deal with it satisfactorily contact
the Drinking Water Inspectorate★, the regulatory body for drinking water
quality.

If you incur extra expense because the water does not seem clean and healthy
to drink, or worse, if you are made ill by it, you may be able to recover compensation from the water company, if the company was to blame for the problem, or
could have prevented it. However, if the cause was a problem with your own
water pipes, say, the company would not be liable. If you have trouble getting
your claim sorted out, you should follow the complaints procedure (see above).

Q *There is a leak from the water supply pipe under my front garden and the grass is always sodden. The water company says it's my responsibility. Is this right?*

A The water company is legally responsible for keeping the following pipes in good order:

- the water main in the road
- that part of the service pipe from the mains up to a point at or near the boundary of your property, at which location, underground, there will usually be a stop tap; and
- the stop tap itself.

The rest of the supply pipe which goes from the stop tap into your property is normally your own responsibility (or that of the landlord or freeholder), so you are obliged to keep it in good repair. This is so even where that pipe runs under a neighbour's land before it reaches your property. As the leakage is from your pipe, it is your responsibility to have it repaired. The water company may ask you to repair it, and, if you fail to do so, may carry out the repair and charge the cost to you. If your water is metered, you will have to pay for the water lost through the leak.

Q *In what circumstances may a water company disconnect a water supply?*

A Under the Water Industry Act 1999 a water company is not allowed to disconnect your supply because of non-payment of a bill. In such circumstances the company must pursue the debt through the courts and is banned from using the threat of disconnecting or reducing your supply to force you to pay any outstanding amount. However, apart from unplanned cuts in the water supply, a company can disconnect you if it is necessary to carry out repairs to the water system; unless it is an emergency, the company must give you reasonable notice of the repair work and must pay compensation if it fails to do so, or fails to reconnect the supply within specified time limits.

Q *Do I have to allow officials from the water company to come into my home?*

A Water officials may enter your home with your permission to install, read or repair meters, inspect fittings, or test or alter your supply. If you refuse to let them in they can apply for a warrant, which allows them to use reasonable force to gain entry. To obtain a warrant for entry the water officials must have shown that they have given you notice, that entry is necessary to carry out the work, and that you have refused to let them in or that the house is unoccupied. Water officials can also enter in an emergency.

Q *We've been told by our local water company that our water will be metered from early next year. Does it have the right to impose metering?*

A For many years charges for water have been based on the rateable value of the individual property. In England and Wales, when the water authorities were abolished and the industry was privatised, the newly formed water-supply companies were given the power to decide how to charge their customers for water in the future. New legislation allowed the companies to come up with an 'approved method of charging'. The old rating system was replaced with the council tax in 1990 and the rateable value basis of assessment is becoming increasingly out of date. In the first instance, following privatisation, companies were given until 2000 to come up with an alternative to rateable value. The only one so far is metering. That deadline has been extended indefinitely and you could still be paying water charges based on the old rating system well into the current century.

Until 1999 water companies could require customers to move to a metered supply. You didn't have the right to choose, although where a company did decide to install a meter it had to be done free of charge. If you wanted a meter and the company agreed to your request it sometimes used to charge for installation. Since the Water Industry Act 1999 things have changed. Now consumers can require their water company to install a meter and it has to be installed free (see below). Equally companies can't force you to have a meter installed if you don't want one, unless you have water fittings in your home which use considerable amounts of water, or if you have a sprinkler in your garden, say. But it is worth considering how a meter would affect your bills as there is a possibility that it could save you money.

The water industry in Scotland and Northern Ireland has not been privatised. In Scotland services are provided by Scottish Water, and nearly all domestic consumers have their water bills based on their council tax bands and have the option to have a meter installed. In Northern Ireland services are provided by the Northern Ireland Water Service and domestic water charges are part of the 'regional rate' (a form of local taxation). Meters are not encouraged as an alternative.

Q *Can my water company insist on having a water meter installed if I want one?*

A Most households in England and Wales are entitled to a free meter on request. And you have the right to switch back to the unmeasured charge within 12 months of installation if you want to. But there are some circumstances in which you can't choose and you may be denied one. A water company can refuse if it would be unreasonably expensive or impractical to install a meter. For example, they could deny you a meter if plumbing alterations, such as separating shared supply pipes, would be needed. But, if you pay for the necessary work, the supplier should then fit the meter free of charge.

It it's impossible to fit a meter — for example, if you live in a block of flats — your supplier should offer you the right to pay an 'assessed charge'. This would usually be based on what other metered customers in your area pay, or an estimate of your usage.

Q *My phone bill is far too high. What should I do?*

A The first step is to contact the local office of the telephone company concerned (British Telecom or Cable & Wireless, for example), at the address on the bill. The company will then usually test its meter and check the readings to trace any inaccuracy. It will also check for any recently located faults in the network that could have affected the metering. If you are not satisfied with the response, contact the new communications industry super-regulator OFCOM★. This body came into being at the beginning of 2004, and has wide-ranging powers under the Communications Act 2003 to deal with all complaints against all phone companies, including mobile phone operators. It can insist that the company replies to your complaint and provides evidence for its claims. It can also force the company to abide by OFCOM's decision on complaints.

You can also complain to the Office of Telecommunications Ombudsman (Otelo)★ if the company is a member. Otelo is separate from OFCOM and provides an alternative avenue for complaining.

If you're still dissatisfied, you may have a choice between court or arbitration. Most claims would be well within the small claims limit of £5,000 (£1,500 in Scotland, £1,000 in Northern Ireland). Alternatively, The Communication Act now requires companies to offer alternative dispute resolution for residential customers. For example, British Telecom (BT)★ offers an Arbitration Scheme run by the Chartered Institute of Arbitrators★, which is totally independent, and is a fixed-cost alternative to court. If you use this service:

- all the evidence is submitted in writing, so you will not have the chance to argue in person (if you use the small claims procedure you will have to give evidence in court)
- the decision of the arbitrator is legally binding on both you and the company, so you cannot start legal proceedings if you do not agree with the decision. The small claims judgment is also binding and rights of appeal are limited.

There is also a new Communications and Internet Services Adjudication Scheme (CISAS), administered by the Chartered Institute of Arbitrators, which offers a free service if your complaint is about a member company. At the time of publishing, members included Orange, Telewest and T-Mobile.

Q *I was without a phone for a while due to a fault, which I reported to my phone company. Should they have repaired it within a specified time?*

A Some telephone companies promise to repair faults within specified time limits and to pay compensation if they fail. And some companies offer a repair service with very short timescales if you agree to pay an additional cost in advance for your phone service. As it still maintains the largest share of the UK telephone market, a good example is provided by British Telecom (BT)★. BT is committed to providing **guaranteed standards** of service, and you will receive compensation if it misses its targets. BT will make a payment of one month's rental for **every day** you are without a service:

- if you report the fault to BT and it fails to repair the faults on the line by the end of the next working day
- if you make an appointment for a phone line to be installed but BT fails to stick to it.

BT will pay up to £1,000 if you can show that you have incurred a financial loss as a result of BT missing a target, but you must have proof that you have suffered the loss.

Q *I am disputing my telephone bill. Can my phone company cut me off?*

A Your bill becomes payable as soon as you get it. The practice is for reminders to be sent out around 21 days later. Rather than go straight to complete disconnection for an unpaid bill, the Office of Telecommunications (OFTEL)★ requires companies to take alternative action to recover monies, for example by barring all outgoing calls and allowing only incoming calls. But if this fails a phone company can then send a final demand giving you seven days to pay:

- if you do nothing in reply to this notice, your phone may be cut off
- if you dispute the bill you should follow the complaints procedures, but you should pay the portion of the bill that is not disputed (say, an estimated amount based upon your previous bill). If you do not pay anything while the dispute is being considered, the company may disconnect you.

Q *Can BT or other telephone company officials enter my home without my permission?*

A No. When you rent a telephone line from BT or any other telephone company you agree to let its employees enter your home at all reasonable times to check that the line is working correctly. This does not mean they can come in without your permission, but if you do not give them reasonable access you will be in breach of your contract with the company, and that will allow the company either to claim compensation or to terminate its contract with you and cut you off.

Q *My daughter posted a birthday gift to a friend. It never arrived and despite a search it has not been traced. The Post Office says it cannot pay any compensation as it was sent by ordinary post. Surely this is a breach of contract?*

A For parcel deliveries there is a lot of competition in the UK, with many companies offering their services under their own contract terms and conditions. It is up to you to make sure that the company you use does not exclude liability for loss and damage without at least offering you a chance to take out adequate insurance. Parcelforce is the arm of the Post Office that competes in this area.

However, at present the Post Office, in the guise of the Royal Mail, holds the monopoly on the delivery of letters within the UK. The Post Office Act 1969 makes it clear that even though you pay to post letters and packets, this does not give rise to a contract between the Post Office and the sender or the receiver. The Act also explains that no one can bring a claim in tort (pp. 17–18), for example, by claiming that a loss or damage is due to the negligence of the Post Office because of something it either did or failed to do. However, there are some circumstances where you may get compensation if mail is lost or damaged:

- when you use ordinary first-class, second-class or recorded delivery services you may get compensation up to £26, or the 'market value' of the item sent, whichever is the lower. But you will not get compensation if you have lost items such as money, jewellery, gift vouchers, cheques, etc. It is up to the sender to make sure valuables of this sort are insured (see below)
- you can increase the compensation available by using one of the various 'schemes' offered by the Post Office. These give you the option to pay an extra fee for insurance cover. Hence, using registered post means you get up to £500, or the market value of the item if this is lower. And using 'Registered Plus' allows compensation of up to £2,200, or market value
- you can increase the protection still further by paying extra for 'consequential loss' cover. This is particularly useful where the item may not have a market value in itself, such as a bundle of documents, but where any delay, loss or damage would cause additional expenses or losses (say, because it is an important contractual document).

So if you send an item using a Post Office scheme you will be covered up to the amount you agree at the time of sending. The amount of cover depends on the fee you pay. Consider carefully what cover you need, bearing in mind always the market value of the item. If you have a problem with the services supplied by the Royal Mail or Parcelforce contact either the Royal Mail Customer Service Centre (address in phone book) or the Parcelforce customer services manager at the branch you dealt with. If you remain unhappy with the response, make your complaint known to the consumer watchdog, Postwatch★.

Q *When I moved home I redirected my mail to my new address. But it became clear this wasn't working when my new cash point card didn't arrive, and a bill that I didn't know about arrived three weeks late. By that time I had to pay interest. What are my rights?*

A When you fill in the postal redirection application form you have to give your address but you should also give all the possible variations of your name (for example, Dr J Smith, Joe Smith, Mr Joseph Smith, J Smith, and so on). Problems can arise when letters are sent with people's initials, middle names, or shortened names that haven't been made clear on the application form. Royal Mail has no legal liability for redirection failure. The Post Office regulator, Postcomm★, has proposed a statutory compensation scheme to cover loss, delay, damaged mail, and redirections. But the current scheme only covers delayed letters and not redirections.

So, it's up to Royal Mail to decide what, if any, compensation to offer for redirection problems. Usually, it offers a book of stamps, an extension of the service or, if there have been several failures (assuming you find out), a refund of the redirection fee. But this will not cover the actual loss you've suffered, let alone the inconvenience. Postwatch★ can intervene in cases where Royal Mail is unable to resolve a problem and can ask Royal Mail to take remedial action, but this is only a recommendation.

Chapter 4

Legal services

Most of us have little to do with lawyers and therefore little practical knowledge of how to go about using one. You may use a solicitor to help you to buy your first home, or draw up a will, but only rarely will most people get involved in litigation. It is likely that you will have to consult a lawyer at some stage for general legal advice, however, or to help sort out a dispute. You're likely to trust what your lawyer tells you and to act on it, so it is essential that the advice you get is reliable. Hiring professional services is not like buying goods. When you buy something in a shop you usually know the price first. Yet with legal services you may not know how much the service will cost in advance, and you may have little opportunity to shop around to compare price and quality. And what if, for example, a solicitor advises you on your claim against someone else and that advice is wrong? Any shortcomings in professional advice may not be obvious until it is too late.

Q *I'm looking for somebody to do the conveyancing on my house. How can I find a competent professional?*

A There are never any guarantees that the person you choose will do the work competently, but all professional conveyancers, whether solicitors or licensed conveyancers, must meet minimum standards in training and competence. The most effective way of finding a lawyer or conveyancer is by personal recommendation. Failing this, contact the Law Society★ or the Council for Licensed Conveyancers★ for a list of practitioners in your area, or visit your local library, which should have a regional directory of solicitors indicating the sort of work undertaken by each practice.

Even with professionals things can go wrong. If you do have reason to complain about the services offered by a solicitor or conveyancer, contact the relevant professional body or complaints bureau, and, if you're still unhappy, the Legal Services Ombudsman★.

Q *What questions should I ask before hiring a lawyer and what information am I entitled to have?*

A Whatever the nature of the problem, the object of the initial interview is to establish what has to be done and lay down the ground rules for doing it. Under the Solicitors' Costs Information and Client Care Code solicitors must give you relevant information on a number of issues, in particular on costs and the firm's provisions for client care and complaints handling. All of this is usually set out, together with the firm's terms of business, in the **letter of appointment** or **client care letter**, and you must agree to these before work starts. For an efficient relationship try the following:

- as lawyers tend to charge by the hour, if possible obtain a written estimate of the likely number of hours' work involved
- set a ceiling on the costs charged and find out whether other costs will be involved, such as search fees and barristers' charges
- ask to be billed at regular intervals so that you can keep tabs on mounting fees and decide as necessary whether or not to carry on
- ask for a clear timetable showing when you will have to pay
- make sure any advice given to you is confirmed in writing and take notes of what is said at the meeting. Also ask for copies of all letters that go out on your behalf.

Q *I need a lawyer but I don't think I can afford it and I doubt if I qualify for Legal Aid. How can I get help?*

A If you can't afford to pay privately for help and advice with your own money then state funding for solicitors' fees (or 'Legal Aid' as it's commonly known) is available – but it's hard to qualify. It is administered by the Legal Services Commission⋆, is means tested and is unlikely to be available for the majority of the population. But there are a variety of other ways to get access to advice and to pay for it, and plenty of good websites providing excellent reference material – notably the Government Community Legal Service (*www.justask.org.uk*) and Citizens Advice (*www.adviceguide.org.uk*):

- **conditional fees** allow a solicitor or barrister to take on a case on the basis that if your case is lost the lawyer gets no fee for the work undertaken and has to write off the time spent on the case (pp. 112–3). However, if you win the case the lawyer is entitled to the usual fee plus an extra amount which is based on a percentage of the normal fee, which can be up to an extra 100 per cent (see below). All of this must be agreed in writing in advance. And the amount of compensation you get has no bearing on the level of fees
- **contingency fees** give the lawyer a direct share of any compensation you recover. So, the arrangement could be that if you lose the case you pay your

lawyer nothing, but if you win the case the lawyer gets the normal fee plus a percentage of the compensation you have recovered. This is relatively new in the UK as until recently lawyers were simply not allowed to do work on this basis. These agreements aren't allowed for court work (criminal or civil), but can be used for general legal negotiations, tribunal work, property selling etc.

- free or cheap legal help is available from Law Centres, Citizens' Advice★, voluntary organisations or Which? Legal Service★. And many trade unions, professional bodies and motoring organisations provide 'free' advice to their members
- **legal expenses insurance** (LEI) can be a very useful way of funding standard disputes and may already be part of your household or car insurance.

Q *Is it worth buying Legal Expenses Insurance (LEI)? I've never had a legal dispute where I've needed a lawyer so I'm loath to pay for insurance cover just in case.*

A Generally it is worth having because the premiums are so small but the cover, including general legal advice, can be valuable. In fact, you may already have LEI cover – many people are simply unaware that they have this insurance as it is usually sold as an add-on to home contents or car insurance. LEI policies attached to car and contents insurance cover most common disputes. Car LEI covers things like the cost of pursuing a claim for injury and subsequent loss of earnings; damage to your car or property in it; uninsured losses and so on. Household LEI deals with a much wider range of disputes and cover will vary between policies. It usually covers you and your family for death or injury due to negligence; disputes you might have over products or services you have bought or sold, including home improvements such as double glazing or a new kitchen; disputes over your contract of employment (such as unfair dismissal); and disputes with neighbours.

Always be aware of the following:

- check you're not paying twice for cover – you may already have access to free legal advice through a union or a trade or professional body
- don't assume the insurer will always take on your case – if it doesn't believe you have a 'reasonable' chance of success it may refuse (see Q&A below)
- there will be small print so make sure you understand the extent of your cover, and if it's not clear, ask for an explanation. There may, for instance, be a time exclusion which means you might not be covered for something if you didn't report it to the insurer in time (usually six months), even though it happened since you took out the policy
- if you have LEI to cover your 'family' check carefully the policy definition of 'family' as this can vary greatly – it may not cover everyone in your household

- if you do pursue a claim and receive an offer to settle, most policies state that you must accept any reasonable offer by the other side. If you don't want to and continue the case against advice you may no longer be covered by insurance and may have to pay future costs yourself
- any dispute over decisions made by the insurer or the handling of the case can be dealt with by the Financial Ombudsman Service★ (pp. 229, 234). And complaints about a solicitor should be referred to the Law Society's Consumer Complaints Service★ (pp. 114, 118) (or the relevant Law Society★ in either Scotland or Northern Ireland).

Q *I have LEI and know a very good solicitor I'd like to use to fight my case. But the insurers won't let me instruct him and they say I have no reasonable chance of winning the claim anyway. What can I do?*

A Some policies do allow you to choose your own solicitor, others don't. Those polices which do allow choice usually say you can do this only once legal proceedings have started. Until then – while your case is being investigated or negotiations are going on, say – you may have to accept advice from in-house staff or a solicitor appointed by the insurer. The policy will probably also give the insurer a veto if the person who is your choice seems to be too expensive or to lack the relevant expertise.

If you do want to challenge the insurer's choice of solicitor the policy may have a procedure which refers the matter to another solicitor for an independent opinion, or even to the Law Society – and if the decision goes against you it could be expensive as you may have to pay the costs of getting that decision.

Just because you have LEI you can't assume that the insurers will take on your case. Insurers will only accept and continue to support a claim if they judge you have a reasonable chance of success. Some policies don't say that the insurer has to give you its reasons for its decisions and sometimes cover can be withdrawn without explanation.

You can dispute the insurer's decision, and some policies helpfully explain how to do this. If you have to argue to convince the insurer to take on your claim, you may have to pay for any evidence needed to make your case – this could be expensive for you, although if you succeed in getting the insurer to change its mind you should get these additional expenses back.

Q *Can I make an agreement with my lawyer that means I pay him only if he wins the case and nothing if he loses?*

A It depends on the type of dispute you have. In civil cases solicitors are allowed to offer what are commonly called 'no win, no fee' (or conditional fee) arrangements in all types of legal work, except family disputes. So, if you have a dispute over building work, or a personal injury claim (this could be a claim of medical negligence or any situation where someone has suffered any kind of injury), this kind of arrangement might be useful.

Under these arrangements you are free to agree with your lawyer (whether a solicitor or a barrister) that the lawyer will take on your case on the understanding that, if it is lost, the lawyer will not receive any payment. This arrangement removes some but not all of the uncertainty and financial risk of going to law.

If you lose you will pay your own lawyer nothing, but you will still have to pay your own expenses such as experts' reports, court fees and counsel's fees (if the barrister is not also on a 'no fee' arrangement). You will also have to pay your opponent's costs after they have been taxed by the court (p. 114).

You can take out insurance cover to pay the other side's costs and your expenses should you lose. For example, if the solicitor you use is a member of the Law Society's Accident Line★ Scheme you can pay a one-off fee for cover in personal injury cases. The Law Society★ also has details of cover for other disputes. Alternatively, you may have your own legal expenses insurance cover.

If you win, you will pay your own solicitor's normal charges plus a **success fee** which you will have agreed in writing at the start. This is not linked to the amount of compensation you are awarded, but will be a percentage of the solicitor's 'normal' bill. It could be up to an extra 100 per cent on top of the normal charges, effectively doubling the bill, although most will agree to limit the success fee to the normal rate plus an extra 25 per cent, say. And, if you win, any insurance premium you have paid and any **success fee** you agreed to pay to your solicitor can be recovered from the other party.

Shop around and contact the Law Society for a copy of its model conditional-fee agreements and details of its insurance policy to cover opponents' costs.

Q *I have a 'no win, no fee' arrangement with my solicitor but what happens if I decide to settle the dispute without going to court?*

A It may be a breach of the Trade Descriptions Act for lawyers to advertise conditional-fee arrangements as 'no win, no fee' as this isn't entirely accurate – you do usually have to pay fees to the other party if you lose. Most disputes never get to court but are settled through negotiation. And the lawyers doing the negotiating may be on a conditional-fee arrangement. If the dispute is for a fixed amount, a claim for an unpaid debt, say, then it should be clear, while claims for general compensation are less obvious. To cope with this the written conditional-fee agreement must spell out what constitutes a 'win'. But remember that while you may have an incentive to hold out for as much as possible, and even go to court, the solicitor may wish you to settle for a smaller amount and not take the risk of the case being thrown out by a judge. In the event of a dispute over the terms of a fee arrangement, contact the Law Society's Consumer Complaints Service (CCS)★. Details of how to complain should be set out in the letter of engagement or client care letter (p. 111).

Q *I have just received a bill from my solicitor. It seems unreasonable and is way above the original estimate I was given. How can I* **challenge the bill?**

A You cannot rely on an 'estimate' as a guarantee of the final bill. But a solicitor's bill must be **fair and reasonable**, although it is not possible to calculate solicitors' fees exactly as there is no set scale of costs and much will depend on the time spent on the matter. If you feel the charges are too high, write to the head partner of the firm setting out your reasons for dissatisfaction. If that doesn't work there are formal methods for challenging a bill, but how you go about it depends on the type of work done – that is, whether it was classified as **non-contentious** or **contentious**. It is possible that substantial overcharging could amount to shoddy work, so you should think about complaining to the Law Society's Consumer Complaints Service (CCS)★, or the Law Society of Scotland★, as appropriate (p. 118).

Contentious work is any for which court proceedings have been started (even if you never actually got to court):

- you should request a **detailed breakdown** of the bill. The solicitor is obliged to provide this under section 64 of the Solicitors Act 1974 (although in Scotland this obligation does not exist, it is always worth asking for a breakdown)
- if you're still not happy, you can apply for the costs to be **taxed** by the court. This means that a special bill is drawn up and the court decides whether each item is fair and reasonable. 'Taxation' can be expensive – not only will you have to pay a fee to the court to have the bill assessed, but if the bill is reduced by less than one-fifth, you will lose the court fee and have to pay the solicitor's costs of going to court as well as your own. In Scotland taxation is done by the Auditor of the local sheriff court, whose decision is binding on both sides.

Non-contentious work is any work done where the case does not involve court proceedings, like conveyancing:

- ask the solicitor to apply to the Law Society's Consumer Complaints Service (CCS)★ for a remuneration certificate. This states whether the bill is fair and reasonable, and, if it is not, suggests another sum that would be reasonable. This procedure is free
- if you feel that the certified amount is still too high, you still have the right to apply for the costs to be taxed by the court (see above).

The complaints system for solicitors' charges is broadly the same in Scotland. However, there is no procedure for a remuneration certificate, so regardless of whether there have been court proceedings you will have to go for taxation.

Q *A solicitor did some work for my mother which she was happy with. He had told her his hourly rate before he started, which she accepted, and had mentioned that the sum might be subject to an* **uplift** *for skill and care involved. His final bill has arrived and he has added another 60 per cent on top of the agreed rate as 'care and conduct'. Can lawyers really do this?*

A A solicitor's bill reflects the cost of the time spent on a case. The bill may also include an 'uplift' – a percentage of that cost – which solicitors may charge if they think the case was particularly complex or needed specialist knowledge, say. This is sometimes called a 'mark-up', 'profit element' or 'care and conduct'.

Solicitors must tell you in advance whether they are likely to charge an 'uplift' and what the likely percentage will be. However, very often it is not separately identified, even though it can increase the bill by as much as 100 per cent. If the matter were not so serious, some of the pronouncements made by judges attempting to set out the rules that permit solicitors to charge uplift fees would be laughable. One judge stated that 'No professional man ... stops thinking about the day's problems the minute he lifts his coat and umbrella from the stand and sets out on the journey home. Ideas, often very valuable ideas, occur in the train or car home, or in the bath, or even whilst watching television. Yet nothing is ever put down on a time sheet, or can be put down on a time sheet adequately to reflect this out-of-hours devotion of time.' Spoken like a true member of the profession.

You can challenge it by asking for a remuneration certificate or having it taxed. But if you were warned in advance your challenge is unlikely to succeed.

Q *I went to a large law firm and asked them to provide a specialist solicitor to advise me on my building contract. However, I am now disputing the legal bill as I was dissatisfied with the service given by the person I assumed was a specialist solicitor. But when I checked with the Law Society I discovered the adviser was a trainee and not a fully qualified solicitor. What are my rights?*

A Many people provide legal advice without being solicitors or barristers. As long as you know the status of your legal adviser in advance there should be no problem with this. When you instruct a firm of lawyers, make sure you get a copy of the firm's terms of business. These should be contained in the 'client care letter' or 'letter of appointment' (see above). You must agree to these terms before the work starts. The Solicitors' Code of Conduct says that the letter should contain details of the hourly charge or fixed fee, whatever is agreed, and also contain the status of the person taking on your case.

It is common practice for many firms of solicitors to use trainees, legal executives or other para-legal employees to do a lot of the work, even when this work goes out in the name of a qualified solicitor or even a partner in the firm. It's good practice for the letter of appointment to tell you if some but not all of the work will be delegated to a junior member of staff, and their name.

These requirements of the Code have been given legal weight by the courts. The Court of Appeal decided that if you specifically ask for a solicitor and instead the firm provides another adviser without telling you that the adviser is not a solicitor, the firm cannot recover the fee for any of the work done by that adviser. This applies even if the standard of the advice given is as good as that expected of a solicitor. So if, despite telling the firm that you specifically wanted a 'solicitor', you didn't in fact get one, you can refuse to pay the bill at all.

Q *My solicitor was handling my dispute with a builder. He failed to start court proceedings on time and I've just discovered that the claim is* **statute barred**, *so it's now too late to sue the builder. Surely the solicitor was negligent?*

A Solicitors are paid to do a good job for you and you have every right to complain if they let you down. As with any other service under the Supply of Goods and Services Act 1982 (common law in Scotland) they are obliged to exercise the care and skill that you would expect from a reasonably competent professional. So the solicitor should give such advice and take such action as the facts of that particular case demand. Negligence arises when your solicitor fails to exercise that care and skill and you suffer financial loss as a result.

Complaints about solicitors generally fall into three categories:

- **negligence** – where you have suffered loss as a result of the actions or omissions of the solicitor
- **shoddy work** – where the work may be inadequate, slow or generally substandard, causing inconvenience or distress, but no financial loss (p. 000)
- **professional misconduct** – where the solicitor is in breach of the professional code of conduct (which may or may not cause you loss).

Your solicitor's duty is to protect your interests. Failure to take certain actions which a reasonable solicitor would do, and which cause damage as a result, constitutes negligence. By failing to start a claim against the builder within the legal time limits (p. 22), thereby losing you the chance of taking that claim to court and recovering compensation, your solicitor has been negligent. However, if you want financial compensation your only option may be court action. There are some alternatives, and whichever course you take it is as well to get some detailed advice on your legal position first:

- if your claim does not exceed £5,000 (£1,500 for the sheriff court in Scotland, £1,000 in Northern Ireland) it is likely to be allocated to the small claims track of the county court. If it exceeds this the claim is likely to end up in the fast track, which is more formal than small claims

- if you cannot find another lawyer with experience of negligence work to help you, contact the Law Society's Consumer Complaints Service (CCS)★ and insist on seeing a member of the Law Society's★ Negligence Panel, who will give you up to an hour's free advice. This service may be limited to those who genuinely cannot find a solicitor to take on their case, but many consumers who face a possible claim against their solicitors will not want to spend more money on another solicitor, so it's important to find out whether your case is worth pursuing (in Scotland the Law Society will appoint a solicitor called a 'troubleshooter')

- under the Solicitors' Indemnity Rules all principals in a law firm – that is, partners or sole practitioners – are required to be insured for the risk of professional negligence claims against the firm. This means that they are covered whether the negligence was their own fault or that of their employees or former employees. If you feel confident enough to argue your own case and your complaint involves negligence which has caused you financial loss, go direct to the solicitors' insurers, who may negotiate direct with you over your complaint. As long as you bear in mind that the insurance company is acting for the solicitor and not you, you may well short-circuit the system. You may need the help of Citizens' Advice★, a Law Centre★, or Which? Legal Service★ (see p.4 for more information) in order to do this, and perseverance may be necessary, but if you have all your evidence and arguments worked out persistence is likely to pay off. Out-of-court settlements are reached in many cases.

Q *I wasn't happy with the work done by my solicitor and decided to change to another, but the old one is refusing to hand over my papers until his bill is paid. Can he do this?*

A As a general rule, a client can change solicitors whenever he or she wishes to do so. If you are already involved in court action, there may be formalities which your new solicitor should complete for you. But if you do owe a solicitor any fees for work done, he or she has the legal right to hang on to your property, and that includes all documents, money, deeds, etc., if it came into his or her possession as part of the professional employment. The principle is the same as the right of a garage to hold on to your car if it has done work for which money is owed. There are circumstances in which you can get the papers back without paying the disputed bill:

- the Law Society★ can recommend that the papers should be released subject to a satisfactory undertaking on your part to pay the outstanding fee
- your new solicitor may agree an undertaking with the original solicitor as to payment once the dispute is resolved
- it may be possible to make a payment of the disputed amount into an 'escrow' account, which will only be paid out, in part or in full, when the dispute over the bill is settled
- if the papers are vital for your case and you would be prejudiced by the solicitor withholding them, you may get a court order for their release: your new solicitor should advise on this.

Q *My solicitor never returns my calls. He has taken three months to prepare my will. How can I speed things up?*

A All firms of solicitors are required to have a system for handling disputes of this sort and to nominate a senior person to deal with complaints, so write to the senior partner of the firm. If that doesn't solve the problem, you should send a brief account of your complaint to the Law Society's Customer Complaints Service (CCS)★. The CCS cannot deal with complaints of negligence (although it can refer you to a negligence solicitor); it limits itself to complaints of incompetence or **shoddy work**, that is, work which has caused you frustration, inconvenience, annoyance or distress, but not financial loss. The CCS provides a system aimed at sorting out disputes quickly and informally and will contact the solicitor on your behalf in an effort to solve the problems you are experiencing. If appropriate it can take **disciplinary action** against the solicitor; it also has powers to award compensation of up to £5,000 and can order the solicitor to reduce a bill.

In Scotland you should contact the Law Society of Scotland★, whose Client Relations Office has powers broadly similar to those of the CCS, under which it can make a finding of 'inadequate professional service', order a refund of the fee charged, and award compensation.

If you are still unhappy with the way the complaint has been handled by the solicitor or by the CCS, or if you are unhappy with the decision reached, you can then ask the Legal Services Ombudsman★ to investigate on your behalf. But you must have exhausted the complaints procedure of the CCS. You must complain within three months of the CCS reaching its decision. The Ombudsman can recommend that the solicitor or the CCS pay you compensation for financial loss, distress and inconvenience, and there is no limit on the amount that can be awarded. Awards are not strictly binding, so the solicitors or CCS may not have to abide by the decision. In Scotland contact the Scottish Legal Services Ombudsman★.

Q *The lawyer who represented me in court didn't put forward all the evidence. He seemed totally unprepared and didn't ask the other side's witnesses the right questions. As a result I lost my claim which I'd been told I'd win. What can I do?*

A If you receive negligent service from a solicitor, barrister or licensed conveyancer which causes you financial loss, then you can claim compensation (pp. 116–7). But until recently if the negligent act that caused the loss took place during court proceedings, the lawyer was **immune** from any claim by you.

This much-criticised protection of legal professionals has now been swept away and you can make a claim for compensation for work done badly in court. The hurdles you face are that you must prove that the lawyer was negligent in not putting all the evidence forward, and that you lost your claim because of that and suffered a loss as a result. You must show that no reasonably competent lawyer would have conducted the case in the way your lawyer did, so you may have to get another lawyer to testify to this.

It may also be worth referring the facts to the Law Society's Consumer Complaints Service (CCS)★ or General Council of the Bar★: if the lawyer's work was bad enough it may amount to **professional misconduct**, which could mean that the lawyer will be banned from practising law, although this course alone won't get you any compensation.

Q *I took advice from a barrister about my claim for compensation against a hospital. My solicitor agrees with me that the barrister's attitude was rude and uncaring. We are sure this affected the outcome and the amount of compensation I got. How can I complain about this – or even just reduce his large bill?*

A You should send the details to the Bar Complaints Commissioner★ within six months of the complaint arising. You will have to satisfy the Commissioner that your complaint amounts to either misconduct or, more likely here, inadequate professional service. If there is a case to answer it will then be considered by the Professional Conduct and Complaints Committee of the Bar Council. 'Inadequate professional service' means conduct falling significantly short of that which would normally be expected of a barrister in all the circumstances. The fact that your solicitor agrees with you will help your case. Complaints of misconduct are referred to a disciplinary panel and 'service' complaints to an adjudication panel. You cannot get any compensation for your distress and frustration alone. But these panels do have the power to require the barrister to reduce or waive the fees, apologise, or pay compensation of up to £5,000 if you have suffered a financial loss.

Chapter 5

Property

Buying a home is the single biggest purchase most people ever make, so getting it right is crucial. You may spend a lot of time and money travelling to see properties which don't match up to the estate agent's prose. And when you buy your home, you may discover more problems than the surveyor pointed out, with disastrous consequences. So what are your rights when buying property? This chapter looks at the law relating to estate agents and surveyors, at the guarantees that come with most new houses, and at the legislation allowing leaseholders the right to buy their home.

Q *I've never bought a property before and I'm worried about things going wrong with the purchase or the subsequent move. I'm borrowing most of the purchase price and spending most of my own money on the surveyor and solicitor. How can I make sure that problems don't arise?*

A There are no guarantees and things could go wrong no matter how careful you are. A large number of different people can be involved in buying property – lawyers, surveyors, estate agents, banks and building societies, to name a few. Choosing the people to help can be a bit of a lottery. But there are some steps you can take to reduce the risks:

- ask friends and colleagues if they have personal experience of a particular individual, firm or company and can make a personal recommendation. But remember that a solicitor, say, who is good at family disputes may not necessarily be able to deal expertly with other types of legal work
- many professionals specialise in certain types of work, and it pays to find people with the right expertise. For example, some lawyers deal with leasehold conveyancing and certain surveyors may have specialist knowledge of Victorian buildings or of a local area
- membership of a trade association may give some protection. The British Association of Removers (BAR)★, for example, provides conciliation and arbitration for disputes if they arise

- interview a number of practitioners in each of the areas where you need help and, even though money may be tight, do not simply choose on price alone

- check whether you have any existing legal expenses insurance cover (p. 111). As this is your first purchase it is unlikely that you have any policies that would cover you for the sort of problems that could crop up. So think about taking out insurance to cover any legal expenses that may arise from the process of buying your home. Home Buyer Legal Protection, for example, specifically covers the legal expenses you may incur if you end up in dispute with your surveyor, removal firm, mortgage adviser, etc., or even over bills that should have been paid by the previous owner. As for any insurance policy, always ask to see the full terms and conditions before you agree to buy.

Q *What should we be wary of if we want to do our own conveyancing?*

A Doing your own conveyancing is quite possible. But it can be both tricky and risky. The simple purchase of a freehold house, for example, is reasonably straightforward but it is advisable to follow instructions on how to go about this (*Doing Your Own Conveyancing*, published by Which? Books★, gives information on the process of buying a freehold house in England and Wales). With leasehold flats or with enfranchised property where leaseholders own a share of the freehold, the process can be complicated and to do the legal work you will need an understanding of land law, trusts, contract and planning law. Leasehold transactions will also involve covenants in respect of repair and maintenance, the rights of the tenant to use common areas, services provided and the liability to pay service charges: all of these are important issues requiring careful consideration. When the purchase is completed both sides are bound by their legal agreement and all the continuing obligations it may contain, so it is essential that the conveyancing is done correctly. Even professionals make mistakes, but at least they are insured and will be in a position to compensate for any loss that arises (see Chapter 4).

Q *I'm buying a property and would like to do the conveyancing, but I'm not confident about doing it myself. Would I have to use a lawyer to help me?*

A Before 1987 conveyancing for payment could be undertaken only by qualified solicitors. Since then it has been lawful for 'licensed conveyancers' to offer their professional services to the public. Licensed conveyancers can set up in business alone or work for solicitors' firms, estate agents, building societies and the like. It is worth shopping around for a good deal as there is now strong competition for conveyancing. For help with your conveyancing work, get details of both licensed conveyancers and solicitors in your area, from the local phone directory or from the Law Society★ or the Council for Licensed Conveyancers (CLC)★. Try to agree a fixed fee for the work, but note that if it is a leasehold property many lawyers and conveyancers may be reluctant to commit themselves to a specific sum as there may be hidden problems. Whatever you agree, make sure you get full details in writing in advance.

Q *I'm thinking of buying a house and I'll need a mortgage. Do I have to pay for a structural survey?*

A No. But you will probably have to pay the mortgage lender (the building society or bank) for its valuation report. You are not obliged to have any other type of survey done, although it is sensible to have a more detailed report. The types of inspection available are as follows:

- **valuation** This is usually carried out on behalf of the lender and is simply an assessment of what the property is worth. It is based on a purely visual inspection and takes into account only the age, size and type of property, the location and amenities, the construction and general state of repair. Some lenders won't let you see their valuation report, or they might not even do one. If you buy a new house, and only rely on the scant information in a valuation report you'll be taking a gamble as it is unlikely to tell you everything you want to know. The valuation is not an indication that the house is structurally sound. The report is addressed to the lender, not to you, and gives you very little protection

- **Homebuyer survey and valuation (HSV)** This is carried out on behalf of the purchaser. It gives more information than a valuation, on a standard form from the Royal Institution of Chartered Surveyors (RICS)★. It doesn't include details of every minor defect. Major faults, such as damp and signs of subsidence, should be included, but the report will cover only those parts of the property which are reasonably accessible and visible. So the surveyor is unlikely to lift carpets or inspect the loft if access is difficult and may recommend you carry out other checks before you exchange contracts – such as asking a specialist to look at the drains, the roof or central heating

- **building survey** These used to be called full structural surveys and are carried out on behalf of the purchaser. This is the most thorough (and expensive) type of survey. It should cover all the main features of the property from the roof to the foundations, commenting on the wiring, plumbing and central heating as well as garden fences and problem trees. This type of survey will give you extra protection, and is particularly useful with older houses. If the surveyor has been unable to lift carpets, etc. then this should be stated in the report.

A survey is a form of insurance. If it shows major defects you may not want to go ahead with the purchase and will be thankful to have been saved the headaches of dealing with such problems. If there's nothing alarming to report, you are paying for peace of mind. When the position is somewhere in the middle, with defects that need attention but may not be severe enough to put you off, a survey is a useful way to negotiate a reduction in price. If you don't have your own survey done then you may have no basis for a compensation claim if the property turns out to have serious defects: you will not be able to claim against the seller. However, if it becomes clear that the surveyor has missed some defects that should have been spotted then you could have a claim against the surveyor.

Q *The building society gave me a copy of its **valuation**. This said there was a small damp patch in the hall wall and a rotten end on a joist in the cellar ceiling. It also said that the cellar was relatively dry. Six weeks after I moved in the cellar floor and walls were covered with mushrooms and mould. I've been quoted up to £10,000 to put it right. Can I claim this from the building society which carried out the valuation?*

A A valuation report is for the benefit of the lender (the bank or building society offering the mortgage), not you. It helps the lender to decide whether the property is good security against the mortgage. But never confuse a valuation with a survey (see above). Many defects will not affect the value of a property or the lender's decision to grant a mortgage. However, if in making the valuation the surveyor has missed something of importance, like a major structural defect or severe damp, which should have been apparent from a visual inspection, or could make the valuation unreliable, you can sue for compensation. It doesn't matter if you paid for the report or not. To claim, you must prove that you relied on it, went ahead with the purchase and then found you had been misled.

You can also complain about the bank or the building society to the **Financial Ombudsman Service***. This scheme is free.

Q *I bought a house after having a homebuyer survey and valuation (HSV) done. Now I find that there is serious trouble with the roof which will be costly to repair. I've written to the surveyor and he says that he didn't manage to inspect every part of the property, so he's not responsible. Is this correct?*

A A surveyor must exercise **reasonable care** and **skill** in carrying out the work. If he or she does not and you suffer loss and damage as a direct result then you have a claim for compensation. However, look in the HSV and you'll find words that stack up against consumers seeking redress. Typical wording states that 'furniture, floor coverings and other contents *are not* moved or lifted'. So there need be no attempt to move bits of furniture, rugs or carpets that may be concealing the signs of damp rot, say; no attempt to even ask the current occupant for permission to move a few things to inspect more fully. If the surveyor can't be bothered, he doesn't have to. The survey terms allow him to get away with this, although descriptions that limit the surveyor's responsibility have to be fair and reasonable. If they are not, they will be invalid under the laws that offer consumer protection against unfair contract terms (pp. 88–9). It may also be possible to argue that these are not legally binding if the surveyor didn't show them to you before the survey was carried out.

The HSV makes it clear that if there are any parts of the property 'which have not been inspected' by the surveyor then it assumes that 'no significant defect' would have been revealed by such an inspection which would alter the property valuation.

If you think that your surveyor has been negligent you will need to prove that he or she failed to see the faults or the tell-tale signs in the property that would have revealed trouble to an observant and knowledgeable surveyor, so you may have to get a report from another surveyor, concentrating on what the first surveyor could have seen and what should have been mentioned in the first report. In the small claims track no expert evidence is permitted, unless the court allows it, and the expert fees you can recover if you win are limited. However, an expert's report may be the only way you can get the other side to accept your claim. So, try to get the surveyor to agree to instruct one expert jointly with you and to give the report some serious consideration.

Even if you can prove your case, you cannot claim the cost of repairs. The test used by the courts is not 'How much will it cost to put matters right?' but rather 'How much less might I have paid for the house had I known of the defects?' (the **difference in value**). As some defects will have little or no effect on the market price of the property, there may be no claim for compensation even though the repairs may be expensive.

Q *I'm claiming compensation from my surveyor but his insurers are saying that I have no claim. I want to pursue this further. Is court my only option?*

A If the surveyor (usually through his insurance company) disputes your claim, you may have to go to court. Negligence cases are often costly and complicated, particularly if your claim is for more than the small claims limit of £5,000 (£1,500 in Scotland, £1,000 in Northern Ireland), so you may have to go to a solicitor. The Royal Institution of Chartered Surveyors (RICS)★ has an arbitration scheme run by the Chartered Institute of Arbitrators★ covering allegations of negligence arising in England and Wales for claims up to £50,000 (above this you have to go to court). Its great advantage is that for a fixed fee you can get an independent decision on a claim against your surveyor without all the hassle and possible costs of a lengthy court case – although costs for large claims may be high if you lose.

If you win, the decision is binding on both parties, and you may get the fee back, plus compensation. If you lose you cannot refer the same case to the courts. Arbitration is compulsory for RICS members. So if the consumer wishes to use it against a RICS member the surveyor will have to consent.

There is a £235 registration fee for arbitration but if your claim is for less than £3,000 there are no other charges if you lose. For claims above this, you have to pay the arbitrator's costs (up to £1,325) if you lose. The scheme applies to all types of survey, including mortgage valuations.

Whichever way you get the complaint dealt with, you will need all the evidence you can get concerning whether the surveyor should have spotted the defects and the effect the missed defects have on the value of the house. For more information contact the Chartered Institute of Arbitrators, or the Professional Practice Department at RICS.

Q *I sold my house to someone who didn't have a survey done. There has been a long-standing subsidence problem but I didn't disclose this to the buyer. He's now discovered it and has written demanding compensation from me. Everything was handled by my solicitor. Do I have to pay up?*

A Currently, the principle of **caveat emptor** ('let the buyer beware') still applies to property purchase, although from 2007 sellers will have to disclose details of the condition of the property they are selling. That is why the burden is always on the buyer to make any inspection and enquiry that seems necessary, hence the riskiness of buying a property without having a structural survey done first. The standard form of contract normally used for selling houses states specifically that the buyer takes the property in the state and condition it is in – so if the buyer didn't do all he or she could to check that state and condition, he or she can't claim against you.

There is only one situation where you might be responsible. If the buyer (or more usually the conveyancer or solicitor) asks a straight question about the state of repair, or whether something is in working order, you must either give a truthful answer or simply say that the buyer should find out for himself or herself (the usual response is 'Make your own enquiries'). If you do mislead the buyer, and that causes him or her loss, you will have to pay compensation, or the contract of sale could even be rescinded – this means the sale would be cancelled and you'd have to take back the property. But you wouldn't be able to cancel the purchase of the new property so you'll end up with both. This means that if you are selling a house you must be careful to be scrupulously accurate. If the prospective buyer asks about something you do not know, do not guess, because if you are wrong you could be held liable for a costly mistake.

Q *The **newly built house** I have just bought has many problems. Can I claim the cost of repairing the defects as the house is not of satisfactory quality?*

A There is no legal requirement that a newly built house should be of satisfactory quality – the Sale of Goods Act 1979 does not apply to property (see above and pp. 31–2). Fortunately, however, almost all new homes are covered by a **warranty** which guarantees that they have been built to certain standards and that any problems will be put right either by the builder, or, if the builder will not co-operate, or has gone out of business, by the warranty company. It is very unlikely that you would be able to borrow money for a new home that does not have warranty cover of some sort (see below).

Q *I've just seen a newly built house I'd like to buy. The developer says it has **housing warranty cover**. What is this?*

A When you buy property you do not have the same rights as when you buy goods, and there is no implied term that the property will be of satisfactory quality. So it is important to carry out your own investigations and some form of survey on the structure is advisable. Even with a new house there's no guarantee that it was constructed properly. So look for a house that is covered by a warranty which guarantees that it was built to certain standards. The notable warranty schemes for new homes are the National House Building Council (NHBC)★ 'Buildmark' scheme and the Zurich Insurance★ Building Guarantee (known as the '10' warranty policy). Both of these offer similar cover whereby during the first two years after purchase the builder undertakes to put right any defects which result from failure to comply with the minimum standards of workmanship stipulated. For the next eight years any major defects in the load-bearing structure of the property will be put right free of charge. The Zurich scheme can be extended by another five years if Zurich agrees.

It is always important to meet the time limits set out in your warranty cover. Any problem should be notified to the builder and to the insurer in writing as soon as possible.

Q *What **fixtures and fittings** will I have to leave behind in my house when I sell it?*

A What you leave behind and what you take with you is completely a matter for agreement between you and the purchaser. If the matter is dealt with in the formal contract of sale, you can spell out in that what you have decided. However, in practice it is difficult to deal with each and every item, so if nothing is said about particular items:

- what are properly called **fixtures** automatically go with the property, and should therefore be left behind. A fixture is something that is firmly attached to the building or the land and not simply put up for display (a light switch is a fixture, but many light fittings are not)
- to avoid a dispute over what constitutes a fixture, list all the items that the purchaser will have seen fixed in place when he or she viewed the property but which you specifically want to take with you, then give the list of items to the conveyancer and ask him or her to add it to the contract of sale
- if you do leave things behind which are not normally considered fixtures – curtains, carpets, cooker, say – it is up to you to decide whether to ask a separate price for these or to include them in the selling price.

Q *Are there any legal controls over what estate agents can do and say? And how can I complain about their work?*

A The legal controls which govern estate agents' work are various:

- breach of contract
- breach of agency obligations
- Estate Agents Act 1979: this is designed to make sure that agents act in the best interests of their clients and that both buyers and sellers are treated honestly and fairly
- Property Misdescriptions Act 1991.

Some agents may be members of professional associations, such as the National Association of Estate Agents (NAEA)★, or the Royal Institution of Chartered Surveyors (RICS)★. These operate codes of practice governing how their members work. The relevant body can reprimand member agents and also take disciplinary proceedings against them. They risk being thrown out of the association, but you're unlikely to get compensation.

Check whether the agent belongs to the Ombudsman for Estate Agents★ scheme. This was started by the large agency chains run by banks, building societies and insurance companies, and many thousands of smaller estate agents are eligible to join, although there are still many that haven't. For complaints about scheme members the Ombudsman can order the agent to pay up to £50,000 compensation.

A voluntary code of practice for those who have signed up to the Ombudsman scheme sets out what is expected of estate agents. For example, agents must:

- give written details of fees and business terms before the client agrees to use the agent

- give written details of any conflict of interest
- explain technical terms such as 'sole agency', or 'ready, willing and able purchaser' in writing
- keep client money in a separate account and not hold money at all without adequate insurance cover
- not directly or indirectly harass anyone to gain instructions
- only erect a 'For Sale' board with the client's permission
- tell clients as soon as reasonably possible about all offers received at any time until contracts are exchanged (or in Scotland missives have been concluded).

If your estate agent is not a member of the scheme your only option is to pursue your claim for breach of contract or breach of agency obligations in court.

Q *Although I used estate agents I feel my house was sold largely through my own efforts. Someone saw the 'For Sale' sign and called in, and I persuaded him to buy. The agents did virtually nothing. Do I still have to pay them their full commission?*

A You probably do. If you instruct an estate agent to sell your home, your legal position is governed by the law of contract. If estate agents abide by the promises they make in their contracts, you have to abide by your promise to pay them. However, agents do not generally make promises about exactly what they will do to sell your house. Instead, many agreements just state that you will pay *them* if they 'introduce' a buyer to you. So, if you found a buyer because of the agent's sign, even if putting up the sign was all they did, they are entitled to their commission. On the other hand, you do not have to pay if no buyer is found, in spite of the agent's efforts, unless the agreement says you must pay a certain amount or that you will pay, for example, for marketing costs, such as advertising.

   Some estate agents' contracts are different (see below), and an agent may specify that he or she will do or not do certain things, or will charge for specific items, such as advertisements, even if the property is not sold. If an agent breaks the contract by not doing what he or she agreed to do, you would, strictly speaking, be entitled to compensation for any loss you suffer. But if you pull out of the contract before paying or end up selling the house through the agent, then you probably won't have suffered any loss. However, if the agent was to incur costs without your authorisation, he or she would have no right to make you pay for them.

Q *I'm thinking of selling my house. When I've instructed an estate agent, can I pull out of the agreement and sell the house privately or through another firm if I decide that agency is not getting the job done?*

A This may be difficult as there are no hard and fast rules about what an agent actually has to do to find a purchaser. Whether you can pull out of the contract depends on the agreement you have, so check the terms and conditions carefully:

- if you choose a no-sale, no-fee deal, you are liable for commission only if the agent introduces you to someone who actually buys your home
- many agents' contracts say that you will have to pay the fee 'in the event of our introducing a purchaser who is **ready, willing and able** to complete the transaction'. Under this arrangement you could end up paying a fee if the agent claims to have found someone who was able to buy the property but didn't go ahead because you took it off the market, or if you simply found the eventual buyer yourself
- normally you can pull out and will owe the agents nothing except any agreed costs such as those incurred for advertising in the local press, provided you do not go on to sell to a buyer who was 'introduced' to you as a result of their efforts (see above)
- some agents now agree to a programme of action for you, and may expect to be paid something at the outset. With that sort of agreement it may not be so easy to pull out and avoid paying, but if the agents have done little or nothing of what they agreed to do, you may have a legal case in this instance for suing for the return of your payment, whatever the terms of the agreement say.

Q *My estate agents want me to sign an agreement giving them 'sole selling rights'. If I do, I will pay less than I would if I were to use other agents as well. Isn't this the same as 'sole agency', so if I sell the house by my own efforts I won't have to pay the commission?*

A These two arrangements are very different:

- **sole selling rights** means that however your house comes to be sold, even if you come to a private agreement which has nothing to do with the agents, you will have to pay them their commission. Never agree to sole selling rights unless you are sure you will not find a purchaser through your own efforts
- **sole agency** leaves you free to sell privately by your own efforts without paying any commission, but not through other agents. You can instruct other agents, but if they sell the house you will have to pay commission to the original sole agents and the agents who have sold the property.

Other types of agency arrangements you can opt for include:

- **joint agency**, whereby you instruct two agents. Both have to agree to this, and on who gets the commission on the sale, which may be shared
- **multiple agency**, whereby you instruct as many agents as you like: the one who comes up with the buyer earns the commission. The fee for this type of arrangement will normally be the highest of all the options available.

Whether sole, joint or multiple agency is best for you depends on circumstances – for instance, what charges are to be made, the merits of the firms involved, how quickly you wish to sell, etc. If you instruct more than one firm of agents, you will generally pay higher commission levels to whichever of them may ultimately sell the property, but you have the advantage of more than one agency being at work on your behalf. On the other hand, a sole agent may have more incentive to sell, and may use sub-agents without any extra charge to you, thus giving you the same advantage at no extra cost. If you do agree a sole agency arrangement, make sure you put a time limit on it – six weeks, say – as this will allow you to spread your options if it's not proving to be the best arrangement.

Q *I heard by chance that a couple were interested in buying my house and had got as far as trying to make an offer for it. Yet the offer was never passed on to me by my estate agents. What is more, it was higher than the offer I actually accepted. Surely that can't have been right?*

A It certainly wasn't. Your agents owed you a legal duty to find the best available sale for you and to pass on all offers promptly and in writing – it sounds as if they were in breach of that duty. Furthermore, under the Estate Agents Act 1979 it is an 'undesirable practice' for agents to fail to pass on offers (or to misrepresent them) or in any other way to discriminate against one potential buyer in favour of others. Agents can be banned from their profession if they are found to have engaged in 'undesirable practices'. You should certainly tell your local Trading Standards Department about this situation (at your local council offices; in Northern Ireland contact the Department of Enterprise, Trade and Investment★). And if the agent is a member of the Ombudsmen for Estate Agents★ scheme you should seek compensation there.

What happened here could of course have been simply poor service. But it could also be more disturbing. It may be that the potential buyer of whom you heard was not interested in arranging finance through the agents and was put off by them in favour of someone else who was. Agents can make large sums of money in commission on arranging mortgages for purchasers. That is why the Estate Agents Act obliges an agent to tell you in writing, in advance, if he or she is going to offer services such as arranging mortgages for people who express an interest in buying the house you have placed with his or her firm. This does not mean that if agents offer such services your interests are bound to be prejudiced, or that this is even likely. But it is as well to be aware of the possibility of a **conflict of interest**.

Other examples of 'undesirable practices' and matters which should be referred to your local Trading Standards Department are as follows:

- failure to disclose promptly and in writing any **personal interest** in a transaction: for example, if the estate agent wants to buy the house himself or herself, he or she may not encourage other offers
- failure to tell the client if a prospective purchaser is seeking financial or other services from the agent.

Q *I put an offer down on a house, had a survey carried out and arranged a mortgage, then the seller pulled out leaving me with a lot of wasted expense. I believe he did this because the estate agents found him a better offer. Do I have any redress against them?*

A This is what is known as **gazumping**, which tends to be common in a booming property market. It is rarer when houses are difficult to sell. In a buyers' market the boot is more likely to be on the other foot, with buyers refusing to go ahead at the last minute unless the price is dropped (sometimes called '**gazundering**').

Unfortunately, there is no legal redress for gazumping and gazundering. A contract for the sale and purchase of a property is not binding unless it is in writing and signed by both parties. (Contrary to popular opinion, this is *not* true of most contracts − land, or property, is an exception.) That means that until both parties have signed a contract for the house, either can withdraw without the other having any right to compensation, whether an offer has been made and accepted 'subject to contract' or not.

Buyers who are gazumped and blame the agent should remember that the agent acts for the seller, and is paid by him or her in commission, and therefore has a legal duty to get the best deal possible for the seller. Agents don't owe any such duty to buyers. If a buyer with a better offer comes along after an offer has been accepted subject to contract, it is actually the agent's legal duty to pass that offer on to the seller and to recommend that the seller accepts that offer, leaving the first purchaser 'gazumped'.

The opportunities for gazumping and gazundering could be reduced − for instance, by speeding up conveyancing in England, Wales and Northern Ireland. In the near future sellers rather than buyers will commission the survey. In 2007 the Home Information Pack (HIP) will become mandatory. This is to be compiled by the seller and is an information pack that includes a type of home-buyer survey and valuation report.

However, in Scotland the whole system of land purchase is different and there is less opportunity for problems of this nature to arise, because once an offer has been made, and accepted by the seller, a binding contract exists, which prevents buyer and seller alike from withdrawing before exchange of contracts.

Q *I've put in an offer on a house which has been accepted 'subject to contract'. How can I stop the seller accepting any higher offers that may be made before we exchange contracts?*

A Gazumping not only causes frustration but also wastes money. Potential buyers can spend money on surveyors, lawyers and search fees but still not buy the property, and have no right to claim the expenses back from the seller.

Proposals have been put forward to speed up the conveyancing process, but that would not remove the problem altogether. Other ideas include the payment of a pre-contract deposit by both parties which would be forfeited if one party withdrew from the transaction without good reason. The government is currently looking at ways of combating the problem of gazumping by reviewing the whole conveyancing process in England and Wales. Currently the most realistic option is to draw up a 'lock-out' agreement. This takes the form of a written contract that both buyer and seller sign. If both sides sign, then, as with all contracts, it would be legally enforceable. The Royal Institution of Chartered Surveyors (RICS)★ has a model contract for use by house-buyers and sellers. In essence, it says that the seller must not show the property to anyone else, or must not accept any other offers, for a period of, say, 14 days. The contract gives the buyer breathing space to have his or her survey done, arrange a mortgage and have the legal work carried out without worrying about being out-bid. If the seller breaks the agreement the buyer can claim compensation for the losses suffered as a result. But if the buyer has not exchanged within the agreed period the seller can go ahead and consider other offers.

Q *I was interested in buying a house described in the agents' particulars in glowing terms – deceptively spacious, immaculate, located in a quiet cul-de-sac close to all amenities etc. When I went to see it, it turned out to be small, in only fair decorative condition, and though the cul-de-sac was quiet, the motorway on the other side of the house wasn't! Also, there was a long trip to the shops, because they were on the other side of the motorway. Wasn't this a breach of the Trade Descriptions Act?*

A No. The Trade Descriptions Act 1968 doesn't cover sales of land. But the Property Misdescriptions Act 1991 fills that loophole. It sounds as if there certainly has been a breach of this legislation.

The test under the Act is whether the description (verbal or written) would **mislead** a reasonable person. If it would, then the agent has committed an offence. It is doubtful whether 'deceptively spacious' would be misleading, so that phrase is probably not a breach of it. Descriptions of decorative condition tend to be subjective and are not covered by the Act. But the other two descriptions you mention sound very misleading, even though they may not have been literally false. If an agent's description of a property (verbal or written) misses out some crucial fact which means that what he or she has said is misleading, then he or she has committed an offence. Here, it would have been quite reasonable to assume that the house was in a quiet location, and that the shops would be a few minutes away, neither of which was the case. This is a matter for Trading Standards Officers (at your local council offices; in Northern Ireland contact the Department of Economic Development★) and the Ombudsman for Estate Agents★ if the agent is a member.

Q *I live in a flat, and I've always felt at a disadvantage having a leasehold rather than a freehold. The landlord hasn't maintained the building satisfactorily, and I'm worried about my flat falling in value as the lease starts to run out. Can I buy the freehold to my flat from my landlord?*

A If you and your neighbours in the building own your flats – i.e. you bought them on long leases, rather than renting them on short tenancies – then you and they may well have the right to get together to buy the freehold of your block. This is called **enfranchisement**. But the legislation puts some hurdles in your way.

First, you must be the owner of an **eligible long lease**, which may mean (among other things) paying only a very low ground rent, if you are to join in an enfranchisement. Moreover, you cannot just buy the freehold of your own flat: freeholds of blocks cannot be split up – they have to be bought as a whole.

Secondly, therefore, your **block as a whole must be eligible**. At least two-thirds of the leaseholders must have eligible long leases, so if you have several neighbours who rent you may well not qualify. A block can also be ineligible if more than a small part of it is given over to use as shops, offices, etc., or if it is a small 'conversion' (not purpose-built as flats) and you have a resident landlord. Moreover:

- if a block is eligible for enfranchisement, at least **two-thirds of the eligible flat-owners** will have to sign a written proposal to buy the freehold. This document will commit those who have signed it to come up with the full cost of purchase, or to paying the landlord's costs if the deal falls through. That will start the enfranchisement process
- at least half of those who sign must have lived in their flats for a year or more
- those who sign must represent at least half of all the flats in the block (whether eligible or not)
- most leasehold house-owners already have the right to enfranchise (see below).

Q *How much will enfranchisement cost?*

A The prices of freeholds will be determined by negotiation between the flat-owners who are seeking to buy and the landlord. If agreement can't be reached, a price will be set after a hearing by a Leasehold Valuation Tribunal, a body resembling an informal court.

Enfranchisement will not be cheap: the legislation lays down that a landlord will be paid:

- all that he or she would have got if he or she sold the freehold on the open market, plus
- at least a half-share of any special value that it has for the flat-owners as opposed to anyone else (called 'marriage value' because it arises from the marriage of leases with the freehold), plus
- compensation for any loss which the sale causes him or her to suffer, and
- all his or her costs.

In areas where property values are high, and especially where there are fewer than 60 or so years left on flat-owners' leases, then the special 'marriage value' could be many thousands of pounds per flat. Enfranchisement will also be expensive if flat-owners have to buy any shops and offices, and/or the rented units, in their block. And where less than 100 per cent of the flat-owners take part in the enfranchisement (at least 67 per cent must participate), the costs per person will be proportionately higher because they will be shared amongst fewer people. Where all these factors combine, enfranchisement may be very expensive indeed.

But, by the same token, in a straightforward suburban or provincial block, with leases that still have 90 years or more to run (as many do), where there are no renting tenants or shops, then the cost should be only a small percentage of what you paid for your flat in the first place – especially if everyone joins in the enfranchisement bid.

Q *We want to enfranchise but can't, under the rules in the legislation. Are we just left out in the cold? Won't that affect the value of our flats?*

A If you have an eligible long lease, you will have an individual right to buy an extension to that lease from the landlord, provided you have lived in your flat for at least three years (or three years out of the past ten). This will leave him or her in control of management, but should help to avoid the problems which can arise when the lease starts to run out (problems can start as early as 60 years or more before the end of the lease).

It is not certain whether flats which remain on unextended leases will end up worth less than flats sold with a share of the freehold or with new, longer leases.

But it is quite likely that they will, especially if the right to enfranchisement and extensions is widely taken up within a block.

Q *What will happen if, although eligible, I don't join in an enfranchisement bid, but it still goes ahead?*

A You will end up with a new landlord – your neighbours. Otherwise, nothing will change: you will have the same lease, the same rights and duties, and the same rules to comply with as before. Note that you might be able to join in the enfranchisement at a later date if those who have already enfranchised agree.

Q *I think my mother's landlord is trying to sell the freehold of the building to one of his friends to stop my mother and the other flat-owners from buying it. Can he do this?*

A No. As long as your leasehold interest and the property itself are eligible for enfranchisement (p. 133) it is a criminal offence for a landlord to sell the freehold of leasehold flats without first making a formal approach to the residents to find out whether they wish to buy it. If the landlord tries it he or she could face prosecution in the magistrates' court and a fine of up to £5,000. And the same sanction is available against any advisers who have been helping in the wrongful sale, such as auctioneers, solicitors and surveyors.

If the illegal sale does go ahead your mother must be contacted by the new landlord and, more important, he or she must tell her that she has a right to buy the freehold back at the same price. If the landlord fails to do either of these he or she commits a criminal offence and faces a hefty fine.

Q *Where can I get advice to help me and my neighbours enfranchise?*

A You can find leaflets and booklets at your local Citizens Advice Bureau and some Bureaux can offer more specific advice. The government has set up the Leasehold Advisory Service (LEASE)★ to help those wishing to take control of their property. Once you decide you may be eligible and you seriously want to go ahead, it is essential to have the advice of both a solicitor and a surveyor or valuer. Enfranchisement is a difficult and complex process, like conveyancing but with far more potential pitfalls.

Q *Is enfranchisement the same as* **commonhold**?
A No. Enfranchisement gives you some of the basic advantages of commonhold, such as control of your property, and will be a necessary first step to commonhold, but it is not the same thing.

Enfranchisement brings about one simple, but crucial, change: you buy out your landlord. You still have leases and the law of leasehold still applies to you.

You still have a landlord – the only difference is that the landlord is now you and your neighbours (usually, it is in fact a company owned by the flat-owners). A form of **commonhold** has now been introduced under the Commonhold and Leasehold Reform Act 2002 and at the time of writing the Act was being brought into force via various stages. When fully in force it will create a whole new way of owning flats, which will be tailor-made for collective ownership and the management of blocks of flats by those who live in them. The Leasehold Advisory Service★ can provide more detailed guidance.

Q *I've seen some articles in the press recently about 'sellers' packs'. What are these?*

A At the time of writing the government had announced its intention to bring in sellers' packs – or Home Information Packs (HIPs), to give them their proper title. The aim of these is to make the process of buying a house less problematic. These will be mandatory from January 2007. The seller must make the pack available to buyers as soon as a property goes on sale. This pack would include documents such as the deeds and lease, search enquiries, planning consents, copies of guarantees and insurance policies, a draft contract and a home condition report based on an inspection of the property by an independent home inspector. The aim is to reduce the time between offers being accepted and the exchange of contracts – the stage when most problems and delays occur. Until these are introduced on a compulsory basis the buyer has to take full responsibility for checking out the property (pp. 125–6).

Q *I am buying a property and I want to know what repairs the seller has done over the years. Does he have to give this information to me, my solicitor or my surveyor?*

A The government has made a number of proposals designed to make home buying and selling more streamlined and straightforward, and to reduce unnecessary delays and stress. Its main proposal is to require the seller to prepare a Home Information Pack (HIP) before putting the property on the market. However, there's no duty on the seller to give you any of this information until 2007. At the moment, all the responsibility rests with you to check out everything to do with the property (pp. 125–6). You can check the physical condition of the property at the time you buy it by getting a survey, and also check that the seller is the legal owner, usually by carrying out a search with the Land Registry★. But a history of repairs to the property is a different matter. Unless the owner voluntarily kept a log book for the property that you can see, you will have no source of information. There is no obligation on house-owners to keep records of work done or tell you the property's history, even if major repair work has been carried out.

You or your solicitor will therefore have to ask the seller questions and hope that the seller answers them. The Law Society★ produces a 'Sellers Property

Information Form' (SPIF) for this purpose which prompts the seller to provide a good deal of information. Legally the seller does not have to answer these preliminary enquiries. If some of the sections are left blank or if a non-committal answer is given, you might be rightly suspicious. Where the seller does provide answers, they must be true. Deliberately untruthful answers would give you the right to take legal action against the seller for misrepresentation if you were to suffer a loss as a result.

Q *The flat we bought is blighted by the constant loud music and shouting from the neighbours above. We have learnt that the previous owners had a long-standing dispute with them and even took them to court. Should we have been told?*

A Some of the questions on the Law Society's★ standard form (the SPIF described above) ask about 'disputes'. Had this been used, the previous owners would have been asked, for example, if they knew of any dispute about the flat or any neighbouring property and if they had made any complaints to any neighbour about the neighbour's activities. There is no definition of what amounts to a 'dispute', so it is not clear whether this includes an informal word with the neighbour or something more formal such as a letter of complaint. Although the sellers would not of course be expected to list every single time they had spoken to the neighbour about the noise, if they had complained to the council or, as here, taken court action, this would clearly fall into the category of a 'dispute'. If the owners answered 'no' to any of the questions, that would have been incorrect and could give you the right to claim for misrepresentation. You would need to take legal advice to help work out your loss. However, if the owners simply chose not to say anything about the dispute there would be nothing you could do. They did not have to tell you anything. If you have any concerns about this, talk to as many neighbours as possible before you buy and try to get some information on any local problems.

Q *The people to whom we are selling our house want to do some minor building work before they move in. I'm worried about letting them do the work after we've exchanged contracts but before completion. What is the legal situation if we agree to this?*

A There is nothing to prevent your agreeing if you wish but there are important potential problems. Even after you have exchanged contracts the house remains legally yours until you complete the sale. You remain responsible for handing over on completion exactly what the buyer has contracted for and is legally entitled to. If something goes wrong with the building works serious problems could arise if you have to argue over the damage to a ceiling, or floor, and whether it was already there or caused by their builders.

You may be able to persuade the buyers, or even their builder, to agree to insure the property and its contents against damage from the date of exchange or from the start of the work. If they will not, it would be better to make them wait until they move in on completion.

Q *Why is the process of buying property quicker in Scotland? Is it just that the lawyers work faster?*

A No. Although there are proposals to speed up the process south of the border, it's simply that property laws and procedures are different in Scotland from those in England, Wales and Northern Ireland. Research by the government has shown that the average time in Scotland between having an offer accepted and the conclusion of missives (the equivalent of exchange of contracts) is about four weeks – less than half that taken in England and Wales. The difference is largely because the survey and mortgage are usually sorted out before an offer is made. The range of types of survey is similar to that in England, Wales and Northern Ireland. If the survey report is favourable, you then make your offer to buy the property.

These are the other main differences between Scotland and the rest of the UK:

- most properties in Scotland are sold by solicitors through their property centres or offices, although there are also estate agents that operate similarly to those in England and Wales
- property in Scotland is offered for sale at an 'offers over' price, and you put in a blind offer above this asking price, usually in a sealed envelope, without knowing how much other people will offer
- in making the offer, you will have to be clear when you want to move in and what extras you want to buy (the sale particulars will normally specify what is, and what is not, included)
- if an offer is accepted in Scotland, final terms are agreed between the buyer's and seller's solicitors, by exchanging letters. The written offer and these subsequent letters are known as 'missives'. These make a binding legal contract, after which neither party can withdraw without liability to pay compensation. So, in theory a contract can be concluded within a few days of making the offer.

Q *How can I make sure that the architect I use to design the extension to my house is properly qualified?*

A The use of the title 'architect' is protected by law. No one is allowed to practise as an architect unless he or she has been accepted on to the register of the Architects Registration Board (ARB)★. Registration is allowed only after applicants have proved that they meet the educational and training standards required to call themselves 'architect'. The ARB was set up under the Architects Act 1997 and has the statutory responsibility of approving and monitoring courses of architectural education and maintaining proper standards within the profession. The ARB has a majority of non-architect members. It has published a Code of Professional Conduct and Practice which lays down the standards expected of registered architects. Examples of the requirements under the Code are that:

- where an architect has custody of monies belonging to a client they should be kept in a separate interest-bearing account
- where the client owes money for unpaid fees the architect cannot simply deduct those fees from any money he or she holds on behalf of the client
- an architect must keep to specific time limits when handling a complaint from a client
- an architect should observe the confidentiality of his or her client's affairs and should not disclose confidential information without the client's prior consent.

The ARB also performs the function of taking disciplinary action where a breach of the Code or any other action by an architect amounts to either:

- unacceptable professional conduct – that is, conduct which falls short of the standard required of an architect – or
- serious professional incompetence.

Neither the ARB nor the Royal Institute of British Architects (RIBA)★, the main professional association for architects, can make an architect pay compensation or help you to challenge a disputed architect's bill. You will have to start your own legal action to do this. The Supply of Goods and Services Act 1982 says that the services provided by anyone acting in the course of a business or profession must be carried out with reasonable skill and care, within a reasonable time, if no specific time was agreed, and at a reasonable price, if no specific price was agreed.

RIBA does have an arbitration scheme although it is not compulsory.

Q *I rent out my property using a letting agent. They find the tenants and then manage the let. But they consistently fail to keep me informed of what is going on and I'm not sure they are totally honest about the money they receive on my behalf. Who can I complain to?*

A Some agents are members of trade or professional bodies and these can offer some protection. Look for membership of the National Approved Letting Scheme (NALS)★, or of one of the professional bodies that support it – the Association of Residential Letting Agents (ARLA)★; the Royal Institution of Chartered Surveyors (RICS)★; or the National Association of Estate Agents

(NAEA)*. Each of these bodies has its own code of practice which member agents must comply with.

In addition to its code, NALS members must also:

- already be a member of ARLA, RICS or NAEA
- operate an internal complaints procedure
- be linked to a legally binding arbitration service
- maintain professional indemnity insurance which covers them against the chance of being sued
- have a client's money protection scheme (which means that, if money that belongs to a landlord or tenant is lost or misappropriated by the agent, the client will get their money back).

It's not compulsory for letting agents to belong to any particular trade body and there is no ombudsman to oversee agents. So, apart from taking unscrupulous agents to court there is little else you can do. But if you've lost money or received poor service from an agent, and any internal complaints system has failed to solve your problem, you can claim up to £5,000 through the small claims track of the county court (pp. 275–6). If the case is more complicated, you may need to consult a solicitor – but this could be expensive.

Chapter 6

Finance, credit and money disputes

Money, whether you've invested it, borrowed it, or you're trying to recover it from someone else, is important to everyone. This chapter explains how the financial services industry is regulated; your rights if a purchase you make on credit is not up to scratch; what to do if your cheques, or credit cards, fall into the wrong hands; if you can't get credit in the first place; how to check your credit rating; how to complain if your bank or building society provides bad service; the options you have if a company you are dealing with goes out of business but owes you goods or money; and how to complain if a debt-collector is hassling you. And with an estimated £100 million-worth of 'cardholder not present' credit fraud committed every year it's important to know what you're liable for if a fraudster has information about you and your credit cards.

Q *What is the procedure for buying on credit or hire purchase?*

A Most contracts become legally binding as soon as they are made, even if they are entirely verbal, and you cannot get out of them simply because you have changed your mind. However, a credit or hire agreement must always be in writing. The procedures are strict and are defined in the Consumer Credit Act 1974:

- the consumer signs a credit/hire purchase application form or the credit agreement itself (usually at the bank or the finance company's premises, or in a shop) and retains a copy of the document signed. The creditor then checks the creditworthiness of the applicant – for example, by making enquiries with credit reference agencies. If all is satisfactory, the creditor will agree to grant the credit and will then sign the contract. The creditor must deliver to the applicant a second copy of the agreement form, signed by both parties, within seven days of the creditor signing

- if the customer signs at a bank or in a shop, and the creditor signs at the same time, the agreement becomes legally binding there and then, and the customer is entitled to only one copy of the completed agreement
- where the form is signed by the consumer at home (or anywhere other than the trader's or creditor's place of business) following face-to-face discussions between the customer and the trader, the situation is similar but the customer has a right to cancel the agreement (see below) during the 'cooling-off' period.

Q *I've just signed a credit agreement for some new furniture. I now realise I can't afford the payments. Can I get out of the deal?*

A Broadly, the answer depends on where you made the agreement and whether it was signed by the trader at the same time you signed:

- if you signed at the furniture store and, most importantly, the trader signed the credit agreement at the same time you cannot cancel (see above)
- some credit agreements do not come into force as soon as you have signed since the company also has to sign before the agreement becomes binding. The trader may want to run credit checks on you to see whether you are a good loan risk before he or she goes ahead. So if you change your mind you may be able to get out of the deal even if you signed the contract at the trader's premises. Tell the trader as soon as possible that you are withdrawing, before he or she has completed the credit checks and signed the agreement, then you should have no problem
- if you signed face to face with the trader, say, at your home or a friend's, you have a right to cancel. But you must act quickly. The **'cooling-off'** period lasts for five clear days. Note that:
  - when you sign up for credit you must be given a **notice of your cancellation rights** along with a copy of the credit agreement, and you have five days in which to send your cancellation in writing
  - the five days does not start to run until you receive the second copy of the agreement from the company with a notice of your cancellation rights. So, if you don't receive the notice of cancellation rights the five days doesn't start to run until you do
  - both copies of the agreement must mention the right of cancellation
  - the second copy must be delivered by post. The countdown to the fifth day of the cooling-off period does not begin until the debtor has received the second copy and does not include that day of receipt
  - if the trader fails to comply with the formal procedures set down by the Consumer Credit Act 1974 the credit agreement cannot be enforced by the company.

To cancel you must give written notice to the creditor or an agent who conducted the negotiations, such as the salesperson. If you mail the cancellation it will take effect as soon as it is posted, so make sure you get a certificate of posting from the Post Office. The effect of cancellation is to bring the whole agreement to an end and to absolve you from any future liability. If you have paid a deposit, that must be refunded to you. (For getting out of the agreement after the cooling-off period, see p. 148.)

Q *I want to buy some new kitchen appliances and have seen lots of 'buy now, pay later' offers. Are these genuine?*

A Check the small print of these and other 'interest-free'-type offers very carefully. If you simply have to pay a deposit with the balance divided into equal monthly direct-debit payments, this can be a good way to spread paying for something. But always look out for the following:

- some deals may be offered over, say, five years, but the interest-free period may be much less. With many deals you have to sign a credit agreement when you buy the item. You may have to start making monthly payments almost immediately (they're then knocked off the balance if you pay in full at the end of the qualifying period); in other cases they're deferred

- shops know that a proportion of customers won't be able to pay off the balance when it becomes due, or will simply forget about it. If this happens, you'll probably start paying a very high annual percentage rate of interest (APR) on the balance

- watch out for payment protection tie-ins – the shop may insist you take this out on any credit deal, though payments involved should be included in the quoted APR

- if you don't think the small print is fair or clear enough, refer it to the Office of Fair Trading (OFT)* under the Unfair Terms in Consumer Contracts Regulations (pp. 88–9).

Q *How do lenders decide whether to lend money or enter into credit agreements?*

A When you apply for a loan, or for any other kind of credit, including a credit or store card, whoever puts up the money bears the risk that you might not pay it back. So lenders often use their own system of **credit scoring** and/or a **credit reference agency** report to sort the mass of credit applications they receive into good and bad risks, or they may simply use their own judgement.

- **credit scoring** The answers you give on an application form will be given marks from a score card. Traditionally lenders have kept their scoring systems secret to prevent cheating. However, it is common knowledge that indicators of personal stability, such as being at the same address or in the same job for a long time (over three years, for example), tend to score highly. The process of scoring is generally automated, making the process efficient. So, a computer will allocate points to each answer you give on the form. The total number will determine whether you get credit, and if so, at what level

- **credit reference agencies** Lenders may use these to obtain information on your credit history (see below).

The final decision will be made, on a commercial basis, by the lender. Opportunities are now increasing to find out why a certain decision was made, and to correct any errors which could change that decision. In the end, however, you can't force the lender to give you credit (see below).

Q *My application for hire purchase was refused. The reply from the finance company said that no outside agency had been used in considering my application. What does this mean?*

A No outside agency means that no credit reference agency has been consulted in making the decision concerning your request for credit. The finance company has probably used its own scoring system when assessing your answers to questions on the application form to score you. However, the vast bulk of the credit industry is bound by the Finance and Leasing Association (FLA)★ code of practice, which states that customers who feel they have been refused credit unreasonably have a right to go to a senior official for a final decision. Proposed amendments to the code mean that there will be a way of discovering the basis for the first ruling. Also, if you think you have been refused on the grounds of race, sex, marital status or disability, complain to either the Commission for Racial Equality★, the Equal Opportunities Commission★ or the Disability Rights Commission★.

The FLA's 'Guide to Credit Scoring' was updated in 2000 and is worth reading. The Data Protection Act 1998 is a major catalyst here (pp. 261–2). It introduced legal safeguards for individuals and puts requirements on those who process data. This includes lenders who use automated credit scoring to make their decisions. One thing is certain, you are entitled to know when credit scoring is being used, how it works, the principal reason why you were turned down, and that you have a right of appeal which will be considered by a human being, not a computer.

This extra knowledge may help you to identify when the company has based its decision on wrong information, has made an error or is guilty of unlawful discrimination – and a manual review of the decision may persuade the finance company to change its mind. But you cannot force a company to give you credit. It is a purely commercial decision for the company to make.

Q *I applied for a bank loan but I've been turned down. I know they use a credit reference agency. Can I find out why this has happened?*

A No one has a legal right to credit. But you do have a right to see any information from a **credit reference agency** file on which the lenders may have based their decision.

It is possible that there has been a mistake on your credit reference agency file. The Consumer Credit Act 1974 gives you a right to know what information agencies hold on you. To find out:

- write to the credit company within 28 days of refusal, asking for the names and addresses of any agencies it used
- if the credit company confirms that it used agencies, you are entitled to see a copy of your file(s); to obtain this, write, enclosing the fee of £2, with your full name and address and any previous addresses over the last six years, or apply online. Within seven working days of receiving your request the agency must send you a copy of your file and a statement of your rights
- if the file contains incorrect information you have the right to ask for its removal or amendment. If the agency does not reply within 28 days, or refuses to alter the file, you have 28 days in which to write a notice of correction
- the agency must place the correction on the file and may send a copy of the correction to other credit reference agencies and anyone who consulted it about you within the last six months
- unfortunately the correction on the file does not guarantee that you will be given credit: this is still at the discretion of the lender, but once the correction has been made you can re-apply for credit
- if the lender (your bank in this example) is still refusing you a loan despite your having written to a senior official, contact the Information Commissioner★, or the Office of Fair Trading (OFT)★.

Q *How do I find out what my credit score is, and is there anything I can do to increase it?*

A Unfortunately, you won't be able to find out what your credit score is – banks and credit companies each use their own scoring systems and keep them confidential to help prevent fraud. It's very difficult to improve your credit score but there are some things that will help boost it. Make sure you're registered on the electoral roll – companies use this information to confirm your current and previous addresses, and not being on it will affect your credit score. Avoid making too many applications for credit. Each time you apply for credit, a company will carry out a credit search and a search will be registered on your credit file. Too many will count against you. How you handle your existing credit has a big effect too, so make your payments on time and don't exceed your credit limits.

Q *Will sending off for a copy of my credit file affect my credit score?*

A No. In fact, it's a good idea to check your credit file with each credit reference agency from time to time. The £2 charge per check is a small price to pay to make sure you know the information held on you is correct and that there isn't anything listed erroneously that you weren't aware of – county court judgments or payment defaults, say.

Q *I owe money to a number of companies and have managed to keep most of my payments up to date. But I keep being contacted by a firm of debt collectors on one loan where I've been late paying. They are very menacing. How can I stop them harassing me?*

A If you don't pay off the debt, or can't make regular payments on time, the creditor is entitled to enforce the loan agreement, and many creditors use debt collection agencies to help them recover any outstanding money. You're not alone. Around 75 per cent of UK households have credit facilities of some kind (ignoring mortgages), such as overdrafts, credit and store cards etc. But debt management is an increasing problem.

And with debt come the debt collectors, who may employ dubious tactics to get the money back and may claim to have more powers than they actually have. The company may be harassing you and this would allow you to take action under section 40 of the Administration of Justice Act.

The Office of Fair Trading (OFT) has issued guidance to debt collectors about unfair practices, suggesting they should not :

- use official-looking documents, often falsely made to look like court claims, to mislead debtors
- contact debtors too often and at unreasonable times
- refuse to deal with a third party you may appoint to help you, such as Citizens Advice or a money adviser
- enter a property uninvited and/or not leave when asked to
- ignore and/or disregard claims that debts have been settled or are disputed and continue to make unjustified demands for payment.

In reality, debt collectors have no greater legal powers than anyone else. They have no right to enter your home without permission and have to rely on persuasion. If that fails, they have to take court action on behalf of the creditor, get judgment and only then, if you still fail to pay, can they ask the court to grant an enforcement order for a bailiff to come and seize goods to pay the debt.

But even court bailiffs aren't allowed to break into your home. They have to come armed with a court order, and, even then, their entry has to be 'peaceable'. They commit a criminal offence if they break and enter (if they happen to find an unlocked door or window then they can make their way in). Although the OFT guidance is simply that, it is backed up by other powers. Not everyone can lend money as a business – to do so requires a consumer credit licence and the power to grant and withdraw these rests entirely with the OFT. The guidance applies to all consumer credit licence holders and also to licence holders who employ third-party collectors to act on their behalf.

Creditors are expected to take responsibility for the businesses they use to collect their debts; they are, after all, acting on the creditors' behalf. If a business fails to treat its customers fairly the OFT could ultimately remove their credit licence.

Q *What does 'APR' mean and how can this information help me compare different loan and credit-card rates?*

A **APR** stands for **Annual Percentage Rate**. Comparing the costs of different types of credit is not easy. The aim of the APR is to give you a yardstick by which to compare the cost of one type of credit with another so you cannot be fooled into thinking you have a really good deal by confusing figures and different rates. A flat interest rate is no basis for comparison because it takes no account of the different ways in which interest can be charged (for example, daily or monthly), which will affect how much you actually pay, and it ignores one-off charges such as arrangement fees. The APR, which must be quoted for most forms of credit, provides a better basis for comparison than the flat rate because all lenders are required (in theory) to quote credit costs in the same way. It takes into account the size, number and frequency of repayments you make, together with one-off costs. It's not a perfect tool for comparing the costs of credit, but if it's used in conjunction with the **total charge for credit** (which shows all the interest and other costs payable when you borrow) it will provide an indication of the deals to consider and those to avoid. The lower the APR the better the deal.

With credit cards, for example, APR is not a good guide to finding the cheapest deal. Even though the cheapest cards do tend to be those with the lowest APRs, credit cards calculate interest in many ways, and the APR doesn't take this into account. For example, if you don't pay your bill in full when you get your statement, one card might charge interest from the date of the purchase, while another might charge interest from the date the transaction reached your account. The government is currently planning to standardise the way APR is calculated and presented to consumers, to allow easier comparison between cards (*www.dti.gov.uk/ccp/topics1/consumer_finance.htm*).

Q *Last year I took out a **personal loan** from a finance company to buy a new car. It was repayable over a four-year period, but I now want to pay it off early. Can I do this?*

A Yes, but with a fixed-term loan you are still liable to pay some of the interest you would have paid had you kept the loan up for the full term. The Consumer Credit Act 1974 gives you, the debtor, two related rights:

- the right to pay off all amounts due at any time during the agreement, and
- the right to a rebate of the credit charges to take into account the earlier receipt of the money by the creditor. The rebate is calculated in accordance with formulae set out in regulations made under the Act. A word of warning: repaying a loan does not simply mean paying off the outstanding capital. The creditor would have received the capital plus all the interest charges over the full loan period, so you are required to pay a proportion of the interest the lender would have got if you'd kept to the original period.

The most common way to exercise your right of early settlement is to send **written notice** to the creditor. The creditor is obliged to send a statement, free of charge, setting out the amount required to pay off the loan after taking into account the rebate allowable. The statement must set out the basic calculations involved in arriving at that sum. You can then pay off all you owe under the agreement, less the rebate. At the time of writing the government's review of the Consumer Credit Act was considering ways to give consumers a fairer deal when paying off a loan early.

Q *I recently took out a loan. I checked my bank statements and discovered that I'm also paying for insurance. It seems this is to cover the repayments should I fall sick or become unemployed. But I didn't ask for insurance. Can the lender do this?*

A When filling in any application form, especially for a long-term commitment such as a loan, always read it very carefully. Insurance policies of this sort are often sold through **negative-option tickboxes** – this means you are said to have agreed to buy the insurance unless you tick a box saying you do not want it. Although this may seem unfair, it is perfectly legal.

Q *I bought a second-hand car on **hire purchase** three months ago. The car has broken down three times now but when I complain to the garage where I got the car they just fob me off. I'm fed up with the car. Can I get rid of it?*

A When you buy on HP your legal rights are against the finance company which lends you the money, not the retailer with whom you originally dealt. This is because in effect the retailer sells the car to the HP company and it then sells the car on to you. The goods will not legally become yours until you have paid all the instalments. However, if you have been sold faulty goods:

- you have the same basic rights as if you had paid cash. For HP these rights are laid down by the Supply of Goods (Implied Terms) Act 1973, which states that goods supplied on HP, like goods sold in the normal way, must be of **satisfactory quality, fit for their purpose**, and correspond with any **description** given of them

- your rights in the event of faulty goods last longer if you buy on HP than if you buy for cash: on HP you have the common law right to reject faulty goods throughout the duration of the agreement as long as you have not 'affirmed' the contract by, for example, carrying on using the car and paying the instalments even after discovering a defect

- to reject the item(s), tell the finance company that the goods are unsatisfactory, that you are rejecting them, and that they are available for collection by the company

- you are then entitled to a refund on instalments already paid, although there may be a deduction for the use you have had of the car. While you could argue that you do not have to pay any more instalments, the best course of action may be to continue paying under protest until you reach an agreement amicably or a court makes a decision for you

- you don't have to reject the car: if you want to keep it, but would like a free repair, say, write to the finance company explaining what is wrong, what you want done about it, and that you will continue paying only 'under protest' until the faults have been put right

- you are entitled to claim compensation for any expenses you incur which were reasonably foreseeable by both you and the company at the time when you entered the HP agreement: for example, the cost of alternative means of transport while your car was being repaired.

Once you have paid all the instalments on your goods, your rights become the same as if you had paid cash.

Q *I have a motorcycle on hire purchase. Do I have to pay all the instalments before I sell it, or can I sell before I finish paying?*

A You cannot sell until you have finished paying. The motorcycle is still owned by the finance company, and it will not become your property until you have paid all the instalments and thus purchased it. You have only the right to use the motorcycle until then. If you do sell, you will automatically be in breach of your obligations as a seller under the Sale of Goods Act 1979. That Act says that you must have title to the goods (i.e. own the motorcycle) before you sell. You would also be liable to the finance company for wrongfully selling its property.

The situation is different where you have bought goods on credit using a loan or credit card, as you will become the owner of the goods as soon as you start paying. If the amount of credit is £25,000 or less, your HP agreement is a consumer credit agreement regulated by the Consumer Credit Act 1974. This gives you the right to settle the agreement early and to obtain a rebate on the interest charges to reflect the early payment. So, if you want to sell, you must pay off the outstanding instalments first.

Q *I paid for my TV on credit. Now I can't keep up my repayments. Could the company come and take it away?*

A No. Only certain people have the right to enter your home, and may do so only for specific reasons (pp. 264–5). You should contact the finance company straight away, explaining your circumstances and asking for your repayments to be rescheduled. If it will not agree new terms or you cannot afford to pay anything, you can be taken to the county court. However, the court may allow you time to pay.

If you break the credit agreement by not paying, the finance company has to serve a 'default notice' on you before taking any action to enforce the agreement. This notice must say what you have done wrong and what you must do to put things right, giving you at least seven days in which to do so. The finance company is not allowed to increase the rate of interest on the amount owed. If you do not comply with the notice or get in touch to sort things out you could be taken to court.

If you are buying on HP and you have paid more than a third of the total price the finance house has no automatic right to recover the goods, and may only do so with a court order. If the TV was not bought on HP or being rented, but you just arranged a loan to pay for it, then the TV is legally yours. But you can still be taken to court by the loan company for defaulting on loan repayments. If you do find yourself in financial difficulties, contact your local Citizens Advice Bureau or Money Advice Centre.

Q *I lost my wallet with my credit card and debit cards in it. Will I have to pay if the finder or thief uses the cards?*

A You should notify the card company of the loss immediately. However, it is worth noting that:

- you will not be liable for any loss arising after you have notified the company

- you must confirm any oral notice by giving written notice within the following seven days
- if you are quick enough to contact the credit-card company before the thief has had time to use the card, you will have no liability at all
- under the terms of the Consumer Credit Act 1974 and the Banking Code you will be liable for no more than £50, even if you fail to notify the credit-card company or the thief is quick off the mark (see below).

Q *I ordered some goods over the Internet and sent details of my credit-card number. The goods came quickly, but when my credit-card statement arrived I noticed some extra amounts I hadn't authorised. I have never let my card out of my possession and still have it now. I can only assume that my card details have been picked up either by someone over the Internet or used by the company. The amount is over £700. What should I do?*

A Tell your card issuer immediately. You will not be liable for the extra amounts that have appeared on your statement. If you lose your credit card and someone else uses it without your consent the Consumer Credit Act 1974 limits your liability for that misuse to £50 (p. 155). That liability will only increase beyond this limit if the card issuer can show that you have acted fraudulently or 'without reasonable care', for example, by keeping your Personal Identification Number (PIN) or password with the card.

Where you have never let your card out of your possession and an unauthorised debit appears on your statement, you don't even have to pay the first £50. This is because the £50 liability applies only to unauthorised debits while your card is no longer in your possession. And in any case where a cardholder alleges that any use that has been made of the card was not authorised by him or her, the 1974 Act makes it clear that the card issuer must prove that the use was authorised. In addition, the Banking Code says that where a card transaction is disputed the card company has the burden of proving that you have acted fraudulently or without reasonable care.

There are a number of initiatives designed to combat the potential problems for consumers of trading on the Internet. Consumers want to be sure that electronic payments are secure, that goods ordered will turn up, and will be of good quality and as described. The government has been looking at issuing electronic hallmarks for authorised traders to use. TrustUK, the body set up to do this, helps ensure that these traders are legitimate traders, who use clear information with clear confirmation of contracts, delivery costs and prices; that personal data will be protected; that there's a clear policy for returns, cancellations, and refunds and so on. The Direct Marketing Association UK Ltd★ and the Association of British Travel Agents (ABTA)★ are both examples of TrustUK code-owners. And all of this is allied to the EU Directive on electronic commerce (pp. 59–63).

Q *I bought goods on my credit card which I've tried to reject because they are faulty. The retailer has gone out of business and I'm told that there is unlikely to be any money to pay my claim. Is the credit-card company responsible?*

A Whether you pay for faulty goods or services in cash or by credit card, your rights are against the seller. However, the Consumer Credit Act 1974 provides added protection where you buy goods or services by credit card, as long as the price of the individual item purchased was over £100 and up to £30,000. Note that:

- the credit-card company as well as the retailer is also liable for any breach of contract and/or misrepresentation. So you can claim for faulty goods or services against the retailer, the credit-card company, or both. If you are making a claim for faulty goods bought on credit, write to both parties. You will not get two lots of compensation, but you will increase your chances of getting the problem sorted out
- if the retailer goes bankrupt, your claim against him or her is unlikely to result in any return of your money, or compensation, for the faulty goods or service. You will remain an unsecured creditor. But if you paid by credit card this allows you to claim against the credit-card company. This cover is particularly useful if you have paid a deposit in advance to a company that subsequently closes down for goods with a cash price of over £100 (even if the deposit itself was below £100).

Q *While on holiday in Italy I went to pick up the hire car which I had paid for by credit card in the UK. I was asked to sign a blank voucher in case of fines or damage to the car. After protesting I agreed to leave a signed blank voucher. What happens if the car hire firm processes it with unjustified amounts?*

A Avoid signing blank vouchers if possible, and always remember to complete the totals box on the credit-card slip. Usually if a voucher you have signed is processed you'll have no comeback on the amount that goes through since your signature is evidence that you authorised the transaction. If a voucher has been processed for something you were not warned about or for an expense that is not yours, complain straight away to both the credit-card company and the car hire firm and produce whatever evidence you have – for example, the agreed hire charge quote. The card company should take things up with the car hire company, although things may not be sorted out for some time since the disputed incident happened abroad.

To prevent problems, when you return the car, get it checked there and then so you can agree if there is any damage that will be added to your bill. If not, get a statement from the car hire company confirming that there's nothing more to pay.

If you do make credit-card payments abroad, you should be protected by the Consumer Credit Act 1974 (the Office of Fair Trading (OFT)★ supports this principle). While some credit-card issuers have announced that they do accept liability, many are unclear and some say they won't. So, be persistent as you may have a bit of negotiating to do before your card company gives in.

Q *I used my credit card to buy a computer. It hasn't been delivered, but the trader has gone bust. Have I lost my money?*

A You can try to recover your money from the trader as part of the bankruptcy or liquidation process, but it's very unlikely that you will get anything back. You can get your money back from the credit-card company, provided the price of the item is more than £100 but less than £30,000, and the credit advance up to £25,000. The credit-card company, along with the trader, is liable for any breach of contract such as non-delivery of an order. But this protection doesn't apply to **charge cards**, **debit cards** and usually to **credit-card cheques**. Credit cards give you the facility to pay by instalments rather than settling the whole balance at the end of each month. Charge cards do not give you this facility, so there is no credit element.

Even if you pay only the first part of the price by credit card (and the balance by cheque, say) and even if that initial deposit was less than £100, you can recover the whole amount from the credit-card company – it's the price of the item that's important, so as long as the total price is £100 or more you are protected.

Q *I closed my credit-card account six months ago and I've just received a statement for a purchase I made when on holiday last year. Do I have to pay?*

A Yes. Although you 'closed' the account you are still legally obliged to settle up for transactions that were authorised during the life of your account, and also for any 'Continuous Authority Transaction' (CAT) on that account. An example of a CAT could be a book club which has your old card number; if you authorised it to charge your subscription to the card account it can continue to do this unless you stop the arrangement and pay by another means. Payments like this are the credit-card equivalent of direct debits, regular payments that you have authorised a company to take from your card. But unlike direct debits the card issuer will carry on paying them and sending you statements after you have closed your account, unless and until you contact the individual companies direct to cancel them. So if you do not pay up, the credit-card company can charge you interest on the outstanding amount. Pay up now and check that you have not authorised anyone else to take out annual subscriptions or payments from that account.

If your statements show that money is still being debited from your account after you have cancelled a CAT, you should send your card issuer a copy of your cancellation letter. If should then arrange to refund the money.

Q *My mother was sold a loan by a doorstep salesman. The interest seems incredibly high. Is there anything she can do?*

A It is illegal for lenders or credit brokers to call uninvited to offer loans unless the loan is for goods and services that they are also supplying. Even then, if your mother did not ask for a visit from whoever sold her the loan, or she didn't sign the loan on their premises, she is allowed five full days after receiving a copy of the agreement in which to change her mind and cancel the loan.

If she can't cancel and so is committed to the loan, because she signed at the trader's premises, say, and it seems a complete rip-off, she may be able to get a court to change the terms or set the loan aside altogether. But she must be able to convince the court that the loan is in some way '**extortionate**'. There is no legal definition of this since the court assesses how expensive the loan is in relation to the risk to the lender that the loan may not be repaid. The court would also consider your mother's financial know-how, and whether the lender somehow took advantage of her – for example, by asking her to sign a blank application form. But be warned, court action can be slow and expensive. If you have financial problems contact a local Citizens Advice Bureau or Money Advice Centre.

Q *I paid for some repairs to my car by cheque and now the car has broken down again only two days after the servicing. I told the bank to **stop the cheque** and now the garage is threatening to sue me. Can it do this?*

A It is dangerous to stop a cheque, especially if you are not sure, as in this case, that the garage is at fault. So the golden rule is, in most cases, not to do it. If you give someone a cheque the courts will not generally intervene – it will be assumed that since you gave the cheque to the garage you did owe it the money. This means the garage can take you to court for the value of the cheque and will win simply by saying that you paid for the work by cheque and then cancelled it. You will only be able to challenge the garage if you have clear evidence that the garage's repairs were sub-standard. Since you do not know whether the car broke down because the garage failed to do its job properly or for some other reason, it is unlikely that you will be able to challenge the garage if you are taken to court. So get the car inspected by an independent mechanic who can back up your suspicion that the garage did something wrong. If you cannot get such back-up, pay up by sending the garage another cheque and investigate the cause of the problem later.

Q *I've got a **multi-purpose plastic card** – debit, cashpoint and cheque guarantee card in one. A few weeks ago I bought a computer by mail order, giving my card details over the phone. The company has not delivered the computer, though the payment of £900 has cleared. I cannot get any response from the company. I've heard that if you pay by plastic you can get your card company to sort things out or even to refund money if the seller has done something wrong. Does this apply to me?*

A No. Debit cards, like Switch or Visa Delta, are like paperless cheques, not credit cards. If you give your debit card number the money comes directly out of your bank account, so there is no credit involved. You don't get the same protection as you would if you had paid by credit card (p. 152). Write to the company requesting delivery within a specific time limit, say, 14 days, and make this 'time of the essence'.

Q *What rights do I have when dealing with banks and building societies?*

A When you open a bank or building society account you are making a contract, and all the usual rules governing contracts to supply a service apply (pp. 67–8). The Supply of Goods and Services Act 1982 (common law in Scotland) states that the bank or building society must carry out the contract with reasonable skill and care.

The Banking Code was last updated in March 2003. It aims to improve the service offered by banks and building societies. The main areas covered are:

- **fair conduct** Banks and building societies should always act 'fairly and reasonably' in dealings with customers
- **information on changes to your account** You must be told of any changes to the terms and conditions, charges and interest rate of your account within specified time periods, and if your savings and investment account is superseded by a different one your account will either be kept at the same interest rate as a new account with similar features, or it will be switched to another with similar features
- **plastic cards** For any type of plastic card – credit card, cash withdrawal, debit card and so on – the maximum liability for money taken without your agreement before the card issuer has been informed is £50, or nil if the card is lost or stolen before it reaches you in the post. You will lose this protection only if you have acted without reasonable care (by, for example, writing

your Personal Identification Number – PIN – on the card), and it would be up to the bank or building society to prove that this was the case

- **confidentiality** Your personal financial details will not be passed to other companies in the banking group, such as its insurance or investment arm, without your consent (but check that such use of information was not made a condition of opening the account)

- **complaints** All institutions must have proper complaints procedures and must tell you what these are. If your complaint is about an overseas finance provider you can use Fin-Net★. This was set up by the European Commission and gives consumers access to alternative redress mechanisms across the EU. For example, if your dispute is with a bank or insurer in another European country you can get access to the relevant ombudsman or other complaint scheme in that country by looking up *http://europa.eu.int/ comm/internal_market/en/finances/consumer/intro.htm#countries*

If you have a complaint, ask for details of the complaints procedures, and write to the branch or area manager of the bank or building society. If this proves unsatisfactory, take your complaint further by writing to the head office, then to the Financial Ombudsman Service★. This was established under the Financial Services and Markets Act. The Ombudsman is free to consumers and can award customers compensation of up to £100,000. The bank or building society must abide by the Ombudsman's decision, but the consumer has the choice of accepting or pursuing the matter further through the courts or ADR.

Q *I've just checked my bank statement and I dispute a couple of the* **cash-card withdrawals***. The bank says that the cashpoint machine definitely paid out the money to me and that there is no mistake. How can I convince the bank that I didn't make these withdrawals?*

A If your bank statement shows a cash dispenser withdrawal which you know you have not made, and you have not given anyone your PIN (Personal Identification Number), informing the bank is the first priority, so you were right to tell yours immediately. Under the **Banking Code,** banks and building societies have to show that the withdrawal was made by the cardholder or someone authorised by the cardholder. If, in this case, the bank insists that you made the withdrawal, that its technology is infallible, and it will not make any sort of refund to you, then the bank must prove these points. It would help sort things out more quickly if you could produce any evidence to back up your claim that it was not you. So try to remember where you were at the time of the **'phantom' withdrawal** and, if possible, try to prove that you had your card with you at the time. Statements from friends who were with you at the time could help.

If the bank accepts what you say, you should get back all the cash taken. If the bank does not accept that there was a phantom withdrawal, you can complain to the Financial Ombudsman Service★.

Q *Are cheques a safe way of paying?*

A If your cheque book is stolen, provided you let your bank or building society know of the theft as soon as possible, you will not be liable for a penny in the event that someone forges your signature: the cheque would be invalid and the bank has to bear the total loss. But if your cheque-guarantee card is stolen at the same time, you may fall foul of your contract with the bank, which requires that you keep the cheque book and the card separate, so you may be held liable for the loss.

If you have written out a cheque which then falls into the wrong hands, it is possible for the thief to forge the signature of the person to whom you were paying the money (the '**payee**') on the back of the cheque, pay it into his or her own account and, when it clears, withdraw the money and disappear. All cheques are transferable, and even if it had been a crossed cheque, you would have no redress against either the bank where the cheque was paid in or your own bank which paid the cheque.

The Cheques Act 1992 states that if you write the words 'Account payee' or 'a/c payee' with or without the word 'only' on the face of a crossed cheque, you are protected against the cheque being transferred to a thief's account. If the bank where the cheque is paid in negligently credits an account other than that of the payee named on the face of the cheque, it will have to make good your loss. All cheques issued by banks and building societies now have the protective words already printed on them.

Q *My current account balance was a bit low last month because I hadn't been keeping an eye on my spending. I knew that I had a direct debit due to go out on the 26th so I paid in a cheque for £100 on the 25th from my savings account to make sure I would have enough money to cover the direct debit and other outgoings. To my horror I got a statement from the bank saying that there had been insufficient funds to meet payment of the direct debit so it had been refused. The bank is also charging me for an unauthorised overdraft of £20 from the 26th to the 28th. Why should this have happened when I'd paid in the money on time?*

A Banks and building societies require at least three days (and in some cases a week) for cheques to clear. So unless you take this into account when paying in money, you could get into trouble. If you go overdrawn without agreement, it may be worth writing to the bank manager explaining the circumstances and asking for the charges to be withdrawn since you had no intention to go overdrawn without authority. If you have kept your account in credit previously the bank may refund the charges if you're lucky, but it is not obliged to do so.

If you know that you are going to overdraw, always get your bank's agreement beforehand. If you do so, you'll pay lower charges.

Q *Why, when I use online banking, does it take three or more days to transfer cleared funds from one bank to another? Surely the Internet is supposed to speed things up?*

A Banks use the BACS (Bankers Automated Clearing Services) system to transfer funds between accounts. They transfer the funds on day one and, on day three, deposit them in the second account. In between, they earn interest on the money. The Association for Payment Clearing Services (APACS) runs BACS but claims there isn't sufficient demand to offer instant Internet transfers. The system is slow and works in the banks' favour – the longer they hold your money, the more interest they earn.

Q *I've lost out on some investments I made, in my view because I was badly advised by my financial adviser. How can I complain?*

A Anyone who carries out investment business must be authorised to do so by the Financial Services Authority (FSA)★. The FSA is now the UK's single statutory financial services 'super-regulator', providing regulation of banks, building societies, mortgage lenders, insurers, life assurance, finance and investment advisers, personal pensions, unit trusts, and many other personal finance products.

Under the FSA rules, intermediaries must ask you for detailed information about your circumstances since they must recommend only suitable invest-ments. All advisers should also tell you whether they receive a commission for selling a particular product.

If you feel you have been badly advised and cannot agree a solution with your intermediary, send the details to the Financial Ombudsman Service★. What you can't complain about is the way an investment has performed just because it's done badly, unless the advice you were given was obviously wrong.

Q *A builder did some work for me which wasn't up to scratch. He is still trading but says that when I had the work done he was the director of a company that has now gone bust. He says I can't take him to court as it was a limited company. Is this true?*

A This is generally correct. But what action you take depends on whether you made your contract with a company or with the builder personally. When you deal with a limited company or a plc (public limited company) this usually means that your contract is with the company, not the individual directors who run it. So if you have a compensation claim the company will pay you out of company money. The director's personal money is not generally involved or at risk. So when a company goes out of business you may lose out on any compensation claim.

If the trader is not a limited company and your contract is with a partnership, firm or one-man band, the trader's personal money is at risk if you have a compensation claim, and you may be able to pursue him. So, check your paperwork to see whether the contract was made with a limited company, a firm, a partnership, or a sole trader. If it was with a company, check with Companies House★ to find out whether the company has gone out of business. If it has, you have probably lost out even though your builder is still trading on his own account.

Q *I've just received a statutory demand from someone who lent me money. What does it mean?*

A If you owe more than £750 and the debt is not a secured loan (like a mortgage, say) you can be made bankrupt, at the instigation of the creditor, if you do not pay up and the bankruptcy court believes you cannot repay the money. So if you get a statutory demand you should pay any debt you owe to avoid bankruptcy proceedings. You generally have three weeks from the date on which the statutory demand is served to pay up or arrange for payment. If you do not or cannot pay, the person or business you owe can present a bankruptcy petition to court.

If a bankruptcy order is made, a trustee in bankruptcy is appointed by the court, or the Official Receiver is appointed to manage your property. The trustee or receiver will take over the running of your financial affairs and can sell off your property to help clear your debts. As an undischarged bankrupt you will be deprived of the ownership of your property. But you can keep some things, such as your clothing and tools of your trade. Generally the bankruptcy is automatically discharged after three years. On discharge you are no longer responsible for bankruptcy debts.

Q *I've got a court judgment against a builder who made a mess of fitting my kitchen. I've been chasing him for the £700 compensation I was awarded by the court. He now says that he's **bankrupt**. Does this mean I've lost my money?*

A To check whether he is telling the truth, telephone the **Insolvency Service**★ (a section of the Official Receiver's Department) to obtain the name and address of his trustee or receiver. You can then send the trustee or receiver information about the money you are owed. Any funds that are collected will be distributed according to a 'pecking order'. This means that preferred creditors (often banks and the Inland Revenue) will get all their money before you. Only if there is anything left after the preferred creditors have been paid will you get anything. So if the builder has gone bankrupt it is likely that you will lose out. It also depends on whether you paid by credit card or bought an insurance-backed guarantee that covers this situation.

Q *When I paid for a new rug the sales assistant put it in the storeroom with a label on it with my name and address. Before it could be delivered the store went bust. Can I get my money or my carpet?*

A When a business collapses and cannot pay all its debts, there is a strict order of priority for creditors. As an ordinary customer, you are an 'unsecured creditor' and unfortunately you come at the back of the queue behind other creditors such as the bank, the Inland Revenue and company employees who are owed salary. You'll miss any chance of getting your money back if you do not get in the queue quickly, so contact the receiver or liquidator straight away. Often there is not enough money to go round so you could end up getting less than you paid or nothing at all.

Whenever you buy goods but don't take them away with you, always make sure you know where your goods are, and insist that they are clearly marked with your name. If they are, and the shop goes bust, you can go to the shop or warehouse and demand to collect them. As you can point to an item which has been clearly labelled as yours it makes it easier to prove you own it, instead of it being just part of the general assets of the business. But if the goods haven't been marked as yours you cannot insist on collecting them.

Q *What is the difference between **receivership** and **liquidation**?*

A When a company is in receivership one of its big creditors – a bank, say – has put its own employee in to run the company. It is the receiver's job to collect enough money to pay off the debt owed to the bank. This could mean that any money you have paid to the company (as a deposit, for example) goes straight to the bank. But you are still entitled to your goods or cash, and should eventually get them if the company does not subsequently go into liquidation.

If an administrator is appointed instead, you could be better off in the long run: a serious attempt to save the company might be under way.

When a liquidator is put in charge the company is going to be wound up completely (liquidation). If any cash is left at the end of this process you might get something back, but you will be with all the other unsecured creditors at the back of the queue. So it is unlikely you will get anything.

Q *Is the **guarantee** on my recent re-roofing work worth anything now that the builder has gone bust?*

A When a company goes bust its own guarantees generally aren't worth the paper they're written on. But if another company buys out the failed business and agrees to take over its liabilities (although this would be rare) your guarantee should be honoured. Check to see whether you paid for your guarantee to be backed by insurance. If you did pay a premium when you agreed to have the building work done, then the insurance should cover the cost of any work that needs doing if the builder did a bad job.

Q *A year ago, I lost a lot of money when I paid a deposit to a company that went bust. The same people have now set up again using the same name. Is this allowed?*

A There's nothing to stop the former directors buying back the assets (including the company name) and starting again. However, it is against the law for those involved in the original company to use the old name (or a similar name) of the liquidated company for five years following the liquidation. And if anyone who was a director of the old company is taking the important business decisions at the new one, even if not officially a director (i.e. a 'shadow' director), he or she is breaking the law. It's unlikely to be noticed by Companies House – unless you complain. So report this to the Companies Investigations Division of the Department of Trade and Industry (DTI)★.

Q *The garage that was restoring my classic car didn't do the work properly. A couple of months ago, after much wrangling, I was offered £1,500 in '**full and final settlement**' of my claim. I accepted the money on that basis, but now discover it will cost £3,000 to put the work right. Can I claim some more?*

A No. When you agree to accept compensation in 'full and final settlement' you cannot go back and ask for more at a later date. So if you are unsure of whether an offer is fair, get advice and do not be pressured into accepting less than you are entitled to. If, during negotiations:

- **the other side hassles you** Write saying that you are seriously considering the offer but are seeking expert or legal advice before you finally decide whether to accept. Most traders will be reasonable and will understand that you need time to make a decision. However, you should remember that an offer can be withdrawn at any time before it is accepted, so don't leave it too long before getting back to the other side
- **you receive a cheque in 'full and final settlement'** Don't simply bank it, as to do so may be interpreted as acceptance. You should send a letter rejecting the offer on those terms but making it absolutely clear that you are banking the cheque in part-payment only.

Q *I am going abroad for six months and want to let out my home. I contacted my mortgage company and it has approved this. But a charge for 'administration costs' has now
appeared on my mortgage statement completely out of the blue. How do I complain?*

A At the time of writing the Financial Services Authority (FSA) has not yet
taken over full responsibility for regulating mortgage providers, which will
begin to happen at the end of October 2004. After that date, it will be illegal for
any firm that is not FSA-authorised or an appointed representative of an authorised firm to continue doing mortgage or general insurance business.

Almost all mortgage lenders have signed up to the Mortgage Code, and are
members of the Council of Mortgage Lenders★. The Mortgage Code commits
lenders and intermediaries to minimum standards in the conduct of your mortgage. The principles include dealing with you in a fair and reasonable manner,
making it clear when they are advising you (not just giving information) and
helping you to understand how your mortgage account works. In particular the
code says that lenders must:

- give new borrowers a tariff and make it available to existing borrowers. This
  should cover the operation and repayment of your loan, including any
  changes and additional interest payable if you are in arrears with your
  payments. It also means that you should be told if there is a charge for grant-
  ing approval to let out property, or for supplying information to you that is
  contained in the deeds, say. Lenders must send you a new tariff each year, if
  there have been changes to it
- set out terms and conditions in plain language, wherever possible, and
  ensure that they are fair to borrowers
- operate an internal complaints procedure for handling complaints fairly and
  speedily, and give borrowers details about which ombudsman or arbitration
  scheme is available
- promise to consider cases of financial difficulty and mortgage arrears sympathetically.

The Financial Ombudsman Service★ uses this and other financial services codes
when ruling on complaints. If you're unhappy with the service you receive you
should contact the Ombudsman.

Q *I have money in bank and building society accounts and also have some income
bonds and other investments. What protection do I have if any of the businesses go bust?*

A The protection you have depends on the level of your investment and
where the money is invested.

The Financial Services Authority (FSA)★ has set up a single compensation
scheme which pays compensation if an 'authorised firm' can't meet its liabilities to

investors, depositors or policyholders. The **Financial Services Compensation Scheme (FSCS)** covers deposits, investments and insurance where the money is invested with a company regulated by the FSA. This includes the high-street banks and personal investment products:

- with deposits, if the bank goes bust the maximum you can receive for a deposit claim is £31,700 – you'll get back the whole of the first £2,000 and then 90 per cent of the next £33,000. These limits are the amount payable for each individual, not for each account, so it does not matter how many accounts you have with the bank – you'll only get one payout. Similarly, joint account holders can each claim 90 per cent of their total investments

- for personal investment products the scheme covers two kinds of loss. First, when an investment firm authorised by the FSA goes out of business, and second where you suffer loss because of bad investment advice, or poor investment management. In these cases the scheme pays out all of the first £30,000 of a valid claim and then 90 per cent of the next £20,000 invested. So if you have, say, £25,000 invested, you will get the full amount back. The maximum any individual investor can recover out of his or her total investments with the company is £48,000. Joint investors can claim up to a maximum of £48,000 each

- for insurance the scheme covers you provided your policy was issued in the UK. If an insurance firm goes out of business the maximum amount of compensation you'll get depends on the kind of insurance. Compulsory insurance, like third party motor insurance, is covered in full. The scheme protects home insurance and other non-compulsory insurance for the first £2,000 and then 90 per cent of the remaining claim or policy. The figures are the same for long-term insurance such as pension plans and life assurance, with £2,000 of a claim fully protected and 90 per cent after that.

Q *My wife died 17 years ago but I have just discovered she had a number of **premium bonds** which have continued to be entered in the draw. I moved home shortly after she died. How do I find out whether any of the numbers have come up in the meantime and am I entitled to any winnings?*

A Premium bonds are not transferable. Only the person who is registered as the original holder is entitled to claim any prize. When a bond-holder dies, his or her bonds can be cashed for their face value and that amount becomes part of the bond-holder's estate. There is no time limit on when the bonds can be cashed. If they are not cashed immediately they remain valid for any prize win for 12 months from the date of death. Prizes during that time will be paid into the estate. After that the bonds can be cashed only for their face value and any 'wins' will not be paid.

Details of the winning numbers of major prizes are shown on Teletext and all winners are notified by post. Cheques remain valid for three months and must be signed for by the original bond-holder. There are unclaimed prizes going back to 1957, and all unclaimed prizes remain valid. It may be worth checking with National Savings★ in case any of the numbers came up during the 12-month period after the death.

Q *I went to pay several cheques into my bank account last week and the bank staff refused to accept one of them. They said it was more than six months old and showed me the date. They were right. I realise now that it must have been lost in my handbag and I must have just picked it up when I paid the others in. I had forgotten about it. It's not a large sum but does it mean that I have lost my right to the money?*

A Some cheques actually state that they must be cashed within three or six months of the date on them. You will see this on dividend payments, for example. But there is no law which says that cheques become out of date after a particular period. It is a matter of banking practice aimed at preventing cheques from lying around for too long. If you do leave some time before cashing it, you may find that the bank refuses it.

You should get some form of verification from the person or company who issued the cheque before you pay it in. Although the cheque has been allowed to go 'stale' you are still entitled to the money. Hence, if the person or company issuing the cheque were to refuse to verify it or to issue another one it would be exactly the same as if they had never paid you in the first place and you would be entitled to take the claim to court. But beware: there is a six-year limitation period on claims for unpaid debts (even if it is unpaid because of your mistake). So if you leave it this long you will not even have the option of taking legal action. There is also a danger that by the time you ask for a replacement cheque the company may have gone out of business. You will then only get your money if funds are available, which is very unlikely.

Q *I have been told that I can't claim for defects in a sofa I bought with my credit card as my husband is the principal cardholder and I am only an additional holder on his card. The credit-card company denies liability. Is this right?*

A Strictly speaking it is. Under the Consumer Credit Act 1974, your rights may be weaker if things go wrong with goods or services you have bought as an additional cardholder. The main or principal cardholder can claim compensation for faulty goods or services from either the supplier or the card issuer if they cost more than £100. If an additional cardholder buys the goods that person does not have the legal right to claim money from the card issuer.

Some credit-card issuers do voluntarily extend protection to additional card-holders but many do not. To make sure you get full protection each of you should be a principal cardholder.

Q *I used to get a good rate of interest from my bank but I've recently discovered that the rate was reduced six months ago and is now much less than I can get elsewhere. Why wasn't I kept informed?*

A The Banking Code (p. 155) lays down some specific guidelines for banks and building societies to follow when changing the interest rate on accounts or changing accounts themselves:

- as an account holder you must be told of any interest-rate changes within 30 days of the changes, either by letter or some other form of notice, such as a personal email, or by prominent signs in branches and through advertisements placed in the press within three working days of the change. You should be told the interest rate applicable to your account and a summary of other accounts and interest rates at least once a year so that you can compare them more easily
- you may have a variable-rate account which the bank or society decides to withdraw. Once a year the bank should send you a summary of all its interest rates, marking those types of account that have been withdrawn, to give you the chance to compare interest rates and switch your money into another account.

If you have not been given full information you should complain first to the head office of the bank or building society, and then to the Financial Ombudsman Service★. The Ombudsman will consider the requirements of the Banking Code when investigating your complaint. You can get details of the Code at banks and building societies, or on the Internet at *www.bankfacts.org.uk*.

Q *If the Banking Code says that banks and building societies must keep customer information confidential and not pass it on to anyone else, why do a number of credit reference agencies have details about my finances?*

A The Banking Code says that your personal information will be kept private and confidential, and this applies even after you cease to be a customer. It also means that no details about your account or your name and address can be disclosed to anyone, even to other companies in the same group. But there are some exceptional circumstances which allow information to be disclosed:

- where the bank or building society is legally compelled to do so, or
- where there is a public duty to disclose, or
- where the interests of the bank require it, or

- where you request or consent to the disclosure, or
- where you have fallen behind with your payments and you do not dispute the amount owed: if you have not made any acceptable proposals to repay the debt, the bank can disclose the details to a credit reference agency as long as it has given you at least 28 days' notice.

Q *How are financial advisers regulated and how can I make sure I'm getting good, impartial advice?*

A The Financial Services and Markets Act 2000 completely overhauled the whole system of regulating all those involved in selling and administering financial products and services. This is due to change again in 2005. At present, the **Financial Services Authority (FSA)**★ is the 'super-regulator', providing a 'one-stop-shop' for regulation, and making the process of complaining less confusing for those affected.

Two of the FSA's statutory objectives are to protect consumers and to promote public understanding of financial services. A compensation scheme is also available if you lose money because your adviser goes bust or turns out to be a fraud.

The financial products and services regulated include banks and building societies, pensions, life assurance, investment management, securities and derivatives business, buying shares, and insurance.

It is a criminal offence for an investment business to operate unless it is authorised by the FSA. The FSA also has the role of setting and enforcing rules to ensure good standards within the investment industry, and dealing with problems through formal complaints procedures and disciplinary action. General rules of authorisation include the following measures to protect customers when dealing with salespersons or advisers:

- at the start salespeople must make it clear whether they are independent or tied to one company
- in most cases they must comply with the 'know your customer' rule: this means they must find out enough about you to put themselves in a position to be able to recommend suitable products; usually this is done by carrying out a written fact-find
- they must give you 'best advice': this means recommending only products which are suitable for you, in accordance with the details from their fact-find
- with some products there is a cancellation period during which you have the right to change your mind and pull out of the deal.

Q *I withdrew some cash from an ATM of a bank that is not my own. Just before the money came out a message flashed up on screen to say that I was being charged for the service. Is this legal?*

A Trying to work out whether you'll be charged a fee for using a cash machine is not always easy. Most bank-owned machines don't charge debit-card users for withdrawing money. But more and more 'convenience' cash machines are appearing in places such as shops and petrol stations, and they do charge for withdrawals. These machines are usually owned by companies other than banks, and they charge hefty fees – often £1.25 to £1.50 a time, and sometimes more.

You will be warned of the fee, but only just before receiving your cash. You will usually have an opportunity to cancel at this stage but most people will be reluctant. Most of these machines should tell you before you start the transaction but the messages may be confusing. Under the Banking Code (p. 155) banks have to tell you of charges only if you have been charged for using a machine. They don't have to make it clear that there is no charge so some banks cover themselves in case you're using a credit card, instead of a debit card, for which the card issuer may charge a fee.

Q *I have trouble remembering all the security passwords and PIN numbers for my cards and accounts so I have them written down in my own secret places and disguise them as phone numbers and names. Does this mean that if I lose my card or if there's an unauthorised withdrawal from my account I'll have to suffer the loss?*

A You're not alone in doing this. Normally such losses are limited to £50 if you've taken reasonable precautions and reported a theft to the bank as soon as possible. But a bank would probably argue that you'd forfeited this protection by writing down the PIN, even if it is disguised. Normally if you've been 'grossly negligent', acted fraudulently or the card had been used with the owner's consent, the bank doesn't have to pay up.

The Banking Code tells you never to write your PIN down. But the Financial Ombudsman has made it clear that in judging a complaint it wouldn't consider you liable automatically just because you'd done so. In judging a case, the Ombudsman would also look at whether you'd taken care and acted reasonably – including how well the number was disguised. If you keep the PIN written down near your card it's clear that you're very unlikely to get any money back.

Q *I read in the newspapers about thieves getting details of credit-card numbers and other information from domestic bins and then pretending to be the card holder. How can they do this and would I be liable for what a thief spent?*

A At least when your handbag is stolen, or your wallet snatched, you know and you can cancel those cards immediately to prevent the thief from tapping into your funds and damaging your credit rating. In fact, when your plastic is stolen the Consumer Credit Act 1974 offers consumers good protection. You're only liable for up to £50 of any amount run up by the thief. Report it quickly, before the thief has an opportunity to use the card, and you could avoid any liability at all (p. 151).

But things may be different if, unbeknown to you, a thief has all the information needed to pass himself off as you, so he can buy goods over the phone, or the Internet, using your card details – even though your cards are still safely tucked inside your wallet. All a fraudster needs is a card number, an expiry date and a billing address, and he's got buying power even if he doesn't have your card. It is estimated that 40 per cent of domestic bins contain a whole credit- or debit-card number, and 80 per cent of these bins also contain a card expiry date. The rubbish is probably outside your house anyway, or contains utility bills with your address on – both are a dead giveaway to the billing address for your cards. Put these together and a fraudster has all he needs to spend your money.

You can take some comfort in the law, but it's comfort that's easily lost:

- if you can show that you've had your cards all along, the law presumes that any transactions are 'unauthorised' and so not your responsibility. The credit-card company has the burden of proving that those payments were made with your permission
- additionally, under the voluntary Banking Code, if the company can prove that you either acted fraudulently or without reasonable care you could be liable for all amounts spent by the fraudster on your card. The danger is that by putting documents containing personal details in the bin without properly destroying them, you may be acting 'without reasonable care'.

It's up to the bank or card company to show that you acted without reasonable care, and if it can't then you won't be liable for anything. Assuming the company can prove that the fraudster got your details from the rubbish, and can show you were careless by simply throwing out all your old receipts and statements without concealing or destroying them, the law may no longer protect you.

If you are the victim of an identity thief who has rummaged through the bins and used your card details to make 'cardholder not present' transactions in your name, a judge or the Ombudsman could find you responsible for picking up the whole tab.

The Banking Code offers guidance on how to protect your accounts and states that 'if you act without reasonable care, and this causes losses, you may be responsible for them'. It cites as an example of carelessness the failure to 'carefully' dispose of card receipts. The best advice is to destroy all credit-card receipts before throwing them away. If you don't have a shredder, tear documents into small pieces and spread the bits around various rubbish sacks. You should also destroy old utility bills, bank statements – in fact, anything with personal information about you. If you don't, then simply throwing these out with the general rubbish may well amount to acting 'without reasonable care' and you could find yourself liable for anything a fraudster spends using your personal information.

Q *I received some credit-card cheques from my card company with the assurance that they allow me to pay cheques up to my credit-card limit and then pay them off over time. Do I get all the same protection with these cheques as I do with my credit card?*

A No. Credit-card cheques are treated as cash advances – you'll incur a cash advance fee and be charged interest on the amount as soon as the cheque is cashed. So, even if you pay off your bill in full, you'll be charged a month's interest on the cheque's full amount. And for purchases using these cheques you don't get any protection from section 75 of the Consumer Credit Act.

Chapter 7

Health

How do you change doctors? What are your rights when your treatment in hospital goes wrong, or if your dentist doesn't provide an acceptable level of service? This chapter explains the legal duties of doctors, opticians, dentists, nurses, pharmacists and complementary therapists.

There can be few consumer services as important as the National Health Service – a bewilderingly large organisation in which it can be difficult to know where to turn if you experience problems. Contact your local Independent Complaints Advocacy Service (ICAS) who can provide free help and guidance on presenting your complaint about NHS services. ICAS work very closely with your local Patient Advice and Liaison Service (PALS) in England and Wales who may phone your local hospital, clinic, GP surgery or health centre (Local Health Council in Scotland, Health and Social Services Council in Northern Ireland).

Your rights, and the correct complaints procedure to follow, will differ depending on the outcome you are seeking and if you received NHS or private treatment. For example, you may simply want an apology, an explanation and an assurance that what happened to you will not happen to others, or you may seek disciplinary action against the person involved, or you may be trying to obtain financial compensation.

If you opt for private treatment – in a private hospital, or by a private dentist, GP, optician or pharmacist – the avenues for complaint may be limited (pp. 179–183).

Q *If I have a problem concerning medical treatment, to whom should I complain?*

A Whatever your complaint, and whether the treatment received was NHS or private, follow these golden rules:

- clarify the situation with the person responsible for the treatment – this might prove the simplest and quickest way of getting things put right
- try to resolve your complaint informally, if possible, but once you decide to start a more formal complaint, act quickly – a delay could cause diffi-

culties with evidence and may lead people to doubt the seriousness of your grievance

- keep copies of letters and other written records concerning your complaint
- ask for a copy of your medical records
- seek advice, at any stage, from the Patient Advice and Liaison Service (PALS) at your local NHS Trust or Primary Care Trust (PCT) (Local Health Council in Scotland, Health and Social Services Council in Northern Ireland) or other organisation or pressure group which might be able to help
- be persistent, and prepared for a process which may prove both frustrating and time-consuming
- be sure in your own mind about the **subject** (GP, dentist, hospital nurse, etc.), the **substance** (wrong kind of treatment, or rude and uncaring behaviour on the part of a health professional), and the **object** of your complaint (do you hope to receive an apology, a change of treatment, financial compensation, or simply to prevent a recurrence of what happened to you?)
- what makes the greatest difference is whether the treatment you are complaining about was from medical staff in hospital ('hospital medical care') or from medical practitioners out of hospital ('community medical care'), by dentists, GPs, opticians, pharmacists, etc. There is a different process for each category (see pp. 172–4).

Q *Is there an Ombudsman for the NHS who can look at my complaint?*

A Yes. The official title is the **Health Service Ombudsman**★. He is independent of the NHS and the government and the services he provides are free. Although he cannot award compensation, he can ask the NHS Trust or Primary Care Trust (if it's a complaint about a GP or dentist, for example) to remedy or compensate for any injustice or hardship suffered.

Before making a complaint to the Ombudsman you must first take it up with the appropriate NHS Trust or Primary Care Trust (pp. 172–3). You need to show that the failure in service or maladministration has caused you injustice or hardship. Complaints may be about the attitude, as well as the actions, of a health practitioner. It is up to the Ombudsman to decide whether to investigate a complaint – the decision will depend on its merits. The main purpose is to ensure that you receive an apology and that the NHS Trust or the Primary Care Trust agrees to change policies or procedures to prevent the problem happening again.

Q *What powers does the Ombudsman have?*

A The Health Service Ombudsman★ is able to look into certain types of complaint about failures in service or maladministration, such as not following proper procedure, rules or agreed policies; poor care; staff attitudes; poor communications; and poor handling of a complaint. Those lodging a complaint will need to show that the failure or maladministration has caused injustice or hardship.

Patients can complain to the Ombudsman if they are not happy with the response to their complaint or if they are unhappy with a decision not to convene an independent review panel (p. 173). The Commissioner also has jurisdiction over cases involving clinical judgment and those involving primary care services. If the Commissioner decides to take on a case, he will undertake a thorough and rigorous investigation (he has legal access to NHS records), and make recommendations to the relevant NHS bodies. If you have a complaint:

- it must first have been made to the Primary Care Trust or NHS Trust as appropriate, following the normal complaints procedures (pp. 172–3)
- it must be made in writing and supported by all background papers
- it should be made within six months of the incident coming to notice but at least within one year of the event.

If you have any doubt about whether the Commissioner can deal with your complaint, contact the Commissioner's office first. He has the power to investigate complaints that a Primary Care Trust or NHS Trust:

- has not provided a service which it has a duty to provide
- has failed to provide service of sufficient quality, e.g. late arrival or non-availability of ambulances
- is guilty of maladministration in any action it has taken or authorised – such as not following proper procedures, not explaining the care being given to a patient, or giving wrong information, or carrying out an unsatisfactory investigation into your original complaint.

The Ombudsman can also investigate complaints concerning a clinical decision about the care or treatment of a patient (p. 174), although no award of compensation can be made for any harm or inconvenience suffered.

Q *I feel that my NHS dentist is rather off-hand and impatient with me and on one occasion recently he was downright rude. Is there anything I can do about this?*

A If you're not happy with the treatment you or your family have received from the NHS, misunderstandings may be resolved by complaining directly to the person concerned. If you do not get satisfaction or you would rather not discuss the problem with the person face to face, your local **Primary Care Trust** (PCT) should be able to help you (Local Health Council in Scotland; Health and Social Services Councils in Northern Ireland). PCTs deal with complaints about GPs, dentists, opticians, pharmacists and their staff.

PCTs act as local commissioners or purchasers of hospital and community services.

Q *Two weeks ago my son developed severe abdominal pain during the night. Our family doctor didn't think it was serious enough to warrant a visit. I took my son into casualty the next morning and acute appendicitis was diagnosed. I am very unhappy about the GP's attitude and wish to make a formal complaint. How do I go about it?*

A Family doctors (GPs), dentists, opticians and general pharmaceutical services from your chemist are all independent of the NHS, but offer NHS services under a contract with the local **Primary Care Trust** (PCT). A family doctor must treat you with reasonable care, which would include visiting you at home if necessary although responsibility for out of hours cover now rests with the PCT if your GP has opted out. If you have a complaint about family health services, including your GP or any member of the primary care team, a process aimed at local resolution should be the first step. So follow these steps:

- make your initial complaint to the practice within six months (soon to be one year). If you would prefer to talk to someone not involved in your treatment you can phone or write to your local Primary Care Trust's Complaints Manager. Most complaints should be dealt with at this level. You should get acknowledgement of your complaint within two days and receive a full response within ten working days
- if you are not satisfied you can ask the Trust to carry out a further review, which may include the setting up of an independent review panel. You must make your request for this within 28 calendar days of the written reply to your complaint. The decision on whether to convene a review panel is taken by a non-executive director of the relevant Primary Care Trust, known as a convenor, and the decision will be made within ten working days (20 if it's a complaint about a hospital)
- if no panel is set up you can complain to the Health Service Ombudsman★ at this stage (pp. 171–2)
- if the convenor does agree to set up a panel this will be done within ten working days. The panel has access to background papers, your health records and any written statements. The investigation should be over within three months of your first approaching the convenor. You will get a copy of the draft report to comment on. The final report is sent to you and the others involved. The chief executive of the Primary Care Trust will write to inform you of any action it will be taking as a result
- if you are still unhappy with the result you can appeal to the Ombudsman (pp. 171–2) or take legal action if appropriate (Chapter 13).

Q *I had to undergo hospital treatment recently. Generally the staff were rude and uncaring and I don't think the treatment was carried out properly. I think this gave rise to complications in my condition. What can I do?*

A In NHS hospitals, complaints which involve clinical judgment – for example, if you think a doctor gave you the wrong treatment, or a nurse or other health service medical professional gave you the wrong medication – and complaints about generally poor service are dealt with in the same way as complaints about family health services (see above). What you should do is:

- wherever possible, tell someone close to the cause of your complaint (e.g. a doctor, nurse or receptionist). Or contact your local Patient Advice and Liaison Service (PALS)★. Give your name and date of birth or hospital number. Also give the date of the incident, the names of the staff involved or a description of them, and the main points of the case, stating what points you want investigated. The complaints guidelines state that you should normally get a full response from the chief executive within 20 working days. Most complaints can be dealt with satisfactorily at this stage
- if you are not satisfied, the reply you receive to your complaint will let you know whom to contact if you want to request an independent review panel. If it does not, ask the Complaints Manager. You must make your request within 28 calendar days of the written reply to your complaint. The convener will set up an independent review panel within 20 working days. This panel will gather together information about you and other evidence and may involve independent clinical assessors in appropriate cases
- if the decision is made not to convene a review panel, or if you are unhappy with the outcome, you can complain to the Health Service Ombudsman (pp. 171–2), or take legal action (Chapter 13).

Q *If I want to try for compensation, do I have to follow the Primary Health Trust or NHS Trust procedures first?*

A No. But they are a useful first step *before* you decide whether to claim compensation later. The complaints procedures against hospital practitioners and community health practitioners (pp. 172–3) will not get compensation for you. You can seek guidance on pursuing the claim from Action Against Medical Accidents (AvMA)★ or a specialist medical negligence lawyer (see below).

Q *The operation I had recently has left me in an even worse condition. I'm not satisfied with the explanation I've received from the consultant in charge of my case, and I feel I'm entitled to some sort of **compensation**. What should I do?*

A Pursuing a **medical accident** or **negligence** claim is certainly not something to be undertaken lightly, even if you qualify for Legal Aid. Besides being expensive and protracted, such cases are notoriously difficult to prove. Your lawyers will have to show that the doctor was negligent rather than just making a professional misjudgment. They will also have to show that this negligence caused your subsequent medical problems. In medical negligence cases, proper legal advice from a specialist lawyer is essential to ensure you obtain all the evidence you will need and to negotiate the best settlement terms. Legal Aid is available only to a very few, so consider trying to find a solicitor who will take on your case on a 'no win, no fee' basis (pp. 112–3), or check to see whether you already have any legal expenses insurance to help fund the case (p. 111). If you want to claim compensation:

- before going to a solicitor, seek advice from the Patient Advice and Liaison Service (PALS) at your local NHS Trust, or contact Action Against Medical Accidents (AvMA)★. AvMA can give you free basic legal and medical advice, and, if appropriate, refer you to a solicitor with substantial experience in such cases

- your solicitor will take a statement of what happened and discuss Legal Aid and costs with you. If the case seems worth pursuing (and if you have the financial means to proceed, have legal expenses insurance, or are eligible for Legal Aid) (pp. 288–9) your solicitor will obtain the medical records, identify the issues and then send them to a medical expert so that a report can be prepared. The report may then be sent with your statement and records to a barrister for advice as to the strength of your claim and on how to proceed

- if your case is a strong one, the Primary Care Trust (or other defendant) may be willing to settle your claim without the need to go to court. If it is necessary to start court action, you must do this within three years of the date when you first realised you had suffered damage (p. 22).

Q *Is there an NHS Code of Conduct or Charter which sets out what I'm entitled to expect from the National Health Service?*

A The Patient's Charter was scrapped a few years ago and many of the patient rights it contained disappeared with it. Instead, the Department of Health has issued *Your Guide to the NHS* (*www.nhs.uk/nhsguide/nhs_guide.pdf*). This contains a number of Core Principles, which promise that the NHS will:

- provide a comprehensive range of services
- shape services around the needs and preferences of individual patients, their families and carers

- work continuously to improve quality services and to minimise errors
- provide a universal service for all based on clinical need, not ability to pay
- respect the confidentiality of individual patients and provide open access to information about services, treatment and performance.

What is missing is a list of national standards of care setting out commitments on performance, but at the time of writing these are in development. There are already standards for cancer, mental health and coronary heart disease (*www.doh.gov.uk/nsf/cancer.htm*; *www.doh.gov.uk/nsf/mentalhealth.htm*; *www.doh.gov.uk/nsf/coronary.htm*).

The Guide does put an emphasis on your responsibilities as a patient and stresses such things as the importance of letting your surgery know when you can't keep an appointment, say.

Every GP practice should have a practice leaflet setting out details of opening hours, the staff, how to get out-of-hours help, the policy on home visits, etc. The government has also promised that by the end of 2004 the following standards will be in place:

- you will be able to see a health professional (a practice nurse, say) within 24 hours, and have a GP appointment within 48 hours
- people with chronic conditions will be able to pick up a repeat supply of their medicines from their pharmacist, without having to go back to their GP each time
- you will be treated in a GP practice instead of having to travel to hospital for treatment.

Q *Is there anything I can do to shorten the time I have to wait for treatment on the NHS?*

A *Your Guide to the NHS* (see above) states that you should be kept informed about how long you'll have to wait for hospital treatment, GP, dental or optician appointments. The general guidance on time scales is as follows:

- as an outpatient, you can expect to wait no more than 26 weeks
- at the outpatient clinic you should be seen within 30 minutes of your appointment time
- as an inpatient you can expect to wait no more than 18 months depending on your condition
- if your GP or dentist refers you urgently with suspected cancer, you will be seen by a specialist within two weeks
- if you are suffering from chest pain for the first time and your GP thinks this might be due to angina, you will be assessed in a specialist chest pain clinic within two weeks.

Q *I don't feel I have a good rapport with my GP. Can I change to another, and if so how do I go about it?*

A You are allowed to change your GP for any reason – because you're moving, you want a certain kind of GP, such as a woman, or even because you don't like your current doctor. Just turn up at the new doctor's surgery and register (providing the practice is willing to take you). There may be several reasons why a new GP may refuse to put you on their list (see Q&A below). You do not need permission from the old doctor and you need not take pot luck with the surgery either as you can find out about GPs before choosing, by:

- getting **personal recommendations** (or warnings) from friends and neighbours
- looking at **practice leaflets**. All NHS GPs are required by law to produce a leaflet for patients which describes their practice. These include the doctor's gender, the year he or she qualified, surgery hours, other practice staff (for example, nurses), and services provided (for example, ante-natal care). You can get leaflets from practices or read them at the local Health Authority offices
- looking at **Primary Care Trust (PCT) lists** of doctors. All PCTs are required by law to produce a directory of all local GPs. These detail the doctor's gender and age or date of qualification, services the practice provides and who works there. Contact your local PCT for a list of GPs in your area. Some give information over the phone. You may be able to see the whole directory at the authority's offices or a local library
- getting a **pre-registration interview** with the GP. Some GPs may be willing to meet and discuss your needs and see whether you both get on before you register. GPs are not obliged to give these interviews, and there is a risk that such a meeting could be used by the doctor to vet you. If you have a long-term condition that may take up a lot of the practice's time or money, it is possible that the doctor will not accept you
- the Patient Advice and Liaison Service (PALS) at your local PCT (or the Local Health Council in Scotland, Health and Social Services Council in Northern Ireland) may have information about GPs in your area.

Q *I've just moved to a new area and tried to register with a local GP in a practice a short walk from my home. But he refused, saying his patient lists were full. Apart from him, the only other GP is a mile away. Can I challenge his decision?*

A GP surgeries are not legally obliged to accept you on to their patient lists and turning away new patients is not uncommon across the UK. The more usual reasons for refusal are that you're outside their catchment area or that they have closed their list because they are 'full'. Surgeries can decide when to close their lists – although at the time of writing the government was expected to publish new formal procedures for closing lists. This is likely to concentrate on the lists of the practice as a whole and not individual GPs.

Surgeries that feel unable to add you to their list will suggest you contact your local Primary Care Trust (PCT) in England (local Health Authority in Wales, Health Board in Scotland, or Health and Social Services Board in Northern Ireland). This body must allocate you to a surgery if you can't find one and can force a surgery to take you. But if a surgery has closed its list, allocations put strains on staff who already feel their service is stretched. All allocated surgeries can turf you off their list, too, without explanation. They'll still be able to do this under the new contract.

Q *I feel my GP is uncertain about his diagnosis of a medical problem I've been experiencing recently. Do I have the right to be referred to a specialist?*

A You don't actually have the right to a second opinion. All you have is the right to ask for one. Many doctors would probably agree that a second opinion is justified if:

- your symptoms persist, and you cannot get a diagnosis
- a diagnosis has been made, but the treatment is not working
- you are worried about the risks or side effects of a treatment that has been proposed, or would like more information about it
- you want to know whether there is any alternative to major surgery or other proposed treatment
- you simply feel the need for specialist confirmation that the proposed treatment is right for you
- you are not confident that your doctor knows enough about your condition.

Since you do not have an automatic right to a second opinion, it could be counter-productive to go into the surgery demanding one. Here are a few tips for how to go about it:

- write down the points you want to make before you go to see the doctor. Remember to say why you feel you would like to see someone else
- say that you are not questioning your doctor's judgment, you'd just like the reassurance of having it confirmed
- listen to what your doctor says. There may be good reason for suggesting that you don't need a second opinion, or that you should wait a bit longer before seeing one – for example, to see whether changes in your lifestyle will help solve the problem
- try to be assertive, but not aggressive if the doctor refuses.

Q *I've discovered that my GP has been talking about my personal medical problems to his other patients. I think it's very unprofessional. Is there anything I can do?*

A The relationship between a medical professional and a patient is a confidential and intimate one, governed by ethical principles set out in the rules of conduct of the professional regulatory bodies. A practitioner found guilty of a breach of professional conduct may have his or her right to carry on practising withdrawn. Whether you are complaining about a private or an NHS practitioner, complaints about **professional misconduct** are dealt with by the following bodies:

- General Medical Council (GMC)★ for doctors
- General Dental Council (GDC)★ for dentists
- General Optical Council (GOC)★ for opticians
- Nursing and Midwifery Council (NMC)★ for nurses, midwives and health visitors
- Health Professions Council (HPC)★ for physios, paramedics and other nursing professions.

Q *What difference does it make to my claim if my hospital treatment was private rather than on the NHS?*

A All NHS hospitals have procedures for dealing with patients' complaints. The complaints procedures (see pp. 170–4) apply only to complaints about treatment from doctors, dentists, opticians and pharmacists within the NHS.

The National Care Standards Commission (NCSC)★ is responsible for regulating independent hospitals. It requires all independent hospitals to have a complaints procedure and it will investigate any complaints arising from a breach of its regulations. Hospitals must give patients full written details of the cost of their treatment, and any terms and conditions that apply. However, while independent hospitals should investigate any complaints about consultants working on their premises, they are still not responsible for problems arising from treatment. And, although each hospital must have its own complaints procedure, patients still have no recourse to an ombudsman.

All complaints are best dealt with as amicably as possible, but if you cannot get a satisfactory response, and if you wish to claim compensation, you will need to take legal advice with a view to possible court action (see p. 175). Within the NHS you could sue the hospital or NHS Trust. In the private sector you have to sue the practitioner personally because doctors, dentists etc. are rarely employees of private hospitals and clinics: they tend to work independently, using such facilities on a private basis. If you feel strongly that your private treatment was unsatisfactory, you could try to withhold payment. If you are in a private insurance scheme you could ask the insurance company (before you receive any treatment) whether it is prepared to send the payment cheque to you rather than to the hospital or doctor concerned.

However, if you do consider withholding payment or starting court action you will have to establish that the treatment provided was negligent and/or that there was a breach of contract (p. 175).

Q *The crown my dentist fitted to my front tooth has come loose but when I complained I was told that this was a risk and I'd have to have more treatment, and possibly a denture. How do I complain about this?*

A Complaining to the dentist's practice is the first step to take in any complaint. If this fails to solve the problem, the system for making complaints depends on whether the treatment was private or on the NHS.

NHS patients can use the NHS complaints procedure and, if unhappy with the dentist's response, can complain to their Primary Care Trust (PCT). The local Patient Advice and Liaison Service (PALS) is also available to help when patients need advice or have concerns. Contact your local PALS by:

- phoning your local hospital, clinic, GP surgery or health centre and ask for details of the PALS
- phoning NHS Direct on 0845 46 47
- Visiting the website *www.nhsdirect.nhs.uk.*

But if it's compensation you want, the NHS complaints procedure won't help. You will have to seek legal advice on further action. In fact, the NHS process will refuse to deal with your problem if you take legal action. Action Against Medical Accidents (AvMA)★ offers information and advice about medical accidents.

Private patients can only complain directly to the dentist's practice or seek legal action, unless the complaint constitutes 'serious professional misconduct'. Both NHS and private complaints of this nature should be taken to the General Dental Council★ (p. 179).

If the complaint is about serious professional misconduct, such as failing to carry out necessary treatment satisfactorily, or if there was a lack of skill and attention, then write to the General Dental Council (GDC)★ with the dentist's details, a note of why you're complaining, and send any relevant documents. After investigation, if the GDC agrees with the complaint it can give the dentist a formal warning, suspend him or her or strike him or her off. But this won't get you compensation.

Q *Can I influence local NHS policy?*

A Patient and Public Involvement (PPI) Forums in England and Wales (Local Health Councils in Scotland, Health and Social Services Councils in Northern Ireland) are probably your best point of contact if you have strong views about the way local services are run. PPIs are new bodies independent from Primary Care Trusts and NHS Trusts and are designed to make sure the views of patients and the public are heard and acted on within the decision-making process. Anyone can apply to become a member of a PPI. Contact the Commission for Patient and Public Involvement in Health★.

Q *I am thinking of going to a private hospital for what should be a routine cosmetic operation. Despite delays and a few complaints I have always felt confident of the quality of care in the NHS. What can I do to reduce the risk of a bad experience in the private sector – it all seems a bit of a lottery?*

A The Registered Homes Act 1984 currently regulates private hospitals. Under the Act, hospitals are registered by the National Care Standards Commission (NCSC), which must inspect them at least twice a year. The only real sanction against a hospital which fails to meet its requirements is to close the hospital down, although this can be a very lengthy process.

There are some steps you can take before checking into a private hospital:

- ask what safeguards exist to cope with an emergency (an intensive care unit, say) and whether a senior medical officer is on the premises at all times. Many private hospitals and clinics simply provide hotel-type facilities and administrative services and have neither the necessary facilities, nor adequate specialist medical and nursing cover, to cope with emergencies. This is especially so when the consultant is no longer on the premises

- there are requirements for private hospitals to have a complaints system in place and to comply with regulations laid down by the National Care Standards Commission★ (p. 179)

- don't be afraid to make a fuss. If you have any concerns at any time ask to see the consultant as soon as possible

- you might consider if you'd be better in a private wing of an NHS hospital where specialist and senior staff would be on hand. And in future, new regulations currently being established in the NHS mean that NHS paybeds and private wings will be treated separately from the rest of the private sector. So, you could have more rights to redress and safeguards against bad practice.

Q *If something does go wrong with my private treatment how do I complain?*

A More and more of us have private medical cover, paying for it ourselves or as a benefit from our employer. But if you have cover, or simply opt to pay for one-off private medical treatment, complaining may not be as straightforward as under the NHS (pp. 170–2). You can't complain to the Health Service Ombudsman★ (the name for the NHS Ombudsman) if the complaint is about private treatment by a dentist, doctor, hospital or any other private practitioner (pp. 71–2). Fewer safeguards are in place, and complaints systems are completely different. Often your only comeback is through the courts, which can be costly and complicated, so enforcing any rights you do have may not be easy:

- many private hospitals are used to dealing only with complaints about their facilities or their own staff, general issues of poor service etc., although they are obliged to have a complaints procedure in place to investigate any complaints
- consultants have no responsibility for patients' clinical care and while private hospitals have to investigate complaints they will not take responsibility for the clinical care undertaken by the consultants who work there. There are no procedures for consultants to respond to complaints about them. The only option is to complain in cases of serious professional misconduct to the General Medical Council (GMC)★ about a doctor, the General Dental Council (GDC)★ for private dentistry, or to sue the consultant concerned.

If you do want to complain about your medical treatment in a private hospital, there are a number of steps you can take:

- always follow the 'golden rules' of complaining (pp. 170–1)
- ask for copies of all your medical and nursing records from the hospital and the consultant – you're entitled to see them under the Access to Health Records Act 1990 (pp. 186–7)
- ask for details of the hospital's complaints procedure (see above). If it claims not to have one, complain in writing to the hospital manager. It's important to do this, even if you're referred to the consultant. The hospital should inform its Medical Advisory Committee of any clinical negligence complaints
- inform your medical insurer, too, if you have one. Although insurers tend not to get involved with complaints about clinical care, they should be made aware of any serious complaints about hospitals or consultants recognised within their schemes
- you can complain to the National Care Standards Commission (NCSC) if you think the hospital is in breach of its registration requirements (see above). Although these are mostly to do with non-clinical matters, some may be relevant. For example, the requirement for hospitals to make adequate arrangements for the care of patients in medical emergencies

- if your complaint is directly about the consultant responsible for your treatment, and the hospital won't get involved, then you can make a complaint to the GMC. However, it will generally deal with complaints only about serious professional misconduct or where a doctor repeatedly fails to meet professional standards
- if you have been injured as a result of medical treatment, Action Against Medical Accidents (AvMA)★ can provide free independent advice.

Q *I've been asked to go into hospital for tests to investigate a lump in my breast. I'm worried that if it's found to be malignant the surgeon may remove my breast without my express* **consent**. *Could he lawfully do this?*

A Without your permission doctors aren't even allowed to touch you. Consent does not have to be given formally – rolling up your sleeve for a blood test can be enough. But if, as in this sort of case, an invasive form of treatment like surgery is planned, you'll almost always be asked to sign a consent form, to provide evidence of agreement. The type of forms currently in use aim to ensure that patients know they are entitled to full information concerning their medical condition.

The consent form will probably ask you whether you have made known to the doctor or dentist any procedure you do not want carried out straight away. If the standard form does not adequately deal with this, make a written amendment to the form before signing it, stating, for example, that you do not want the breast removed. If the doctor or dentist were to disregard an express prohibition by the patient, he or she would be committing the offence of 'assault and battery' and would be liable to pay compensation for negligence, unless the procedure could be justified on the grounds that it was immediately necessary to preserve the patient's life or health.

Q *How much does my doctor have to tell me about the* **drugs** *he's prescribed for my arthritis?*

A Even if you have agreed to take a particular course of drugs, or to undergo some other procedure, the doctor will be responsible if he or she has failed to give you adequate information about the treatment, possible side effects and so on. You will not receive compensation for any injury you suffer as a result unless you can show you would not have agreed to that type of treatment had you been given additional information. Deciding how much information you are entitled to is a tricky issue, and if other doctors are prepared to say that you were told enough, the doctor will not be liable.

Q *I am suffering from a heart condition and my doctor has asked me if I would be willing to take part in a drug trial. He has told me something about it but I'd really like more detailed information before agreeing to take part. Would I be able to pull out if I wanted to during the trial and would I be entitled to know the results? I'm concerned about confidentiality too.*

A If you do agree to participate in the drug trial you should know that there are some safeguards:

- **adequate information**: you have the right to know all about the trial before you start. Don't agree to take part until you are satisfied that your questions have been answered. Make sure you are aware of all known risks. Ask your doctor about what side effects to look out for
- **pulling out**: you have a right to pull out of a trial at any time without giving a reason. You should not have to worry that your future health care might suffer. It is wise to find out beforehand whether pulling out of the trial early could have any adverse effects on your health
- **results**: you should be able to see a copy of the results of the trial. But you may need to be patient, as production of a research report can take years
- **confidentiality**: your case details and clinical data should remain confidential. In practice, this may be difficult since a drug company monitor or official auditor may also be involved. If you are concerned about confidentiality make it clear to your doctor that you would like your records to be seen by as few people as possible and made anonymous.

Q *I'm seriously considering trying some form of **alternative medicine**. How do I know what is on offer and whether the person I choose is competent?*

A Doctors, nurses and certain state-registered professionals (for example, dentists and physiotherapists) must by law have a certain minimum training before they can practise. **Alternative** or **complementary medicine** includes therapies which are not usually taught at medical schools. However, note that:

- anyone in the UK can set themselves up to practise most complementary therapies without qualifications
- there are no government requirements for training in complementary medicine
- some complementary practitioners choose to join registering bodies which require certain levels of training, but there may be several organisations for any one therapy, all of them claiming to register practitioners
- for many therapies there is no agreement on the training needed to be a competent practitioner, and some practitioners are not registered with any organisation

- if a practitioner is not properly trained the treatment could injure you, or he or she may not spot a problem which should be brought to a doctor's attention.

Letters after a practitioner's name could mean that he or she has had many years of training or has been on little more than a weekend course. Consult the organisations listed in the address section at the back of this book to find out what the various qualifications actually mean. And if you want advice on finding practitioners in other therapies, or information on other registering bodies, you can get information from the British Complementary Medicine Association★, the Institute for Complementary Medicine★ or The Prince of Wales's Foundation for Integrated Health★.

Q *I've suffered from back trouble for several years and recently it's got worse. My GP doesn't seem able to help. I'd like to try an osteopath or a chiropractor. Is it possible to be referred to a complementary therapist on the NHS?*

A It is for the individual GP to decide in the case of each individual patient whether a complementary therapist offers the most appropriate treatment for that patient's condition. Any GP may employ a complementary therapist to offer NHS treatment within his or her practice.

Many medical professions, including psychiatry, physiotherapy, osteopathy, chiropractic, occupational therapy and chiropody have statutory regulatory bodies. These maintain standards for the education, training and conduct of registered practitioners in the UK. So all osteopaths and chiropractors have to be registered with the professional body in order to practice – either the General Chiropractic Council★ or the General Osteopathic Council★. It is illegal for anyone to use the title of osteopath or chiropractor unless they are on the register.

However the law doesn't regulate most complementary therapies. For example, anyone can register themselves as a reflexologist, say, even if they're unqualified and have no training or experience. But the Health Act 1999 has made it simpler for voluntary bodies regulating health professionals or complementary therapists to gain statutory recognition. The process takes time and it will probably be several years before we see other new statutory bodies for complementary therapies – herbal medecine and acupuncture are likely to be the next in line.

In the meantime, if you want to try complementary ('alternative') medicine always check the following:

- Is the practitioner registered with a governing body?
- What qualifications does the practitioner have, if any?
- What was the training that led to the qualifications?

- How many years has he or she been practising?
- Does he or she have professional indemnity insurance? Without it you might not be able to get any compensation if the practitioner is negligent (see p. 175).

Once you have established whether the practitioner belongs to a registering body, check whether that body is professionally managed by asking if it has:

- a code of ethics specifying the professional conduct required of members
- disciplinary procedures for practitioners who break the code
- a complaints scheme for dissatisfied customers.

Q *Am I entitled to see a copy of my hospital records?*

A Yes. The Access to Health Records Act 1990 gives you a legal right to see your paper medical records (i.e. those not held on computer) written after November 1991. The Data Protection Act 1998 also gives you the legal right to see any records held on computer as well as certain 'structured' manual paper records (pp. 261–2). To get a copy you should write to the holder of the records – NHS Trust (Local Health Boards in Scotland and Northern Ireland) for hospital records, your GP or NHS dentist for non-hospital health records, for example. For records of private treatment, write to whoever it was that treated you. Both laws apply to privately held medical records as well as NHS ones. If you encounter any problems, contact the Information Commissioner★.

Q *The doctor who treated my teenage son is refusing to let me see my son's medical records. As a parent, can I not insist?*

A No, you can only insist on seeing your own records. Children can normally see their own records, but a parent can see his or her child's records only with the child's consent, or, should the child be too young to give consent, if the holder thinks it is in the child's best interest to show the record to a parent.

Q *Three months ago I wrote asking to see my medical records. How long do I have to wait?*

A The record holder must give you access to your records within 40 days or, if fresh information has been recorded in the last 40 days (because you've been treated during that time, say), you must be shown the information within 21 days of your application. You can choose either to go and inspect them in person, or to be sent a copy although you will be charged for these. If your records have not arrived it may be easier to pay a visit.

Q *I don't think the records I saw were complete. Am I entitled to see all of my medical records?*

A No. Parts of the record can be withheld if the holder thinks seeing them would seriously harm your or another individual's physical or mental health, although examples of this will be rare and difficult to justify.

Q *My GP let me view my medical records, but they refer back to records that were made several years ago. Am I entitled to request those earlier records too?*

A You have no legal right of access to medical records recorded on paper before the start date of 1 November 1991 (see opposite), so you can only insist on seeing records made after that date. If your health records were held on computer a different law gives a right of access to those records but only those held from 1987 onwards. If your GP thinks that you need to see earlier records to make sense of those made subsequently, he or she may be persuaded to disclose them.

Q *Can I see health records written by other health professionals as well as my doctor?*

A Yes. As long as the records relate to you, you are legally entitled to see records held by a wide range of health professionals – dentists, opticians, pharmaceutical chemists, nurses, midwives, health visitors, chiropodists, dieticians, occupational therapists, orthoptists, physiotherapists, clinical psychologists, child psychotherapists, speech therapists, art or music therapists employed by a health service body, and scientists employed by a health service body as head of department. If you have any doubt whether you are entitled to see records held by a health professional, contact your local Patient Forum (Local Health Boards in Scotland and Northern Ireland). And before taking it further you can get advice from your local Independent Complaints Advocacy Service (ICAS) or Patient Advice Liaison Service (PALS).

Q *My optician has charged me £20 to see my records. Do I have to pay?*

A If you ask for a copy of any paper record made within the last 40 days, this must be provided free of charge. For older records the holder is entitled to charge up to £10 (the maximum charge is the same for access to computer records). You may also be charged if you have photocopies sent.

Q *I've just been shown my medical records, and there is an entry in them that is wrong. Should the holder alter the records?*

A If your medical records are incorrect, misleading or incomplete, you are entitled to apply to your GP for a correction to be made. If the GP thinks that the record is inaccurate he or she should correct it. If your GP disagrees with you and believes it is accurate, he or she should make a note in the records saying why you feel it is inaccurate. In either case your GP should send you a copy of the correction or note free of charge. If in doubt contact your local ICAS or PALS.

Chapter 8

Holidays, travel and transport

Travel problems never seem to be out of the news – rail delays causing upset for commuters, air rage, DVT, terrorism, or simply poor-quality holidays. Things can and do go wrong. The descriptions in the holiday brochure may not be accurate, the accommodation may not be of the standard you expected, you may not get the room with the view that you requested, the flight may be delayed or your luggage may not turn up. Holidays are meant to be enjoyed but enjoyment is an extremely subjective concept. A noisy, sleepless night for one person is a lively evening in the hotel disco for someone else. Similarly, a pleasant, quiet hotel for some guests will seem deadly boring to others. The same can be said of most of the facilities provided by a typical tour operator; it all depends on your own personal tastes and, most importantly, your expectations.

But wherever we take our holidays and whatever their duration, holidays are something we look forward to, and often involve considerable outlay, so we do not want anything to spoil them. When your booking is accepted by the hotel, tour operator or airline, a legally binding contract is made between you and the company providing the accommodation, holiday package, air transport or indeed any other travel arrangements. For most package holidays abroad, your contract is with the tour operator. The contract is not with the travel agent, although travel agents do owe you a legal duty of care and you will have a claim if they do not do a competent job (p. 199).

Q *What can I do to protect myself against problems arising when I book a holiday with a tour operator?*

A You cannot guarantee that problems won't crop up, but to reduce the risks as far as possible, follow these tips:

- make sure that any special requirements which you consider important (such as a balcony or en suite facilities) are noted on the confirmation invoice. If all it says is that these items are a 'special request' the tour operator may say you have no entitlement to such facilities. But some requests are an essential part of your holiday and should not simply be optional (p. 198)

- consider paying at least part of the deposit by credit card. Then you will have rights against the credit-card company if something goes wrong, provided the holiday itself is priced at more than £100 (pp. 152, 205–6). Make sure the payment is made to the tour operator, not to a travel agent, although some card companies will still accept liability (pp. 196–7)

- choose a tour operator which is **bonded** – look for Association of British Travel Agents (ABTA)★ or Air Travel Organisers' Licensing (ATOL)★ bonding, and if you buy scheduled airline tickets from an agent look for the International Air Transport Association (IATA)★ logo. These schemes protect your money or your travel arrangements if the travel agent or tour operator goes out of business (pp. 196–8)

- always take out a good travel insurance policy at the time you book, so that if you or someone close to you becomes ill before the holiday, you are covered in the event of cancellation (p. 240)

- make sure the policy provides adequate medical cover, especially if you are visiting a country where medical bills can be very high, such as the USA (p. 240)

- take your policy with you, and if anything goes wrong whilst you are away read the conditions of the policy and make sure you comply with them, especially time limits

- if something goes wrong on your holiday, complain to the tour operator's rep as soon as possible. Ask to be moved if your accommodation is unacceptable (pp. 199–200)

- if possible, take photos or get the names and addresses of your fellow holidaymakers to help establish your allegations

- when you get home, write to the company's head office without delay, quoting your holiday reference number, and seek compensation (pp. 199–200)

- be polite but firm in your dealings with the tour operator. Do not be deterred by its first letter if it refuses you compensation. If you have a good legal case, it is worth being persistent

- take advice if you feel unsure of your legal position

- correspond with the company, sending your letters by recorded delivery, and keep copies

- if correspondence fails, consider bringing legal proceedings in your local county court (sheriff court in Scotland). Claims of £5,000 and less (£1,500 or less in Scotland) qualify for the quicker and cheaper small claims track (p. 279). ABTA also offers an arbitration service which adjudicates on disputes between disgruntled customers and its members.

Q *What is the difference between a **charter flight** and a **scheduled flight**?*

A Although the difference is becoming increasingly blurred there are some general points to distinguish these:

- for **charter flights** a tour operator will charter, or hire, a plane or seats on a plane from an airline. The whole plane is usually reserved (sometimes by a number of operators) and it is up to the operator whether it fills all the seats. Whether you book a complete package holiday or just buy the flights from the tour operator, if things go wrong you need to direct your complaint to the tour operator. In the case of lost baggage your rights are against the airline (see below). But if the tour operator changes your flight your claim is against the operator (check the booking conditions in the brochure first, however pp. 197–8)
- for **scheduled flights** it is usually the airline which sells the seats and the airline's sole responsibility to make sure your seats are available, and that you arrive on time (see below and pp. 192–3). However, some tour operators offer packages with scheduled flights, so for these complaints you should first contact the operator.

Q *I recently flew to the USA, but my expensive suitcase went missing and was never returned to me. What can I claim against the airline, and what against my travel insurance company?*

A The Warsaw Convention (incorporated into English law by the Carriage by Air and Road Act 1979) governs the liability of airlines for luggage which is **lost, damaged or delayed** on all international flights (scheduled or charter). Compensation for lost luggage is very low because claims are settled according to weight rather than value of the case and contents. The current Warsaw Convention limitation applies whether your case is full of expensive designer clothes or old T-shirts and jeans:

- at present you are entitled to around £15 per kilo of checked-in baggage, so for a standard baggage allowance of 20 kilograms the claim would be around £300
- if your luggage is more valuable than this you should make what is called a 'declaration of interest in delivery' when checking in. This will entitle you to higher compensation for delay or loss. You may have to pay a small premium for this
- to make a claim, you must report any loss or damage to the airline whilst you are still at the airport, by filling out a **Property Irregularity Report (PIR)**. Keep a copy of the PIR and your baggage stubs (which are attached to your tickets on check-in)

- you may also be able to claim from the airline for essential items such as toiletries and underwear (below)
- the limits set by the Warsaw Convention are low, so it is important to see whether your travel insurance policy covers baggage problems. Many policies do provide cover for lost, damaged or delayed baggage. Again, make a claim on the policy as soon as possible, but remember that you cannot claim twice over for the same loss, so the insurer will only agree to pay out for loss of damage which comes within the policy cover, and which is not adequately covered by the Warsaw Convention limits. Send a copy of the PIR with your luggage stubs to the insurance company.

The current weight-related compensation should change later in 2004 when the government brings the Montreal Convention 1999 into UK law (at the time of writing the exact date was not known). Once this happens the weight of the baggage will no longer be relevant. Instead claims will be payable up to a maximum of around £850. You will have to show the value of the contents to claim the appropriate compensation – this may be difficult without receipts for everything.

Q *My luggage was delayed on my recent trip to Florida. It didn't arrive until four days into the holiday. I had to buy clothes and toiletries to keep me going. From whom should I claim the cost of these purchases?*

A As long as you reported the baggage missing and filled in a Property Irregularity Report (see above) before you left the airport, you should be entitled to claim against the airline for the essential items you had to buy to tide you over until your luggage arrived. In fact, many reputable airlines will make an interim payment. You'll have to ask for it, but for a delay of between 12 and 24 hours an amount of up to £75 is normally acceptable, so don't rush out and replace all your clothes and jewellery – the baggage may turn up and you will lose out. Some other useful tips are:

- if the airline will not pay up in advance, keep the receipts for your purchases and claim a refund later
- if the bag does not turn up later, the amount paid for the essentials will be deducted from your final compensation claim for the lost luggage of around £15 per kilogram (p. 191)
- if the essential items cost you more than the maximum, look at your holiday insurance policy to see whether it provides cover for delayed baggage. If so, put in a claim.

Q *Our flights to New York were fine but, coming back, we were held up by over 12 hours. Does the airline have to compensate us?*

A Under the Warsaw Convention, airlines are obliged to compensate you if they fail to get you to your destination within a reasonable time of your scheduled arrival. On long-haul flights, a 'reasonable' time is usually considered to be about six hours. But the strength of your claim depends on what causes the delay: if your flight was delayed due to an event outside the airline's control, such as bad weather, for example, you are unlikely to be able to claim substantial compensation. However, a reputable airline should offer you meals during any lengthy period of delay, and should keep you reasonably well informed about the delay. If you were delayed overnight, it ought to provide you with accommodation.

It is worth taking out **holiday insurance** which provides cover for flight delays, although the amounts provided are rarely high and some may only cover delay on the outbound flight. Check your travel insurance policy carefully, and if cover is provided make a claim as soon as possible (p. 240).

Q *We booked scheduled flights to Spain. When we arrived at the airport, we were told that our flight was already full due to* **overbooking**. *We had to wait 14 hours before there was room on another flight. Can the airline do this?*

A Airlines deliberately overbook some scheduled flights to take account of what they call 'no shows' – people who have a ticket that is refundable or transferable and choose not to travel on the flight they have booked. This is unlikely to happen on charter flights. Using previous flights as a guide, airlines try to match seats to passengers. When they get it wrong and too many passengers turn up, somebody has to be **bumped off** the flight:

- under European Community Regulations, which currently only cover scheduled flights from European destinations (but see below), if you check in on time and are **bumped**, you must be offered either a full refund, a seat on the next available flight to your destination or another flight at a later date of your choice. The airline must also offer you on-the-spot cash compensation of around 150 euros for flights up to 3,500 km, and 300 euros for longer flights
- these amounts are halved if the airline can get you to your final destination within two hours (or four hours for flights over 3,500 km) of your original scheduled arrival time
- you must be given a free telephone call to your destination, meals during your wait, and overnight accommodation if necessary
- as it was a scheduled flight, your claim is against the airline.

Q *I've heard that the European Commission has introduced better air passenger rights. What do these say?*

A New regulations from the EC will indeed increase and broaden the current compensation scheme for air travellers who are denied boarding, or where a flight is cancelled or delayed. At the time of going to press these were not yet in force, but were likely to be so from early 2005. The new rules will apply to both scheduled and non-scheduled flights (including air travel sold as part of a package holiday):

- **for overbooking (denied boarding)** the following rights seem likely: (to qualify passengers must have a confirmed reservation on a flight and present themselves for check-in as required by the airline or tour operator, or 45 minutes before departure if no other instructions given)
    - when it's likely that all passengers won't be able to board, before doing anything else airlines must call for volunteers to surrender their seats in exchange for advantages – in short, they will try to strike a deal with passengers interested in giving up their seats. The idea of this is to create an incentive to make volunteering attractive and a powerful deterrent to denying boarding. Only if there are insufficient volunteers would the airline be allowed to deny passengers their seats
    - if the airline has to deny any passenger boarding it must pay cash compensation at the following level: 250 euros for flights of less than 1,500 km, 400 euros for intra-community flights of more than 1500 km (and for other flights between 1,500 km and 3,500 km), and 600 euros for all other flights
    - in addition to the right to financial compensation, passengers denied boarding will continue to be given the choice between reimbursement of their ticket or an alternative flight, together with meals, refreshments and hotel accommodation
- **for cancellation by the airline or tour operator** passengers will have the right to cash compensation at the same levels as those for denied boarding, unless:
    - they are informed two weeks before the scheduled time of departure, or
    - they are informed in due time and rerouted at a time very close to that of their original flight.
  In addition, when a cancellation delays a passenger for at least five hours passengers will receive meals and refreshments, and hotel accommodation, when cancellation obliges passengers to stay overnight, and reimbursement of the ticket.
- **for delays of at least five hours** airlines will be obliged to give passengers meals and refreshments, and hotel accommodation, when a delay means passengers have to stay overnight, and reimbursement of the ticket.

Q *I saw an ad in a travel agent's window for two weeks in Venice for £160. When I went in they told me it was no longer available and offered the same holiday for £250. The ad is still there two weeks later. Can I insist on paying only the price advertised?*

A No. You cannot insist that any trader sells goods and services to you at the price marked (pp. 26–7). But it is an offence knowingly to mislead consumers about the price of goods or services on offer. If an advertised holiday is no longer available, travel agents should remove all material promoting this holiday from their windows and not use it to entice customers into the shop. You should report the matter to the Trading Standards Department at the local council offices (in Northern Ireland, the Trading Standards branch of the Department of Economic Development★).

Q *I saw a flight advertised for £60 but when I went to book I suddenly found another £80 added. The airline told me this was for government tax, or Air Passenger Duty. Surely the advert should have included this?*

A Yes it should. The Consumer Protection Act 1987 makes it a criminal offence for any trader to give a misleading price indication to consumers. And it doesn't matter what form the price indication takes – it can be in a television or press advert, on a notice or billboard, on the Internet, in a shop window or on the edge of a shelf, in a brochure, catalogue or leaflet, and even given orally over the phone.

The Act allows the government to approve a code of practice giving practical guidance to traders. The current 'code of practice on price indications' is due to be reviewed and updated. What it currently says is that any price indication for holiday or travel arrangements must include in the basic price all non-optional extra charges which are for fixed amounts.

Air Passenger Duty (APD) is a tax payable by all people departing by air from a UK airport, so it's a compulsory extra charge. And increasingly your airfare will also include similar taxes charged by the destination country. The amount you pay is fixed, depending on whether you're flying within Europe or outside the EU. So, APD must be included in the price you see quoted whether it's an advert for a package which includes the flight, or simply for the flight alone. Enforcement is by Trading Standards (see above). You should also refer the matter to the Advertising Standards Authority★.

Q *I recently booked a holiday, but the tour operator is now demanding another £100. Can it do this?*

A Check the tour operator's booking conditions to see if they mention **surcharges**. Some brochures boast 'no-surcharge guarantees', which they must honour. Operators must explain what the surcharge is for (usually the reason is changes in exchange rates or increases in fuel prices), and under the ABTA Code of Conduct and the Package Travel Regulations 1992 they must not impose any surcharge less than 30 days before your departure.

The tour operator should absorb increases of up to two per cent of your holiday cost, but may pass on amounts above this. If the surcharge represents a 'significant' change in price (over ten per cent, according to the ABTA 'standards on surcharges') you are entitled to cancel, and are entitled to a full and prompt refund.

Q *When a travel agent or tour operator goes bust, what sort of protection do its customers have?*

A The protection you get when a tour operator or travel agent goes bust depends on the type of travel arrangements you made and with which company you booked. Bonding schemes are financial guarantees intended to prevent you losing your money, or being stranded abroad, in the event of a travel agent, tour operator or airline going out of business. The Package Travel, Package Holidays and Package Tour Regulations 1992 make it a legal requirement that all tour operators must protect their customers so that if they go bust before you travel you will get your money back, or if you are on holiday you will be brought home. However, the regulations implementing this law are confusing and there are significant holes in the umbrella of cover that holidaymakers have. For example, there is currently no compulsory financial protection for full-fare scheduled flights (opposite), or for services such as car hire or hotel accommodation booked as part of an independent holiday.

Many consumers book airline seats on the Internet and then book accommodation from a linked website – but this does not mean you've bought a package and your arrangements are not protected under the Package Travel Regulations. The easiest way of ensuring that your money is safe is to look for one of the established bonding schemes:

- when booking charter flights, or a package holiday which includes flights, use a company with an Air Travel Organisers' Licence (ATOL)★ and make sure you get either the airline tickets or an ATOL receipt with the name and licence number of the ATOL holder. ATOLs are granted by the Civil Aviation Authority (CAA)★. Any travel firm based in the UK selling air travel must hold one of these licences. The protection applies to all payments made to travel firms for a flight or a package holiday that includes a flight. Under the ATOL scheme there is no automatic protection if you book direct with an airline, rather than with a travel firm (see below)
- all members of the Association of British Travel Agents (ABTA)★ are backed by a bond to protect the money you pay the company for your holiday

arrangement. So if the tour operator or travel agent goes bust holidaymakers abroad will be brought back at no extra cost (in most cases at the end of their holiday) and people who have booked and paid for their holidays or flights but have not yet travelled will receive a full refund

- tour operators who are members of the Association of Independent Tour Operators (AITO)★ are also covered by bonds to protect against the insolvency of member companies. The Federation of Tour Operators (FTO)★ and the Association of Bonded Travel Organisers Trust (ABTOT)★ also provide similar protection for your money
- as an extra source of protection, if your flights or holiday cost more than £100 each, and you use your credit card to book direct with the tour operator or airline, you can make your claim against the credit-card company provided that the voucher is made out to the tour operator or airline (p. 152). Some banks promise refunds even if the voucher is made out to the agent. Alternatively, if the tour operator is a member of the ABTA your money will be protected by the Association even if the credit-card company is also liable, as long as there is a booking in place.

Q *When I book a flight is my money protected if the airline goes bust?*

A It depends on the kind of flight and who you paid the money to. The points to consider are:

- if you book a **charter** or **discount scheduled flight** from a travel agent, the person selling the seats must be covered by an Air Travel Organisers' Licence (ATOL)★. If you do not get a ticket immediately when you book, make sure the agent hands over an ATOL receipt giving the name of the ATOL-holder and the licence number. The agent itself may simply be acting as a retail agent for the ATOL-holder so the receipt is the documentation that makes it clear who the ATOL-holder is. It also confirms that you are covered by the financial bond administered by the Civil Aviation Authority (CAA)★
- there is currently no ATOL-like scheme to protect you if a scheduled airline goes bust when you book a scheduled flight direct from the airline, or pay the official published fare. For a couple of pounds you can take out scheduled airline failure insurance but this is not always readily available – ask your travel agent.

Q *Our holiday plans were changed by the tour operator after we had booked. Can the tour operator do this?*

A Most booking conditions and the ABTA★ code let operators make changes they consider small without paying compensation (check the conditions in the brochure). But if the change is a major one or 'significant', the operator must tell you as soon as possible. If you are not happy, you can cancel and get a full refund, or opt for compensation (often on a rising scale set out in the brochure). **Major changes** include moving you to a different resort or altering your flight time, although the significance of the effect of the time change on your holiday will depend on how long you are away for. If it involves extra expense, such as booking into a hotel to catch an early-morning flight, accept **under protest** and **reserve your rights**. Then write to the operator for additional compensation (pp. 199–200).

Q *Can I challenge the tour operator's decision to change my flight to an early-morning one?*

A If your tour operator changes your flight, or any other aspect of your holiday arrangements, check the booking conditions in the brochure: unless the conditions allow such changes, the tour operator is not entitled to make them without breaching your contract. Most booking conditions, and the ABTA★ code of conduct, do allow minor changes to flight times.

Any attempt by the tour operator to limit your right to complain, or to make changes to your holiday arrangements after booking, must be fair and reasonable, otherwise you may have a claim under the Unfair Contract Terms Act 1977 (p. 81) or may be able to complain to one of the 'qualifying bodies', such as the Office of Fair Trading (OFT)★, under the Unfair Terms in Consumer Contracts Regulations 1999 (pp. 88–9).

Q *I asked for a hotel room with a sea view. When I arrived I found the room overlooked the car park. What can I do?*

A It is not generally enough to fill in the 'special request' box on the booking form because the tour operator will only be agreeing to try to provide you with a room with a view, rather than guaranteeing it. Check the brochure terms and booking form. If the operator knew of your requirement and guaranteed it before you booked, it will be part of the contract. So you must ensure that it was shown on your confirmation invoice. If it was guaranteed but was not provided, and things were not put right when you complained, claim compensation (pp. 199–200).

If you've asked for something which is essential to your holiday it would be difficult for the operator to argue it was just a request if it fails to come up with the goods. For example, if you booked a skiing package including car hire from the airport, the roof rack you said you needed to transport your skis would be essential for your journey and not just a nice thing to have. The same could be said of the child seat you asked for if the tour operator knows that you and your young family can't use the car without it. Where things are clearly essential for you to access or enjoy your holiday arrangements, don't be put off pursuing your claim just because things like these have been listed as only on 'special request'.

Q *We booked a holiday via the travel agents in the high street. We also asked them to arrange car hire for the week, with the car being picked up on arrival. When we arrived the car hire had not been arranged. It was high season and so we had to pay more to hire the car than the rate we'd already agreed with the agent. Can we claim this from the agent?*

A Even though you do not have a contract with the travel agent, it is legally obliged to perform its job competently. If it fails in this duty, and you suffer loss as a direct result of its negligence, you can claim compensation from the travel agent. The agent's duty is not only to pass on your holiday booking, but also to make all the other arrangements on your behalf. If it costs you more to hire the car on arrival (because of lack of availability etc.) than you paid by booking in advance, then you are entitled to recover the extra from the agent. This may mean using the small claims procedure, or, if the agent is a member of ABTA★, the independent arbitration scheme (pp. 273–6).

Q *We've just returned from a dreadful package holiday abroad. The first few days were a nightmare, but after complaining to the representative we enjoyed the rest. Our letter to the tour operator produced an offer of £50. But the holiday cost us £1,400. How do we assess the amount of compensation?*

A A tour operator is legally obliged to provide the type and quality of holiday booked, taking account of the price paid, the description in the brochure and any specific requirements. However, the booking conditions may allow for changes of hotel or resort (pp. 197–8). The amount of compensation you can expect to receive following holiday dissatisfaction depends largely on how much the problems affected your enjoyment. Assessing disappointment is not an exact science, however, and if your claim has to go to court or arbitration you may not be able to recover what you want if you were asking for an unreasonable sum.

None the less, there are three basic components of holiday compensation, so add together whichever of the following apply:

- **loss of value** – the difference between the value of the holiday you got and the one you paid for. If, for example, you were put into a cheaper hotel for the first week because the one you booked was full, work out what a week in the cheaper hotel would have cost. You must also take account of those parts of the holiday that were not affected by the problem. If it was only the room that was unsatisfactory, and you were on the beach or out exploring most of the day, the effect will not have been so great. So, if three days out of a total of seven were totally ruined, say, or if there was a continuing problem which partially spoiled the whole of the holiday, the amount in this instance might be about two-thirds of the cost of the holiday

- **out-of-pocket expenses** – the refund of any reasonable expenses you incurred as a result of the tour operator's breach of contract, such as taxi fares incurred because the replacement hotel was farther away from the resort attractions

- **loss of enjoyment** – to compensate you for the disappointment and frustration of your holiday going wrong, and for the hassle involved in trying to sort it out. You must ask yourself whether the holiday was a complete disaster as a result of the tour operator's breach of contract, or OK apart from the unpleasantness of the room, plus the inconvenience of moving to the new hotel. This is the hardest part to assess in any claim as it is highly subjective.

You should complain to the representative when the problems arise, and write as soon as you return (p. 204). If you do not get a satisfactory result, you can either take the tour operator to court, using the small claims track if the amount of your claim is below £5,000 (£1,500 in Scotland), or, if the tour operator is a member of the Association of British Travel Agents (ABTA)★ (most are), you may decide to use ABTA's independent arbitration scheme which can deal with claims up to £25,000. The arbitration scheme is available online (*www.arbitrators.org/ ABTA/*). You cannot do both, as both are final and binding, so you cannot go to court later if you are unhappy with the arbitrator's decision.

Q *The food at our hotel in Spain was very disappointing – poor choice, and either lukewarm, burnt or tasteless. After the first week, we decided to eat out every night. Can we claim this cost from the tour operator?*

A In a package tour which includes meals, there may be a specific promise about food standards in the tour operator's brochure. If so, the tour operator will be in breach of contract if this promise is not kept. And even if no specific promises are made, there is an implied term in your contract with the tour operator that food should be of a reasonable standard, in accordance with the type and price of the holiday. But complaints about food are very subjective. You can certainly argue that your costs of eating out should be reimbursed, but you will have to prove that the food on offer was of a sufficiently poor quality to justify your decision to eat out. Photographic evidence, sample menus, or supportive evidence from fellow holidaymakers may help you win the argument, but cases about poor food are notoriously difficult to prove.

Q *The holiday brochure described our Italian villa as 'peaceful and secluded'. When we got there, it turned out to face directly on to a busy main road, with a big supermarket opposite. Do we have a valid complaint?*

A When you book a holiday from a tour operator's brochure, the Supply of Goods and Services Act 1982 says that the accommodation and facilities must be as represented in the brochure, in both the words and the pictures. Similar requirements are set out in the Package Travel Regulations 1994 and in ABTA's Code of Conduct for its members. The tour operator should notify you of any significant changes. In future, read the description of your accommodation in the *DG & G Agents' Gazeteer* – ask your travel agent to show you a copy. If you do have any sort of complaint:

- tell the tour operator's representative immediately so that, if at all possible, the problem can be put right on the spot. The representative may be able to move you to a quieter villa
- make sure your complaint is recorded in writing to show that you tried to get something done at the time, and ask for a copy of the complaint form
- note the names and addresses of other holidaymakers who can back up your complaint, and take photographs if you think they will be helpful in showing what was wrong; you might also record evidence, including noise levels.
- as soon as you get home, write to the tour operator, setting out the ways in which the villa failed to deliver what the brochure had led you to expect
- ask for compensation for disappointment and inconvenience, and for reimbursement of any additional expenses incurred (pp. 199–200)
- report the tour operator to the Trading Standards Department at the local council offices. Under the Trade Descriptions Act 1968 a tour operator that publishes a brochure which makes untrue representations is guilty of a criminal offence: this will not in itself earn you any compensation but it will encourage the company to be more accurate in future
- report the tour operator to ABTA★ if it is a member of the Association, as it will investigate the matter and may discipline or fine the company for a breach of its Code of Conduct. Complaining to ABTA will also give you access to an independent arbitration scheme which is compulsory on ABTA companies if you choose to use it (pp. 273–6).

Q *We picked what the tour operators described in their brochure as a '3-star' hotel. But it was shabby and dilapidated and had no restaurant. We complained to the tour operators but they said that they had rated it as 3-star, and that was the end of the matter. Can they get away with this?*

A The problem with star ratings is that they vary between countries, even within the European Union. Therefore many tour operators choose to use their own rating system to assess the accommodation they offer. This means that a claim against the tour operator based on the star rating system alone is difficult to argue, unless you can prove that it failed to meet even its own criteria in assessing the accommodation.

However, you may still have a viable claim for compensation, based on the fact that the accommodation was not of a reasonable standard in view of the price paid and/or the descriptions given in the brochure (pp. 198–200).

Q *We booked a last-minute trip to the Greek islands – five days before departure – at a bargain price. We were not told where we would stay, only that it would be at a 2-star hotel. The hotel was extremely simple. There were no en suite facilities and our room was cramped and dingy. It didn't deserve even one star. The tour operator has come up with a letter from the Greek tourist authorities, assessing the hotel as 2-star. What can we do?*

A For a last-minute cheap booking your expectations must reasonably be lower than for a more expensive booking made in advance when you choose a particular hotel on the basis of its brochure description. You cannot base your complaint against the tour operator on the question of the hotel's fitness for a 2-star rating, since it is clear that it was in fact locally rated as being 2-star. Nevertheless, you can argue that the hotel was not of an acceptable standard and that you should be compensated for your loss of enjoyment.

The Package Travel Regulations 1992, which came from a European Union Directive, state that brochures must include the following information:

- the type of accommodation, its location, rating or degree of comfort and the hotel's main features, and
- where the accommodation is to be provided within an EU member state, its approval or tourist classification under the rules of that member state. So the official tourist category must normally be given (although that does not prevent the tour operator from also using its own rating scheme).

But for last-minute bookings (made within 14 days of departure) an organiser or agent need not give full details to the client before the contract is made. This exemption has been included to enable telephone bookings and late bookings like your own to continue.

Q *We'd booked a 4-star hotel as part of our family package holiday to Spain. We chose the hotel for its numerous facilities and pools. When we got there the hotel was full. The tour operator took us to another hotel, but it was of a much lower standard with no children's facilities. We complained at the time, but nothing else was available. Did the tour operator have the right to do this?*

A Accommodation should not be overbooked. When a tour operator confirms your booking for a specific hotel, it is obliged to accommodate you there. If it does not, it is in breach of contract under the Package Travel, Package Holidays and Package Tour Regulations 1992, and the ABTA code:

- if the operator knew about the overbooking before you set off on holiday, you should have been informed and given the option of cancelling or choosing another holiday
- if the problem only became apparent on your arrival, you should have been offered other accommodation of at least equivalent standard. If it is of a lower standard you are entitled to be brought home, or you may opt for compensation (pp. 199–200)
- check the booking conditions in the holiday brochure. These may contain a term which allows the tour operator to put you in a different hotel from the one booked. If it does, you can still insist on coming home, or claim compensation if the alternative was not of the same standard or had fewer facilities etc.
- if you were unhappy with the change of hotel, you were right to complain to the rep immediately and accept the cheaper hotel only **under protest**, ideally in writing (p. 221)
- when comparing your new accommodation with the original, consider convenience of location, quality of surroundings, facilities provided and any extra expense, such as increased travel costs to the beach, or car hire
- you can claim compensation for your loss of enjoyment and the disappointment and inconvenience caused (pp. 199–200).

Q *We booked our summer holiday at a hotel in Tenerife. When we got there, it was still being built. Only the wing we were staying in and one pool (out of three) were completed and only one of the three advertised restaurants was open for business. We asked to be moved, but it was high season and everywhere was full. What should we do?*

A The tour operator's brochure descriptions should be accurate, and it should warn you of any significant factors that could affect your holiday. In this case, the tour operator should definitely have warned you that the hotel was not completed, and arguably should have offered you an alternative hotel since the one offered was essentially not the accommodation you had chosen. You can certainly complain and seek compensation for the difference between the holiday you were promised and the holiday you actually got, as well as compensation for loss of enjoyment, disappointment and inconvenience (pp. 199–200).

Q *Our self-catering apartment was totally unacceptable. It was dirty, had virtually no cutlery, and contained only one cooking ring and a tiny grill in the kitchen. The representative refused to move us, and now we are home the tour operator is refusing to pay us compensation on the grounds that it was a cheap holiday. Does it have the right to refuse?*

A However much or little you paid for your holiday, you are entitled to reasonable standards of cleanliness and adequate facilities. Obviously, your expectations of a holiday should be related to the type and price of package, and the brochure descriptions. But whatever the price and description your apartment should not have been dirty, and if it was advertised as self-catering there should have been enough suitable equipment for you to prepare meals.

Make sure you keep receipts for any expenses to support your claim. You were right to complain to the rep, but since she did not move you, you can now claim compensation from the tour operator. If it refuses to offer compensation, consider the small claims track of the county court, which can deal with claims of up to £5,000 (£1,500 in Scotland, £1,000 in Northern Ireland) (pp. 279–80) or ABTA★ arbitration, which can deal with claims up to £25,000.

Q *The tour operator's representative for our holiday was rude, unhelpful and hardly ever available. Can we complain to the tour operator about her behaviour?*

A Yes. If a tour operator provides you with the services of a representative, he or she should be reasonably courteous and as helpful as is reasonably practicable, as well as being available to a reasonable extent. The services of the rep form part of your holiday contract, so if the rep fails to do his or her job properly you are entitled to compensation, based on an estimate of how much of your holiday it has affected. Make sure you follow up your complaint in writing (p. 201).

Q *We had no hot water for 11 out of the 14 days of our stay in a Portuguese hotel. The tour operator has refused to compensate us, saying that we should have complained to the rep at the time. Will this scupper our claim?*

A You may have seriously damaged your right to compensation. The lack of hot water is undoubtedly a serious matter, and worthy of compensation. But there is a general duty on you to keep your losses to a minimum by complaining on the spot at the earliest possible opportunity. Had you complained at the time, the matter could quite possibly have been rectified by the rep, thus saving you several days of aggravation and saving the tour operator a substantial claim. If the tour operator did not know you had a problem, and could therefore not try to do something about it, the company cannot be held responsible for the full extent of your disappointment and distress. So even if you do succeed in getting some compensation from the operator, the amount is likely to be reduced to reflect your failure to complain at the time.

Q *I had problems with my holiday accommodation and filled in a complaint form at the time, but because of work commitments I didn't follow up my complaint for a fortnight after my return. The holiday company has pointed to a term in the booking conditions which says that complaints should be made in writing within seven days of return. Can the tour operator hold me to this?*

A Normally, the law allows you a period of six years from a breach of contract to bring a claim. Only after the six years have elapsed does it become too late to issue proceedings, so that effectively your claim is time-barred (p. 22). In some circumstances a company can alter this general rule – as the tour operator has attempted to do – by putting its own time limit in its contractual conditions. This term attempts to limit your right to claim compensation, but by virtue of the Unfair Contract Terms Act 1977 such an attempt to limit or exclude liability will be valid only if it is fair and reasonable in all the circumstances (p. 81). It would ultimately be for a court to decide whether in the circumstances this seven-day time limit is reasonable.

As limits for claims are quite common in holiday booking conditions, the tour operator may cite it as part of its defence and it is possible that the court will rule in the tour operator's favour. A seven day limit would however be exceptional. You can challenge the term (the time-limit clause) as part of your claim for compensation (pp. 199–200) or refer it to the Office of Fair Trading (OFT)*, say, under the Unfair Terms in Consumer Contracts Regulations 1999 (pp. 88–9). Under these Regulations the company could be forced to remove the term from all its standard contracts so that no one will fall foul of it in future. The advice is to complain as early as possible in writing, and always to read through contractual conditions, preferably before a problem arises.

Q *My husband and I booked a holiday to Africa six months ago. We paid a 50 per cent deposit to the tour operator and were due to travel next month. We have just heard that the company is **insolvent** and no longer trading. The company was not ABTA-bonded, but we paid the deposit (£2,000) by credit card. Is there anything we can do?*

A Possibly. Under the Package Travel Regulations 1992, all tour operators must have in place a system of financial protection to ensure you get a refund, or to bring you home from your holiday destination, if they cease trading. You should have been given details of the cover provided. If you have these details, contact the body or company that arranged the financial protection. However, measures taken to enforce the regulations are still inadequate, so there is in such a case no guarantee of protection. Meanwhile:

* until it is shown that the regulations work in practice, it is worth choosing a holiday company which is ABTA- or ATOL-bonded, to maximise your protection should the company cease trading (p. 196)
* if you have paid for at least part of your holiday by credit card, and things go wrong, under the Consumer Credit Act 1974 you can claim from the credit-card company as well as the tour operator (though you cannot recover compensation from both). This is particularly valuable in cases where the supplier goes out of business as it means that you can pursue the credit-card company for the return of your money (p. 151). But:

- your holiday must cost more than £100 per person
- the credit-card slip must usually have been made out to the tour opera-tor, not the travel agent, although some credit-card companies have voluntarily accepted liability in these cases
- debit cards, charge cards and some gold cards do not offer this protection as the protection only covers credit cards.

Q *Following an accident my wife has recently become a wheelchair-user. What service can she expect from travel agents and airlines? I'm wary of booking and flying now as so many things can go wrong.*

A All the services provided by travel agents and tour operators in the UK are covered by the Disability Discrimination Act (DDA) (pp. 89–90). So brochures, websites, booking forms etc. must all be reasonably accessible. Airports, travel agents and tour operators' premises are also covered by the DDA and they must make reasonable adjustments to the way they provide their services so that disabled people can get access. You cannot be made to pay for individual assis-tance at the airport from check-in to boarding, say. When the final phase of the DDA comes into force in October 2004 reasonable adjustments will have to be made to business premises to remove or alter any physical obstacles which prevent access to the premises.

As the DDA is a piece of domestic law, overseas services such as hotels, car hire, etc., are not covered. Aeroplanes themselves are not currently covered by the legislation although current government proposals could see airlines brought within the law if access isn't improved within the aviation industry voluntarily. The government is currently monitoring the effect of the voluntary aviation code – 'Access to Air Travel for Disabled People – Code of Practice' which was published in March 2003. This sets out what is expected from travel agents, tour operators, airports and airlines. The full code is available at *www.mobility-unit.dft.gov.uk/airaccess/index.htm* and includes a 'checklist for disabled and less mobile passengers' developed by ABTA★. The checklist is aimed at ensuring that travellers can give relevant information about their needs and that service providers such as tour operators, airlines and hotels understand what is needed to provide services which are enjoyable and safe.

The Disabled Persons Transport Advisory Committee (DPTAC)★ has also produced a guide for disabled consumers. The full guide is available at *www.dptac.gov.uk/pubs/aviation/access/index.htm*.

The DDA gives you the right to take action direct against the service provider (p. 90). You can also refer your complaint to the Disability Rights Commission (DRC)★, which can provide guidance and, in some cases, take legal action on your behalf.

Q *I'm always being pestered by* **timeshare** *touts when on holiday. The idea seems so attractive, but there must be a catch. How can I protect myself if I go to one of the presentations?*

A Timeshare reps offer inducements to attend a presentation in the hope that you will be persuaded to make an on-the-spot financial commitment, often for many thousands of pounds. And it is even more enticing when you are in a hot and sunny country away from home. Whether you are at home or abroad, follow these guidelines:

- do not go along unless you're really interested in buying
- be prepared for a long, hard sell
- **never sign anything** on the day – even if you are offered a large 'today only' discount
- always ask for copies of all the documentation – brochures, plans, terms and conditions, finance agreements – so that you can take them away and think them over after taking advice
- if you are interested in a timeshare, do some research among resale agencies to find out how easy or costly it would be to resell your timeshare later – you may find that resale agencies offer more competitive prices than developers on the spot
- if you are buying a timeshare abroad (or even one in the UK that says it is not governed by English or Scots law) be very careful. Your rights, should anything go wrong, will be governed by the law of the country stated, so you would need to find a lawyer in that country to help you, which could prove extremely inconvenient and expensive, although there are regulations for countries within Europe which lay down ground rules for consumer protection (pp. 208–9)
- if the timeshare contract is made in the UK, the Timeshare Act 1992 gives customers a right to cancel the contract (pp. 20–1 and below) within 14 days
- if the timeshare contract is made elsewhere in the EU, or where the property is in the European Economic Area (EEA), the Timeshare Regulations 1997 spell out the information you must be given and the form the contract must take (pp. 208–9).
- in recent years many 'holiday clubs' have also sprung up. These are not covered by timeshare legislation, so be very wary about any promises they might make.

Q *I attended a timeshare presentation and signed an agreement for two weeks at a development in Wales. Now I realise how foolish I was. Is it too late to cancel?*

A There are some golden rules to follow if you attend a timeshare presentation or are offered a timeshare agreement (see above). The Timeshare Act 1992 not only gives you more protection for timeshares purchased in the UK than is available if you buy a timeshare property or sign a timeshare contract in other European countries (see below), but has also been amended and strengthened by new European regulations. The Act provides for a 14-day (minimum) cooling-off period in timeshare contracts provided that *either*:

- the contract is signed by either party within the UK, or
- the contract is subject to the laws of the UK.

Before you make the agreement, the timeshare company must give you notice of the right to cancel the contract at any time during the cooling-off period. It is a criminal offence for the timeshare company not to do this. Furthermore:

- a cancellation form should be attached to the notice setting out your cancellation rights
- the seller is not allowed to ask for or take any money from you during the cooling-off period, for him- or herself or for anyone else. A reputable company will not ask for a deposit. If you have paid over any money, and if you cancel during the cooling-off period, you are entitled to recover any money you have paid under the contract
- the same cooling-off period applies in the case of most timeshare credit agreements in which credit is offered to pay for the timeshare, although it is not a criminal offence if the company fails to hand over a notice of your rights to cancel a timeshare credit agreement.

If you have any problems relating to timeshare, contact your local Trading Standards Department or the Organisation for Timeshare in Europe★, the trade association which represents many British timeshare companies. The Timeshare Consumers Association★ is also a useful source of information.

Q *There are so many horror stories of people signing timeshare contracts while on holiday around the world. Aren't there any international laws to protect timeshare buyers?*

A International laws do not offer any consistent minimum protection, but there is certainly good protection within the European Economic Area (EEA). This comes from the Timeshare Directive 1997. The EEA includes all countries that are members of the European Union (including the Spanish islands making up the Canaries and Balearics) as well as Norway, Iceland and Liechtenstein. For consumers buying timeshare in the UK, protection has been in place for a number of years in the form of the Timeshare Act 1992. This has been amended and extended by the 1997 Regulations, and on some issues still provides better protection than you get elsewhere in Europe. It doesn't matter whose the property is, as long as the contract is signed in the UK and as long as it doesn't claim to be governed by the laws of any other country. The main elements of consumer protection are as follows:

- a cooling-off period of at least ten days from the day you sign the timeshare contract. With contracts in the UK you have the right to cancel within 14 days and you will not have to lose a penny. Elsewhere in Europe you may have to pay any necessary legal costs of making the contract, such as the cost of a lawyer witnessing the signatures, say, but these should be clearly set out in the contract itself
- it is illegal for a seller to ask for any money from you up-front, so if you want to sign you are entitled to refuse to pay a deposit
- if you ask for information on the property before deciding whether to buy, the seller must supply a document accurately describing the accommodation. This must give realistic deadlines for completion of construction if the property has not yet been built, and describe the state of services such as telephones and gas connections, shared facilities such as swimming pools, the timeshare periods that can be bought, and whether those periods can be swapped or resold. If the sale goes ahead this information becomes part of the contract
- if you ask for it the seller must give you the brochure and contract in your own language and a translation in the language of the country where the timeshare is situated (you may need this if you have to go to court).

A European trade association exists and operates a code of practice. Membership includes many British timeshare developers and marketing companies. Contact the Organisation for Timeshare in Europe (OTE)★. Another contact is the Timeshare Consumers' Association★.

Q *We went along to a holiday presentation which was very exciting and claimed that we could afford a holiday every year if we joined the holiday scheme. So we signed up and paid a membership fee. But when we tried to book we had trouble getting through to the company. And when we did there was little we could afford despite the initial promises of cheap holidays for life. My husband and I are elderly and can't afford to buy foreign holidays every year so this looked very attractive. But nor can we afford to lose our money. Can we cancel and get our money back?*

A That's unlikely. This sounds like a holiday club, which differs from timeshare in a number of important ways – the most important is that there is no law to protect consumers as there is with timeshare (pp. 207–8).

Holiday clubs are marketed as a flexible alternative to timeshare and offer consumers the facility to make reservations in timeshare accommodation.

A deposit (usually a few hundred pounds) and a fee (usually a few thousand pounds) are payable up front. These buy you 'membership' of the holiday club.

On top of these you then pay an annual subscription. The membership is said to give you access to discounted holidays over a specific period of time. What you don't buy is the right to use a specific property or to choose from a specific pool of property. This takes it outside the current timeshare law. So, if you sign up you can't always change your mind because there's no automatic cooling-off period as there is with genuine timeshare (p. 207).

High-pressure selling is common here, backed up with offers of a free holiday or prizes. You may find you're the holder of a 'winning' ticket which entitles you to attend a VIP presentation to get your prize. You'll then have to sit through a long presentation, usually for a number of hours. Or you'll get a phone call at home claiming you're the winner of a prize draw and inviting you to a 'presentation'. You will receive exciting promises in return for a deposit and your signature on the agreement.

Some consumers are asked to pay in return for a specified number of points which can be used to buy holidays through the holiday company's website. But there is no guarantee that the points have a particular value or that they will keep their value. Many consumers find it difficult to contact the company to make a booking. And the promises don't always match the reality. When this happens your comeback depends largely on the policy of the company you have your contract with. There are no laws to protect you in the way there are with timeshare.

Underlying all of this is the fact that there is no financial protection in place for your money if the company goes into liquidation. Not all holiday clubs are disreputable but to avoid being caught always consider the following:

- Can you take the contract away and come back in a few days' time with your decision?
- Do you have cancellation rights, and are they written down in the contract?
- Is everything in writing in the contract that was promised to you at the presentation?
- But with little protective legislation in place, it is wise to consider whether signing up is worth the risk.

Q *Our hotel in Tunisia was very pleasant, with good food and facilities, but our holiday was marred by the building work going on across the road – a massive new apartment complex was under construction. The work started at 5 a.m. every day and we could not sit on our balcony due to the noise and dust. The tour operator is refusing to compensate us for this, claiming that it is not responsible for circumstances outside its direct control. What can we do?*

A The tour operator may be right. But you would certainly be entitled to compensation for the loss of enjoyment (and sleep!) if:

- the building work was going on within the hotel itself, in which case you could reasonably have expected at least to have been warned in advance and to have been offered an alternative hotel if the disruption to your holiday would be great
- this new complex had been under construction for some considerable time before your holiday, in which case you could argue that the tour operator, via its rep, ought to have known about the proximity of the work and should at least have warned you.

ABTA's* Code of Conduct says that where a tour operator becomes aware, or ought reasonably to have become aware, of building works which may reasonably be considered to seriously impair the enjoyment of a holiday, it must, without undue delay, tell clients of the situation and give them a chance to transfer to another hotel at the appropriate price or to cancel without penalty. The operator must also make sure that all prospective clients are alerted to the situation. Where imminent works are known about, relevant information should appear on the appropriate brochure page.

Q *Our holiday was spoiled by the group of loud holidaymakers in the next apartment. They played their ghetto-blasters from 1 a.m. till dawn every night for a week. We complained to the rep after the first occasion, but he was only able to find us somewhere to move to after the first week of our fortnight's holiday had gone by. Shouldn't the tour operator compensate us?*

A The tour operator is not liable for the activities of other guests, even those who are its own clients. However, assuming that alternative accommodation was available somewhere in the resort at an earlier stage than one week into your holiday, you could argue that the company should have responded positively to your complaint much earlier and should have moved you in the first couple of days. In addition, if the troublesome party was travelling with your tour operator, it would have been reasonable for the rep at least to have asked them to pipe down. It is worth your trying to obtain compensation for the poor quality of the first week's holiday on this basis. However, you don't have a watertight case.

Q *After booking a room in a Brighton hotel I had to cancel. I told the hotelier immediately, but he kept my deposit and wrote asking for extra compensation. Is he entitled to this?*

A If a hotel accepts your booking (whether it is made by phone, letter or in person), you have made a binding contract whereby the hotel agrees to provide the accommodation for the specified dates at the agreed price, and you agree to pay for it. If you later back out, or fail to turn up, the hotel can keep your deposit to cover its administrative costs. The hotel must try to re-let your room, but if it cannot it may claim the profit it has lost from you, and this is likely to be a high proportion of the total price.

Q *While I was staying at a hotel my video camera was stolen from my room. Is the hotel liable?*

A Hotel owners owe you a duty of care and must look after your property while it is on their premises. They are liable for any loss and damage as long as it was not your fault (your claim would be unlikely to succeed if you left the camera clearly visible in a ground-floor room with the door and window unlocked). However, under the Hotel Proprietors Act 1956, providing the hotel owners display a notice at reception, they can limit their liability to £50 per item or £100 in total. They cannot rely on this limit if the loss was caused by the negligence of their staff, although you will have to prove such negligence to make a higher claim. Check whether you are covered for your loss on the all-risks section of your house contents policy.

Q *The cottage we stayed in in the Lake District was dirty, badly furnished and dilapidated. We had paid over £400 for the week, and had expected much better. When we complained, the tour company said we should take it up with the owner, since their small print says that they act only as agents for the proprietors. Whom should we sue?*

A Strictly, the wording of the booking conditions is conclusive, as it forms part of your contract and is binding upon both parties. Therefore, be prepared to pursue the matter with the proprietor. Whatever the contract says about ownership, however, the agents are responsible for the accuracy of brochures that they publish and could be liable for a breach of the Trade Descriptions Act 1968, so report any inaccuracies to the Trading Standards Department at the council offices local to the tour company.

Q *The hotel brochure promised floodlit tennis courts. When we arrived the courts were neglected and uneven, the nets were down and we couldn't play. Do we have any redress?*

A Under the Supply of Goods and Services Act 1982 a hotel must provide the advertised facilities. If it fails to do so you can claim compensation, or ask for an appropriate reduction from your bill in respect of the disappointment suffered, which will depend on the emphasis placed on the facilities by the hotel in the brochure and the amount you intended to use them. Keep receipts for any extra outgoings incurred to make up for the lack of tennis courts. Photographs of the court would also be useful. You should also report the matter to the Trading Standards Department local to the hotel, which may prosecute the hotel under the Trade Descriptions Act 1968.

Q *When I arrived at the hotel where I'd booked a weekend break, I was told that they had made a mistake and the hotel was full. The only other hotel in the area that had room for me was a more expensive one in the next town, so I'm out of pocket. What are my rights?*

A The hotel accepted your booking and was obliged to keep a room available for you. It is in breach of contract and liable to compensate you for the additional expenses arising out of that breach – the difference in cost between what you were expecting to pay and what you ended up having to pay in the more expensive hotel, plus any extra travelling costs. You should write to the hotel manager explaining what happened, and enclosing copies of receipts for your additional expenditure (pp. 199–200).

Q *While I was in bed in my hotel room a section of the ceiling caved in. I was shaken and slightly injured, but it could have been worse. Can I claim for the shock and injuries?*

A Under the Occupiers' Liability Act 1957 hotel owners are responsible for the physical safety of their guests (pp. 256–7). You have a claim for compensation and would be wise to seek legal advice to have your injury claim properly assessed.

Q *When I called to book a room the hotel told me it would cost more if I wanted to pay by credit card. Is this legal?*

A Yes. **Dual pricing** has been legal since 1991, and some hoteliers have increased their charges to guests who pay by credit card in order to recover the commission they pay to the card company. But to be entitled to the increased charge hoteliers must draw it to your attention when you book and indicate it on the tariff displayed in the reception. If you were not informed, contact the Trading Standards Department at the council offices local to the hotel.

Q *My hotel room was shabby and dirty with soiled towels and grubby sheets. I refused to pay the whole bill, but then the hotel refused to let me remove my luggage until I settled up in full. Was the hotel within its rights to hold my luggage hostage like this?*

A Any hotel room, whatever its price, should be clean and safe and offer a reasonable standard of accommodation for the price paid. As yours failed to do so it is reasonable to seek a reduction in the bill. However, the hotel does have a right to hold on to your luggage until the bill is paid.

It is probably easier to pay up in full but give written notice that you are paying **under protest** and are reserving your right to seek compensation in the courts (pp. 230–1).

Q *I've booked three places on a flight to Spain but I've been told that I can't pre-book the actual seats. I know that other customers have specific seat reservations on the same flight. What is the legal position?*

A There is hardly ever a guarantee that you will get specific seats, and you certainly have no legal right to insist on a particular seat unless your specific demand is accepted or if you have paid for the service. Some airlines and tour operators will pre-book seat allocations on payment of £5–£10, allowing you and your companions to sit together. Only if you do manage to get a specific guarantee of particular seats will a promise have been made that you can enforce. But in most cases your 'request' will be just that – a request which the airline or operator will honour if it can. If it cannot there are no grounds for complaint. At present much depends on the policy of the tour operator, airline and agent.

Q *I was due to go on my annual holiday next week but there has been a terrorist attack in the country I'm going to. I want to cancel as I don't want to put my family at risk, but the tour operator is saying I'll have to pay cancellation charges. What is my legal position?*

A In most cases no one is at fault when world events change our desire to travel. In practice what consumers are entitled to is dictated by a combination of the law and, if it's an ABTA company, the ABTA Code of Conduct. Some typical scenarios may help make sense of it all:

- where it has become impossible to get to the country, cancellation of the holiday will be the only option. For example, war in your chosen destination, or a natural disaster in the resort, means that nobody would be expected to holiday there – indeed civilian flights would probably be grounded anyway. This would represent what in law is known as a 'frustrating event'. In short, something happens to make it impossible to perform the holiday contract. Another legal term, 'force majeure', would also cover it. This is an unusual and unforeseeable event beyond everybody's control which prevents you travelling. Either way, you'd be entitled to a full refund and would not be subject to any cancellation charges
- where there's been a terrorist attack, or where the country or resort is close to, but not directly involved in, a war, say, and flights are still going – travel may be physically possible, but you may be disinclined to travel because of fear for your safety. In law this is a little more tricky. Risk is very subjective, and if you simply decide you don't want to travel the law and ABTA's Code may not help. You may be subject to the travel company's cancellation charges.

Everything depends on what the UK Foreign and Commonwealth Office (FCO) travel advice says. The FCO is considered the arbiter in such matters, and your rights are governed by the practice of travel companies and airlines of following this advice. But even this can be confusing for consumers. A blanket warning saying that there's a high risk in the destination doesn't give you the right to cancel your holiday and demand your money back, nor to postpone your travel plans. Only if the FCO advises specifically against 'non-essential' travel to a particular destination do your rights kick in. Then tour operators and most airlines will allow customers to transfer their booking to a later date, a different destination or, at the very least, cancel and get a refund. The law doesn't allow additional compensation claims for disappointment, say.

Because FCO advice can change at any time the right to cancel covers short periods at a time. If you've booked to travel in six months' time, say, and the FCO advice is currently against travel, don't think about cancelling now unless you want to lose your deposit.

If you're already in a destination at the time the FCO advice changes, your operator or airline will either encourage you to move to another destination or to return to the UK. Again, no compensation is payable but you're entitled to a refund of any unused services, such as hotel costs.

Q *When I went to claim on my holiday insurance I was told that due to my pre-existing medical condition my policy wouldn't cover me so I had no valid cover at all. Who can I complain to?*

A The regulation of general insurance has been through a series of shake-ups over the last few years and is still in transition. Ultimately regulation will be under the Financial Services Authority (FSA)★ (p. 166) although the General Insurance Standards Council (GISC)★ (p. 238) will continue to regulate most general insurance until January 2005. Under the new regime insurance brokers and insurers will be subject to FSA regulation, but insurance sold by travel agents and tour operators in conjunction with travel arrangements will be exempt from FSA regulation until 2007, when the government will review the exemption. So if the policy was sold with travel arrangements by an ABTA agent or operator, complain to ABTA★. You can make use of the independent arbitration scheme. If it was a non-ABTA company you'll have to refer it to Trading Standards for help.

Q *My mother suffered from deep vein thrombosis (DVT) which I'm convinced developed because of the cramped seating on her holiday flight. What are her rights against the airline?*

A Estimates suggest that one in ten of us will develop blood clots after long flights. This may be hard to prove as most DVT sufferers tend not to show symptoms (or in extreme cases, die) while on the aircraft – it usually happens some time later and if there is a death DVT is not always recorded as the cause. Although it's not an exclusive air travel problem – sitting in a car, on a bus or train for long periods without any exercise can also present risks – the press has labelled air travel as the culprit and given prominence to a number of cases, including some tragic deaths.

To succeed in a claim you would have to prove that the DVT was caused by sitting for a long time on a cramped aircraft. You would also have to show that the airline failed to warn you of the dangers. But, even if you could prove these things, as the law stands at the time of going to press, the airline will not be legally responsible to compensate you for death or injury caused by DVT.

In 2003 the Court of Appeal considered a group action brought by passengers and dependants against 27 airlines, but threw out their claim. Passengers' rights are governed by international convention. If you want compensation for death or personal injury the airlines are only liable if you can bring a claim under the 1929 Warsaw Convention. Article 17 of the Convention says that the airline 'is liable for damage sustained in case of death or wounding of a passenger or any other bodily injury suffered by a passenger, if the accident which caused the accident so sustained took place on board the aircraft'. The crucial question for the Appeal Court judges was whether DVT was an 'accident' as defined by the Convention. They decided that 'accident' means that the death or injury must result from an 'event' which is external to the passenger – yet DVT is a result of a passenger's own internal susceptibility to thrombosis, or a reaction to the normal operation of the aircraft. So the claims failed. The fact that an airline gave no warning about the dangers of DVT made no difference under the Convention. In practice, the decision means:

- when a passenger is injured the airline's sole legal liability is under international convention – there's no claim for negligence, and no Human Rights Act liability; only the Warsaw Convention applies. If a passenger can't make their claim fit under the Convention, then they have no claim at all
- if you do suffer DVT it's unlikely your travel insurance will cover you for the same reason – most policies cover 'accidents' and injuries. As the Court of Appeal decided that DVT is not an 'accident' there can be no insurance claim. DVT is also increasingly specifically excluded by many policies. In law, a claim only arises where the passenger can prove that there has been death or injury caused by an 'accident' while on board an aircraft or while getting on or off
- travel insurance cover may not be available for a number of reasons – your policy may specifically exclude DVT, and you're unlikely to be covered for this under 'accident'. Or if DVT didn't arise until you got home it will not be covered under illness on holiday. And a claim for illness could be excluded under the policy as an 'existing condition' which simply came to light as a result of the flight.

Q *What rights do airlines have to deal with air rage or disruptive passengers?*

A Although you may be flying through the airspace of different countries, the law which applies to aircraft remains fairly constant during the journey. Around 170 countries, including the UK, signed up to the 1963 Tokyo Convention. The effect of this is that the country where the airline is registered has the authority to apply its own laws to passengers on board. So, with a UK-registered plane, if anything happens once the doors are shut it's British law that applies until the plane lands and the doors are opened at the destination. The UK can also assume jurisdiction over aircraft arriving in the UK, and therefore over any disruptive passengers on board.

Passengers may be detained on arrival and sent home immediately, or even locked up and then tried in the destination country's courts. Other passengers have received a life-long ban from travelling on planes, trains and ferries. So the punishments for bad behaviour can be pretty harsh and difficult to predict. The UK's Civil Aviation Authority (CAA) now requires all UK-registered airlines to report every incident.

After the catastrophic terrorist attack of 11 September 2001 there has been a massive increase in heightened security at airports and on aircraft – and there's no longer a light touch to legal action. Apart from criminal prosecution, the airlines have civil rights too. When you buy a ticket and you make a contract with the airline, you agree to be bound by the standard 'conditions of carriage'. Airlines can refuse to let you on the plane, and even ban you from travel, for a whole host of reasons. They range from using threatening, abusive or insulting words or behaviour, to being drunk, or simply that your presence on the plane may affect the comfort of any person in the aircraft.

Once on board, there's a no-nonsense approach to 'unacceptable behaviour', which includes failing to obey the seatbelt sign, and causing discomfort or inconvenience to other passengers. And if the aircraft has to be diverted to an unscheduled place of destination you may have to pay the reasonable costs of the diversion.

Q *My train to work is consistently about a quarter of an hour late, and sometimes even later. Aren't there supposed to be standards for trains to make sure customers like me get a good service and compensation if those standards are not met?*

A Every rail company must have its own **Passengers' Charter**. This means that each company must set and publish its own performance targets for punctuality, reliability and compensation. It must also tell customers how to complain. Details should be displayed at all staffed stations and updated at monthly intervals (this does not always happen in practice). If you have suffered poor service you may be entitled to compensation. The amount depends on what sort of ticket you have bought and the extent of the problem:

- **season ticket holders (for a month or longer)** For generally poor punctuality or reliability, compensation is payable if the company fails to meet one or both targets by more than a few per cent over the period of a month or longer. But this depends on the overall targets of the company. The company may operate a number of lines. If you are on a particularly bad line, yet on average the company's routes are all right, you will get nothing. Compensation is paid in the form of a 5 per cent discount off your next season ticket (or 10 per cent if both targets are missed). Confusingly, most companies are allowed to miss their punctuality target by 3 per cent and the reliability target by 1 per cent before discounts are paid. For a one-off delay of an hour or more on any single journey, compensation is paid according to the limits for season ticket compensation set out in the rail company's Passengers' Charter. If this doesn't make provision for season ticket compensation you're entitled to claim 10 per cent of the total price of your season ticket, divided by the number of days for which it was valid when you bought it. You must complain within two working days of the delayed journey

- **one-off journeys and weekly tickets** If your train is delayed by more than an hour the precise level of compensation differs between train companies, but you are entitled to travel vouchers worth at least 20 per cent of the value of your journey, whichever train company you have travelled with. However, this is not paid automatically – you will have to contact the company to ask for a refund. Either get a complaint form from the station, or phone or write to the company. The phone number and address should be displayed on trains and at stations. Some companies offer more than the minimum compensation required, sometimes giving vouchers worth up to 40 per cent for an hour's delay. You have to get your claim form in within two working days of the delayed journey.

Q *I'm not getting anywhere with my complaint against the rail company I use to get to work. Is there a central body to which I can complain?*

A For any complaint you should first write to the customer service section at the head office of the train operating company (TOC) concerned. Details should be on display on notices at the station or in the phone book (staff at the station must have this available). If you remain unhappy contact the secretary of your local regional Rail Passengers Committee★. There are eight around the country and they will mediate in any complaint with the TOC which you can't resolve on your own.

The Committees are co-ordinated centrally by the Rail Passengers Council (RPC)★ and deal with issues such as punctuality and reliability of train services, overcrowding, cleanliness, fares, facilities on stations, timetables and access. Make sure you enclose copies of all correspondence. All eight Committees and the RPC are sponsored by the Strategic Rail Authority (SRA)★ which has many powers to ensure that the TOCs do not neglect their commitments to the travelling public in providing services and running trains. It can impose financial penalties and ultimately withdraw the franchise of a TOC if it doesn't comply with the terms of its franchise.

If your complaint concerns the condition or maintenance of the railway network contact Network Rail★. This is the railway network operator which replaced Railtrack in 2002. And if you're unhappy with the response contact the Office of the Rail Regulator (ORR)★. The regulator was set up as part of the privatisation of the industry to protect rail users' interests and deals with companies' relationships with passengers, including matters such as whether they are giving correct information about ticket prices.

You can complain directly to the ORR, but it is unlikely to help with individual problems unless you have first taken your complaint to the TOC and then your local Rail Passengers Committee.

Q *My local train company has a tendency to terminate late trains before the advertised end of the route, and I have often been left stranded. Surely this isn't allowed?*

A The Passenger Service Requirements lay down the minimum service level a train operating company (TOC) must provide, both in terms of overall frequency and first/last trains. When any train is cancelled, or terminated short of its destination, the TOC has to pay a penalty to the Strategic Rail Authority (SRA). Similarly, the TOC has to compensate passengers under the National Conditions of Carriage and/or its own Charter, regardless of the type of train, and, in the same way, has an obligation to get passengers to their final destination. This could involve anything from paying for a taxi, say, to overnight accommodation. Unresolved complaints should be made to the RPC★ (see above).

Chapter 9

Eating and drinking

Health and **hygiene** are important issues in restaurants. What are your rights if the meal makes you ill, or if the food is not properly cooked? And whether it's called a '**tip**', '**optional gratuity**' or '**compulsory service charge**', are you legally obliged to pay extra for the service you've had? What if you book a table and don't turn up, or turn up and find there is no table for you?

Q *We recently had **appalling service** at a restaurant – the waiter was rude and took ages to serve us. We complained at the end of the meal but paid the bill because we felt we were under pressure. Does this mean we can't get our money back?*

A Possibly, yes, although it is still worth writing to the manager of the restaurant to ask. You should always try to speak to the manager or head waiter at the time, and if you fail to reach an agreement you can deduct a suitable amount from the bill.

The bill is made up of two main parts – a charge for the food and drink, and a charge for the service (with VAT on top). If the food and drink are acceptable but the service is not of a reasonable standard, you can deduct a reasonable sum from that part of the bill, and leave your name and address with the restaurant (p. 225). It will then be up to the restaurant to claim against you for the rest if it does not agree with the deduction:

- if the service charge is **compulsory** and automatically **added** to your bill, you are legally obliged to pay it unless the service was unsatisfactory, in which case you can deduct all or part of that charge
- if the service charge is not added because the prices **include** service, again you are legally obliged to pay. But you can deduct a reasonable sum, say 15 per cent, from the total bill for the service element if it is not up to scratch
- if the service charge is not included and not added, and is entirely **optional** or **at your discretion**, there is no legal obligation on you to pay anything extra, so it is up to you to decide whether to tip and, if so, how much.

If you do decide to pay the bill inclusive of service in full, then you can pay **under protest** (put this in writing – on the back of the cheque, say) and write to the restaurant as soon as you can afterwards (p. 240). Make sure you keep a copy of the letter. By paying under protest you are keeping open the option of claiming the money back later, if necessary by taking the matter to the small claims court (pp. 279–80).

Q *We went to a local restaurant which had been recommended by friends. It was only when we sat down that we were able to check the prices and realised that everything was very expensive. Shouldn't information about prices be clearly displayed?*

A It is best to check prices before you sit down. If you turn up without a booking you are within your rights to leave if you haven't ordered. However, if you have booked in advance but on arrival decide it is too expensive and leave, even if you haven't yet ordered, the restaurant may sue for loss of profit if it cannot re-fill the table (p. 222). If you are not sure you can afford it, ask about the prices of the food and any extra charges, such as cover or service charges, before you book.

There are rules as to what information a restaurant or bar should give you before you make any commitment. These are mainly contained in the Price Marking (Food and Drink Services) Order 2003. If the information below is not clearly displayed you should report the establishment to the Trading Standards Department at the local council offices:

- a restaurant must display prices on a menu at, or near, the entrance, so that you can see them before you sit down
- in a pub, the menu can be on or near the bar counter or at the table, depending on where you order the food
- all prices on the menus outside and inside a restaurant must **include VAT**
- the menu displayed at or near a restaurant entrance must also show any **service, cover or minimum charges**.

Q *In a restaurant recently I was served chicken that wasn't properly cooked. The waitress took it away, but when it came back it was still almost raw and certainly inedible. Was I obliged to pay for it?*

A The Supply of Goods and Services Act 1982 (common law in Scotland) obliges restaurants to prepare food (and provide service) with reasonable skill and care: if they don't you are right to stop eating and tell the waiter. If you are unable to get things put right, you can deduct a reasonable sum from the bill – in this case, the cost of your chicken, for example – and refuse to pay some or all of the service charge if the service was not up to scratch. But you must pay for the food you did eat and the wine you drank, and the other parts of the meal which were all right. Alternatively you can pay the full bill **under protest** and effectively reserve your right to make a claim later.

Q *We had booked a table for four but had to cancel because one of the party fell ill. The restaurant wants to charge us for the likely cost of our meal. Can it do this?*

A When you book a table, you are making a contract with the restaurant: it has to provide a table, and you have to turn up at or near the time booked. If you are very late – or don't turn up at all – the restaurant can claim reasonable compensation for its loss of business if it is unable to fill the table again. The restaurant must prove that it made reasonable efforts to fill the table to reduce its loss, so it cannot simply sit back, turn people away and claim the cost of the meal from you. If it does fill the table – because it is a very popular and busy restaurant, say – then it can't charge you.

Q *The restaurant asked for my credit-card number when I booked over the phone. If I don't turn up, can it charge anything to my credit-card account?*

A An increasing number of restaurants now ask for your credit card number when you book. They may then use it to deduct a sum to compensate them for loss should you fail to keep your booking. By giving the number over the phone, you may be authorising payment for the meal, or for compensation should you not arrive. And you may then find it harder to dispute the sum. If you do not want to leave your card number, try leaving your name and address as security instead: this shows good faith and the restaurant knows where to contact you to take the matter further.

Q *I had booked a table in advance for my mother's birthday, but when we arrived there was no table for us. It was such a disappointment. What are our rights?*

A When you book a table in advance, you make a contract with the restaurant and it is obliged to provide you with the table you have booked for the requisite number of people at the specified time. As there was no table for you, despite your booking, the restaurant was in breach of contract and you can claim a reasonable sum to cover any expenses you incur as a result, such as travel costs. You can also claim a reasonable sum as compensation for the disappointment and inconvenience suffered. The amount you claim depends on the importance to you of eating at that particular restaurant, whether it was a special occasion, and the trouble involved in making alternative last-minute arrangements.

Q *We went to a smart restaurant last week. The prices displayed outside said: 'Lunch – 3 courses – £12 all in'. Later we discovered that we would have to pay a **compulsory 15 per cent service charge** on top of the £12. Can the restaurant do this?*

A No. Any compulsory service charge that is automatically added to your bill must be displayed clearly on a menu at, or near, the entrance to the restaurant (p. 221). If it was not on the menu and you were not informed at the time you made your order, then you can refuse to pay it as it does not form part of your contract with the restaurant. If it was displayed, you must pay it – unless the service was not of a reasonable standard for that type of restaurant (p. 220).

By failing to mention the compulsory service charge, the restaurant risks prosecution for publishing misleading prices. There is a statutory Code of Practice on misleading price indications, made under the Consumer Protection Act 1987. This gives guidance to traders, including bars and restaurants, on how to avoid giving misleading prices. During 2003 the government consulted on strengthening the Code but at the time of writing no changes have been announced. You should tell the Trading Standards Department at the local council offices for the area where the restaurant is located about your experience, as the Trading Standards Officers have the responsibility of policing this bit of law (pp. 23–4, 29–30).

Q *My lunchtime pot of tea set me back £10! It turned out that the restaurant had a* **minimum charge** *of £10 between 12 and 3 p.m. Could I have refused to pay the full £10?*

A Restaurants must display any **minimum** or **cover charges** as prominently as the prices of the food on the menu, at or near the entrance. If the minimum charge did not appear on the menu at all, and you were not told about it when you ordered your tea, you could have refused to pay it. Whether you can now claim it back depends on the conditions under which it was paid (see p. 220). If the minimum charge was not prominently displayed, contact the Trading Standards Department at the council offices local to the restaurant. The restaurant may be committing an offence for publishing misleading prices (see above).

Q *We wanted a leisurely and relaxing meal, but this was not to be. The waiter brought each course before we had finished the last, and the coffee, dessert and bill all arrived at the same time. Was he within his rights to hurry us up like this?*

A You should be given a reasonable amount of time to finish your meal. This varies according to the type of restaurant and the price of the meal (you cannot expect to take as long in a pizzeria as you would in an expensive restaurant). If you do feel you have been unreasonably hurried, and were not advised when you booked that the table would be needed for another sitting, complain about the bad service and deduct a sum from the service charge, or refuse to pay any service charge (p. 220).

Q *We left our coats in the cloakroom at our local bistro. When we went to collect them both coats were gone. The owners say they are not responsible. Are they right?*

A When you leave your possessions in the care of a restaurant it is under a duty to take reasonable care of them. In law this situation is known as **bailment**. If your possessions were lost or damaged whilst in the restaurant's keeping it has to prove that it used reasonable care to prevent the loss or damage (p. 82). If it cannot prove this you are entitled to the value of the lost or damaged item.

If there was no clear notice in the restaurant excluding liability for loss or damage to customers' belongings, it is likely that you can hold the owners responsible. Even if they had such a notice, under the Unfair Contract Terms Act 1977 you may be able to challenge the notice as being unfair and unreasonable in all the circumstances. If a court finds such an exclusion or restriction clause unreasonable, it will be struck out (pp. 81–2).

Q *The waiter was so clumsy that he spilled a bowlful of soup down my suit. Can I claim the cost of cleaning?*

A Yes. If you can prove that the waiter was **negligent** by failing to take reasonable care while serving you, the restaurant will be responsible for the cost of cleaning. And if the soup had been hot and scalded you, its liability would be much greater. Make sure you get evidence from witnesses and send the cleaning bill to the owner as soon as possible.

Q *We were most upset to discover pieces of bacon in a 'vegetarian' salad which we ordered in a café. We did not eat it but the café insisted that as we had ordered the salad and it had been made for us we had to pay. We did pay as they threatened to call the police. It was all very nasty. Would I have been within my rights to leave without paying for the salad?*

A Yes, and as long as you paid for the food and drink you did eat, the police would have had no authority to get involved. It would only have been a matter for the police if you had gone to the café with no intention of paying for anything. You are entitled in these circumstances to complain and to refuse to pay for the dish. If you do pay, you should do so '**under protest**' so that you can still claim back the cost of the salad later:

- descriptions of food and wine on the menu form part of your contract with the restaurant – 'home-made soup', for example, must be home-made, not canned or out of a packet
- under the Supply of Goods and Services Act 1982 (common law in Scotland) any food or drink you order should be as described. Your 'vegetarian' salad clearly wasn't

- if there is a genuine dispute, and the police are called, you should pay whatever you think is reasonable for anything else you did eat (the starter, drinks etc.) and deduct the cost of the disputed dish (p. 221). If you leave your name and address and show proof of identity the police cannot intervene as you are not committing any crime. It will then be up to the café to pursue you for the amount it says you owe

- a restaurant is misleading customers by not serving food (or drink) as described on the menu. The Trade Descriptions Act 1968 makes it a criminal offence to give a false description of food in menus or other promotional literature. So tell the local Trading Standards Department that the restaurant might be deliberately misleading customers.

Q *A 15 per cent service charge was added to the price of a meal I had in a restaurant recently. I was happy to pay this and used my credit card. I've now received my credit-card statement, which has a higher amount for the meal. I checked the voucher I signed and noticed that the total box had been left blank. It seems that the restaurant has filled in the total and added an extra charge after I signed it. Do I have to pay the extra?*

A No. This practice of leaving credit slips 'open' where service has already been charged is iniquitous because customers may fail to notice, as you did, or may feel morally obliged to add something extra. But under your contract with the restaurant you agreed to pay only the price shown on the bill and credit voucher you signed. Any extra would be unauthorised and the restaurant may not assume that you agree to pay more *after* you have signed:

- write immediately to the restaurant with a copy of the slip: the restaurant is legally obliged to reimburse you for the extra charged
- contact the credit-card company straight away and send a copy of the credit slip you signed with the blank total. The company may agree to remove the extra charge from the statement and recover the amount from the restaurant on your behalf
- if need be you can take action against the restaurant under the small claims track of the county court (pp. 279–80) (sheriff court in Scotland).

Q *If I'm bothered by smokers at tables nearby, can I get the restaurant manager to stop them from smoking?*

A There is no legal obligation on restaurants to provide no-smoking areas. Normally it is at the manager's discretion whether or not to stop people smoking. However, if you specifically booked your table in the no-smoking area and other diners are smoking in that area, the manager should ask them to stop or move them to a smoker's table. If not, you may be able to reduce the bill by a small amount for the effect the smoking had on your enjoyment of the meal. If there is no separate no-smoking area then you have no legal right to complain.

Q *A local wine bar refused to serve my sister, saying it would only take orders from a man. In the end I gave the order to save embarrassment. But surely they weren't entitled to do this?*

A It is a criminal offence to discriminate against anyone in the supply of goods or services on the grounds of sex or race. This is clearly sex discrimination and as such is illegal. The wine bar can be prosecuted. Contact your local Trading Standards Department (at the council offices) and the Equal Opportunities Commission★.

Q *After eating at the local bistro, the whole family was ill for two days. The cause was obviously the food served at the bistro. Is there anything that we can do?*

A Yes. If you think the food you ate in the restaurant made you ill, tell your doctor immediately. Although it can be difficult to pinpoint the cause of illness, since symptoms can take up to three days to appear, the fact that you were all ill after this particular meal makes it more likely that the food was substandard.

You can claim compensation for your pain and suffering, and any loss of earnings and other expenses you incur as a result, including a refund of the cost of the meal. Tell your doctor and get a report on the cause of your illness.

The Food Safety Act 1990 makes it a criminal offence for a restaurant to serve food which is unfit for human consumption. You should also tell the local Environmental Health Department (EHO) at the council offices for the area where the bistro is. The EHO can investigate the incident and the restaurant could be fined and forced to compensate you. The EHO can even close down the restaurant if it is found to be in a dirty condition.

Q *When I arrived at the restaurant my friends had booked I could not get in. I am in a wheelchair and the restaurant was on the third floor. The lift was too small for my chair. Doesn't the law say that restaurants have to provide access for disabled people?*

A Laws to prevent discrimination on the grounds of race and sex have existed for some time (see above). The Disability Discrimination Act 1995 aims to prevent discrimination on the grounds of disability in the provision of goods and services (pp. 89–90).

If a restaurant offers a lower level of service, or treats you less favourably than others, because you are disabled in some way, it will be breaking the law. It is not just a simple matter of physical access (wheelchair users account for less than 10 per cent of people registered as disabled). If you have a serious speech impediment or are facially disfigured, say, the restaurant cannot choose to tuck you out of sight at an obscurely placed table just because it is more convenient for its staff or will cause less distress to its other customers. You are entitled to exactly the same quality of service and treatment as any diner who has no disability.

Since October 1999 restaurant owners have been obliged to consider whether it is reasonable to provide 'auxiliary aids' such as temporary ramps, or making staff available to help you physically overcome any hurdles you face in getting to your table. Furthermore, the Disability Discrimination Act requires restaurants, or other buildings to which the public have access, to permanently improve physical access by widening doors or installing ramps by October 2004. Try persuading the places you want to visit to make voluntary improvements now – in the long term the law says they will have to. If you feel discrimination is taking place, contact a solicitor and seek advice on making a claim.

Q *Does the law allow us to take our children with us when we go to a restaurant or bar?*

A The law lays down age limits for the consumption of alcohol in licensed premises such as restaurants and pubs. If the age limits are broken it is not just the person who has the licence who has committed the offence. The 'underage' drinker may be guilty as well as the parent or person in charge of the youngster. The watershed age is 18, and it is illegal:

- to serve alcohol to anyone under 18 – whether to take away or to consume there and then
- for an adult to send an under-18 to buy alcohol from a shop, and
- for an adult to buy alcohol for an under-18.

If you are under 18 the law allows you to enter licensed premises with an adult, and actually to drink alcohol, in certain circumstances:

- if you are 16 or over you can be served cider or beer with food in a restaurant
- if you are 14 or over you can go into a bar, but may only drink soft drinks
- if you are under 14 you can go into the gardens and separate 'family rooms' of pubs and wine bars if the premises have been granted a 'children's certificate' and you are with an adult.

Chapter 10

Insurance

While you cannot prevent things happening by taking out insurance, proper and adequate insurance cover can soften the blow when problems arise. It is important to decide what you want to insure and how much cover you need as opposed to what somebody wants to sell you. You may want to insure your home, its contents, your car, other specific possessions like a caravan or boat, your forthcoming holiday, yourself and your liabilities to others.

The insurance profession is highly regulated both by statute and by voluntary codes providing protection for the public. The right choice of insurance policy or scheme will depend on the circumstances of each individual case, so professional advice is essential. Whether you take advice from an insurance broker, an accountant, a solicitor or any other professional, it is preferable to choose an adviser who is personally recommended to you by a friend or colleague. It would be unwise to rely on someone who is not a member of one of the many professional associations in the insurance field. If need be, take advice from more than one adviser.

All insurance policies have exclusions, so as well as checking that a policy offers the right level of cover, always insist that you see the full policy. You must tell the insurance company about anything that might affect its decision to insure you, even if the information is not specifically requested on the form (pp. 231–2).

For claims on homes (buildings and contents), holidays, cars or private health insurance, this chapter explains the terms in frequent use and answers the most common queries on how to proceed, what hurdles you are likely to face, and to whom to complain.

Q *I wish to make a claim on my insurance policy: what should I do?*

A First, obtain a **claim form** from your insurance company or your insurance broker without delay. Always check the terms of your policy for **time limits** within which claims must be reported or claim forms completed and make sure you comply with them. If you have doubts about whether to include information and/or certain items of claim, consult with your broker if you have one. In general, disclose everything that could possibly be relevant, and get the relevant **evidence** to back up any claim:

- you may need to show that a theft has been reported to the police, so get a police report or incident number from them
- if your luggage goes missing while you are travelling, fill in a 'property irregularity form' (p. 191), and if you have to make emergency purchases, keep the receipts
- get medical evidence if your claim depends on this – a report from a doctor or specialist, for example. And if you are claiming for medical expenses, keep receipts for medication, etc.
- take photographs, and get statements from other witnesses about any event that may give rise to a claim.

Q *I've been arguing with my insurers for six months over my claim. Should I sue them?*

A An insurance contract is a contract like any other and you can take the company to court for breach of contract if it refuses your claim. Consider the following:

- if you've reached a deadlock with the insurance company you can take your complaint to the Financial Ombudsman Service (FOS)★ (see below)
- if you are claiming £5,000 or less, use the **small claims track** of the county court (see pp. 279–80). You can pick up free leaflets from your local county court (sheriff court in Scotland). Even if your losses are for slightly more than the small claims limit of £5,000 (£1,500 in Scotland, £1,000 in Northern Ireland), it could be worth restricting the amount of your claim to that limit to take advantage of this informal and low-cost procedure
- claims for over £5,000 would be heard in the 'fast' or 'multi' track of the county court or in the High Court, which could be expensive, lengthy and risky (pp. 279–80).

Q *What powers does the Ombudsman have?*

A The Financial Ombudsman Service (FOS)★ has the power to award up to £100,000 against an insurance company. Using the service is free to the consumer. You do not need the consent of your insurer to go to the FOS and the Ombudsman's decision is not binding on you, so you can still go to court afterwards if you are not satisfied, although it's unlikely the courts will take a different view. You normally have to bring your case before the FOS within six months of reaching a stalemate in your negotiations with the insurance company at Head Office level.

Q *By how much can the insurers increase the premium when I come to renew my policy?*

A As much as they like. Insurance contracts usually last for one year and every time you renew you make a new contract (although often on the same or similar standard terms each year). So at the date for renewal you can decide if you want to pay the premium, or accept any new terms the insurer may want to put into the agreement, or you can shop around for another company.

Q *Can I rely on the quote that I'm given by an insurer for cover?*

A If you accept the quote and pay your premium, a binding contract comes into existence so long as you have disclosed everything you should have (see p. 231). The insurer may not try to raise the premium after the event unless it has previously warned you that the quote is only provisional.

Q *The insurers say they want to send a **loss adjuster** round. How does this differ from a **loss assessor**?*

A **Loss adjusters** are independent professionals who are qualified to decide how much *insurers* should pay towards the cost of claims. For example, they may be called upon by your insurer to assess how much of the damage to a roof was done by a storm, and how much was due to poor condition in the first place.

    Loss assessors specialise in negotiating the settlement of claims on behalf of *policyholders*. It is you, the insured, who pay the assessor (usually on a percentage basis). They are usually only necessary in complicated claims. The advantage of an assessor is that he or she will make sure the claim is properly prepared and dealt with quickly, and will be able to get values quickly for your damaged property, stolen jewellery etc.

Q *My insurance company is not paying my claim. They say I didn't take reasonable care to prevent the damage arising. What does **reasonable care** mean?*

A There is no fixed meaning, so it depends on the circumstances. In house buildings insurance, for example, it means that you've got to maintain the build-ing to prevent avoidable accidents from happening – an insurance contract is not a maintenance contract, so wear and tear will usually be excluded. For contents insurance this means – among other things – that you must lock your doors when you go out. And if, for example, while on holiday you decide to lock your jewellery in the boot of the car and the jewellery is stolen, your claim might well succeed if you could show that you had considered the choices available and chosen what you thought best. You may, in such a case, have decided that it would be unsafe to take your jewellery with you, and it might well be considered reasonable to have locked it in your boot; so as long as you can show that your decision was not 'reckless', it could be worth challenging the insurance company's refusal to pay (p. 229).

Q *One of the clauses in my insurance policy seems very unfair. Can I challenge it?*

A Yes. The general rule is that once the contract is agreed you are bound by all of the terms contained in it. In most contracts you make as a consumer, you can challenge certain terms which try to take away or limit your rights under the Unfair Contract Terms Act 1977 (see pp. 88–9). Contracts of insurance are exempt from this Act, so you cannot take your own case to court to challenge the contract on the grounds that it is unfair. But that should no longer be a problem. Unfair terms in standard contracts can now be challenged, on behalf of all those affected, by the Office of Fair Trading (OFT)★, Consumers' Association★ and other 'qualifying bodies' (pp. 88–9). You should refer the policy to one of the 'qualifying bodies', which may decide to take action. Even if you are stuck with a 'get-out' term, it may be worth referring the matter to the Ombudsman: often, the interpretation of a clause is crucial.

Q *I made a claim on my policy. The insurers have pointed to an exclusion clause, but I don't agree with their interpretation of it. The clause isn't entirely clear but I think I'm covered. Who's right?*

A It is up to insurers to make sure their policies are clear, and if they fail to do this they should bear the financial risk. A special legal principle, the **contra proferentem** rule, applies in cases like this. What this says is that where an exclusion clause in a standard form contract (which insurance policies always are) is ambiguous, that ambiguity must be interpreted against the person who drew the contract up, and in the policyholder's favour. So the interpretation that favours you is the one that should prevail in this case. If the insurance company sticks to its own version, contact the Financial Ombudsman Service (FOS)★ if the company is a member (pp. 276–7).

Q *My insurers say they won't meet my claim and they're going to declare my policy void because I didn't tell them about a minor conviction five years ago. Can they do this?*

A They probably can. A particular feature of insurance policies is that they are considered by the law to be contracts where the requirements of **utmost good faith** apply. So when you take out an insurance policy, you obviously have to answer truthfully all the questions you have been asked. Less obviously, you have got to tell the company about anything not asked which might possibly be relevant. If you do not, the company can refuse to pay out. 'Relevant' means anything that could conceivably affect its decision to insure you, even if you do not regard it as relevant. And you are not only required to 'disclose' when you fill in the proposal form, but also when you confirm that you want to be covered and when you renew the policy. If you do not, you could be guilty of making a **material non-disclosure** and your insurer always reserves the right to cancel the policy if this happens.

Q *What is the difference between third party cover, third party fire and theft, and fully comprehensive insurance?*

A **Third party cover** is the minimum cover for vehicle drivers required by the law. If you have no insurance you are committing a criminal offence by driving. Third party insurance covers you for any damage you cause to another person (the 'third party'), whether by injuring them or damaging their property. This includes not only other road users and pedestrians but also passengers in your own car. Any damage you or your car may suffer will not be covered.

Third party fire and theft means that in addition to the basic third party cover you are also covered if your own car is stolen or destroyed by fire. Such a policy will not usually cover the contents of your car.

If you also want to cover accidental damage to your car or injury to yourself you will need **fully comprehensive insurance**. With this you also get cover for theft of car radios and cassette-players (often limited to a specific sum – see p. 234), and cover for theft of personal possessions from your car; however, valuable items such as jewellery and cameras may be excluded from cover entirely, so always check your policy. You should also normally get cover for medical expenses, and personal accident benefit if you are killed or permanently disabled in an accident.

Q *Do I lose my **no-claims discount** if I have an accident but it is not my fault?*

A It all depends on how you seek to recover your losses:

• if you are comprehensively insured, you have the right to claim your own repair costs from your insurer. The advantage of doing so is that a claim against your own insurance policy will usually be paid more quickly. The main disadvantage of claiming on your own insurance is that to do so is likely to affect your no-claims discount (or 'bonus'), even though the accident was not your fault. This is because it is a **no-claims**, not a **no-blame**, discount. In some cases, claiming against your own policy may be the only practical option: for example, if the other driver is unknown or has no proper car insurance (p. 235). If you know the identity of the other driver and you decide to claim for your repairs from your own insurer, you can try to recover your uninsured losses (such as your excess, loss of no-claims discount or transport costs while the car is off the road) from him or her

- if you are not comprehensively insured, or you simply decide to pursue the other driver for all your losses, including your repair bills, then your no-claims discount should not be affected, as you are not making a claim. You are, however, under an obligation to notify your insurer of the accident
- traditionally, some insurers have operated 'knock-for-knock' agreements between themselves. The effect of such an agreement is that in the event of an accident taking place between parties insured by the respective companies, the companies agree that each will meet its own policyholder's losses, regardless of fault. Although these schemes are now going out of vogue, if there is one in existence you may be put under pressure to agree settlement on these terms (see p. 235).

Q *What happens when insurers declare a car a* **write-off,** *and how can they be forced to increase their offer for the value?*

A If the garage estimate for the cost of repairs is more than about three-quarters of the value of the car, the insurance company may decide that the car is a **write-off.** This is because it is quite likely that when the garage starts repairs, it will find further damage, and a car that has been repaired after an accident will usually be worth less than it was before the accident. So you could end up with a car worth less than the amount spent to repair it.

If your insurance company decides to declare a car a write-off, it will pay the full value of the car and sell the wreck for scrap. The amount you are entitled to is the value of the car before the accident, i.e. the amount you would have to pay to buy an identical car in a private sale (second-hand car dealer prices will be higher than private sale prices). This may not be the amount you said it was worth when insuring it. Insurers simply use that as a guide.

When deciding the value of a written-off car, the insurer will start by looking in one of the guides to second-hand car prices, such as *Glass's* or *Parker's.* To challenge the amount offered you will need proof that it is worth more. The following will all help to persuade the insurer:

- advertisements for similar models in newspapers
- statements of its worth from a number of car dealers
- proof of modifications that would have added to its value.

The Institute of Automotive Engineer Assessors★ will give you the name of a value assessor in your area. If you are a member of a motoring organisation such as the RAC or AA, either will help with your claim. But if the insurer will not budge you may have to take it to court or to the Financial Ombudsman Service★ (pp. 276–7).

Q *Do I have to make a claim if I have a car accident?*

A No. If you want to preserve your no-claims discount and pay for the repairs yourself (or attempt to recover them from the other driver) you do not have to submit your claim to your insurer. Sometimes the cost of losing your no-claims discount is more than the cost of paying for repairs yourself. If so, you would be better off not claiming. However, you do have to inform your insurer that you have been in an accident. Send a letter telling the insurer what has happened, but make it crystal clear that it is for 'information only' and that you do not wish to make a claim. This should ensure that the insurer does not make a knock-for-knock or compromise settlement without your knowledge (p. 235).

Q *Someone broke into my car whilst it was parked outside the house. As well as breaking a window they took my radio-cassette system. Is it worth claiming for this from my insurers?*

A It is not always advisable to make an insurance claim following this type of incident, even assuming you are comprehensively insured (pp. 232–3). You should always report any incident involving your car to your insurer. But you are not obliged to make a claim for your resultant losses. Instead, look at your home contents insurance policy. You might find that this provides cover for your car radio/cassette-player. If you do claim on your motor policy, you may lose your no-claims discount, so you need to calculate whether it is worth doing so. It may be cheaper to replace the radio and the window yourself to protect your no-claims discount unless you have a policy which allows a certain number of claims without your discount being affected.

Q *Some of my losses aren't covered by my policy, such as car hire and the first £200 excess. Can I claim these back from anyone?*

A If the other driver involved in an accident with your vehicle was to blame, you can sue him or her for your **uninsured losses**. These could be:

- your excess – any amount you have to pay for repairs
- cost of alternative transport while your car is off the road, so long as it is reasonable and justified (very few policies, if any, cover this)
- compensation for personal injury (most insurance policies pay out a small amount in the event of serious injury such as loss of limbs)
- loss of earnings
- loss in value of the car.

Start by writing to the other driver giving details of your uninsured losses and ask him or her to pass your claim on to his or her insurer. If the driver refuses to co-operate, you will have to take him or her to court. If the claim is for £5,000 or less (£1,500 in Scotland, £1,000 in Northern Ireland) you can use the small claims procedure (pp. 279–80). If you are successful and the courts make an award in your favour, but the other driver does not pay up, his or her insurance company must pay you.

Q *I was badly injured in a collision with another driver who was not insured. Is there any way I can get compensation without going to court?*

A If your injuries were due to the other driver's negligent driving, you are entitled to claim compensation through the courts. Even if he or she is not insured but you think he or she has the money to pay, this may be worthwhile. But if your claim is for more than the small claims limit of £5,000 (£1,500 in Scotland, £1,000 in Northern Ireland), taking a case to court can be very expensive, and there is a risk that the other driver may not be worth suing (pp. 279 and 286–7). The **Motor Insurers Bureau (MIB)**★ was set up in 1946 to help people injured in road accidents who are having difficulty in obtaining the compensation to which they are entitled. All motor insurance companies are members of the MIB, which may meet a claim:

- for **personal injury** caused by an uninsured driver, whether or not the driver can be traced (this would cover, for example, a hit-and-run incident)
- for **damage to property** where the guilty driver is known but uninsured. You will have to pay the first £185 of all property damage yourself, rather like an 'excess'.

Q *What does the insurance company mean when it says my claim will be dealt with on a* **knock-for-knock** *basis?*

A The so-called knock-for-knock agreements that exist between insurers mean that each company pays the expenses incurred by its own policyholder. Where two people are involved in an accident and each holds a **comprehensive** policy with different insurers who are participants in a knock-for-knock scheme, if all parties involved are at fault to some extent each insurer pays for its own policyholder's damage, regardless of precise liability and blame. From the insurers' point of view, this avoids the cost that would be involved in arguing about liability (and in theory this allows premiums to be lower). But as far as a no-claims discount is concerned, the question of liability is relevant: if liability is clear and a recovery could have been made from the other insurance company had it not been for the knock-for-knock agreement, you can try to persuade your insurer to reinstate or preserve your no-claims discount. Evidence that you were not to blame will help.

But if liability is not clear, unless you show that the other party is to blame (by getting some payment, witness statements or other evidence of liability from the other driver) your insurer will reduce your no-claims discount after paying out under a knock-for-knock agreement. Where there is any doubt about who is liable, or where liability for the damage is clearly shared by both parties, your no-claims discount will be reduced in the ordinary way.

Q *The insurers' loss adjusters are reducing our claim to take account of the age of our stolen property. Can we argue about this?*

A Yes, but only if your policy stipulates that contents are covered on a '**new for old**' basis. This means the policies will pay the full cost of repairing items or pay to replace them with new items (except for clothes, bedlinen and some-times bikes) so you can go out and buy brand-new replacements. Many policies provide cover on an **indemnity** basis, i.e. to replace the lost item with an item of the same age and condition. Check your policy cover. Indemnity cover should be cheaper than 'new for old', but could leave you much worse off if you have a large claim.

Q *Our neighbourhood is becoming a high-risk area for burglaries. Could the insurers decide to raise our premiums?*

A Insurers are always within their rights to raise the premium on renewal of a policy. Each year's renewal is a new contract and the offer of insurance can be made on any basis. The particular risks in your area are highly relevant to an offer of household insurance. But it is up to you to accept or reject as you see fit. If the amount seems too high, you will have to shop around for an alternative policy. Most insurers will offer a discount if you fit approved locks to doors and windows and install a burglar alarm – check that your locks and alarm meet the standards set by the insurer. A typical discount is 5 per cent for locks and 5 to 10 per cent for an alarm. But if you live in a high-risk area for theft you may have to fit these locks or a burglar alarm before an insurer will cover you or renew your cover.

Bear in mind that security discounts come with conditions. You'll usually have to agree to set the alarm and use the locks at night and while you're away from home. If you don't and your house is broken into, your excess for the claim may increase or, in extreme cases, your insurer may not pay out at all.

Q *The sofa forming part of my three-piece suite was completely ruined when my house was flooded. The two chairs were undamaged. We made a claim against our household insurance policy for a new three-piece suite, because the original style has been discontin-ued, but the insurers are only agreeing to replace the sofa. Are they within their rights?*

A As with any insurance case, much depends upon the written terms of your policy. But unless the policy specifically states that a three-piece suite should be seen as a single entity for insurance purposes, you are unlikely to be able to insist that the whole suite should be replaced. The Financial Ombudsman Service (FOS)★, which deals with cases like yours, takes the view that a policyholder should not be allowed to claim for a whole new suite when one item of it is damaged, or for the re-covering of the whole if one item is damaged and the material cannot be matched. This is worth bearing in mind if you decide to take your case to the Ombudsman or to court.

Q *For what amount should I insure my house?*

A Most policies are geared to insuring you for the full cost of **rebuilding** the house rather than just its market value. You must ensure that it is insured to a sufficient value because if it is not any claim, even if it is not for complete rebuilding, will be averaged. This means the amount claimed under the policy will be reduced in proportion to the extent to which your house is under-insured.

The Association of British Insurers (ABI)★ produces a free leaflet on insuring a house and an interactive online calculator to help (*www.abi.org.uk*). If you're not online most insurers will supply a table based on the charts in the ABI leaflet, so ask your insurance company.

Q *Will index-linking guarantee that my house is always insured to a sufficient value?*

A Not necessarily. For example, if you have improved the house in any way, such as by extending it, this will increase the value in a way that is not reflected by simple index-linking. The best way to protect yourself is to check with the insurer on a regular basis that your house or flat is adequately insured for the full rebuilding cost.

Q *Without our knowledge, water was seeping into our cellar for a long period. Does this count as **flood damage**?*

A The risks covered by insurance policies are defined very precisely. In the case of flood, water seeping in like this does not come within the term. This will depend on what your policy says but your property is unlikely to be covered: normally flooding is regarded as a relatively **sudden and substantial** influx of water. The damage may be excluded under the policy in any event because of your failure to maintain the property to a reasonable standard (p. 230), as well as your failure to take the necessary remedial steps to rectify the problem. The moral is that it pays to keep an eye on your property's general condition.

Q *We had **storm damage** but the insurers won't believe us. How can we persuade them?*

A You will have to prove that the property was damaged as a result of strong winds accompanied by rain. For this you should present evidence that there was a storm at the time that the damage occurred: the Meteorological Office★ will be able to help you with this. In addition, it may help to have an independent expert opinion from a builder or a structural engineer confirming that the damage you have claimed for could only have been caused by a storm.

Q *My insurers say that my illness was a pre-existing condition and they won't pay for my treatment. Can I challenge them?*

A You can do this but you will need a report from a consultant or your GP supporting your claim. Unfortunately, this may not necessarily be enough to persuade your insurer if its expert says the opposite. There may be some connected illness in your past either which you disclosed but assumed was totally irrelevant to this particular claim, or a past condition or treatment which, if you failed to disclose it, could make your insurance policy invalid (p. 231).

Q *My doctor reckons my illness is covered by my private health insurance policy. Does this mean the insurers have to pay up?*

A Not necessarily. The insurer does not have to accept the recommendation of your doctor or consultant that the treatment is within the cover offered. It may get its own expert to examine you and base its decision on that. Your own doctor's opinion will help, but if the insurance company refuses your claim your only option will be to contact the Financial Ombudsman Service (FOS)★, or to take the matter to court.

Q *Whenever I buy my holiday or an electrical appliance I tend to take out the insurance cover offered by the travel agent or the shop. Who can I complain to about the way an insurance policy was sold by an intermediary like this?*

A The current system of regulation of the sale of 'general insurance' is about to change. General insurance covers insurances for individuals and their families (such as home and contents, motor, travel, medical, extended warranty and payment protection). The General Insurance Standards Council (GISC)★ is a voluntary scheme which currently covers all major insurers and a large number of 'intermediaries' (which could be insurance brokers as well as those who sell insurance as an add-on to their main product, such as high-street shops, banks, car dealers, etc.).

You can take your complaint to the GISC about the sale, advice and service provided by a GISC member. The first stage in any complaint is to exhaust the company's own internal complaints process. All insurance companies are already regulated by the FSA (p. 166) so if your complaint is about the insurance company itself (for example over the non-payment of a claim) you can refer the matter to the Financial Ombudsman Scheme (FOS) (p. 229). For complaints about all other GISC members you can get assistance under the GISC Dispute Resolution Facility (*www.gisc.co.uk/consumer*).

In January 2005 most businesses wishing to sell general insurance will also have to be regulated by the Financial Services Authority (FSA)★. Only businesses authorised by the FSA will be allowed to sell general insurance (although some areas will not be required to have FSA authorisation, such as travel agents and tour operators who sell travel insurance usually at the same time as the holiday arrangements themselves). Where these companies are ABTA members the sale of insurance will be regulated by ABTA★ (p. 215). For all others you should refer the complaint to your local Trading Standards.

Q *I have been having treatment for the same illness for many years, and my private health insurance has been covering the cost. Now the insurers say my condition is a* **chronic, long-term illness** *and my policy does not cover me for this. Surely this can't be right?*

A Many policies do exclude treatment for conditions if they become chronic and in a sense the insurer is penalising you for turning out to be a bad risk. An insurance company can also insert exclusions for specific conditions when it renews the policy. If you have been receiving treatment and the insurance company decides to classify your condition as **long-term** or **incurable**:

- get evidence from your consultant that your illness is not incurable or long-term: for example, you could argue that each time you received treatment in the past the illness was 'cured' for a time, and that each flare-up is a separate and curable condition
- write, enclosing all your evidence, to the managing director of the insurance company
- if that fails refer the matter to the Financial Ombudsman Service (FOS)★
- If you don't want to use the Ombudsman, or if you don't like the Ombudsman's decision, think about taking the claim to court, especially if the amount of your claim is £5,000 or less (£1,500 in Scotland) (pp. 274–6) and can therefore be dealt with under the small claims procedure. Just one word of warning. If you go to court having failed to explore alternatives such as the Ombudsman Scheme first, the judge could delay the case and send you and the insurer away to consider this option.

Q *What sort of cover should I look for in a holiday and travel insurance policy?*

A It is important that the level of cover offered by a policy is enough to meet your needs. The cover you should look for in a holiday policy includes the following:

- **for cancellation** This comes into operation as soon as the premium has been paid and should give you back everything you have paid out in advance. The minimum cover should be the full amount of your liability under the contract and should include cancellation in the event of your illness or death, or the illness or death of a close relative or business associate, or travelling companion; redundancy; jury service or being called as a witness in court; severe damage to your home by fire, flood, storm, burglary or other criminal acts against you which require you to stay at home

- **for curtailment** This covers you if you have to cut short your holiday for broadly the same reasons described under 'cancellation' above, or because of illness or accident while on holiday, and should also include the additional costs of earlier return travel

- **for medical expenses** This covers the possibility of high medical bills for illness or an accident while abroad. The minimum you should look for is £250,000 in Europe and £1 million in the USA and the rest of the world

- **for belongings and money** This depends on how much you will be taking but in general a minimum of £1,500 is recommended to cover loss of, or damage to, your baggage and currency

- **for personal accident** A specified sum to be paid if as a result of an accident you should die, or lose a limb or an eye, or suffer permanent total disablement

- **for delays** In the event of your baggage being delayed you need minimum cover of £75 to buy emergency supplies. The delay usually has to be for 12 hours or more on the outward journey. Delayed departure should give you at least £20 after the first 12 hours' delay and the option to cancel and get a full refund of the holiday cost if you are delayed for more than 24 hours

- **for personal liability** This covers you if you have to pay compensation for accidentally injuring other people or damaging their property. Look for minimum cover of £1 million in Europe and the rest of the world, £2 million for the USA.

Q *When I was on a touring holiday I locked my camera in the glove compartment of my car while I went for a walk. The camera was stolen and the insurers are refusing to pay up. How can I get the money?*

A It is a general principle of insurance law, and it is often repeated in insurance policy conditions, that valuables are covered only if you took **reasonable care**

of them – by keeping the jewellery, say, in a locked safe (p. 230). There is no legal definition of what amounts to reasonable or due care, as it depends on all the circumstances, so you can certainly challenge the insurer's decision. Follow the procedures for making a claim (pp. 238–9), and if the insurer still refuses to pay, consider the Financial Ombudsman Service (FOS)★.

Q *I booked a package holiday and filled in the booking form. When the confirmation invoice arrived I discovered that I'm being charged for holiday insurance. Do I have to pay this?*

A Usually you can choose whether or not to buy your tour operator's insurance, although the brochure and booking form do not always make it clear that you have a choice. But some booking forms may use **negative option** selling. This means you will automatically be charged for insurance when you book unless you make it clear that you do not want it by deleting a word or phrase. So if you did not notice the 'option' and did not indicate that you did not want the tour operator's insurance, you will have to pay. Although this may seem unfair, it is perfectly legal.

Q *My car was parked outside my house when it was damaged by a van owned by a local building firm. It was clearly the other driver's fault. I have been trying to get the money out of the firm but they simply ignore my letters and calls. Can I claim against their insurance company (I have their address and policy details)?*

A When an accident occurs owing to another driver's failure to take care, your right to claim compensation for the loss and damage you have suffered is against that other driver, not the insurance company. Assuming you can prove it was the other driver's fault you are entitled to compensation. All drivers are legally required to have insurance that at least covers their liability for damage or injury to a third party, in this case your car. But insurance is simply a contract between the insurance company and the insured person – you have no rights under that other person's contract. The driver may decide to pay your claim out of his or her own pocket or pass the claim on to his or her own contract of insurance. It is the driver's choice, although he or she will have to notify his or her insurer of the accident, and so will you (p. 235). If the driver is simply refusing to pay up or pass the claim to the insurer you will have no option but to commence legal action in the courts.

However, if the reason you have heard nothing from the other driver is because he or she has gone out of business, the law will step in to help. If it is a company or firm, check first with Companies House★ or the local Trading Standards Department (pp. 158–9). The Third Party (Rights Against Insurers) Act 1930 is designed specifically to help victims of road accidents caused by insured drivers who are, or subsequently become, insolvent or bankrupt. If this is the case here you will acquire the rights that the other driver had against his or her insurer under his or her contract of insurance for third-party liability, so contact the insurer to make a claim.

Q *I received the renewal reminder for my insurance but decided to shop around. I found a better deal with increased cover so I took out a different policy. But a couple of weeks later I received a letter from my original insurer thanking me for renewing my policy again. I checked my bank account and discovered the premium had been taken already. Surely it can't do this?*

A It can, if there's a clause in your insurance contract which says that the policy will be automatically renewed unless the insurer hears to the contrary. The reminder notice should set this out. If it does and gives you a reasonable time to respond, then it can automatically renew and use the charging details you'd already provided for previous premiums.

What is a 'reasonable' time depends on the type of contract. If you don't think the time was reasonable, or you missed the deadline because it wasn't clearly explained, then contact the company and ask for a refund.

It would be possible to challenge automatic renewal clauses like this if you can persuade the Office of Fair Trading (OFT)★ that it's legally unfair under the Unfair Terms in Consumer Contracts Regulations (pp. 88–9 & 231). Go to *www.oft.gov.uk* for more advice.

Q *My mobile phone was stolen and before I noticed the thief had made lots of expensive calls. Will my insurance cover this?*

A All policies will insist that you tell the phone company and the police of the theft. So that you don't lose the right to claim, you should do this immediately, and certainly within the time limit set out in the policy, usually 24 hours.

Not all policies insure against unauthorised calls or will have a low limit on the amount of cover, so check. As far as the theft itself is concerned the level of cover can vary substantially. Check your policy for the following:

- cover for theft from secure premises, such as a house, or if you're mugged; you're unlikely to be covered if your phone is stolen while unattended in a public place
- cover for theft from a car. Even if it does provide this many will only pay if you can prove it was hidden from view
- accidental damage is usually covered but the policy may exclude loss
- a new replacement phone may be provided but some policies will only replace with a reconditioned one
- not all policies will cover you while outside the UK.

As with all insurance, be wary of exclusions and read the small print, so make sure you get a copy of the policy before you buy, and keep it when you do. Alternatively, you may already have cover, which may be better, on your house contents policy. Most cover the cost of replacing your phone if it's stolen from your home. And if the policy covers accidental damage you may also be covered if you drop it.

Your house contents policy may also cover you if your phone is stolen, lost or damaged while away from home as long as you have personal possessions or 'all-risks' cover. If you don't, it may be more cost-effective to add this to your policy rather than taking out separate mobile phone insurance. It's unlikely that all your losses will be covered by your insurance, so it's worth protecting yourself in advance:

- if you have a contract phone ask the phone company if you can specify a monthly credit limit. This will limit your loss if the phone is stolen.
- make sure you use any security measures that exist on the phone, such as a PIN, to lock it.

Chapter 11

Neighbours

Relations between neighbours are a rich source of dispute – noise, overhanging trees, unreasonably high hedges, nuisance pets, to name a few. Here, unlike with disputes over goods and services, it's often difficult to distance yourself from the cause of the problem – unless you move house. But be warned – what your neighbour does may annoy you, but may be perfectly reasonable and legal. So although there is some legal protection for you and your property, and it is possible to take formal legal action, it's always best to try a friendly approach first.

Before taking legal action try one of the many local mediation schemes available, which aim to resolve disputes through discussion (pp. 273–6). Mediation UK★ will put you in touch with a scheme in your area. Alternatively, if the dispute is over boundaries, you may need to find a surveyor.

Q *Our neighbours often play music too loud. What rights do we have and can we force them to turn it down?*

A This depends on whether the noise is **unreasonable**. You are entitled to enjoy your property and can do whatever suits you, as long as you don't stop other people enjoying their property. The law calls an unreasonable disturbance of the enjoyment of property a **nuisance**. But just because you find the music a nuisance does not mean that the law is being broken. In flats and semi-detached houses some noise from neighbours is unavoidable. You have to put up with what is reasonable, and you yourself must behave reasonably. If you make a lot of noise in retaliation you could be just as guilty of nuisance. If you are unreasonably disturbed:

- don't assume your neighbours are aware that they're disturbing you, and do try to sort it out on a friendly basis
- keep a detailed diary of each disturbance, noting the time, date and duration of the nuisance, and get other neighbours to write statements to back you up

- if the friendly approach doesn't work, send copies of your evidence to the Environmental Health Officers (EHO) at your local council. If they consider that your neighbour is causing a 'nuisance' they have the power to serve an **abatement** notice on the neighbour to prevent the nuisance continuing, or making the neighbour restrict it to certain days, or certain times. If this is not complied with, the neighbour can be fined up to £2,000, and up to £50 each day that it continues

- it may sometimes be hard to persuade the EHO to take this action, but you can do it yourself. You will need to visit your local magistrates' court (sheriff court in Scotland) to ask for a 'nuisance order'. If you can persuade the court to grant one then the consequences are the same as above, so make sure you have evidence from other neighbours and your diary to support your case

- you can get an **injunction** in the county court (an 'interdict' in the sheriff court in Scotland) to prevent the noise continuing. The advantage of this over the magistrates' court process is that you can also claim compensation for the inconvenience you have suffered. But the process can be quite lengthy and expensive and any compensation is likely to be small

- EHOs also have powers under the Noise Act 1996 to confiscate equipment such as music systems. And if the noise is excessive and is being made between 11 p.m. and 7 a.m., the EHOs can issue warnings and follow these up with on-the-spot fines of up to £1,000 for persistent 'night noise offences' (pp. 253–4).

Q *I work at night but can't sleep during the day because my next-door neighbours are noisy. Can I do anything?*

A Probably not. The law won't take into account your particular lifestyle if it differs from what is considered 'normal'. So, unfortunately, if the noise disturbs you only because you sleep during the day, and would not be considered a nuisance to someone who is awake at that time, you'll be unable to do much about it. The only answer may be to sleep in a quieter part of the house. But if the noise is severe enough to amount to a nuisance to anyone who is normally awake in the daytime, you will have a right at least to restrict the noise to more reasonable levels or to specific times of the day (see above). It is unlikely you will get the noise stopped altogether as a certain amount of noise is only to be expected during the day.

Q *We've repeatedly asked our neighbours to prune their tree. It hangs over the fence and the leaves block up our drain. As it is almost touching our house we're worried that it might damage the foundations. Can we prune it ourselves?*

A Trees certainly can cause damage to foundations. It is not so much that they cause direct physical damage, but rather that they take water from the soil, particularly in clay conditions, which then contracts and causes subsidence. The tree's owner is responsible for any damage caused, as long as it is proved that his or her tree was the cause. So if your foundations are damaged you may need expert evidence on the precise cause:

- you may well be covered for this damage by your house insurance policy. If you are, the simplest course is to make a claim under the policy, and let the insurer pursue the claim against your neighbour, or possibly against his or her insurance company
- chat with your neighbour – he or she may be persuaded to trim the whole tree, including the roots, so that it keeps its shape but stops being such a bother
- if a friendly word with the neighbours fails to do the trick, before you start cutting check with your local council whether the tree has a **preservation order** on it. If it does, and you prune it, you are committing an offence and could be fined. Also, if you live in a **conservation area** you must tell the council before you cut. It has six weeks to decide whether to put a preservation order on the tree
- if there's no such protection for the tree, you're entitled to cut off the roots and the branches at the point where they cross the boundary. You then have to offer them back to the neighbour – just because they are on your land does not mean they belong to you. The same applies to tempting fruit that hangs over the fence. If the fruit has fallen into your garden the law assumes it has been abandoned by the neighbour, so it's yours. But don't be tempted to shake the branch!

Q *Do I have a 'right to light'?*

A If you find your garden plunged into darkness by the neighbour's new wall, or your garden becomes shaded by the trees next door, there may be little you can do. Things could be different if it's a high hedge and you live in a residential area (below). But the general rule is that not everyone has an automatic **right to light**. Here's a guide to when you might be able to act:

- if you have enjoyed a particular level of light for 20 uninterrupted years or more, you are entitled to keep a reasonable level of light for normal purposes – but you can't insist on getting the same amount of light as you have had in the past. The legal test is not 'how much light have I lost?', but 'how much light do I still have?'
- you can acquire a right to light to a particular window in your house, or a structure in your garden, like a greenhouse, but never to the garden itself, so if your garden has been cast into shade you can't complain

- you can complain only if an artificial structure, like another house or a wall, interferes with it – no complaint can be made when it is a natural obstacle like a tree that is in the way.

Q *The leylandii hedge that our neighbour planted three years ago is now so high that very little will grow in our garden as it's so dark. And we have to have the lights on in all the rooms on that side of our house during the day. Can we force them to keep the hedge low?*

A Part 8 of the Anti-social Behaviour Act 2003 deals with the problem of 'high hedges' and aims to remedy the effect they can have on a homeowner's enjoyment of their property. At the time of writing Part 8 was expected to come into force sometime during the second half of 2004. Until then, the existing law is of very little help at all as the only argument is that the hedge is interfering with your light (see above).

The 2003 Act now makes it clear that if a hedge is adversely affecting your reasonable enjoyment of your property you can complain. To benefit from the Act the important things to note are:

- it must be domestic property
- the hedge must be formed wholly or predominantly by a line of two or more evergreen trees or shrubs
- it must rise to a height of more than two metres above ground level
- it must represent a barrier to light or to your access to your property
- you must have tried amicable negotiation first.

The Act introduces a new procedure for local authorities to deal with complaints where negotiation has failed. Although the emphasis is on mediation, if it agrees with your complaint your local council can issue a remedial notice for a fee setting out what action should be taken to remedy the effect. The council will not be able to order the complete removal of the hedge or its reduction to a height lower than two metres – but its new powers should be of real practical help to prevent the hedge from becoming out of control and kept to a manageable height. Contact your local council for help.

Q *The side wall of our house stands right on the boundary with our neighbour. We need to do some urgent repairs to the wall but we need to go into his garden to do the work. The neighbour has refused permission, and we don't want to trespass. What should we do?*

A Strictly speaking you cannot go on to the land without the neighbour's permission (p. 248). However, under the Access to Neighbouring Land Act 1992, where the neighbour has refused permission, you can apply to your local county court (sheriff court in Scotland) for an order giving access to do the work:

- you must identify the land, state why access is necessary, when it will start and its likely duration
- you will have to convince the court that the work you have in mind is necessary to maintain your property and that the only way to get it done is to go next door. This includes work to the house, drains, hedges, trees and ditches
- in return for access, you will have to make good any damage to the neighbour's land and perhaps pay a small sum of money for access or compensation
- you may have to take out insurance to cover injury to persons or damage to property during the proposed work.

Q *I have bonfires most weekends to get rid of garden rubbish. My neighbour objects to this. Am I not allowed to carry on with this perfectly reasonable activity?*

A In general there are no restrictions on when bonfires can be lit, but check with your local council for any by-laws. Whether it's a **nuisance** depends on whether the fires interfere with your neighbour's enjoyment of his or her property, and whether they're more frequent than an ordinary person would consider reasonable. Occasional bonfires, even the ritual burning of garden rubbish once a week, may not constitute nuisance. But listen to the objections and try to make an acceptable arrangement. Your neighbour is entitled to complain to the local Environmental Health Department or to the magistrates' court (sheriff court in Scotland) and you may receive an 'abatement' notice. If this happens you must comply with the notice or risk a £2,000 fine (p. 245).

Q *Can I stop people coming on to my land?*

A Yes. Each time people come on to your land without your permission, they are **trespassing**. Some people have implied permission to be there for particular purposes – to call at the front door, to deliver the post and milk, or to collect the refuse. So, unless you specifically exclude everybody, by sign or fortifications, people can cross the boundary within certain limits. But if those people who entered for legitimate reasons start wandering over your garden or into your garage, say, or stay after being asked to leave, they have gone too far.

You can build fences around your home. The general rule is that you do not need any planning permission to build your own fence up to two metres high where it joins your neighbour's land (one metre where it joins a public road, path or pavement) – check with the planning department at your local council first, and also look at your deeds to ensure there are no 'restrictive covenants' preventing the building of fences. Here are some guidelines:

- if a friendly word doesn't stop unwanted visitors you're perfectly entitled to bar their way, by planting a hedge or putting up a fence, or by standing in the way!

- think carefully about what obstacles you put up. You can't set a trap (certainly not one that will harm trespassers or keep them against their will). Nor should you use barbed wire or broken glass around a domestic property because it may injure unsuspecting people, particularly children (pp. 255–6)

- you must always be prepared for trespassers, especially young ones. Children cannot always read warning signs and may not realise how dangerous things like barbed wire are. If they injure themselves, even if they are not meant to be on your land, you could be responsible. The danger comes when you put something unnatural on your land

- when faced with repeated trespass, by a neighbour, say, you can apply to the county court for an injunction (an interdict from the sheriff court in Scotland). If the intruder has caused damage, you can claim compensation as well, but unless the damage is serious this is unlikely to be much. Keep a diary of each trespass and evidence of the damage caused

- trees and animals often cross boundaries without permission: their owner, in each case, is responsible for them.

Q *My neighbour is building an extension. The noise of drills and cement mixers is intolerable. Can I stop the builders causing this nuisance?*

A Whether noise constitutes nuisance in law depends on the type of work, the methods used, and what steps have been taken to ensure that any annoyance to neighbours is kept to a reasonable level. An interference which is temporary may well escape being a nuisance on that ground. However, there always has to be a degree of give and take, and with construction work you will have to expect a certain amount of disturbance. But you don't have to put up with it 18 hours a day, seven days a week – it all depends on what is unreasonable (pp. 244–5):

- check with the local authority planning department: it may well have imposed restrictions on the hours during which construction can take place (normally between 8 a.m. and 6 p.m. on weekdays, and on Saturday morning) and the machinery to be used

- under the Control of Pollution Act 1974, a local authority has the power to serve a notice on property owners restricting hours of working and the type of machinery used, to cut down the disturbance

- if all else fails, and the annoyance is excessive and happens at unreasonable times, you can seek an injunction in the civil courts – and you can ask for compensation (p. 245).

Q *What can I do about my neighbour's garden? It looks like a municipal dump.*

A There is no law which says people have to be tidy. So if the view from your window is spoilt by the state of your neighbour's garden, and a friendly word has no effect, there may be nothing you can do. But the local council has powers under the Town and Country Planning Act 1990 to clean up the areas it controls. It may consider a highly visible mess to be ruining the **amenity** and beauty of the neighbourhood – in which case you may even persuade the council to remove the rubbish (for which the neighbour will have to pay).

The law will certainly help if rats and mice are infesting the rubbish. Under the Prevention of Damage by Pests Act 1949, the council can serve a notice demanding its removal, and your neighbour could face a fine if he or she does not comply. Your local authority officials, such as the Environmental Health Officers, can enter a home if they suspect that there has been a breach of public health regulations, or of by-laws on sanitation. They also have the power to inspect houses for pests such as mice and rats, having given 24 hours' notice. If the householder does not admit them they can apply for a warrant authorising entry by force.

Q *I was walking across a field when the farmer pointed to a sign saying 'Trespassers will be prosecuted' and shouted that he would call the police if I didn't get off. I often walk that way. Can I be prosecuted?*

A No. Contrary to popular belief, trespassers cannot be prosecuted. It is not a criminal offence merely to walk on somebody else's land. If it is a public right of way you are entitled to be there, as long as you stick to the footpath. But if it is private land with no established right of way, the landowner can apply to a court for an injunction to prevent you walking that way again. If you ignore that you will be in contempt of court, and the penalty for contempt is a hefty fine or prison. You may also have to pay compensation for any damage you cause, although if you have been careful this is unlikely to be much. Only if you are deliberately causing damage can the police intervene and prosecute for criminal damage.

Q *I have a **right of way** along a narrow passageway to my back garden. The lady down the street keeps parking her car there and blocking it. What can I do?*

A You have what is known in law as an **easement** ('servitude' in Scotland) – a right to use someone else's land for a specified purpose. This will be set out in the deeds of the property. And many other people may also have separate easements over the same land. Your neighbour probably has a specific right to park there. She may even own the land. But she cannot stop you exercising your right of way.

If the obstruction is serious and your neighbour refuses to move her car, consider mediation as a way forward (p. 277). If that fails you can apply to the county court for an injunction (or, in Scotland, to the sheriff court for an interdict) to prevent her parking there. Anyone who ignores a court order is in contempt of court and risks ending up in prison.

Q *My neighbours have several dogs which are always making a noise and running in and out of my garden. One of them is particularly nasty and has bitten me. Can I make my neighbours control their pets?*

A Noise problems can be dealt with effectively if they amount to **nuisance** (p. 244). But you cannot easily prevent the dogs entering your garden, other than by putting up your own fence or wall; nor can you force your neighbours to fence in their animals. Dogs and cats are expected to roam, and, unlike most humans, they do not respect boundaries – a fence to a dog is something to jump over or tunnel under, and cats can climb just about anything.

If a dog injures you, or damages your property, you are entitled to compensation under the Animals Act 1971 if you can prove that your neighbour has:

- not taken **reasonable steps** to restrain the dog, or
- has **actively encouraged** the dog.

It would be difficult to prove that your neighbour has actively encouraged the dog to come into your garden or to bite you. And as there's no duty on your neighbour to fence the dog in, and as dogs are expected to roam, there is no easy answer to what 'reasonable steps' to restrain the dog would be. But if any harm caused is due to the nasty or dangerous character of that particular dog, or breed of dog, and the neighbour knows it may cause harm not likely to be caused by an 'average' dog, the neighbour is legally responsible.

Under the Dangerous Dogs Act 1991, if you can show a dog is 'dangerous' and 'out of control', a magistrates' court can order that it be kept under proper control – for example, muzzled, kept on a leash, neutered or destroyed. The owner may also have to pay a fine of up to £2,000. One bite could be enough for a dog to be classed as dangerous. The court could also disqualify the owner from having a dog for a specified time. To ignore this would mean another fine of up to £2,000. Contact the police or the Royal Society for the Prevention of Cruelty to Animals (RSPCA)★ for action.

Q *How do I know which of the fences around my garden are mine and which belong to my neighbour?*

A The first and obvious rule about fences is that the person who puts up the fence owns it. But this is not always clear. In many cases the matter can be settled by looking at the deeds relating to the property, which can be consulted at Land Registry★ if the land is registered, or in the lease. Often, you will see on the plan that there is a small 'T' marked against the various boundaries. The convention is that the fence belongs to the owner of the property on the side on which the 'T' is drawn. However, the T mark by itself has no meaning, and it is important to check its definition in the body of the deed.

If it is not clear from the deeds, then see if there is any record of who actually put up the fence or whether anyone in the neighbourhood can recall it. If there's no such evidence the law makes a presumption, although this is not a firm rule and evidence to the contrary would change it. The presumption is that a close-boarded fence with supporting posts every so often, or a timber lap fence or chain link fence built similarly, are assumed to belong to the owner on whose side the supports are. The reason for this is the presumption that anyone putting up a fence would erect it as near his or her boundary as possible, so that he or she fenced in the maximum amount of land. But if the fence line ran along the boundary, and the posts projected on the neighbour's side, the posts would be trespassing (p. 248). The best the person putting up the fence can do is to run the fence along the boundary and have the projections on his or her side. The same applies to a garden wall which has supporting pillars every so often.

Q *I'm sure one of my boundary fences is in the wrong place, giving me more land than I should have. Has that extra land become mine?*

A A word of caution when consulting a registered land certificate to decide where boundaries run: registrations are made with what are called 'general boundaries', which are approximate boundaries. So, although Land Registry★ has very good plans, their accuracy is not guaranteed from this point of view except to about the nearest foot or two.

At the time of writing the law was in a state of change. Under the old law the land may have become yours through what the law calls **adverse possession** (or 'squatters' rights'). The transition from the old to the new law will still allow this to happen.

The old law says that if you are claiming land which is not legally yours, it automatically becomes yours as long as you have been using it without the real owner's permission for 12 years or more and during that time the true owner had done nothing about it. During that period, you have to act as if the land is yours: the most obvious proof that you are acting as if you were the owner is the fact that it is fenced in so that only you can be the owner and the 'true' owner is kept out. Your claim exists even if the fencing was put up (or moved!) by a previous owner of your land; the effect of the transfer is cumulative, so when you bought the land you got the benefit of the previous owner's annexation, and the 12 years includes the whole period since the fence was put up – not just your own period of possession.

Once the 12 years have gone by, the land becomes yours automatically, and the fact that the deeds may tell a different story does not alter that. If it is registered land you can get the deeds changed to include the extra land.

From October 2003, Part 9 of the Land Registration Act 2002 has applied to land where the property owner's title is registered. With unregistered land the old rules will continue to apply. Under the new regime:

- after ten years, of adverse possession of the land you now have the right to apply to be the legal owner – the owner's title is no longer automatically extinguished
- the true owner is given details of this application and can object. If there's no objection then the squatter becomes eligible to be registered as the new owner
- if the true owner does object then he has a further two years in which to take proceedings to evict the squatter
- if no eviction action takes place during that time the squatter can apply again to be the owner and will get registered title to the land.

Q *I have had a long-running battle with my neighbour over the height of his trees. Last year he finally agreed to prune them. Now I am moving and the buyer has sent a questionnaire asking all sorts of questions about the house. One of these asks whether I know of any 'disputes' about this or any neighbouring property. Do I have to tell the buyer about the past disagreement?*

A The buyer will ask you a lot of questions, most of them contained in the standard Seller's Property Information Form produced by the Law Society*. You do not have to volunteer any information at all about the house, its condition, or about your relations with neighbours. You can leave it entirely up to the buyer to do any checking. You can leave the questions blank, but that may appear suspicious. The 'Seller's Property Information Form' specifically includes questions about 'disputes' over the land or with owners of neighbouring property. But it is not clear what would amount to a dispute with the neighbour (p. 137). If you do give answers they must be true. Deliberately untruthful answers would give the buyer the right to take legal action against you for misrepresentation.

Q *I am bothered by constant noise from next door where DIY renovations have been going on for over six months, sometimes at night. I have spoken to my neighbours about the drilling and banging but they simply said it will take them another year to finish. Do I have to put up with this?*

A The fact that the neighbours can be heard through the walls is not enough to warrant legal action (pp. 244–5). But the law does recognise unreasonable noise as a type of pollution. Recent changes to the law show that the best way to deal with these problems is to separate the noise maker from the noise-making equipment. Under the Noise Act 1996, Environmental Health Officers (EHOs) at local councils have powers to confiscate equipment such as drills and hi-fis. And if there is excessive noise coming from domestic premises between 11 p.m. and 7 a.m. the neighbours may be committing a 'night noise offence'. If they ignore a warning from the EHOs, the EHOs can impose on-the-spot fines of £40 for first-timers and up to £1,000 for persistent offenders. Your best course of action is to keep a diary showing the time, date and cause of each disturbance and contact the local council if the friendly approach to your neighbours fails. In many cases problems are caused by inadequate noise insulation, and the council can intervene to demand improvements from the property owner.

Chapter 12

Other problems

This chapter deals with a variety of everyday problems which pose legal questions. Accidents, for example, will happen – but if they are somebody else's fault, what can you do? And can anything be done to stem the rising tide of junk mail, faxes, text messages or email 'spam'? What should you do if you are sent goods you never ordered, or if you are worried about personal data being held on computer? That contract you just signed may not seem such a good idea in the cold light of day, but can you change your mind? And in what circumstances may your home be entered without permission?

Q *The girl who delivers our papers fell off her bike and hurt herself on our drive. Are we responsible?*

A Every 'occupier' of property has a duty to ensure that it is reasonably safe for the people who are there by permission or who have a right to be there – so your duty does not just extend to your friends and relations, but also to people delivering post and milk, collecting rubbish etc. This is laid down in the Occupiers' Liability Act 1957 (in Scotland the Occupiers' Liability [Scotland] Act 1960). That does not mean that every time someone hurts him- or herself you will be liable. Liability will depend on how the accident happened:

- if you have neglected repairs to your drive which you know or should have known were needed, then it is your fault
- if you had done all you could reasonably be expected to have done, then you are not to blame
- visitors are obliged to take reasonable care themselves. If they contribute to the injury by their own lack of care, the compensation you may have to pay will be reduced. For example, if there was an enormous pothole that was obvious to any visitor, or if you put up a warning sign, say, a court could decide that you were 70 per cent responsible for the injury, and the visitor was 30 per cent responsible

- you must expect children to be less careful than adults, particularly if you know children are likely to use the drive, or if you have 'allurements' on your premises – for example, a pond, pets, or anything that is likely to attract children. So, if a child is injured on your land because it was not reasonably safe, it will be difficult to argue that he or she contributed to the injury
- if you are responsible you risk having to pay compensation for the time the injured person has to take off work, and the pain and suffering caused (which could be substantial)
- check to see whether your household insurance provides cover for this kind of 'third party liability' (p. 232).

Q *While shopping in a supermarket I slipped on some yoghurt somebody had spilled on the floor. I broke my wrist and tore my coat as I fell. The manageress told me that the supermarket is not responsible as the yoghurt was dropped by a customer. Is that correct?*

A It depends on whether you can prove that the supermarket was negligent. The Occupiers' Liability Act 1957 (in Scotland the Occupiers' Liability [Scotland] Act 1960) places on **occupiers** – people in control of premises – a legal duty to take reasonable care to see that visitors coming on to their land (and to a lesser extent trespassers – p. 248) are reasonably safe. But if the yoghurt had just been dropped by a customer and the supermarket staff were unaware of it, you would not be able to prove that the supermarket had been negligent; if, on the other hand, the staff had seen the breakage or been told of it by a customer and had failed to take immediate action, the shop could be held responsible.

Your compensation would cover the pain and suffering caused by your **personal injury**, plus the cost of repairing your coat. You may also get compensation for any loss of earnings that result.

Q *I knocked a teapot off a shelf as I was walking through a shop. The assistant pointed out a notice which read: 'All breakages must be paid for.' I hadn't seen the notice and I don't consider that the accident was my fault as the shelves were piled high and I stumbled on a loose floorboard. I didn't pay at the time but left my name and address. I've now received a letter demanding £60. Do I have to pay?*

A Notices like this are misleading as you only have to pay for breakages if the shop can prove that you were negligent or careless, and not otherwise, so it makes no difference whether you saw the sign.

Much will turn on the layout of the shop. If the display shelves were too close together, so that it would be difficult for the ordinary shopper to walk along the aisles without knocking off a piece of china, say, then you can argue that the accident occurred in spite of your being careful. Or it may be that the spout of the teapot was sticking out over the edge of the shelf. If, on the other hand, you were rushing through the shop with your clothes flapping, the responsibility would be yours. Often it is a bit of each – perhaps you were partly to blame, but a contributory factor was the loose floorboard, or the layout of the display shelving in the shop. If so, you would have to pay part of the price, taking into account the contributory negligence of the shop. You were absolutely right to leave your name and address and leave it up to the shop to contact you. Alternatively, had you felt under great pressure to pay up, you could have paid **under protest** and written this on the back of the cheque. You could then have tried to claim the money (or part of it) back later (p. 221).

Q *Last winter my car was showered with grit from the council's gritting lorry. The paint-work was badly damaged, but the council has refused to accept liability for its employees. Am I entitled to compensation?*

A If an employee, acting in the course of his or her employment, causes you to suffer damage or loss, you are entitled to claim compensation from that person's employer, in this case the local council. As long as you can prove that the damage was in fact caused by a gritting lorry driven by a council employee, you should write to the council with details of the damage caused. If it will not pay up you will have to consider either making a claim on your own car insurance, or taking the claim to court (pp. 275–6).

Q *I parked my car in the street next to some scaffolding. When I returned paint had been splattered over the roof and bonnet. I complained to the workmen, who told me that I shouldn't have parked so near the work site. Is this right?*

A If you are injured or your property damaged as a result of the carelessness of others, you can claim compensation:

- the workmen owed you and other passers-by a duty of care not to cause any damage when carrying out their work – for example, they should have taken precautions to shield pedestrians and road-users from paint and debris
- your claim will be against the company or business which employed the workmen, rather than the individual workmen, so you should address your written complaint to the managing director or partners as appropriate
- the trader could argue that you contributed to the damage by parking so close to the work, particularly if there were parking restrictions or other warning notices in the area of the scaffolding. If this is the case then any compensation you are entitled to will be reduced to reflect your own lack of care: a court would be able to divide up responsibility accordingly. If the repairs to your car cost £600, say, the court may decide that you were 50 per cent to blame, and you would only recover £300.

Q *I tripped and fell on the pavement and ruined a good pair of shoes. Luckily I was only shaken. Can I claim for the shoes?*

A If you can prove that the pavement needed repair and had not been properly maintained by the local authority, you will have a claim for negligence. There are no hard and fast rules as to what condition the pavement has to be in to give rise to liability, but as a rule of thumb, if paving slabs stick up by more than one inch from the general level of the pavement, this will indicate that it is in an unacceptable state of repair.

You can claim for any financial losses that result from the accident, such as the cost of repairs to your shoes, or their value if they are beyond repair. If the accident had been worse you would have been able to claim for any time off work, and for your personal injury, for which damages could have been high.

Q *I seem to get a load of advertising circulars and other junk mail, and I don't want them. Is there anything I can do about this?*

A You can write to the Mailing Preference Service (MPS)★ to request that your name and address be removed from the mailing lists of companies sending such material. You will be sent an application form to complete or you can register online at *www.mpsonline.org.uk*. This is a free service, set up and funded by the direct mail industry through its representative body the Direct Marketing Association UK Ltd (DMA)★. It gives consumers the opportunity to have their names and addresses taken off (or added to) lists used by direct mail businesses. There is a similar service for unsolicited phone calls (the Telephone Preference Service★) and faxes (the Fax Preference Service★) (see below).

Q *We have been getting unwanted phone calls and faxes from companies trying to sell us things we don't want. While we've always been able to throw junk mail in the bin, these calls are extremely annoying. Is there anything we can do?*

A As well as using the traditional direct-mail shot, many companies use the phone and increasingly the fax to try to sell their products and services. If you find unsolicited offers for goods or services which drop through the letterbox a nuisance, the Mailing Preference Service (MPS)★ has long provided a way of reducing the amount you receive (see above). The law also now offers protection from junk faxes and phone calls.

The Privacy and Electronic Communications (EC Directive) Regulations 2003 provide the following protection for consumers:

- a complete ban on the sending of unsolicited advertising or marketing faxes to individual consumers unless you have given your consent before the fax is sent. Unlike consumers, companies that receive junk faxes don't benefit from this complete ban but can opt out by registering with the Fax Preference Service operated by the Direct Marketing Association UK Ltd (DMA)★

- individual consumers now have the ability to opt out of receiving unsolicited direct marketing phone calls by registering free of charge (with the Telephone Preference Service★)

- companies that operate by direct marketing by phone or fax must offer a contact address or freephone number so that consumers can contact them to ask to be removed from their database.

The Regulations as well as the Data Protection Act 1998 are enforced by the Information Commissioner★, and any company breaching the Regulations faces an enforcement order, and, if they ignore that, a substantial fine. In addition, if you can show that you have suffered damage as a result of a breach of the Regulations you are entitled to compensation. But as most claims will amount to little more than the extra expense of a letter or phone call, plus possible stress as a result (and it is never easy to claim for this kind of compensation), it's unlikely that many compensation claims will succeed.

The Commissioner has also issued best practice guidelines which bring an end to 'opt-out' and 'soft opt-in' means of collecting customer data for future marketing use. Individual customers now must opt-in to any kind of direct marketing. The penalty for misuse of personal data is £5,000, or an unlimited amount for persistent offenders.

Direct marketers (telephone sales businesses, say) must also provide an address or a freephone number for contact by consumers. If you register with the Telephone Preference Service★, businesses must stop calling you.

The Consumer Protection (Distance Selling) Regulations 2000 also require telephone sales and marketing businesses that cold-call consumers at home to give details of who they are and why they're calling at the start of the call.

Q *I often get text messages on my mobile phone saying I've won a prize and giving me a number to call to claim it. How legitimate are these?*

A These are familiar to most mobile phone users. The phone number you have to ring to claim the prize is usually a 'premium rate' number and these can cost a lot more than calls to a conventional number. You'll then have the chance to enter a draw to win a prize. An effective weapon against premium-rate junk faxers and texters is the Independent Committee for the Supervision of Standards of Telephone Information Services (ICSTIS)★, which has the power to fine and bar companies from using these high-cost lines. While many of these messages may be legitimate, an ever-increasing number of complaints to ICSTIS have shown that the prizes are too often non-existent.

The Privacy and Electronic Communications Regulations 2003 ban direct marketing by email, SMS, fax or phone – in short, unsolicited text messages and 'spam' emails to individuals (see below) – unless the consumer gives explicit consent. The law is enforced by the Information Commissioner★.

Don't reply to them, as you could end up out of pocket. ICSTIS has cracked down on companies that send such texts inviting a reply which could be expensive. 'Reverse-billing' texts usually offer information or chat services but they may not tell you how much you're paying or how to cancel – vital information if you've unwittingly subscribed by replying to an unsolicited text. This is a breach of the ICSTIS code. Registering your mobile number with the Telephone Preference Service★ might help you avoid unsolicited texts.

Q *How do I deal with unwanted emails?*

A In theory unsolicited 'spam' emails or text messages are outlawed in the UK following the implementation of the EU directive on Privacy and Electronic Communications. The law means that customers must give their consent before a company can send them emails or text messages for marketing purposes.

Companies will also have to make it clear that emails are for marketing purposes, and that customers can opt out of future emails free of charge. Companies that breach the law could be fined.

At the time the law came in, at the end of 2003, around half of all emails sent were 'spam'. However, the law won't solve the problem quickly. Although the law covers Europe, it won't apply to spam from outside the EU and even within the EU the enforcement regime in another member country may be at best inconsistent. In the meantime:

* never reply to spam unless it's clearly from a reputable company
* always check privacy and security policies of any websites that ask for personal details.

Similarly, if a company uses cookies to track the Internet activity of customers visiting the company website, they must tell you that they use cookies, clearly state why they use them, and give you the chance to reject the cookies.

Q *I recently received a set of CDs in the post. I didn't order them, but now I've been sent an invoice. What should I do?*

A If you receive goods that you haven't ordered and don't want, sent in the hope that you will buy them, you are certainly not obliged to pay for them. As long as the goods were sent to you in your private capacity (not to your business) and had not been requested or ordered by you and you have not agreed to acquire or return them, the goods become your property and you are free to do whatever you want with them.

The law makes it a criminal offence for a trader to do any of the following to consumers in relation to unsolicited goods or services: demand payment, threaten legal proceedings, place or threaten to place the consumer's name on a list of defaulters, or instigate a debt collection procedure (see also p.266). You are therefore not obliged to meet demands for payment of the goods or services and should report the matter to the Trading Standards Department at your local council (address in phone book).

Q *I'm curious to know what information a company has about me. Can I find out?*

A Under the Data Protection Act 1998 you are entitled to see a copy of any **personal data** held on computer that is about you, provided you make a written request to the company. This law also gives you rights in relation to any personal data that is held about you in 'relevant filing systems'. So, access extends to manual records as long as those records are structured either by reference to individuals, or to criteria relating to individuals so it's readily accessible. This means any card index or microfiche storage system, say, or simply details stored in a filing cabinet where the contents are filed by surname. The Act puts the burden on those who hold and process personal data to follow rules which guarantee good practice and openness.

The Act is the result of an EU directive designed to harmonise data protection laws across Europe. It talks about the responsibilities of '**data controllers**' and '**data processors**' and the rights of '**data subjects**' (that's you).

'Personal data' means any information which relates to a living individual who can be identified from those data – your name and address would be enough. In this case the company is the data controller. If the company gets information about you from someone else, another company you may have bought something from in the past and which sold its mailing list, say, then the new company must contact you quickly, identify itself, and tell you for what purposes it wishes to use the data.

Anyone 'processing' any personal data about you must comply with at least one of a number of possible conditions before he or she can process the data. 'Processing' includes anything from getting hold of the data, recording and holding it, to disclosing it to someone else or destroying it. The required conditions include your unambiguous consent to the processing, or, in the absence of your consent, processing must be necessary for performing a contract with you. Another condition is taking steps at your request to make a contract with you.

You have a right to be told who is processing data about you and why. The Act also prevents data being used for direct marketing if you give notice that it is not to be used (p. 260). While the Act applies to computer records and certain 'structured' manual records, these manual filing systems won't be covered in the full provisions of the Act until 2007, although some parts have applied since 2001. But the Information Commissioner★ has urged companies that hold 'manual records' to follow the Act voluntarily until then.

All companies that hold personal data must abide by the 'data protection principles' (a kind of statutory code of good practice). These say that personal data shall:

- be processed fairly and lawfully
- be obtained only for one or more specified and lawful purposes, and not for any reason incompatible with those purposes
- be adequate, relevant and not excessive in relation to the purposes for which it is processed
- be accurate and kept up to date
- not be kept for longer than is necessary for the purpose for which it was obtained.

And where the information concerns 'sensitive personal data' the data controller must get your 'explicit consent' to it being held or passed on. This kind of data includes information about your racial or ethnic origin, political opinions, religious beliefs, physical or mental health or condition, membership of a trade union, sexual life, and so on.

When you do request information the company may make a charge (currently £10), but in some cases it will provide the information free of charge. Write to the company's head office. State that you are requesting information under section 7 of the Data Protection Act 1998. It may help if you state what relationship you have with the company (e.g. employee, customer, patient, student) and supply other relevant details. The company must respond within a prescribed period (currently 40 days): if it does not, you should complain to the Information Commissioner★, who can enforce your right to know.

Q *If I suffer damage, such as credit blacklisting, because of errors in computer records, am I entitled to compensation?*

A Yes. You are entitled to seek compensation through the courts if damage (not just distress) results from any inaccuracy, loss, destruction (without authorisation from the data subject, that is, you) or disclosure held on computer or in a 'relevant filing system', that is, a manual file. If you can prove damage, and there is no defence, the court may award compensation for the damage and any associated distress. If the court is satisfied that personal data held by a data controller is inaccurate, it may order rectification or erasure of that data, or the inclusion of a supplementary statement clarifying the matter. Contact the Information Commissioner★ if you have problems of this sort.

Q *Yesterday I received a visit from a double-glazing salesman who pressurised me into signing a contract to replace all my windows. I've just been told by a friend that the company has a bad reputation and is very expensive. Is there anything I can do about this?*

A Under the Consumer Protection (Cancellation of Contracts Concluded Away from Business Premises) Regulations 1987, if the visit was '**unsolicited**' then you will have a cooling-off period of seven days during which you have the right to cancel the contract you signed. An unsolicited visit is one that you have not expressly requested the salesperson to make: this includes appointments made as a result of unrequested telephone calls, or after delivery of a card proposing the visit. Even were the salesman to make an initial unsolicited visit during which you arranged for him to return, that return visit is also covered by the Regulations (p. 43). However, if you initiated the double-glazing salesman's visit you will not be protected.

To cancel the contract you should either write stating that you are cancelling the contract in accordance with your legal rights, or send the cancellation notice to the salesperson mentioned in the notice of cancellation rights. Keep any goods safe until they are collected by the trader.

Q *Can I cancel any contract signed at home?*

A No. The Regulations don't apply to:

- contracts signed as a result of a home visit which you have requested (see above and p. 43)
- most cash and credit contracts under £35
- agreements for the sale of food and drink, or other goods supplied by regular roundspeople such as a milkman
- agreements that relate to land (you *can* cancel contracts for repairs or improvements to property signed after an unsolicited visit)
- insurance agreements
- certain catalogue order agreements
- investment agreements and agreements for making deposits which are regulated by other legislation.

With any other agreement, if you sign following an 'unsolicited' visit at home the salesperson must give you a notice of cancellation rights at the time the agreement is signed. If he or she does not do this, the contract is null and void: you would be under no legal obligation to pay any money to the company and you may recover any money already paid.

Q *I cancelled the contract I signed at home but the trader says I must forfeit my deposit. Is this true?*

A No. Under the Consumer Protection (Cancellation of Contracts Concluded Away from Business Premises) Regulations 1987 (p. 263), you should not be penalised for exercising your right to cancel within the cooling-off period: your deposit should be returned in full.

Q *If I don't pay a bill, can the trader or company enter my home without permission and seize the goods in question – or anything else?*

A No. If you owe money, the trader must pursue the dispute with you through conciliation, mediation, arbitration or the courts. If he or she succeeds, he or she will be entitled to be paid the money you owe (and may also be entitled to the costs of pursuing you for the money). But there are some circumstances in which there *may* be a right of entry arising from an unpaid bill. The most common are unpaid bills from:

- a gas or electricity supply company (pp. 95–6, 101)
- water supply companies (p. 101)
- telephone companies (pp. 106–7)
- where a court judgment has been obtained for the unpaid bill and bailiffs are sent to enforce that judgment (pp. 267–8).

Q *Who, apart from gas, electricity, water and telephone company employees, and court bailiffs (as described above), can enter my home without my permission, and in what circumstances?*

A Generally, anyone who comes on to your land without your permission is a trespasser, which means that you can evict him or her and sue for compensation (pp. 248–9) in the event of any damage caused. Some officials can enter your home if they have got a warrant; others can enter anyway in certain circumstances, for example, if there is a gas leak (p. 95). Otherwise, the following personnel could have a right to enter your property:

- **the local council** (p. 250)
- **TV licence inspectors** can, as a last resort, get a warrant giving them the power to enter and search your home, if they reasonably suspect that you

own a TV and have not got a licence, or have a black and white licence for a colour TV. The warrant lasts for a month and allows the TV licence inspectors to enter at a reasonable time. However, they are not allowed to use force to get in

- **the police** normally need a warrant to enter your property. However, in certain strictly defined circumstances, for example if they are trying to stop someone from being seriously hurt, they can enter without a warrant. If they search your house while you are not there, they must leave a copy of the warrant behind, and if they force entry, they must leave your house secure. A warrant allows them to search your house for wanted people or stolen goods. If they want to take away items that they reasonably believe to be connected with a serious crime they must give you a receipt

- **fire-fighters** may, if necessary, force entry to your home to put out a fire or rescue anybody who is at risk from the flames. If they believe a fire has started, or need to get into your home in order to access a neighbour's, they may break in

- **the Inland Revenue** For tax inspectors to be able to come into your home without permission, they will need to have obtained a warrant from a judge, who must be satisfied that there are reasonable grounds for suspecting serious tax fraud. If a warrant is issued the tax inspectors will be able to visit your home at any time, search it and remove any evidence that they reasonably believe to be connected with tax fraud. They are permitted to use force to break in if necessary, and to call in the police to help them. If they take documents or other evidence you are not entitled to an explanation about why they are being removed, but you are entitled to a receipt. If they take documents which you need to run your business, they should give you reasonable access to them.

Q *I parked on a piece of land behind an accountants' office in my town. I saw a sign about wheel-clamping but I did not take any notice. I have parked there many times – the land is always empty, and as it was a Saturday afternoon the offices were closed. When I got back there was a clamp on my car. The man from the private clamping company would not let me have my car until I paid £100. I paid, but can they do this?*

A Recent years have seen an enormous increase in clamping on private land. There are two competing legal rights here – the landowner's right to be free of trespassers and your right not to have your car detained against your will. The law says that it is wrong to trespass, but it also says that it is wrong for landowners to detain goods that belong to someone else, even if this person is trespassing.

The Private Security Industry Act 2001 makes it a criminal offence for any person or business to clamp vehicles on private land and charge a release fee without a licence to do so. Unlicensed clamping carries a fine of up to £5,000. Licences are granted by the Security Industry Authority★. At the time of writing the SIA was in the process of developing a code of practice for wheel-clamping companies.

Before licensing came in, prosecutions for blackmail against unscrupulous clampers succeeded in the English courts where signs warning of the risk of clamping were not sufficiently large, or were simply non-existent. This course of legal action would still be possible.

But if the sign is large enough and prominent enough, and the clamping fee reasonable, the legal principle *volenti non fit injuria* will apply. This means that by parking there you accept the risk of clamping and of having to pay a fee before the clamp is removed. By voluntarily accepting this risk the law also assumes that you voluntarily accept the risk that your car will not be unclamped until a reasonable amount of money has been paid. One crucial factor in all of this is that you must be given a proper means of offering to pay, and once you have paid there must be no delay in releasing your car.

Hence, if the sign was small or hidden away, or the fee exorbitant or unreasonable, or there was no means for you to pay immediately to get your car released, you can argue that the clamping was illegal. You could successfully challenge the fee, and claim extra compensation for 'conversion' – the legal term for wrongful detention of your goods. Scottish law is different: even if there is a sign warning of the risk of clamping, clamping with a release fee has been held by the courts to amount to theft and extortion.

Q *I had my driveway resurfaced some time ago. I paid the bill in full but the company keeps sending me demands for the agreed charge. I have told the company that the bill was paid and they always apologise. Then another demand arrives. Now a debt collection agency has threatened to start court action. Is this* **harassment***?*

A It could be. If you have paid what you owe, the company has no claim against you. It is wasting its time and money by employing the collection agency. As long as you can prove you paid, there is no danger that you will be liable for its wasted expense. This is why it is always important to get and keep receipts for payments. It seems that the company's credit department does not communicate with its sales department: but that is not your problem.

You should send a letter to the managing director arguing that the company's constant demands amount to harassment, quoting section 40 of the Administration of Justice Act 1970 (which makes harassment a criminal offence). Although this Act doesn't apply in Scotland the common law offence of **extortion** or possibly a breach of the peace would cover similar situations. Threaten to refer the matter to the police: a crime will have been committed if demands claiming that payment is due under a contract were made with such frequency or in such a way that they caused you or your family alarm, distress or humiliation. If your letter does not do the trick, follow up your threat with action (pp. 146–7 – debt collection guidelines).

Q *Several years ago a friend left his boat in our driveway 'for a week or two'. We've lost touch with him and the boat is taking up space we need. Would we be within our rights to sell it?*

A The law does not provide any easy solutions. But it is clear on one point – you cannot sell something that does not belong to you. If you do, and the friend turns up looking for his boat, you will be accountable for the money you got for it.

But as the friend seems to have abandoned the boat and as you need the space, you may be prepared to argue that to sell was the only practical solution. If so, you must first do all you can to trace the owner, to support your case in the event of the owner returning and taking you to court. For example, send recorded delivery letters to his last known address or contact his last known employer to ask for any forwarding address.

If you do this, you should be prepared to pay the amount you raise from the sale of the boat to the owner if he demands his property during the next six years. Legally, once six years have passed following the sale, it would be difficult for him to bring a claim against you as it would be 'out of time'.

Q *My late-night cab fare cost £21.50 and I offered the driver two £20 notes. This was the only cash I had. He didn't have change and told me he would only accept the right money – no cheques or credit cards. I had to wake a neighbour to borrow the money. Could I have insisted he took a cheque?*

A No. The law is that not only must all debts be paid in cash, but you must provide the exact amount. If you only have a large note you cannot insist on change. What is more, the taxi driver was entitled to take the note and keep the extra rather than take your cheque. Avoid this predicament by agreeing a fare in advance. If you do not have small notes or change, ask, as you get into the cab, whether the driver can change your large note or will take a cheque. This then forms part of your contract with him or her.

Q *Our 19-year-old son had some unpaid parking fines and we came home one day to find a note saying the bailiff had called 'to seize goods worth £190' – the amount he owed. We paid the fines but we are worried this could happen again. Could the bailiff force entry and take our property?*

A A bailiff may not break into your home – his or her entry must be 'peace-able'. However, if your door is unlocked, he or she can go in whether you are there or not. Your son's unpaid parking fines are his responsibility. The bailiff is entitled to seize your son's belongings only to the value that will cover his fines – your own possessions should be safe.

If the bailiff should seize anything wrongly, you have to inform the court or authority concerned. Independent bailiffs are usually employed to do this work but details of the relevant authority or court to contact will be on the paperwork the bailiffs leave for you. You should also complain direct to the firm of independent bailiffs. If the firm is a member of the Enforcement Services Association★, complain to this organisation too.

Q *I've written lots of short stories for my own children and would like to get them published. I saw an advert in a national paper that made getting into print seem easy. I've been dealing with the publisher for over six months and still haven't seen any evidence of the book or of any marketing. It's cost me £1,500 so far. What should I do now?*

A First you must look at the terms of the contract you agreed with the publisher. The fact that you have actually paid money to the publisher shows that this is not a normal publisher/author relationship. Authors don't usually have to pay money to the publisher. Instead, the publisher assesses the manuscript, works out the risk of publishing it, the costs of printing and marketing, and how well it is likely to sell. The author normally receives an advance and, once the book has earned enough in sales, a royalty from the company based on the continuing sales figures.

The kind of publishing where the author is expected to pay the publisher is called 'subsidy publishing' or, more accurately, '**vanity publishing**'. The money you paid was probably asked for as a 'contribution' to production costs. In return for the money these companies often undertake to have the manuscript assessed by an independent editor who will give an honest assessment of the manuscript's literary worth. Some vanity publishers may be committed to producing a good book and marketing it professionally. But all too often this kind of publishing, as its name suggests, simply feeds off the desire many people have to write a book. Always be wary of a company promising to publish your book for a fee.

For example, the assessment the company gives the manuscript may simply be carried out by an employee within the company. It's likely that the company is going to publish your stories no matter what they are like. The reason is that the money you pay is often far more than the cost of production, and the company may have no intention of marketing the final product.

Whether you can recover your money depends on what promises the company made. As a first step you should write to the company asking for details of the publication date, and also insist on a full breakdown of its costs with evidence to support this. You should also ask to see evidence of the marketing it has done or details of what it proposes.

Depending on the response you get the publisher may be guilty of **misrepresentation**, or a straightforward **breach of the contract** you made. To succeed in a claim of misrepresentation you would have to prove that the publisher made representations which you relied on and which induced you to enter into the contract and pay the money.

It would probably be best to allege both misrepresentation and breach of contract. To succeed with either you may need to prove:

- that you were told there would be an independent assessment of the manuscript, yet there was none, or
- that the company intended to publish the book irrespective of the chances of commercial success, or
- that the money you paid was not simply a 'contribution' but was in fact way above the cost of publishing the book, or
- that the company has made no effort to market the book. The argument here is that the company would make money from you regardless of whether any copies of the book were sold, and so wouldn't need to make any effort to market it anyway.

Q *I'm about to buy a metal detector to search the local farmland for Roman jewellery and coins. Can I keep any treasure I find?*

A The rights of those who do unearth 'treasure' has long been a difficult issue for the law. So difficult in fact that coroner's inquests are usually the only way to resolve questions about whether a find is treasure, who owns what, who should be paid and how much.

The Treasure Act 1997 make sure that finders, and landowners, are paid the market value of any 'treasure' found. The government publishes a 'Treasure Annual Report' which shows that around 220 items of treasure are reported each year. If the real owner or his heirs can be found then it's rightfully theirs. Otherwise anything declared as 'treasure' still belongs to the Crown. Anything that isn't treasure belongs to the finder under the old principle of 'finders keepers'. So the first thing is to decide whether it's treasure or not.

'Treasure' is defined as any object (other than coins) that is at least 300 years old, with a minimum of 10 per cent precious metal content. There are special rules for a large haul of coins. It doesn't matter if you find it on the ground, in a building, in a lake or river, or on the 'foreshore' of a beach (that's anywhere between mean high water and low water marks) – except if it comes from a wreck, but that's a different story.

Treasure has to be surrendered to the local coroner who then arranges for it to be valued (usually by the British Museum). If a museum is interested in acquiring it the market value will be paid and this is usually shared between the finder and the owner of the land. If no museum is interested then it will normally be returned to the finder unless there's an objection by the landowner which will have to be settled first!

Alongside the Treasure Act is a Code of Practice. This says that if you have taken your detector where you've not been invited and find treasure, you're unlikely to get any reward at all, or at best a reduced reward. So the Act is not a charter for gold diggers to tramp all over land without permission and benefit from their trespass. The best advice is to agree with the owner of the land beforehand as to how you'll split the proceeds of any finds.

Before you do venture out, take heed. It is illegal to use a detector on a Scheduled Ancient Monument, just in case you thought you could concentrate on more obvious sites. And if you know you've found treasure and fail to report it you could face a fine or imprisonment. The trouble is that most of us wouldn't have a clue. If in doubt, report it to the local coroner.

Chapter 13

Taking your claim further

Statistics show that one in eight consumers drop their case in the small claims track, due to frustration and confusion, and one in five who are awarded compensation never receive their money. But don't be put off. If the company or trader you are dealing with fails to answer your letters, or refuses to sort your problem out, you shouldn't be discouraged from pursuing your complaint further. Many traders are members of **trade associations** which have **codes of conduct** by which their members should abide, and some codes also have Office of Fair Trading (OFT)★ approval so there is additional weight behind them. Many associations offer a conciliation service to help resolve disagreements between consumers and member companies, and others can offer binding arbitration schemes to sort out disputes (pp. 273–5).

There is now a wide range of ombudsman schemes in the UK. Using such a scheme to settle a dispute may be an alternative to going to court. They are completely free and aim to be less complex and time-consuming than legal proceedings, in many cases upholding the spirit and not just the letter of the law.

Going to court is nearly always an option, but should be considered only as a last resort. Indeed, the courts are now under a duty to encourage parties with a dispute to consider methods of Alternative Dispute Resolution (ADR) and to try to resolve their differences out of court (pp. 277–8). Court action can be lengthy and costly, and legal aid is available only to a few. The small claims track, which is an informal and simplified process, provides a comparatively quick and low-cost way of using the courts. Small claims are dealt with as part of the county court: your local one will be listed in the telephone directory. And for cross-border disputes in Europe, consumers now have access to ADR schemes in all member states through the EEJ-Net and Fin-Net (pp. 291–2).

Q *Over a number of months I have been hassled by a doorstep salesman despite the fact that I have asked him on several occasions not to return. How can I stop him returning?*

A First, check whether the salesman's company is a member of a **trade association**, as the trade association may operate a **code of practice** to which the member should adhere. If it has breached the terms of the code, inform the trade association, which may be able to persuade the trader to comply and, in this case, adhere to proper selling methods. However, the trade association can only put pressure on members to comply: it cannot force them to do so. And if they do not follow the code they risk being thrown out of the association and losing the benefits that membership brings them. If the harassment is serious, contact the Trading Standards Department for the areas local to the trader as they may be able to refer the conduct of the trader to the Office of Fair Trading (OFT)★ which has powers to take action against traders who use unfair trading practices. You could also ask the police to intervene (pp. 87–8).

Q *I've got a dispute with a company over some work it did for me. It has suggested the matter be settled by* **conciliation**. *Does this prevent me going to court if a settlement can't be reached?*

A No. Conciliation is usually offered by the trade association to which the trader belongs, which will try to bring you and the trader together to reach a mutually acceptable compromise. Conciliation is free and informal and may result in the settlement of the dispute. It is often a prerequisite to arbitration in that many trade associations insist on the use of conciliation facilities before the dispute can be referred to their arbitration schemes. However, the outcome of conciliation is not legally binding and the trade association cannot force its members to reach a compromise. If conciliation does not resolve the dispute you can still go to court or refer the dispute to arbitration. In many industries special low-cost arbitration schemes are available or, even if not, you can still agree with the other party to use an arbitrator (pp. 273–5).

Q *My four-bedroomed house needs decoration. I have shopped around to get the best quotes. Of the best two, one firm is a member of a trade association and the other isn't. What would be the benefits in choosing the one that is?*

A Membership of a trade association will not necessarily guarantee you better work or fewer problems. It may offer you some safeguards (see above): for example, conciliation facilities and low-cost arbitration schemes if something goes wrong; also, basic standards of workmanship may be set out in the code of practice. However, generally the recommendations in the code of practice have no legal force and no action can be taken in the court if the code is not followed by a member; although some codes allow the arbitrator to take the requirements of the code into account when deciding the case, and with others there may be a guarantee scheme which pays for work to be corrected or completed, if the original contractor goes out of business (pp. 73–4).

Q *How do I know whether a trader is a member of a trade association?*

A The logo of the trade association should be prominently displayed at the trader's/firm's place of business and is usually displayed on the trader's headed notepaper. If so, check with the association that the membership is genuine. Otherwise:

- contact the trade association which seems most likely to apply, or
- ask the trader if he or she is a member of a trade association, or
- contact the Office of Fair Trading (OFT)★.

At the time of going to press the whole issue of codes of conduct, including the level of help they provide the public and the OFT's support for those that meet certain criteria, was under scrutiny with a view to strengthening consumer protection in this area. For an up-to-date position contact your local Citizens Advice★, the OFT, or visit the DTI's Consumer Gateway★ Internet site (soon to be relaunched as Consumer Direct).

Q *I'm owed money by a firm but it doesn't belong to a trade association. Can I still have the matter settled by **arbitration**?*

A Yes. Any dispute can be sorted out by arbitration, whether through a scheme operated under a trade association code of practice (**code arbitration**) or arranged by you independently of any association. Although it is informal, a fee of some kind is payable. Most of the costs arising from code arbitration schemes are borne by the trader or trade association and consequently your costs should be relatively low. So it is best to deal with traders who are members of trade associations which offer alternatives to court.

However, in cases where there is no existing scheme you can refer the matter to arbitration only if both sides agree. You can request it from the Chartered Institute of Arbitrators★ (Arbiters in Scotland), but because you won't be using a pre-existing low-cost scheme the loser will be paying for the arbitrator's time, charged at an hourly rate, so it could be costly, depending on the complexity of the problem. With arbitration, you and the trader each put your side of the story to an independent person – an arbitrator (arbiter in Scotland), whose decision will be binding (see below).

Q *The company I'm claiming money from wants the claim dealt with by an arbitration scheme run by the Chartered Institute of Arbitrators. Could I still go to court afterwards if I wanted to?*

A You have a choice as to whether you have the dispute settled by a court or an arbitration scheme:

- you can't be forced to go to arbitration. The Arbitration Act 1996 and, in Scotland the Consumer Arbitration Agreements Act 1984, outlaw contract terms which state that consumer disputes which would otherwise be dealt with in the small claims track (up to £5,000) must be referred to arbitration. Such contract terms are simply unenforceable
- arbitration schemes are offered as alternatives to court, not in addition, so you have to choose
- consumer arbitration schemes generally, though not always, use written evidence only, so you cannot present your case in person, and it's not always easy to put your problem clearly in writing. Court gives you the chance to put your side of the case (pp. 280–1, 286)
- once you have made your choice, the decision of the judge or arbitrator is binding, so you cannot have the case re-heard using the other option if you are unhappy with the decision.

Q *I'm owed a partial refund from the double-glazing company which did an inadequate job fitting new windows, but the company disputes this. We have signed the form agreeing to have the dispute referred to **arbitration** supplied by the company's trade association, but I'm concerned about the costs this will involve.*

A Many but not all arbitration schemes run for trade associations are operated on a low-cost basis, so they should not cost you very much. Contact the relevant association for details. Generally:

- you will have to pay a registration fee on submitting your case. This varies depending on the trade association involved and the amount in dispute. But if you win your case, the arbitrator is more than likely to order the other party to refund your registration fee
- since most arbitration schemes generally decide cases on written evidence only, you won't incur travel expenses as there is no hearing to attend
- a number of schemes include free site visits: for example, the Glass and Glazing Federation (GGF)★ and British Telecom (BT)★; or free expert examinations: for example, the Retail Motor Industry Federation★.

Q *What is the process of arbitration?*

A Generally, you and the trader will have to sign a joint application form, an **application for arbitration**, which you can get from the relevant trade association and/or the body that administers the scheme, for example, the Chartered Institute of Arbitrators★. The signed form together with the appropriate registration fee must be returned to the organisation. If the case is considered suitable for arbitration (that is, it fits the rules of the scheme), the organisation will send you (as the **claimant**) a **statement of claim** and an information sheet, detailing the process. Some schemes are also available online. After reading the claim form and any guidance carefully to ensure you comply with all the time limits and procedures:

- you must complete the statement of claim by setting out briefly but concisely the facts of your case. This, together with the appropriate **registration fee** and all supporting documentation, should be sent to the Chartered Institute of Arbitrators, or whichever organisation operates the scheme in question, as indicated on the form
- it is important to ensure that you send copies of all the documents which support your case, for example, receipts, invoices, contracts, brochures, expert reports and photographs, as the arbitrator's decision will, in most situations, be based on the information contained in the statement of claim, and supporting documents. There will be no opportunity to clarify matters at an oral hearing
- the trader (called the **respondent**) will have to do the same by sending in a defence and supporting documents
- having received the documents, the arbitrator will read the papers and if necessary arrange an inspection or site visit. He or she will then make a decision and both parties will be notified in writing.

Q *I won my case at arbitration but the trader has failed to pay the amount he was ordered to pay me. Is there any way that I can force him to pay up?*

A Initially it is a good idea to inform the relevant trade association, which may be able to persuade the trader to comply with the arbitrator's decision and may also be able to take disciplinary action against the trader under its code of conduct. If this doesn't persuade the trader to pay up, then you can go to court to enforce payment of the award as the arbitrator's decision is legally binding and enforceable by law. By agreeing to go to arbitration both you and the trader also agree to accept the findings. So if either side fails to comply the agreement will have been broken (see p. 287 for the various methods of enforcement).

Q *I've heard court action sometimes referred to as 'small claims arbitration'. Is this the same as 'code arbitration' offered by trade associations?*

A No. Confusingly, the term 'arbitration' was often used to refer to an informal means of arriving at a decision on a dispute which is binding on both parties, as well as to small claims court hearings. But the term 'arbitration' is no longer used to refer to the small claims procedure, which is completely different from arbitration schemes organised by bodies such as the Chartered Institute of Arbitrators★.

Civil court cases are governed by the Civil Procedure Rules (CPR) which are designed to make access to justice in England and Wales easier and quicker for all claims. The old system of small claims arbitration has been replaced by the small claims track. This allows cases involving claims up to £5,000 to be allocated to an informal and low-cost court process.

When you start proceedings in the county court, claims of £5,000 or less (£1,000 or less for any personal injury element within that) are 'small claims' and are likely to be referred to the **small claims track** (or, popularly, small claims court). The case is normally heard by a district judge.

Arbitration schemes run for trade associations are operated by independent bodies such as the Chartered Institute of Arbitrators. The arbitrators appointed are independent of the trade association and are usually qualified professionals, for example surveyors, architects, engineers, lawyers or retired judges.

Q *My insurance company won't pay my claim. I've written to the head office but am now at an impasse. Could the* **ombudsman** *help me?*

A It is worth making your complaint to the relevant ombudsman to try to settle the dispute before considering going to court. There is a wide range of ombudsman schemes in the UK. Some are statutory and cover everyone in that industry (e.g. the Legal Services Ombudsman★); others are voluntary and cover only those companies which have joined the scheme (e.g. the Ombudsman for Estate Agents★) (pp. 127–8). So if you have a complaint against a company that is not a member of a voluntary scheme you cannot take your case to the Ombudsman. Generally the following apply to *all* schemes:

- they are completely free for consumers and aim to be less complex and time-consuming than legal proceedings, in many cases going beyond the letter of the law
- there are time limits for complaining, usually six or 12 months from reaching **deadlock** with the company (see below). Check with the relevant scheme
- some ombudsmen can **award** compensation, others can only **recommend** that the company pays up. Some have a maximum of £100,000, but most are unlimited
- these schemes are designed to be independent, accessible and, compared with going to court, quick.

Q *I've complained without success to the local branch of the company with which I'm in dispute. I want to write to the ombudsman, but if I do this, would the decision be binding, or could I still go to court?*

A Generally you have to exhaust all attempts at sorting out the dispute with the company first. Companies in most industries are required to have in place a complaints procedure. So you must usually write to the head office of the company. If there is still no agreement, make sure the company is a member of the relevant ombudsman scheme and send the ombudsman all the details. An ombudsman's decision is binding on the organisation you have complained about, but it is not binding on you, so you can still go to court or to arbitration if you are unhappy with the decision. But you should consider seriously whether a court is likely to take a different view about it.

Q *I wish to refer the dispute I have with my bank to the relevant ombudsman but the bank has refused to issue the necessary 'deadlock' letter.*

A You should not be stopped by a company/organisation from referring your dispute to the ombudsman. If the company tries to stop you by refusing to provide a letter indicating that you have reached stalemate (a deadlock letter), complain to the ombudsman anyway about the way your complaint has been dealt with, as well as about the original matter over which the dispute arose.

Q *I've heard the term ADR mentioned. What does it stand for and how can it help me?*

A ADR stands for **Alternative Dispute Resolution** and means any method of resolving a dispute between two or more parties which does not involve legal proceedings. In April 1999 radical changes took place in the county courts and the High Court in England and Wales. And now, whatever the amount being claimed, judges must place great emphasis on trying to get the parties to resolve their dispute by using ADR before allowing cases to go to a formal court hearing. Negotiation, conciliation, mediation, ombudsman schemes and established arbitration schemes are all forms of ADR.

In mediation, for example, a neutral mediator helps the parties in dispute to negotiate a settlement. The mediator does not make a decision on behalf of the parties and has no power to impose a view on them. The process differs from conciliation in that the mediator takes a more active role in the discussions and will suggest the terms of a possible settlement, but neither side is obliged to accept any of the suggested terms. With conciliation, the conciliator aids or encourages the parties in dispute to reach their own agreement.

A number of organisations such as Mediation UK★, the Centre for Effective Dispute Resolution (CEDR)★ and the Alternative Dispute Resolution Group★ offer ADR facilities. The fees they charge depend on the amount in dispute. At the time of writing CEDR offers a day's mediation for £350 plus VAT per party where the amount in dispute is under £20,000, and the ADR Group charges

£175 plus VAT per party for one-and-a-half hours of mediation where the amount in dispute is £25,000 or less.

Q *I am owed £600 by a trader, who has refused to give me the money even though I wrote asking for it. Can I sue him?*

A As long as you have a genuine dispute with a company or trader you can claim through the courts. However, even if the amount of your claim is below the small claims limit of £5,000 (£1,500 in Scotland, £1,000 in Northern Ireland) you should try to sort the matter out by using any alternative methods first, so contact any relevant trade association and ask if it will conciliate, or refer the matter to an ombudsman if appropriate (pp. 276–7). If that proves unsuccessful, you will then have to decide between arbitration and court (pp. 273–6). If you do choose to start legal action you need to send one last letter to the trader, stating that if he or she does not settle the matter within a reasonable time, usually seven to 14 days, you will start a claim in the county court. Such a letter is known as a **letter before action**. Since radical changes to the civil court procedures were introduced in April 1999 you should be as clear as you can be about your claim, giving a summary of the facts, the nature of the complaint, and how the amount you are claiming is arrived at. If you do not hear from the trader within the time limit, you can fill in the claim form and start the ball rolling (pp. 289–90).

Q *I want to issue a claim in my local county court against a company based over a hundred miles away. Will it definitely be heard at a court local to me?*

A You can start the claim (**issue proceedings**) in your local county court. But if the company (or person) you are suing defends the case, it will automatically be transferred to a county court nearer its place of business as long as the claim is for a specific amount. Claims for unspecified amounts, for example, for 'damages limited to £5,000' (pp. 279–80) will not be transferred automatically.

You will have to fill in an **'allocation questionnaire'** and a judge will then decide which **track** the case goes into (see opposite and p. 280). In the questionnaire you'll have the opportunity to ask for the case to be heard in your local court. Many cases settle out of court, but if you do have to travel a long way and you win your case, you can recover reasonable travelling expenses and currently up to £50 for your loss of earnings (however long the case lasts, but it is likely to be only a matter of a few hours and a maximum of one day).

Q *I had repairs carried out to my boat but the work was very shoddy and I have incurred further costs in having it put right. I want to sue the repairer but I'm worried about what it could cost me. Could I keep costs down by using the small claims court?*

A This is exactly the kind of dispute that is suitable for the small claims track of the county court. The small claims procedure is intended to deal with claims of up to £5,000 in England and Wales (£1,500 in Scotland, £1,000 in Northern Ireland). However, even if a claim is for a very small sum there is no guarantee that it will be allocated to the small claims track. Everybody who wishes to use the courts has to complete an 'allocation questionnaire' after the claim has been started, and also pay an extra fee (currently £80 on claims for more than £1,000), on top of the initial claim fee. This 'allocation fee' is for a judge to tell you which track he or she considers most appropriate. Pick up information from your local county court, Citizens Advice Bureau or legal advice centre. Once in the small claims track there are simplified rules which make it fairly speedy and straightforward for people using it.

The main advantage is cost. First, you won't have to seek the assistance of a solicitor so you won't incur solicitors' charges. Secondly, even if you lose, the only costs which can normally be awarded against you are:

- the defendants' and their witnesses' (if any) reasonable expenses incurred travelling to and from the hearing
- up to £50 per witness for loss of earnings or costs incurred in staying away from home or for childcare, say
- up to £200 to cover the cost of any expert fees.

If you win the judge has discretion to make the loser pay your expenses and those of your witnesses, within certain limits. You will usually get back:

- the court fee for issuing the claim, and possibly the allocation fee as well
- your own and your witnesses' (if any) reasonable expenses incurred travelling to and from the hearing
- up to £50 for your own and your witnesses' (if any) loss of earnings or accommodation or childcare costs
- up to £200 if you paid an expert to provide evidence to support your case (this covers the preparation of any report and attending the hearing).

Q *What are the risks involved in starting legal proceedings for more than £5,000?*

A The amount being claimed will usually decide which court the claim should be started in and also which 'track' the case will follow within the court. There are three case 'tracks' that apply. The **'small claims track'** in the county court will deal with claims of £5,000 or less (except personal injury and housing disrepair cases where the limit is £1,000). The **'fast track'**, also in the county court, will deal with all cases over these limits and up to £15,000 (or up to £50,000 for personal injury claims). And claims for more than £15,000 (or more than £50,000 for personal injury claims) will usually go down the **'multi**

track' in the High Court. However, there's no guarantee as to which track your case will go down – the decision rests with a judge who allocates the case to the most appropriate track.

The 'fast' and 'multi' tracks are subject to formal rules of evidence, and unless you have had experience of presenting cases in court and cross-examination you would be at a severe disadvantage. So legal representation, although not compulsory, is usually essential and as a result you will have to ask a solicitor to act for you. Furthermore, unlike in small claims cases, if you lose your case you face the prospect of having to pay not only your own lawyers' costs but also those of the other side, which could run into several thousands of pounds. Therefore proceedings in any track other than small claims could turn out to be very expensive.

In Scotland the rules haven't changed and claims of up to £1,500 are dealt with in the small claims process, which is intended to provide a quick, straightforward way of settling disputes that does not necessarily require a solicitor. Similarly, in Northern Ireland the small claims limit remains at £1,000 and the risks of incurring costs described above apply to all claims for more than that amount.

Q *I want to issue proceedings for £5,500. I want to avoid using a solicitor. Is there any way the case can still be heard as a small claim, even though it is over the small claims limit?*

A It can still be heard using the small claims track if either you or the other side applies to the court and the court agrees. This way, you can still benefit from the informal procedures (pp. 281–5). However, the 'no cost' rule won't apply as it's over the £5,000 limit. So if you lose you will have to pay the other side's costs, as in the 'fast track' (see above). Alternatively, you can limit your claim to £5,000 and make full use of the benefits of the small claims track. But you will have to accept that you will not recover the extra £500, and there is still the danger that the claim will be allocated to a different track (pp. 278–9).

Q *How do I start a claim using the small claims track?*

A Free leaflets explaining what to do are available from county courts and can be printed off from the Court Service Internet site at *www.courtservice.gov.uk/*. You can also obtain a claim form from your local county court. Reforms of the court system have done away with the plethora of forms there used to be. Now, however much you're claiming, there is one form for all types of claim. It is simple to fill in. If you do need any assistance, the court staff, your local Citizens Advice or Consumer Advice Centre will help you. Otherwise:

- complete the form by inserting the full name and address of yourself (the claimant) and the other side (the defendant) and set out briefly the details of your claim. Finish by stating the remedy you require: these details are called the particulars of claim

- it is important that you sue the right person or company – a name on a letterhead, for example, may only be the trading name, not the name of the registered company
- check that the trader is still in business by contacting the Trading Standards Department for the area local to the trader, or, if it is a company, phone Companies House*
- once you have completed the claim form, take it plus a copy to the court, or send it by first-class post. Also ensure you keep a copy for yourself. You will have to pay an issue fee ranging from £30 to £80 for claims up to £5,000, although if it is above £5,000 it will not be heard as a small claim. If you pay by cheque or postal order, make it payable to 'HMPG'.
- a few days later you should receive a note ('Notice of Issue') from the court telling you the number of the case. The court will send a copy of the claim to the defendant.

For straightforward claims where only money is involved you can now use Money Claim Online – a court-based Internet claims service (p. 285).

Q *I'm owed £5,600 by a double-glazing company. I want to sue them for the full amount but I know it won't be heard in the small claims court. How do I commence proceedings?*

A The process for starting a claim for over £5,000 is the same as in the small claims track but there are further steps which have to be taken before a hearing date is fixed. The court will inform you of what steps you should take as it tends to vary depending on the type of claim and its complexity. You should instruct a solicitor, and bear in mind that if you lose you may have to pay the other side's costs (pp. 279–80).

In Scotland claims for over £1,500 can be dealt with in the sheriff court but formal procedures apply and you start proceedings by issuing an initial writ. You will need the assistance of a solicitor to start such proceedings.

Q *I've received a claim form, form N1, from a company claiming £2,200 for work it did on my garden patio. This work was so bad that I don't want to pay anything. It's going to cost another £2,450 to put the work right. What should I do?*

A If you dispute the full amount claimed, you should send a **defence** to the court within 14 days from the date you receive the claim by completing form N9B; if you fail to do this you risk having judgment entered against you (p. 282). This form and full instructions should be sent to you with the claim. The court will then send the defence to the person making the claim (the claimant). If a defence is not filed with the court within the time limit, the claimant can apply for judgment to be given automatically ('in default'). As you will have to pay £250 more than the claim to put the inferior work right, you will have to fill in the form to make a **counter–claim** against the claimant. Always:

- read everything the court sends you very carefully: court forms and language are not as clear as they could be. If in doubt, ask for help. The court staff should be able to answer your queries
- put your evidence and arguments together carefully and avoid irrelevant elements
- keep receipts for all expenses you intend to claim and make sure you have all the evidence you need to support your arguments, such as estimates, bills and written reports.

Q *I issued proceedings approximately three weeks ago in my local county court for compensation for a spoilt holiday. Although I received a note from the court indicating the case number, I've heard nothing from the defendant. What should I do next?*

A When sending you notification of the case number, the court will also have sent you documents setting out what happens if you hear from the defendant and what you should do if you don't. Read these documents *very* carefully.

You should ring up the court and find out whether the defendant has sent a **defence** to the court. If he or she has, then the case will proceed in a set way. If he or she has not, you can apply to have **judgment in default** entered. You do this by obtaining from the court and completing form N30 (judgment for claimant) or by filling in the form attached to the Notice of Issue which the court will have already sent to you (form N205A for claims for a specified amount and N205B for unspecified amounts). Before you complete the form think carefully about how you would like to be paid. You may prefer the money straight away, but if it's a one-man-band or small firm you may be more likely to get it if you opt to be paid in reasonable instalments. Send or take the completed form to the court, which will enter judgment for you. You will be sent a copy of the judgment, which will indicate a time within which you require payment from the defendant. A copy of the judgment should be sent to the defendant.

Q *Should I be represented by a solicitor at the hearing? If I'm not, and the other side is, will I be disadvantaged?*

A This depends on whether the case is a 'small claim' or not:

- if the case is being heard under the **small claims track**, you will not need the assistance of a solicitor in preparing or presenting the case. The small claims procedure is specifically designed for you to take your own case to court and operates by simplified rules. Therefore, even if the other side is represented by a solicitor you should not be disadvantaged

- if the case is being heard in the **fast or multi track** (pp. 278–80) (sheriff court in Scotland for claims over £1,500), strict rules of evidence and presentation apply and the case is heard in a formal atmosphere, so legal representation is very important. Unless you have had experience of this type of thing before, you may find it difficult to present your case and cross-examine effectively. Clearly, if your opponent is professionally represented you would be at an unfair disadvantage.

Q *I've issued a claim. Will I have to attend a court hearing?*

A Issuing a claim does not necessarily mean that you have to go to court. You can always pull out if, for example, the defendant pays up, or makes an offer that is acceptable (you may need a 'consent order' to agree this outcome formally). The threat of proceedings in a letter before action and/or the issuing of a claim shows you mean business and often results in the settlement of the matter.

Q *I issued a claim and I have now received a form from the defendant in which he admits he owes me money, and has offered to pay the money in instalments. What should I do?*

A If you're not happy with the amount offered you should proceed on the basis that the claim will carry on. If you're happy to accept the amount the defendant has offered and the instalment terms you should fill in the relevant form (the bottom of form N205A if it's a claim for a fixed amount, otherwise form N226). The court will then enter judgment in your favour on the terms agreed. If you object to the instalments suggested you can ask the court to make what's called a 'determination'. Put simply, a judge will decide what is reasonable in the circumstances.

Q *I want to start a small claim. How will my claim be dealt with by the court?*

A Even before filling in a claim form to start legal action the law expects everybody to be up-front and open about a claim as early as possible. To encourage this a number of '**pre-action protocols**' exist to ensure that there is full and early exchange of information so all sides know what the dispute is about, how much is being claimed and what the evidence is. If you do have to start legal action you'll have to fill in a claim form (see pp. 289–90). It's the same form whether you're using the county court or the High Court.

The form should contain brief particulars of your claim, and you should attach a separate sheet with detailed particulars. You'll also have to sign a '**statement of truth**' saying that the facts you've put in the claim are indeed true.

Once you've issued your claim form, and after a defence has been filed, both parties will receive an '**allocation questionnaire**'. You have two weeks to return this to the court. This prompts you to try to settle the claim and also allows the court to decide to which 'track' to allocate the case to. Even if it's well below £5,000 there is no guarantee it will be dealt with as a small claim. You'll be asked what steps you've taken to use Alternative Dispute Resolution (ADR) (pp. 277–8) and will then receive a list of standard directions. For example, these set out the deadlines for exchanging copies of your evidence with the other party, and so on.

Whenever a court deals with a case, whether in the small claims track, fast or multi track (pp. 279–80), it must do so in line with what is called the '**overriding objective**'. This means that courts must deal with cases justly and judges must actively manage cases. The aims are to:

- ensure the parties are on equal footing
- save expense
- deal with the case in ways which are proportionate to the amount of money involved, to the importance of the case, to the complexity of the issues, and to the financial position of each party
- encourage the parties to co-operate with each other
- identify the issues at an early stage; deciding promptly which issues need full investigation at a full trial and disposing of any others that can be dealt with earlier; deciding the order in which issues are to be resolved
- encourage and facilitate the use of ADR procedures if appropriate, and help the parties to settle the whole or part of the case (pp. 277–8)
- deal with the case without the parties needing to attend court, and make use of technology
- give directions to ensure that the trial of the case proceeds quickly and efficiently.

Q *I'm due to attend a small claims hearing in few days' time to defend a case. What can I expect?*

A If you are familiar with the details of your case, the hearing should be informal and quick, so there is no need to be nervous. Taking the following steps should make matters easy for you whether you are bringing or defending a case:

- the day before the hearing you should read your documents so you are clear about the facts of your case
- make notes in point form of the main facts you have to raise in order to prove/defend your case, and flag the documents which cover those points, so you can find them easily during the hearing

- make sure you take with you to the hearing all the documents relating to the case
- ring your witnesses the day before to remind them of the time and place of the hearing
- arrive at the court in plenty of time
- at the hearing keep matters simple and stick to the points you mentioned in your claim/defence.

The clerk of the court will call both parties into the room where the hearing is to take place. Although the case probably won't be in a proper courtroom it will be open to the public. However, it will take place in an **informal** atmosphere before a **district judge** (**sheriff** in Scotland). District judges differ in their approaches: some ask questions and intervene a great deal, while others simply listen. In any event the claimant will be asked to give his or her side of the story and call his or her witnesses, if any. The defendant will then be given the opportunity to ask the claimant any questions. The defendant will then give his or her side of the story and call any witnesses. The claimant will then have the opportunity to ask the defendant questions. Once each side has presented evidence, the district judge will give his or her decision. This will be confirmed in writing a few days later by the court.

Q *The courts are so behind when it comes to using the Internet. Why can't I make a claim online?*

A If you are claiming money and nothing else, the amount you're asking for is less than £100,000 and your claim is in sterling then you can use Money Claim Online (MCOL) at *www.courtservice.gov.uk/mcol*. The other requirement is that there is only one defendant, or, if there are two, the claim is for a single amount against each of them.

Using the Internet, you can fill in a claim form and pay the issue fee. The defendant can file a defence and a counterclaim online or in the old-fashioned way if he wishes. All the forms needed for a traditional claim (pp. 283–4) have their own online versions. If the claim is disputed, then all the parties will have to attend a hearing as normal. You can also apply for enforcement online if the defendant fails to pay up.

Q *If I don't agree with the district judge's decision, can I appeal?*

A Yes, but you have to get the permission of the judge. And you have to give proper reasons for appealing. It's not enough that you don't like the decision the judge made, so if you simply disagree with the outcome there is nothing you can do. And be aware that an appeal could be very expensive as none of the cost benefits of the small claims track apply even though it's a small claim you're appealing against.

Q *I have failed to reach an agreement with a company that owes me £950. It is a member of a trade association which offers arbitration. I don't know whether to go to arbitration or issue a small claim. What are the advantages/disadvantages of arbitration?*

A The advantages of having your claim dealt with by arbitration are:

- generally there is no hearing to attend so you need not take time off work or incur travel expenses
- if you're worried about presenting your case in person, arbitration is better as it is based on documents only and some can be made online
- financial ceilings may be higher than the small claims limit of £5,000 (for example, ABTA's arbitration scheme can deal with claims up to £25,000).

The disadvantages are:

- you won't be able to argue your case in person
- it's not always easy to put your problem in writing and include all relevant facts
- the trader must be a member of the relevant trade association to enable you to use the scheme.

Q *What are the pros and cons of taking court action using the small claims track?*

A The advantages of pursuing a claim through the small claims procedure are:

- costs (see pp. 278–80)
- you present your own case in an informal hearing. It may be easier for you to get across the extent of your case by giving a verbal account of your troubles
- it is relatively easy to make a claim and some can be made online (p. 275)
- issuing a claim shows you mean business and often leads to a sensible offer.

The disadvantages of court action are that:

- you may need to take time off work to attend the hearing
- you may incur travel expenses
- you will have to present your own case at the hearing (some people find this difficult and daunting)
- there is a financial limit under the small claims procedure of £5,000, or £1,000 for personal injury claims (£1,500 in Scotland, £1,000 in Northern Ireland).

Q *I obtained judgment in the court for payment of a debt and although I sent a copy of the judgment to the defendant and have requested payment on numerous occasions, he has failed to pay up. How can I force him to pay?*

A You will probably have to take further court action to get your money. The various procedures open to you are set out and explained in a free booklet from your local county court. The court will do nothing at all on its own initiative so it is up to you to take enforcement action and to choose the best method. The key to successful enforcement is to find out what assets there are and to select a method of enforcement to get at them. The methods of enforcement are currently under review by the Lord Chancellor's Department but at the time of writing the main ones are:

- **attachment of earnings** Payment is extracted from the wages or salary of an employed (as opposed to a self-employed) judgment debtor. The employers are obliged to make specified deductions from pay on a week-by-week or month-by-month basis and pay it to the court
- **warrant of execution** This orders bailiffs to remove and sell sufficient goods belonging to the judgment debtor to pay the debt. Items on hire purchase or belonging to someone else may not be seized. The judgment debtor's clothes, bedding and trade tools up to a certain value may not be seized
- **third party debt order** This process directs moneys that are due to the judgment debtor to be paid to you instead. For example, it can be used to access money held in the judgment debtor's bank or building society account or a trade debt
- **charging order** This can be placed on domestic or business property owned by the judgment debtor, by himself or jointly with someone else. The object of such an order is to have the property sold to pay the judgment debt.

If you do not know anything about the financial position of the judgment debtor or his or her business, it may be in your best interests to find out as much as you can on this before opting for one of the above methods of enforcement. You can do this by applying to the court for an **order to obtain information** from a judgment debtor. This procedure allows you, or the court, to ask the debtor a series of questions to find out how much money/assets he or she has and how much he or she can afford to pay. Once you have such information it will then be easier for you to decide whether it is worth enforcing the judgment and, if it is, to choose the best method.

Q *I was just about to sue a company when I heard that it had gone out of business. Is it worth taking the company to court?*

A Unfortunately, once a company has gone into liquidation it is very difficult to recover any money unless the company is solvent and merely ceasing to trade. Usually the only people who have a chance of recovering any money from such a company are preferential creditors such as the Inland Revenue or those who have secured loans to the company. These groups will be the first to be paid out should there be any money and only if there is some money left over will unsecured creditors be paid.

In the circumstances, your only course of action is to notify the liquidators of the nature and extent of your claim as soon as possible so that they are fully aware of all outstanding debts. If you paid on credit you may have a claim against the lender or credit-card company. And if you took out an insurance-backed guarantee you should not lose out (pp. 73–5).

Q *I have a claim that I'm sure will end up in court. I can't afford lawyers and I know I will not qualify for any kind of Legal Aid. Are there any other ways I can fund my case?*

A Most people in the UK do not qualify for Legal Aid. The qualifications for Legal Aid have been substantially tightened over the last decade and it is now available only to people with income at income support levels. This leaves an increasing number of people having to think even more carefully about taking legal action. So you are not alone. Consider the following:

- if your claim is for £5,000 or less (£1,500 or less in Scotland, up to £1,000 in Northern Ireland) you can use the small claims track, which is designed so that you can represent yourself. There is a 'no legal costs' rule which means that you do not have the threat of having to pay the other side's legal bills if you were to lose your case (pp. 278–80)
- in most kinds of dispute clients are now free to arrange with lawyers that a legal case is taken on a 'conditional fee' basis. This is a contract between the client and lawyer whereby the lawyer agrees that if the claim fails he or she will not receive any payment. More commonly known as 'no win, no fee' agreements, they remove the uncertainty and financial risk of going to law (pp. 112–3)
- in a limited range of legal work contingency fee agreements are also available. Here you could agree that if you lose the case you pay your lawyer nothing, but if you win you give a percentage of the compensation you recover. These agreements aren't yet allowed for court work, but they are for general legal negotiations (pp. 110–11)
- you may already have legal expenses insurance without being aware of it. This is insurance against the possibility of future legal expenses. The cover can pay for a lawyer to claim compensation on your behalf in a wide range of circumstances. Some house and car insurance policies include legal

expenses insurance. Others let you buy it for an extra premium. Car add-ons generally cover compensation for car accident injuries and other uninsured losses, such as hiring a car while yours is off the road. Household add-ons usually cover consumer disputes, and legal problems connected with home ownership, personal injury and employment. Some car breakdown services and travel insurance policies help with legal expenses too, and some cover the many problems which can arise from a specific event, such as moving house (pp. 120–1).

Q *A builder took me to court for a debt and I lost the case. I paid the award but when I recently applied for a credit card the credit reference agency files still showed the judgment and I think this is why I was turned down. Surely the record should be removed?*

A As soon as a judgment is entered in the county court details are recorded at the Registry of County Court Judgements★. As long as the amount of the judgment against you (the 'judgment debt') is paid within one month of the date of the judgment, you can ask the Registry to remove it from the record and this should then be done. Assuming you did pay within a month, send proof to the Registry and to the credit reference agency concerned and ask to see a copy of the corrected entries with the judgment removed.

If you waited longer than one month before you paid, the judgment will remain on the record and you will have to apply for a 'certificate of satisfaction' from the county court that made the judgment. There will be a small fee for this. Although the certificate will show that the judgment debt is no longer outstanding, the judgment will not be removed from the record completely. Both 'satisfied' and 'unsatisfied' judgments remain on the Register until the end of the sixth calendar year following the date of registration. They will also stay on the files of credit reference agencies for six years from the date of judgment (pp. 143–4). Therefore, if you have a judgment against you and want to avoid any knock-on effects (in respect of your credit rating, for example), make sure that you pay within one month.

Q *I tried to start a small claim against a window-cleaner who damaged my car. The claim was returned to the court marked 'not known at this address'. The court bailiff was told the same thing when he tried to deliver it. I know I have given his correct address and he is still working in the area. Why is it not enough for the bailiffs simply to leave the claim?*

A To pursue your claim in the hope of getting a judgment against the window-cleaner you must 'issue' and 'serve' the claim on him (pp. 280–2). In the county court this is usually completed by the simple process of sending the claim form to the defendant's address. You must be able to prove to the satisfaction of the court that the defendant has been properly notified of the claim. As the posted claim was returned, and as the bailiffs could not verify that the defendant would actually get the claim form if they left it at the address, proof of service will be difficult. Bailiffs may not act deviously and if the window-cleaner simply denied his identity and his family gave him cover, there is little the bailiffs could do.

One way to get round this problem is by serving the claim personally on the defendant. Unlike the bailiffs, you know what the defendant looks like and you can identify him. So 'personal service' could be achieved by finding him at home or catching him up his ladder, say. Once you find him it would be enough for you to inform him of the contents of the claim and throw it down in his presence. You must then swear on oath that you found him, identified him, and served the claim on him. You can do this by filling in a standard form of affidavit (form N215) from your local county court. If the defendant does not then put in his defence you can apply for judgment 'in default' in the normal way (p. 282).

Q *My previous experiences of courts and court staff have all been bad. And my recent small claim was no different, with long delays in the correspondence and rude staff. Isn't the Courts Charter supposed to guarantee that I will be treated like a human being and not like a nuisance?*

A That is the idea of the Charter for Court Users ('Courts Charter'). The Court Service Unit⋆ is now an executive agency of the Lord Chancellor's Department providing administrative support to the High Court, Crown Court and the county courts. Magistrates' courts are not covered by the Courts Charter but have their own charters, administered by local magistrates' courts committees (MCCs), which report to the Lord Chancellor.

The Courts Charter covers you in your role as a juror, a witness or a defendant in criminal cases, and has special standards for divorce cases and family disputes. Most important for consumers, it also spells out what you can expect if you have anything to do with the county court (including the small claims court) or High Court. For example, if you are appearing in a county court, you can expect:

- to have your case heard in court within a maximum of 40 days once you have told the court you are ready for trial
- to be sent a copy of the court's decision no more than ten days later
- when you write to the court, a response within ten days.

The courts have many leaflets available, so make use of them: they can work to your advantage. For example, there are leaflets explaining each stage of the small claims procedure as well as family and probate matters. Complaints about any aspect of the service you receive from the courts (but not the outcome of your case) should be made to the customer service manager of the court at the time it arises. Further complaints should be made to the Chief Clerk and if you are not happy with the reply you are given you should write to the Courts Administrator.

The name of the Chief Clerk and the name and address of the Courts Administrator are displayed in every court office. Leaflets contain all the information and addresses you need, as well as describing the complaints procedure in detail. The Courts Charter says that your written complaint will be acknowledged within two working days and you will receive a reply within 20 working days from the date your letter is received.

If you are not happy with the Courts Administrator's investigation you can write to the customer service department of the Court Service Unit for an independent investigation. If you have lost money or incurred costs as a result of a mistake by a member of the court staff, the Chief Clerk is your point of contact. You must provide proof of your financial loss. The Clerk will assess the claim and send a report to the Courts Administrator. Large claims will be passed on to the customer service department of the Court Service Unit. If you have a complaint about the way a judge has treated you personally in court (apart from decisions made in your case) you should write to the Judicial Group at the Court Service Unit address. Quote the name of the court you attended, your court case number, the date of your hearing, if possible the name of the judge concerned, and your reasons for making the complaint.

Q *Why do I have to consider alternatives before going to court? I just want to start legal proceedings as quickly as possible to get my money.*

A If lawyers can't show they've explored the alternative options first judges can put the litigation on hold, send the parties away to explore the alternatives, and penalise one or other side and their lawyers on costs for failing to try. The courts are becoming what they should always have been – the last resort. Lawyers and the courts are also required to use plain language and to explore all the alternatives to court before getting that far: mediation, conciliation, ombudsmen schemes, and arbitration.

So now it's official policy of both the UK government and the European Commission to make it as simple as possible to enforce rights through Alternative Dispute Resolution (ADR) schemes. Anything that makes it easier to sort out disputes without having to go to court is a good thing. In 2001 the European Commission launched 'Fin-Net' – the Financial Services complaint Network (p. 156), and also 'EEJ-Net' – the European Extra-Judicial Network (*www.eej-net.org.uk* or contact *EEJ.Net@nacab.org.uk*).

Although these 'Nets' operate differently they share the same simple objective. With the rise of e-commerce, and with more and more people travelling and buying goods and services abroad, cross-border disputes are increasingly likely. But not many of us have the time, the resources, or the inclination to start legal action against a trader in another country, in another language, and often in a very different legal system to our own. These networks are designed to give consumers access to alternative redress schemes across Europe.

Where the problem relates to retail banking, insurance and investment services, the Fin-Net gives you direct access to the ADR scheme that exists in the other member state for that kind of complaint. To get access you simply contact the relevant UK ombudsman (the Financial Ombudsman Service, say) which will refer the complaint to the ombudsman in the other country.

The EEJ-Net is a bigger and more general initiative. Here you contact your 'clearing house'; in the UK it's the Citizens Advice★, and they in turn refer your complaint to the clearing house in the other country, which then refers it on to the relevant ADR body. Currently there are around 400 bodies listed. A serious intent of the Commission's objectives is to simplify and introduce common rules for enforcement and effective redress mechanisms across Europe.

Addresses

Accident Line
Abbey Legal Protection Ltd
1st Floor
17 Lansdowne Rd
Croydon
Surrey CR0 2BX
Tel: (0800) 192939
Fax: 020-8730 2801
Email: info@accidentlinedirect.co.uk
Website: www.accidentlinedirect.co.uk

Action Against Medical Accidents (AvMA)
44 High Street
Croydon
Surrey CRO 1YB
Helpline: (0845) 123 2352
Fax: 020-8667 9065
Email: admin@avma.org.uk
Website: www.avma.org.uk

Advertising Standards Authority (ASA)
2 Torrington Place
London WC1E 7HW
Tel: 020-7580 5555
Fax: 020-7631 3051
Email: enquiries@asa.org.uk
Website: www.asa.org.uk

Air Travel Organisers' Licensing (ATOL)
Consumer Protection Group
Civil Aviation Authority
Third Floor, CAA House
45-59 Kingsway
London WC2B 6TE
Tel: 020-7453 6350
Fax: 020-7453 6353
Email: claims@cpg.org.uk
Website: www.atol.org.uk

Alternative Dispute Resolution Group (ADR)
Grove House
Grove Road
Redland
Bristol BS6 6UN
Tel: 0117-946 7180
Fax: 0117-946 7181
Email: info@adrgroup.co.uk
Website: www.adrgroup.co.uk

Architects Registration Board (ARB)
8 Weymouth Street
London W1W 3BU
Tel: 020-7580 5861
Fax: 020-7436 5269
Email: info@arb.org.uk
Website: www.arb.org.uk

Association of Bonded Travel Organisers Trust (ABTOT)
86 Jermyn Street
London SW1Y 6JD
Tel: 020-7930 2388
Fax: 020-7930 7718
Website: www.abtot.com

Association of British Insurers (ABI)
51 Gresham Street
London EC2V 7HQ
Tel: 020-7600 3333
Fax: 020-7696 8999
Email: info@abi.org.uk
Website: www.abi.oig.uk

Association of British Travel Agents (ABTA)
68–71 Newman Street
London W1T 3AH
Tel: 020-7637 2444
Information line: (0901) 2015050
(50p per minute)
Fax: 020-7637 0713
Email: information@abta.co.uk
Website: www.abta.com

Association of Chartered Certified Accountants (ACCA)
64 Finnieston Square
Glasgow G3 8DT
Tel: 0141-582 2000
Fax: 0141-582 2222
Email: info@accaglobal.com
Website: www.acca.co.uk

Association of Independent Tour Operators (AITO)
133a St Margaret's Road
Twickenham
Middlesex TW1 1RG
Tel: 020-8744 9280
Fax: 020-8744 3187
Email: info@aito.co.uk
Website: www.aito.co.uk

Association of Manufacturers of Domestic Electrical Appliances (AMDEA)
Rapier House
40–46 Lamb's Conduit Street
London WC1N 3NW
Tel: 020-7405 0666
Fax: 020-7405 6609
Email: info@amdea.org.uk
Website: www.amdea.org.uk

Association of Personal Injury Lawyers (APIL)
33 Pilcher Gate
Nottingham NG1 1QE
Tel: 0115-958 0585
Fax: 0115-958 0885
Website: www.apil.com

Association of Residential Letting Agents
Maple House
53–55 Woodside Road
Amersham
Bucks
HP6 6AA
Tel: (0845) 345 5752
Email: info@arla.co.uk
Website: www.arla.co.uk

Bar Complaints Commissioner
2 Cursitor Street
London EC4A 1NE
Tel: 020-7440 4000
Fax: 020-7440 4001
Website: www.barcouncil.org.uk

British Association of Removers (BAR)
3 Churchchill Court
58 Station Road
North Harrow
Middlesex HA2 7SA
Tel: 020-8861 3331
Fax: 020-8861 3332
Email: info@bar.co.uk
Website: www.removers.org.uk

British Carpet Technical Centre (BCTC)
Wira House
West Park Ring Road
Leeds LSI 6 6QL
Tel: 0113-259 1999
Fax: 0113-278 0306
Email: info@bttg.co.uk

British Complementary Medicine Association
Kensington House
P.O. Box 5122
Bournemouth
Dorset
BH8 0WG
Tel: (0845) 343 5977
Fax: (0845) 345 5977
Email: info@bcma.co.uk
Website: www.bcma.co.uk

British Retail Consortium (BRC)
2nd Floor
21 Dartmouth Street
London SW1H 9BP
Tel: 020-7854 8900
Fax: 020-7854 8901
Email: info@brc.org.uk
Website: www.brc.org.uk

British Telecom (BT)
Head Office
BT Centre
81 Newgate Street
London EC1A 7AJ
Tel: 020-7356 5000
Fax: 020-7356 5520
Email: cceo@bt.com
Website: www.bt.com

British Wood Preserving and Damp-proofing Association (BWPDA)
1 Gleneagles House
Vernon Gate
Derby
DE1 1UP
Tel: (01332) 225100
Fax: (01332) 225101
Email: info@bwpda.co.uk
Website: www.bwpda.co.uk

Building Guarantee Scheme Ltd
143 Malone Road
Belfast BT9 6SU
Tel: 028-9087 7147
Fax:028-9087 7155
Email: bgs@cefni.co.uk
Website: www.cefni.co.uk

Centre for Effective Dispute Resolution (CEDR)
Exchange Tower
1 Harbour Exchange Square
London E14 9GB
Tel: 020-7536 6000
Fax: 020-7536 6001
Email: info@cedr.co.uk
Website: www.cedr.co.uk

Chartered Institute of Arbitrators
International Arbitration Centre
12 Bloomsbury Square
London WC1A 2LP
Tel: 020-7421 7444
Fax: 020-7404 4032
Email: info@arbitrators.org
Website: www.arbitrators.org

Chartered Institute of Environmental Health
Chadwick Court
15 Hatfields
London SE1 8DJ
Tel: 020-7928 6006
Fax: 020-7827 9930
Email: info@cieh.org
Website: www.cieh.org/

Citizens Advice
Website: www.nacab.org.uk
www.adviceguide.org.uk
Look in the phone book for your local office

Civil Aviation Authority (CAA)
CAA House
45–59 Kingsway
London WC2B 6TE
Tel: 020-7379 7311
Website: www.caa.co.uk

Commission for Patient and Public Involvement in Health
Helpdesk Team
9th Floor
Ladywood House
45 Stephenson Street
Birmingham B2 4DY
Tel: (0845) 120 7111
Fax: 0121-222 4488
Email: enquiries@cppih.org
Website: www.cppih.org/

Commission for Racial Equality
St Dunstan's House
201–211 Borough High Street
London SE1 1GZ
Tel: 020-7939 0000
Fax: 020-7939 0001
Email: info@cre.gov.uk
Website: www.cre.gov.uk

Companies House
Crown Way
Cardiff CF14 3UZ
Tel: 029-2038 0801
Fax: 029-2038 0900
Email: enquiries@companies-house.gov.uk
Website: www.companieshouse.gov.uk

Consumer Gateway
Website: www.consumer.gov.uk

Consumers' Association
2 Marylebone Road
London NW1 4DF
Tel: 020-7770 7000
Fax: 020-7770 7220
Email: which@which.net
Website: www.which.net

Council for Licensed Conveyancers (CLC)
16 Glebe Road
Chelmsford
Essex CM1 1QG
Tel: (01245) 349599
Fax: (01245) 341300
Email: clc@conveyancer.org.uk
Website: www.conveyancer.org.uk

Council of Mortgage Lenders (CML)
3 Savile Row
London W1S 3PB
Tel: 020-7437 0075
Fax: 020-7434 3791
Email: info@cml.org.uk
Website: www.cml.org.uk

Council for Registered Gas Installers
(CORGI)
1 Elmwood
Chineham Park
Crockford Lane
Basingstoke
Hampshire RG24 8WG
Tel: (0870) 401 2300
Fax: (0870) 401 2600
Email: enquiries@corgi-group.com
Website: www.corgi-gas.co.uk

The Court Service
Southside
105 Victoria Street
London SW1E 6QT
Tel: 020-7210 2266
Fax: 020-7210 1797
Email:
customerserviceCSHQ@courtservice.gsi.gov.uk
Website: www.courtservice.gov.uk

Department of Enterprise, Trade and
Investment (Northern Ireland)
Trading Standards Section
176 Newtonbreda Road
Belfast BT8 6QS
Tel: 028-9025 3900
Fax: 028-9025 3953
Website: www.detini.gov.uk

Department of the Environment Water Service
Helpline: (08457) 440088
Metered water enquiries: 028-9032 1500
Email: waterline@waterni.gov.uk
Customer.billing@waterni.gov.uk
Website: www.waterni.gov.uk

Eastern Division
Westland House
Old Westland Road
Belfast BT14 6TE

Northern Division
Academy House
121a Broughshane Street
Ballymena BT43 6BA

Southern Division
Marlborough House
Central Way
Craigavon BT64 1AD

Western Division
Belt Road
Altnagelvin
Londonderry BT47 2LL

Department of Trade and Industry (DTI)
DTI Enquiry Unit
1 Victoria Street
London SW1H 0ET
Tel: 020-7215 5000
Fax: 020-7215 3114
Email: dti.enquiries@dti.gsi.gov.uk
Website: www.dti.gov.uk

Direct Marketing Association UK Ltd (DMA)
DMA House
70 Margaret Street
London W1W 8SS
Tel: 020-7291 3300
Fax: 020-7323 4165
Email: dma@dma.org.uk
Website: www.dma.org.uk

Disability Rights Commission (DRC)
FREEPOST MID02164
Stratford upon Avon CV37 9BR
Tel: (08457) 622 633 (DRC Helpline)
Fax: (08457) 778 878
Website: www.drc-gb.org

Disabled Persons Transport Advisory
Committee (DPTAC)
Room 1/14
Great Minster House
76 Marsham Street
London SW1P 4DR
Tel: 020-7944 8011
Fax: 020-7944 6998
Email: dptac@dft.gov.uk
Website: www.dptac.gov.uk

Domestic Appliance Service Association
(DASA)
69 The Maltings
Stanstead Abbotts
Herts SG12 8HG
Tel: (01920) 872464
Fax: (01920) 872498
Email: mail@dasa.org.uk
Website: www.dasa.org.uk

Drinking Water Inspectorate
Floor 2/A2
Ashdown House
123 Victoria Street
London SW1E 6DE
Tel: 020-7082 8024
Fax: 020-7082 8028
Email: dwi.enquiries@defra.gsi.gov.uk
Website: www.dwi.gov.uk

Driver and Vehicle Licensing Agency (DVLA)
Longview Road
Swansea
SA67JL
Tel: (01792) 782341
Website: www.dvla.gov.uk

Energywatch
Head Office
4th Floor
Artillery House
Artillery Row
London SW1P 1RT
Tel: (08459) 060708
Fax: 020-7799 8341
Email: enquiries@energywatch.org.uk
Website: www.energywatch.org.uk

Enforcement Services Association
Park House
10 Park Street
Bristol
BS1 5HX
Tel: 0117 9074 771
Fax: 0117 9074 701
Email: secretary@bailiffs.org.uk
Website: www.bailiffs.org.uk

Equal Opportunities Commission
Arndale House
Arndale Centre
Manchester
M4 3EQ
Tel: (0845) 601 5901
Fax: 0161-838 1733
Email: info@eoc.org.uk
Website: www.eoc.org.uk

Fax Preference Service
DMA House
70 Margaret Street
London W1W 8SS
Tel: 020-7291 3330
Fax: (0845) 0700702
Email: fps@dma.org.uk
Website: www.fpsonline.org.uk

Federation of Tour Operators (FTO)
16 Sussex Road
Haywards Heath
West Sussex
RN16 4EA
Tel: (01444) 457900
Email: *general@fto.co.uk*
Website: www.fto.co.uk

Finance and Leasing Association (FLA)
Imperial House
15–19 Kingsway
London WC2B 6UN
Tel: 020-7836 6511
Fax: 020-7420 9600
Email: info@fla.org.uk
Website: www.fla.org.uk

Financial Ombudsman Service (FOS)
South Quay Plaza
183 Marsh Wall
London E14 9SR
Consumer helpline: (0845) 080 1800
Switchboard: 020-7964 1000
Fax: 020-7964 1001
Email: complaint.info@financial-
ombudsman.org.uk
Website: www.financial-ombudsman.org.uk

Financial Services Authority (FSA)
25 The North Colonnade
Canary Wharf
London E14 5HS
Tel: 0845 6061234 (Consumer helpline)
Fax: 020-7066 1099
Email: consumerhelp@fsa.gov.uk
Website: www.fsa.gov.uk

Fin-Net
Website: http://finnet.jrc.it/en/

Gas Consumers Council (GCC)
Abford House
15 Wilton Road
London SW1V 1LT
Tel: 020-7931 0977
Complaints: (0645) 060708
Fax: 020-7630 9934
Email: gcc@gascc.org.uk

General Chiropractic Council
44 Wicklow Street
London WC1X 9HL
Tel: 020-7713 5155
Fax: 020-7713 5844
Email: enquiries@gcc-uk.org
Website: www.gcc-uk.org

General Consumer Council for Northern Ireland
Elizabeth House
116 Holywood Road
Belfast BT4 1NY
Tel: 028-9067 2488
Fax: 028-9065 7701
Email: info@gccni.org.uk
Website: www.gccni.org.uk

General Council of the Bar
3 Bedford Row
London WC1R 4DB
Tel: 020-7242 0082
Fax: 020-7831 9217
Website: www.barcouncil.org.uk

General Dental Council (GDC)
37 Wimpole Street
London W1G 8DQ
Tel: 020-7887 3800
Fax: 020-7224 3294
Email: information@gdc-uk.org
Website: www.gdc-uk.org

General Insurance Standards Council (GISC)
9th Floor
110 Cannon Street
London EC4N 6EU
Tel: (0845) 601 2857
Fax: 020-7648 7808
Email: enquiries@gisc.co.uk
Website: www.gisc.co.uk

General Medical Council (GMC)
178 Great Portland Street
London W1W 5JE
Tel: 020-7580 7642
Fax: 020-7915 3641
Email: gmc@gmc-uk.org
Website: www.gmc-uk.org

General Optical Council (GDC)
41 Harley Street
London WIG 8DJ
Tel: 020-7580 3898
Fax: 020-7436 3525
Email: goc@optical.org
Website: www.optical.org

General Osteopathic Council
Osteopathy House
176 Tower Bridge Road
London SE1 3LU
Tel: 020-7357 6655
Fax:020-73570011
Email: info@osteopathy.org.uk
Website: wrww.osteopathy.org.uk

Glass and Glazing Federation (GGF)
44–48 Borough High Street
London SE1 1XB
Tel: (0870) 042 4255
Fax: (0870) 042 4266
Email: info@ggf.org.uk
Website: www.ggf.org.uk

Guarantee Protection Insurance Company (GPI) Ltd
27 London Road
High Wycombe
Buckinghamshire HP11 1BW
Tel: (01494) 447049
Fax: (01494) 465194
Email: shirley@gptprotecdon.co.uk

Hairdressing Council
12 David House
45 High Street
South Norwood
London SE25 6HJ
Tel: 020-8771 6205
Fax: 020-8653 9627
Email: registrar@haircouncil.org.uk
Website: www.haircouncil.org.uk

Health Professions Council
Park House
184 Kennington Park Road
London SE11 4BU
Tel: 020-7582 0866
Website: www.hpc-uk.org

Health Service Ombudsman

England

Health Service Ombudsman
Millbank Tower
Millbank
London SW1P 4QP
Tel: (0845) 015 4033
Fax: 020-7217 4160
Email:
OHSC.Enquiries@ombudsman.gsi.gov.uk
Website: www.ombudsman.org.uk

Northern Ireland

Assembly Ombudsman for Northern Ireland
Freepost
Belfast BEL 1478
Tel: 028-9023 3821
Fax: 028-9023 4912
Email: ombudsman@ni-ombudsman.org.uk
Website: www.ni-ombudsman.org.uk

Scotland

Scottish Public Services Ombudsman
4 Melville Street
Edinburgh
EH3 7NS
Tel: (0870) 011 5378
Fax: (0870) 011 5379
Email: enquiries@scottishombudsman.org.uk
Website: www.scottishombudsman.org.uk

Wales

Health Service Ombudsman for Wales
5th Floor
Capital Tower
Greyfriars Road
Cardiff CF10 3AG
Tel: (0845) 601 0987
Fax: (02920) 226909
Email:
WHSC.Enquiries@ombudsman.gsi.gov.uk
Website: www.ombudsman.org.uk

Hire Purchase Information plc (HPI)
Dolphin House
New Street
Salisbury SP1 2PB
Tel: (01722) 422422
Fax: (01722) 412746
Website: www.hpicheck.com

ICSTIS
Clove Building
4 Maguire Street
London SE1 2NQ
Tel: 020-7940 7474 (Mon to Fri 9am-5pm; no
premium-rate number enquiries)
Helpline for premium-rate numbers on bills:
(0800) 500212
Fax: 020-7940 7456
Email: helpline@icstis.org.uk
Website: www.icstis.co.uk

Independent Warranty Association Ltd
21 Albion Place
Northampton NN1 1UD
Tel: (01604) 604511
Fax: (01604) 604512

Information Commissioner
Wycliffe House
Water Lane
Wilmslow
Cheshire SK9 5AF
Tel: (01625) 545700
Data Protection Helpline: (01625) 545745
Fax:(01625) 524 510
Email: mail@ico.gsi.gov.uk
Website:
www.informationcommissioner.gov.uk

Insolvency Service
Official Receiver's Office
Ladywood House
45-46 Stephenson Street
Birmingham B2 4UP
Tel: 0121-698 4000
Fax: 0121-698 4407
Website: www.insolvency.gov.uk

Institute of Automotive Engineer Assessors
Stowe House
Netherstowe
Lichfield WS13 6TJ
Tel: (01543) 266822
Fax: (01543) 266833
Email: secretary@iaea.demon.co.uk
Website: www.iaea.uk.com

**Institute of Chartered Accountants in England
and Wales**
P.O. Box 433
Chartered Accountants' Hall
Moorgate Place
Moorgate
London EC2P 2BJ
Tel: 020-7920 8100
Fax: 020-7920 0547
Email: profstan@icaew.co.uk
Website: www.icaew.co.uk

Institute of Chartered Accountants in Ireland
Quality Assurance Department
11 Donegal Square South
Belfast BT1 5JE
Tel: 028-02 31 541
Fax: 028-9031 9320
Email: qad@icai.ie
Website: www.icai.ie

Institute of Chartered Accountants of Scotland
CA House
21 Haymarket Yards
Edinburgh
EH12 5BH
Tel: 0131-347 0100
Fax: 0131-347 0105
Email: enquiries@ icas.org.uk
Website: www.icas.org.uk

Institute for Complementary Medicine
P.O. Box 194
London SE16 7QZ
Tel: 020-7237 5165
Fax: 020-7237 5175
Email: icm@icmedicine.co.uk
Website: www.icmedicine.co.uk

Institute of Trichologists
Fraser House
Netherhall Road
Doncaster
South Yorkshire
DN1 2PH
Tel: (08706) 070602
Fax: (01302) 380028
Email: admin@trichologists.org.uk

Insurance Brokers Registration Council (IBRC)
Higham Business Centre
Midland Road
Higham Ferrers
Northants NN10 8DW
Tel: (01933) 359083
Fax: (01933) 359077

Insurance Ombudsman Bureau (IOB)
135 Park Street
London SE1 9EA
Tel: (08456) 006666
Fax: 020-7902 8197
Email: complaint@theiob.org.uk
Website: www.theiob.org.uk

International Air Transport Association (IATA)
Central House
Lampton Road
Hounslow
Middlesex
TW3 1HY
Tel: 020-8607 6262
Fax: 020-8607 6350
Website: www.iata.org

Kitchen Bathroom Bedroom Specialists Association (KBSA)
12 Top Barn Business Centre
Holt Heath
Worcester WR6 6NH
Tel: (01905) 621787
Fax: (01905) 621887
Email: info@kbsa.co.uk
Website: www.kbsa.co.uk

Land Registry
32 Lincoln's Inn Fields
London WC2A 3PH
Tel: 020-7917 8888
Fax: 020-7955 0110
Website: www.landregistry.gov.uk

Law Centre
The Law Centres Federation
Duchess House
18–19 Warren Street
London W1T 5LR
Tel: 020-7387 8570
Fax: 020-7387 8368
Email: info@lawcentres.org.uk
Website: www.lawcentres.org.uk
Contact for details of your local centre, or look in the phone book

Law Society of England and Wales
Law Society Hall
113 Chancery Lane
London WC2A 1PL
Tel: 020-7242 1222
Fax: 020-7831 0344
Accident Line: 0800 192939
Consumer Complaints Service: 01926 820082
Email: info.services@lawsociety.org.uk
Website: www.lawsociety.org.uk

Law Society of Northern Ireland
Law Society House
98 Victoria Street
Belfast BT1 3JZ
Tel: 028-9023 1614
Fax: 028-9023 2606
Email: info@lawsoc-ni.org
Website: www.lawsoc-ni.org

Law Society of Scotland
26 Drumsheugh Gardens
Edinburgh EH3 7YR
Tel: 0131-226 7411
Fax: 0131-225 2934
Email: lawscot@lawscot.org.uk
Website: www.lawscot.org.uk

Leasehold Advisory Service (LEASE)
70-74 City Road
London EC1Y 2BJ
Tel: 0845 345 1993
Fax: 020-7253 2043
Email: info@lease-advice.org
Website: www.lease-advice.org

Legal Services Commission
85 Gray's Inn Road
London
WC1X 8TX
Tel: 020-7759 0000
Website: www.legalservices.gov.uk

Legal Services Ombudsman
3rd Floor
Sunlight House
Quay Street
Manchester M3 3JZ
Tel: 0845 6010794
Fax: 0161 832 5446
Email: lso@olso.gsi.gov.uk
Website: www.olso.org

Mailing Preference Service (MPS)
DMA House
70 Margaret Street
London W1W 8SS
Tel: 020-7291 3310
Fax: 020-7323 4226
Email: mps@dma.org.uk
Website: www.mpsonline.org.uk

Mail Order Protection Scheme (MOPS)
18a King Street
Maidenhead SL6 1EF
Tel: (01628) 641930
Fax: (01628) 637112
Email: enquiries@mops.org.uk
Website: www.mops.org.uk

Mail Order Traders' Association
P.O. Box 1023
Liverpool L69 2WS
Tel: 0151-227 9456
Fax: 0151-227 9678
Email: malcomlandu@compuserve.com

Mediation UK
Alexander House
Telephone Avenue
Bristol BS1 4BS
Tel: 0117-904 6661
Fax: 0117-904 3331
Email: enquiry@mediationuk.org.uk
Website: www.mediationuk.org.uk

Motor Insurers Bureau (MIB)
Linford Wood House
6–12 Capital Drive
Linford Wood
Milton Keynes MK14 6XT
Tel: (01908) 830001
Fax: (01908) 671681
Website: www.mib.org.uk

National Approved Letting Scheme (NALS)
Tavistock House
5 Rodney Road
Cheltenham GL50 1HX
Tel: (01242) 581712
Fax: (01242) 232518
Email: info@nalscheme.co.uk
Website: www.nalscheme.co.uk

National Association of Citizens Advice
See Citizens Advice, above

National Association of Estate Agents (NAEA)
Arbon House
21 Jury Street
Warwick CV34 4EH
Tel: (01926) 496800
Fax: (01926) 400953
Email: info@naea.co.uk
Website: www.naea.co.uk

National Care Standards Commission (NCSC)
St Nicholas Building
St Nicholas Street
Newcastle upon Tyne NE1 1NB
Tel: 0191-233 3600
Fax: 0191-233 3510
Website: www.ncsc.gov.uk

National Grid Transco
National Grid Transco plc
1–3 Strand
London WC2N 5EH
Tel: 020-7004 3000
Transco Gas Emergency line: (0800) 111999
Fax: 020-7004 3004
Website: www.ngtgroup.com

National House Building Council (NHBC)
Buildmark House
Chiltern Avenue
Amersham
Buckinghamshire HP6 SAP
Tel: (01494) 735363
Fax: (01494) 723530
Email: reception@nhbc.co.uk
Website: www.nhbc.co.uk

National Register of Property Preservation Specialists (NRPPS)
11 Greenland Road
Barnet ENS 2AL
Freecall Advisory Service:
(0500) 223505

National Savings and Investments
Blackpool FY3 9YP
Tel: (0845) 964 5000
Email: customerenquiries@nsandi.com
Website: www.nsandi.com

Network Rail
40 Melton Street
London NW1 2EE
Tel: 020-7557 8000
National Helpline: (08457) 114141
National Rail Enquiries: (08457) 484950
(timetable and ticket enquiries)
Website: www.networkrail.co.uk

Newspaper Publishers' Association Ltd
34 Southwark Bridge Road
London SE1 9EU
Tel: 020-7207 2200
Fax: 020-7928 2067

Newspaper Society
Bloomsbury House
74–77 Great Russell Street
London WC1B 3DA
Tel: 020-7636 7014
Fax: 020-7631 5119
Email: ns@newspapersoc.org.uk
Website: wwrw.newspapersoc.org.uk

NHS Direct
Tel: (0845) 4647
Website: www.nhsdirect.nhs.uk

NHS Direct Wales
Tel: (0845) 4647
Website: www.nhsdirect.wales.nhs.uk

Office of Communications (OFCOM)
Ofcom Contact Centre
Riverside House
2a Southwark Bridge Road,
London SE1 9HA
Tel: 0845 456 3000
Email: contact@ofcom.org.uk
Website: www.ofcom.org.uk

Office of Fair Trading (OFT)
Fleetbank House
2–6 Salisbury Square
London EC4Y 8JX
Tel: 020-7211 8000
Fax: 020-7211 8800
Email: enquiries@oft.gov.uk
Website: www.oft.gov.uk

Office of Gas and Electricity Markets (OFGEM)
9 Millbank
London SW1P 3GE
Tel: 020-7901 7000
Fax: 020-7901 7066
Website: www.ofgem.gov.uk

Office of the Rail Regulator (ORR)
1 Waterhouse Square
138–142 Holborn
London EC1N 2TQ
Tel: 020-7282 2000
Fax: 020-7282 2045
Website: www.rail-reg.gov.uk
Fax: 028-9031 1740
Website: www.ofreg.nics.gov.uk

Office for the Regulation of Electricity and Gas (OFREG)
Brookmount Buildings
42 Fountain Street
Belfast BT1 5EE
Tel: 028-9031 1575
Supply failure enquiries: (08457) 643643
Payment, connection and billing enquiries:
(08457) 455455
Fax: 028-9031 1740
Website: www.ofreg.nics.gov.uk

Office of the Telecommunications Ombudsman (Otelo)
P.O. Box 730
Warrington WA4 6WU
Tel: (0845) 0501614
Fax: (0845) 0501615
Email: enquiries@otelo.org.uk
Website: www.otelo.org.uk

Office of Water Services (OFWAT)
Centre City Tower
7 Hill Street
Birmingham B5 4UA
Tel: 0121-625 1300
Fax: 0121-625 1400
Email: enquiries@ofwat.gsi.gov.uk
Website: www.open.gov.uk/ofwat/

Ombudsman for Estate Agents (OEA)
Beckett House
4 Bridge Street
Salisbury SP1 2LX
Tel: (01722) 333306
Fax: (01722) 332296
Email: admin@oea.co.uk
Website: www.oea.co.uk

Organisation for Timeshare in Europe (OTE)
78–80 rue Defacqz (4th Floor)
B-1060 Brussels
Belgium
Fax: 0032 2 533 30 61
Email: info@ote-info.com
Website: www.ote-info.com

Periodical Publishers Association Ltd
Queen's House
28 Kingsway
London WC2B 6JR
Tel: 020-7404 4166
Fax: 020-7404 4167
Email: info1@ppa.co.uk
Website: www.ppa.co.uk

Postcomm
The Postal Services Commission
Hercules House
6 Hercules Road
London SE1 7DB
Tel: 020-7593 2100
Fax: 020-7593 2142
Email: info@psc.gov.uk
Website: www.psc.gov.uk

Postwatch
Freepost
Postwatch
Tel: (08456) 013265
Fax: 020-7730 3044
Email: info@postwatch.co.uk
Website: www.postwatch.co.uk

The Prince of Wales's Foundation for Integrated Health
12 Chillingworth Road
London N7 8QL
Tel: 020-7619 6140
Fax: 020-7700 8434
Email: info@fihealth.org.uk
Website: www.fihealth.org.uk

Qualitas
Maxwell Road
Stevenage SG1 2EW
Tel: (01438) 777777
Fax: (01438) 777780
Email: qualitas@fira.co.uk
Website: www.fira.co.uk

Quality Mark Scheme
Website: www.qualitymark.org.uk

Radio, Electrical and Television Retailers' Association Ltd (RETRA)
Retra House
St John's Terrace
1 Ampthill Street
Bedford MK42 9EY
Tel: (01234) 269110
Fax: (01234) 269609
Email: retra@retra.co.uk
Website: www.retra.co.uk

Rail Passengers Committee
Website: www.railpassengers.org.uk

London
London Transport Users Committee
6 Middle Street
London EC1A 7JA
Tel: 020-7505 9000
Fax: 020-7505 9003
Website: www.ltuc.org.uk

Eastern England
Third Floor
Zone 4
Stuart House
City Road
Peterborough PE1 1QF
Tel: (01733) 312188
Fax: (01733) 891286

Midlands
6th Floor
McLaren Building
35 Dale End
Birmingham B4 7LN
Tel: 0121-212 2133
Fax: 0121-236 6945

North-eastern England
Ground Floor
Unit 2
Holgate Court
Holgate Park
Poppleton Road
York YO26 4GB
Tel: (01904) 787711
Fax: (01904) 795689

North-western England
9th Floor
Rail House
Store Street
Manchester M1 2RP
Tel: 0161-244 5982
Fax: 0161-244 5981

Scotland
5th Floor
Corunna House
29 Cadogan Street
Glasgow G2 7AB
Tel: 0141-221 7760
Fax: 0141-221 3393

Southern England
3rd Floor
Centric House
390–391 Strand
London WC2R 0LT
Tel: 020-7240 5308
Fax: 020-7240 8923

Wales
St David's House
Wood Street
Cardiff CF10 1ES
Tel: 029-2022 7247
Fax: 029-2022 3992

Western England
10th Floor
Tower House
Fairfax Street
Bristol BS1 3BN
Tel: 0117-926 5703
Fax: 0117-929 4140

Registry of County Court Judgements
173–175 Cleveland Street
London W1T 6QR
Tel: 020-7380 0133
Email: info@registry-trust.org.uk
Website: www.registry-trust.org.uk

Retail Motor Industry Federation
201 Great Portland Street
London W1N 6AB
Tel: 020-7580 9122
Fax: 020-7580 6376

Royal Institute of British Architects (RIBA)
66 Portland Place
London WIN 4AD
Tel: 020-7580 5533
Fax: 020-7255 1541
Email: info@inst.riba.org
Website: www.riba.org

Royal Institution of Chartered Surveyors (RICS)
12 Great George Street
London SW1P3AD
Tel: 0870 333 1600
Fax: 020-7334 3811
Email: contactrics@rics.org
Website: www.rics.org.uk

Royal Society for the Prevention of Cruelty to Animals (RSPCA)
Wilberforce Way
Southwater
Horsham
West Sussex RH13 9RS
Tel: (0870) 3335 999
Fax: (0870) 7530 284
Website: www.rspca.org.uk

Scottish Daily Newspaper Society / Scottish Newspaper Publishers' Association
48 Palmerston Place
Edinburgh EH12 5DE
Tel: 0131-220 4353
Fax: 0131-220 4344
Email: info@snpa.org.uk
Website: www.snpa.org.uk

Scottish Legal Services Ombudsman
17 Waterloo Place
Edinburgh
EH1 3DL
Tel: 0131-556 9123
Fax: 0131-556 9292
Email: ombudsman@slso.org.uk
Website: www.slso.org.uk

Scottish Motor Trade Association
Palmerston House
10 The Loan
South Queensferry
Edinburgh EH30 9NS
Tel: 0131-331 5510
Website: www.smta.co.uk

Security Industry Authority
PO Box 9
Newcastle Upon Tyne NE82 6YX
Tel: (08702) 430 100
Fax: (08702) 430 125
Email: info@the-sia.org.uk
Website: www.the-sia.org.uk

Telephone Preference Service
DMA House
70 Margaret Street
London W1W 8SS
Tel: (0845) 0700707
Fax: 020-7323 4226
Email: tps@dma.org.uk
Website: www.tpsonline.org.uk

Textile Services Association Ltd (TSA)
7 Churchill Court
58 Station Road
North Harrow
Middlesex HA2 7SA
Tel: 020-8863 7755
Fax: 020-8861 2115
Email: tsa@tsa-org.uk
Website: www.tsa-uk.org

Timeshare Consumers' Association
Hodsock
Worksop
Nottinghamshire S81 OTF
Tel: (01909) 591100
Advice line: (0901) 607 0077
Fax: (01909) 591338
Email: info@timeshare.org.uk
Website: www.timeshare.org.uk

Timeshare Council
See Organisation for Timeshare in Europe
(OTE), above

Trust UK
Website: www.trustuk.org.uk

*United Kingdom Central Council for Nursing,
Midwifery and Health Visiting (UKCC)*
23 Portland Place
London WIB 1PZ
Tel: 020-7637 7181
Fax: 020-7436 2924
Website: www.nmc-uk.org

Water Industry Commissioner
Ochil House
Springkerse Business Park
Stirling FK7 7XE
Tel: (01786) 430200
Fax: (01786) 462018
Email: enquiries@watercommissioner.co.uk
Website: www.watercommissioner.co.uk

Which? Books
Freepost
Hertford SG14 1SH
Tel: (0800) 252100
Fax: (0800) 533053
Website: www.which.net

Which? Legal Service
Castlemead
Gascoyne Way
Hertford SG14 1LH
Tel: (0800) 920123

Zurich Insurance
Galaxy House
Southwood Crescent
Farnborough
Hampshire GU14 0NJ
Tel: (0870) 241 8050
Website: www.zurichmunicipal.com

Index